THE
HOLOCAUST
—— AND THE ——
ENGLISH SCHOOL

BARBARA WOLFENDEN

To order additional copies of this book, contact:
Bookwhip
1-855-339-3589
https://www.bookwhip.com

To the Roughians

Contents

Timeline

T his story ties into the portions of twentieth century history identified today as the Holocaust and World War II. Salient events of each appear below to help the reader position the narrative of Stoatley Rough School's history within the context of the larger historical framework.

June 28, 1919	Treaty of Versailles ends World War I
October 29, 1929	Stock market on Wall Street crashes; world-wide depression
September 14, 1930	Nazis to become the 2nd largest political party in Germany
January 30, 1933	Adolph Hitler becomes Chancellor of Germany; politicization of all governmental agencies; Dachau concentration camp opened
March, 1933	Enabling Act makes Hitler dictator.
April, 1934	Stoatley Rough opens doors to its first pupils
July 25, 1934	Nazis murder Austrian Chancellor Dolfuss; four years of tumult follow

September 15, 1935   Nuremberg Race Laws are enacted by the
                      German Parliament

1936   Germany occupies the Rhineland;
                      Mussolini takes Ethiopia, Civil War
                      erupts in Spain; Olympic Games are held
                      in Berlin; first of several "reconnections"
                      of territories holding significant German-
                      speaking populations.

March 12/13, 1938   Bloodless takeover or *Anschluss* [Union]
                      with Austria

November 9/10, 1938   *Kristallnacht* [Night of the Broken Glass]

December, 1938-   *Kindertransport* - over 10,000 refugee
September, 1939   children taken in by Great Britain via
                      special sealed trains

March 15/16, 1939   Nazis take Czechoslovakia, close borders

1939   Spanish Civil War ends; Nazis sign pacts
                      with Italy and Soviet Union; invade
                      Poland British fleet mobilizes

1939 - 1940   Stoatley Rough reaches peak enrollment of
                      over 100 children

September 3, 1939   Britain, France, Australia and New
                      Zealand declare war on Germany

January 8, 1940   Rationing begins in Britain

May 10, 1940   Winston Churchill becomes British Prime
                      Minister

1940   Nazis invade Denmark, Norway, France,
                      Belgium, Luxembourg, Netherlands

Late May–early June, 1940	Dunkirk Evacuation of British Expeditionary Forces
July 10, 1940	Battle of Britain begins
September 7-December 30, 1940	Blitz begins
1941	Battles take place in North Africa, Greece, Yugoslavia; Stoatley Rough School becomes Red Cross Message Center; Roosevelt and Churchill announce the Atlantic Charter; fighting begins in Soviet Union
June / July, 1941	SS begin mass murders; Göring instructs Heydrich to prepare for the Final Solution
September 1, 1941	Jews ordered to wear yellow stars
1941	Roosevelt and Churchill announce the Atlantic Charter
December 7/8, 1941	Pearl Harbor is bombed; U.S. declares war on Japan; December 11 U.S. declares war on Germany
1941	First all-American attack in Europe; Rommel driven back by Montgomery in North Africa; Fermi sets up atomic reactor in Chicago
January 21, 1942	Wannsee Conference coordinates logistics of "Final solution to the Jewish Question"
June, 1942	Mass murder of Jews by gassing begins at Auschwitz

1943	Germans surrender at Stalingrad; Montgomery takes Tripoli; Jews rise up in Warsaw Ghetto; Allies land in Sicily
1944	Allies land in Anzio near Rome; Hamburg bombed with 3000 tons; Germans surrender in the Crimea; Nazis liquidate Polish concentration camps; Americans recapture France, Soviet pushes from the East
June 6, 1944	D-Day landings
June 13, 1944	First V-1 (doodlebug) rocket attack on Britain
September 17, 1944	Allied airborne (82nd) assault begins on Holland
December 16–27, 1944	Battle of the Bulge in the Ardennes; Concentration camp victims force-marched away from the camps
April 11-15, 1945	Allies liberate Buchenwald and Bergen Belson concentration camps
April 28, 30, 1945	Mussolini captured and hanged; Hitler commits suicide
May 8, 1945	V-E (Victory in Europe) Day
August 9, 1945	Second atomic bomb dropped on Nagasaki, Japan
September 2, 1945	V-J (Victory over Japan) Day
November 20, 1945	Nuremberg war crimes trials begin

Preface

I t is the fall of 1998 on board a cruise ship en route to Alaska. Three friends of my husband's regale me night after night with stories of their time together over sixty years earlier in England during World War II. The four men are celebrating their seventieth birthdays (another friend from Albuquerque had to cancel at the last minute.) Martin's mane is abundant with just a touch of gray, while the hairlines of Wolf, Goldy and Obo have begun to recede. Even though the men live hundreds of miles from each other in the US, they are easy with each other, like brothers.

In 1938, with the world on the cusp of war, each boy found refuge in an English school after Nazi governments had declared them and their families unfit to be citizens. As the ship moves among the glass-green bergs, the men return again and again to the years 1938 – 1945. It is clear that the men received more than just refuge at Stoatley Rough School. It became their home and for the most part, it was a happy home. They were ten-years old when they arrived and would spend the next seven years safe from the murderous grasp of the Nazis in Europe.

As we sit around the dining table, each man expresses gratitude to the School for teaching them to value cultural and religious differences while working and playing even as the School imposed chores and taught the children to take responsibility for each other. The communal living was infused with kindness from the adults.

I am an educator and have taught public and private school children from elementary through college level. As Director of Studies (1974-1977) for the fledgling Tampa Preparatory School, I understand the challenges of building a new school. Listening to my husband's friends on that cruise ship, I was struck by the odds against success of such a venture. Starting a school in 1934 for German-speaking refugees, the Headmistress of Stoatley Rough School and her Board not only had to build a curriculum and acquire a teaching staff, books and materials, but also needed to establish a nurturing environment for parentless children in a foreign country. They needed a building. That the founding staff were flexible enough to establish and keep the School afloat in a constantly changing wartime environment characterized by rationing, lack of adequate heat, scarce funding sources, and the ever-present potential for emotional meltdown within each child, was remarkable.

As we sit at breakfast in the large salon considering the merits of French toast versus Eggs Benedict, the men recall their daily fare of breakfast porridge. They speak of mischief, of pranks, of discovering girls and of watching the RAF fight the *Messerschmidts* overhead, only forty miles from London and under the direct path of aerial fighters from Croydon Air Base. I think about the impact the school has made on their lives as the men express over and over again how their few years in England have been of profound importance. They have lost parents, grandparents and other relatives to the Nazis and their story of survival needs to be documented.

In *The Uprooted: A Hitler Legacy* Dorit Bader Whiteman refutes the assumption by some that only people who spent time in a concentration camp suffered, that they are real survivors and that "nothing happened" to the others whose lives were also irrevocably damaged. She asserts that anybody whose life was interrupted or otherwise injured in the name of Aryan supremacy also certainly suffered. While the book tends to reflect happier memories, the facts are that the children at Stoatley Rough School suffered. They endured homesickness, insufficient heat in the winter, poor wartime sanitation, substandard nutrition and grinding fear. They lost more than can be assessed or compensated for. These children lost their childhood. Yet these men with whom I sit, laughing hard at their drolleries, retain positive memories. In the face of their suffering, the fact that they can smile as witnesses to their kind of survival is owed to the saving graces of a small school on a Surrey hillside in which decades ago they grew up. The Headmistress, the Matron, the faculty and in no small measure, the architecture and gardens of the site itself – all helped to make their survival not only tolerable, but a healing experience.

The material in this book is documented history. I have tried to knit together the many skeins of the anecdotes that have unspooled since the School closed in 1960. Together they recreate a picture of a special time. I place particular but not exclusive focus on the five boys and some of the girls who remained friends for over sixty years after sharing a remarkable time in history.

Finally, this is the story of a beautiful old manor house that still sits in its Surrey aerie, high on a bluff. It is no longer a school, but its beauty has been restored and people inhabit its buildings once more. The house is a sturdy and steadfast reminder that England, herself under siege, found within her soul the generosity to offer safe haven and so much more that cannot easily be articulated, to stranded and desperate children.

Other Refugee Schools in Great Britain

Stoatley Rough was not the only school founded for the specific purpose of taking in German-speaking children. All but one of more than twenty were significantly smaller than Stoatley Rough School; all were boarding schools oriented towards the German progressive educational reform tradition of *Landerziehungsheime* (literally "countryside educational homes"). They all had one common task: "to support the uprooted and confused refugee children as they developed a new and complex identity, and as they came to terms with an alien environment."[1]

Bunce Court in Kent, England, was the largest, with roughly nine hundred students over nine years. (Next in size came Stoatley Rough;

---

[1]   Feidel-Mertz, Hildegard, "Integration and Formation of Identity: Exile Schools in Great Britain" Volume 23, number 1, Fall 2004, pp. 71-84, Purdue University Press

with a cumulative student count of around eight hundred over its twenty-six years.) Bunce Court began life in Germany and was transplanted to England. Miss Anna Essinger, with the help of two sisters and her physician brother-in-law, started the school in Ulm, Germany in 1929 as an alternative to traditional German pedagogy. Like Hilde Lion, she was a progressive educator who believed in child-centered, non-punishing methods of teaching, and she paired vocational training such as carpentry, sewing and cooking, with academics. In 1933 she and one of her sisters (who became her Matron) moved her school (with the heroic help of the Quakers) from Germany, just one step ahead of Nazi defilement. They settled on property that dates to the time of Henry VIII. Bunce Court resembled Stoatley Rough in many ways, using play performance to teach English, holding non-denominational, cultural celebrations, and placing children in the homes of benefactors over pre-war holidays. In June of 1940, the British army requisitioned the Bunce Court estate, forcing most of the school to move. They settled in Trench Hall in Shropshire. Stoatley Rough housed a contingent of Bunce children during the move. The school continued to operate until June, 1946, accepting prisoners from Nazi concentration camps. By 1948 Anna Essinger, almost seventy, closed its doors. Her students remembered with gratitude the kindly Anna Essinger without whose efforts they would have perished.[2]

Other exile schools in England included the Beltane School, moved by its founders Ernst and Ilse Bulowa from Berlin to Wimbledon where it housed thirty children. It closed in 1941. The most famous exile school was Gordonstoun, near Abderdeen, Scotland, still very much in existence. Known for its famous pupils, Princes Philip and Charles, Gordonstoun was modeled by its Jewish exiled founder in 1934, Kurt Hahn, on his German *Schule Schloss Salem*, a school that

---

[2] Anna was a cordial colleague of Dr. Lion's. Correspondence exists between them during the early war years since she was a member of the original Trust group that oversaw the founding of the school. Alan Major, "Bunce Court & Anna Essinger," Stoatley Rough Newsletter issue 14, May, 1997. The article first appeared in *Bygone Kent*, a monthly journal of all aspects of local history, Volume 1, Number 8, August, 1989.

preached self-realization through community service and a Spartan lifestyle. The school moved to Wales during the war and evolved to become an important independent educational institution today.[3] Yet another school was Camp Hill House, founded by Karl König, who moved fifteen colleagues also to Aberdeen to form an educational workshop for handicapped and non-handicapped children.[4] Minna Specht's *Landerziehungsheim* [agricultural educational home] school named *Walkemühle,* was founded in Denmark, then moved to Wales, and finally became situated in a country house near Bristol called Butcombe Court in 1938. It closed in 1940, although Minna Specht herself continued to educate children in a camp school on the Isle of Man. Ms. Specht's building on Man was later used by Quakers to care for half-Jewish survivors of Theresienstadt[5]. Towards the end of the war, a group called the Free German Cultural Alliance created the Theydon Bois School near London under the directorship of Hans Schellenberger. Its purpose was to prepare young German and Austrian refugees for their return home.

Post-War Years

In March, 1945, Mrs. Vernon transferred the use of her property by deed poll to the religious order of St. Mary's Convent in Wantage, Oxfordshire. This Anglican community nurtured overseas communities

---

[3] Research conducted and reported by Manfred Berger, whose original document appeared in the Ida Seele Archive for the Research of the History of the Kindergarten in Dillingen, Germany, translated by Gerda Mayer and reprinted for the Stoatley Rough Newsletter issue 14, October, 1997. Dr. Hahn is credited for having founded Outward Bound, originally created in 1941 for British soldiers facing battle.

[4] A first cousin of Stoatley Rough student Renate Dorpalen [Dorpalen-Brocksieper] where she died.

[5] With the rise of the Nazis in the 1930's, Minna Specht had moved her *Landerziehungsheim* school from Germany to Denmark and then to Butcombe Court in Bristol. She married an English headmaster while waiting out the war in England, returned to Germany and became a member of UNESCO's committee on Education.

in India, Madagascar, and South Africa. A Mr. Jeffries, whose notes on an earlier history of Stoatley Rough are filed with the school's archived materials in the London School of Economics, wrote that the transaction was complicated, the legal status of the house "being almost 'entrusted' to the new owners" who allowed the school to remain without incident. In 1963, after the closing of Stoatley Rough School, a new school moved in. It was part of the Ockenden Venture, a charitable organization formed in 1951 to care for Latvian and Polish girls from displaced persons camps. The mansion became known as Quartermaine House. The Venture eventually took in other children under the War Charities Act of 1940, turning Stoatley Rough into a "reception center," for Vietnamese "boat people" between 1979 and 1988. When the Ockenden organization moved its operations overseas, the buildings in Haslemere lay empty and in disrepair for almost a decade. In early 2001 a development corporation bought the land and buildings and converted the original building into three luxury condominiums. The new owners tore down the Bungalow, Hut, Farmhouse, pump house and other outbuildings, and converted Mr. Phillips' cottage, the Lodge, into a fourth luxury condo. They restored the landscape. Thanks to the efforts of Chris Townson and other Trustees, the new owners agreed to install a plaque at the entrance stating that the site was once Stoatley Rough School.

Today the estate is as grand as ever. The façade of the building is impressive, the view over the Downs still takes one's breath away, and the small brook still runs at the base of the property. A quiet reflecting pool sits where once children cavorted in the home made, sometimes slimy swimming pool. Today its tranquil waters are guarded by a pair of long-legged brass herons. The fields are wild.

In 2004, the Stoatley Rough School Trustees organized a reunion to take place in Haslemere. (The first of several prior reunions was held in November, 1990, in Guildford, Surrey.) The condo owners kindly opened their homes to the crowds of aging alumni and their partners for an afternoon of reminiscing. In attendance were people in their seventies and eighties who had been at the school in the 1930s, as well as the younger post-war Roughians. John and Lyn Orrick, owners of the largest condo, gathered the large group in the Sitting Room and fed them refreshments. Everyone sat down to view a video of a black and white film made in 1937. With the still lovely tiles of the William Morris fireplace shining behind the television set moved in for the occasion, Roughians chortled and exclaimed, laughed and clapped as a sprightly Nore Astfalck led the morning run and a beaming Dr. Lion read to children sitting cross-legged facing the Polynesian shack. When he saw the film, Mr. Orrick declared on the spot that he would restore the gazebo, thatched roof and all.

The view from the mossy-walled terrace (now carved into three terraces partitioned by brick walls) still commands attention, although some alumni reported that the general tree-line looks higher now from the third floor than it had sixty years earlier. The main building itself remains magnificent – quietly imposing, elegant, restful – rising high above the cobbled pavement leading in from Farnham Lane – and ageless. It is comforting to be there. One feels as if the house itself is comfortable in its own remarkable history and will be infused with a special peace for as long as it stands.

Acknowledgements

Many people helped to make this historical record. This material is the stuff of memory. The former pupils of Stoatley Rough School spent many years in building their lives in their new countries before they were able to turn around and look back. Baerbel Guerstenberg [Prasse] wrote, "For so many years I repressed most of my life prior to coming to America and focused on being a good Middle Western wife and mother." Once they began to write, however, they poured out quantities of rich stories.

First and foremost, I must thank my husband and reader, Martin (Friedenfeld) Owens. He was patient to the end and made use of the excellent editing skills he acquired in his Stoatley Rough English classes so many decades ago. A valuable resource for this book was Katharine

Whitaker's and Michael Johnson's excellent short history, *Stoatley Rough School 1934 – 1960,* illustrated by Chris Townson, which they produced for the 60ᵗʰ Anniversary Reunion of May, 1994. Many alumni granted me interviews in the United States, England and Switzerland. Autobiographies, memoirs and oral histories also provided crucial details that brought the stories to life. I gleaned history also from archived materials placed with the London School of Economics by Dr. Lion upon her retirement. I am also indebted to Wolf Elston who spent many hours reviewing and adding to the stories in this book.

A major source of information came from the Stoatley Rough newsletters. On the occasion of the first "official" reunion, Hans Loeser and Herta Lewent Loeser had the foresight to record and distribute *Oral History of Eleanore Astfalck* and *Since Then* (a collection of stories by alumni about their lives after Stoatley Rough. Later a bi-annual *Newsletter* was created, edited, printed and distributed in the U.S. and abroad starting in December, 1992, by Franceska Rapkin Amerikaner. She maintained it until her death in 2002. In October of that year, Dieter Gaupp picked up the job, sending out his last issue (# 28) in August, 2011.

The views in the book are not the whole story. They reflect the thoughts of those who survived to write and of those who chose to write. Countless former students remain unrepresented, some of whom may disagree with my interpretation of the school. Lacking the existence of complete records, I cannot, nor do I claim to account for all of the people who passed through the mansion's halls or for the unrecorded value they were to the Stoatley Rough community.

The pupils themselves provided the story for this book, and they did it well. Renate Dorpalen's account of her return to bombed-out Berlin after the war illustrates the power of an witness report. In this excerpt of her story she has met with her former (Aryan) housekeeper at the ruins of her former home, having seen "children rummaging for food and begging for cigarettes" along the "Kurfuerstendam that had also lost its soul....My dominant feeling on encountering German men and woman was one of distrust, as I could not help but wonder what part they had played in the sadistic drama..the wrecked members of the master race.....I felt no pleasure in watching the misery of the masses who had once shouted *Sieg Heil, Jude Verrecke* [Hail Victory, Jew die.] I was supposed to hate them with all my strength. But I could not hate, or was it in the face of such suffering hatred was silent? I would neither sit in judgment nor would it be in my power to forgive and forget."

SANCTUARY

Martin's heart was beating too fast. Why was he being sent away? In a vague way he understood that his parents were trying to protect him from people in Austria who didn't like Jews. But why would they not come to England with him? The sight of his mother's efforts to stay her tears almost swamped his own resolve not to cry but then he thought of the excitement ahead of him. A trip on a train to a new country! From the corner of his eye he saw the big black engine that seemed to crouch, like an animal, on the tracks in the noisy *Bahnhoff*, chuffing and hissing, impatient to get going. The tangy-sweet smell of hot tar and jets of steam coming from the engine promised unimagined adventure. He tried to be patient as his father droned on with more instructions. Then it was time to mount the steep stairs into the railway car. His mother had the funniest look on her face.

Martin found a seat by the window and turned to wave but *Muti* had turned away. His father waved a handkerchief and was gone. The train gained speed and the buildings of Vienna began to slip away, faster and faster. Martin soon tired of looking out the window and pulled down his backpack from the overhead rack. Let's see what *Muti* gave me, he thought. There was a bottle of 4711 Cologne. He sniffed it and put a drop on his cheek. He took a bite from an apple then put it back. He wasn't really hungry. There, under the lunch bag, was the stupid cardboard sign with his name on it. He was supposed to wear it around his neck when he got to England. Other children on the train were already wearing theirs. The older girl across from him asked if he wanted her to read to him from his book. He scoffed. Why did everybody think he was a baby? He returned his backpack to the overhead rack while outside his window telephone poles raced by in hypnotic regularity. Then a little girl in his compartment began to cry. He thought, I'm not going to cry but within minutes, he was also in tears. The big girl pulled out *Der Letze Mohikaner* (The Last of the Mohicans) and read them both a chapter.

At ten, Martin was wiry and frail, his body spread too thin over big bones. His hands and feet were growing ahead of the rest of him and his broad shoulders rescued him from looking like a waif. He had a wide mouth with full lips, pale blue eyes and his nose, while not a beak, was the most pronounced part of his sharp little face. He was an observing, sensible boy and every time his heart began to hurt again, he told himself that this was an adventure. It was going to be fun acting like a grown up.

He knew the trip was related to what had happened last March. His nanny, Millie, had taken him downtown on the trolley. Afterwards, he had told his parents about the exciting thing that had happened. First they had gone to the *Kaertnerstrasse* and there were probably a hundred or maybe even a million people. They were yelling out the colors of the Austrian flag - "*Rot, Weiss, Rot bis in den Tod* (Red, white, red until death). When he had asked why they were talking about death, his parents had just smiled in a sad way. And then the next day Millie took him downtown again but this time they got to watch a long parade. Tanks, trucks, all kinds of guns on wheels, hundreds of soldiers, and a whole pack of huge red flags – all swept by in rows and rows. He had yelled "*Heil Hitler*" too when the *Fuehrer* came into view but then he felt scared being in the midst of many people all squeezed together. Their shouting grew as the Fuehrer began to speak, and the crowd made a bigger noise than he'd ever heard, a noise that rolled across the *Platz* in thundering waves. He had been glad his nanny had kept a tight grip on his hand.

Martin slept. The shriek of the engine occasionally roused him as his train pushed across Germany, but the rhythmic clacking of the wheels lulled him back to sleep. At one point, uniformed men boarded to check his papers. He slept again, then it was morning, and nice ladies were passing around rolls and hot chocolate talking in words he did not understand. Then he was in a line with other children walking up a gangway and onto a ship.

The air was brisk. He stood at the ship's rail and watched the water traffic. His ship, a large ferry, loomed up over a smaller ferry. Two long blasts said Out of My Way. Martin jumped and shivered. His mother would have insisted he bundle up in six layers of clothes and two hats and three mufflers but his mother wasn't here to tell him what to do. He could stand here without his mittens as long as he wanted. His mother was far away now. His throat started to hurt. He was going away to be safe, his mother had said. *Mutti* had promised she'd meet him in England, later on, she and *Vati* and tiny sister Lisa. Why couldn't they come now, on this ship, with him? He simply could not understand. The ship bellowed once again. The people left their shuffleboard game to peer over the rail.

He was glad he wasn't back in school, though. "Since you didn't know that arithmetic problem, and I'm not surprised since you're a Jew, you'll come up to the head of the class. Right now." The caning hadn't hurt very much – he was used to it. But he didn't know why his teacher didn't like him.

Martin rubbed his hands together. Maybe he'd put on his mittens. His parents expected him to be a big boy now. When he told his parents about all the bad stuff at school, they kept saying to just be brave, that the other children had the problem, not he. Sticks and stones and all that. His father used to say with a very serious look in his eye, "President Hindenburg won't let anything happen to us. After all, I served in the Great War. This Hitler fellow is just a flash in the pan. They'll soon get rid of him."

But *Vati* was wrong.

The engines of his ship thrummed and the thick sea rolled by, pea green and sticky looking. It looked like gelatin. Or snot. Rudi would laugh like crazy if he were here. Snot. A seagull swooped down and cried like a cat.

Once in Paddington Station, Dr. Eisen met Martin because he was wearing his cardboard sign. His father's friend led him to a café where he drank his first cup of tea. Then Martin found himself alone again in a small train heading into the darkness, a warm little cocoon on rails. He thought about home and hoped his little sister would not get into his toy soldiers. *Muti* had promised to keep them safe. Many hours later, the conductor prodded him awake. Time to get out, Lad and he helped Martin, along with his backpack and suitcase, down to the platform. Martin frantically searched his memory for an English word, any of the words that Frau Pfniesl had made him repeat during the last weeks of preparations in Vienna. It was pitch black. And cold. The engine hissed, settled itself, and hissed again before leaving behind a gritty warm tarry smell in its wake.

Martin stood, rigid.

From around a corner of the station house a small woman bustled up.

"Hallo, Kleine Mann. Du müsst ya Martin Friedenfeld sein? Wilkommen. Meine Namen ist Freulein Astfalck." (Hello Little Man. You must be Martin Friedenfeld. Welcome. My name is Miss Astfalck.).

After a short ride up a hill, the car stopped and the nice lady hustled him upstairs and tucked him into bed. The next morning, he awoke to cries of "Der Neue ist hier!" (The new boy is here!) A pillow sailed through the air and hit him on the head. He sat up. Three little boys were looking at him. He grabbed the pillow and sent it back at the one who was grinning. Bull's eye! Everyone cheered and the fight was on, pillows flying, sheets tangling, blankets flung. A small table fell over. He was having the best time until a big girl rushed into the room. She stood by while he washed his face, talking about what he was supposed to do that morning. Then they went downstairs and she put him to work stirring porridge on the large stove. The cook, speaking rapid German was telling some big girls to get the milk pitchers ready. He saw large bowls of brown sugar and stewed fruit on a table. Some big boys stood near the outside door in rubber boots ogling the girls until the cook told them to take their seats at the table. Just outside the half door that led down a corridor, he saw children carrying spoons and napkins; then a big girl started distributing the milk pitchers to the children.

Martin had to stand on a chair to reach the big pot. *Du must das Porridge rueren so das es nicht verbrent. Nein Nein, nicht so schnell! …..*(You must stir the porridge so it doesn't burn. No, not so fast.) He stopped listening because the edges of the pot got blurry and he couldn't help it. He began to cry. The big girl lifted him off the stool and gave him a glass of milk. *There there, it's your first day, after all, you'll be all right, we all had to leave our parents but you get used to it.*

She yelled, *"Somebody go get Miss Astfalck!."*

Martin would remain at Stoatley Rough for the next seven years and in spite of all manner of discomforts - chilblains, mumps, toothaches, plus a pesky and persistent sense that a German parachutist might swoop in at any time to run a bayonet through him or a bomb might land where he lay sleeping - he would emerge a secure young man. He would live with a new family, brothers and sisters he would grow to love. Safe in his new home, he would witness Great Britain engage in her extraordinary rendezvous with a great military power across the Channel: World War II. He would never forget.

The Austrian Exodus

Martin had gone to England because Germany had marched into his country in March of 1938 to claim it for itself. Martin's parents understood at once that Austrian Jews were no longer safe. How had Austria been taken over by Germany? If Martin, only ten years old at the time, had been old enough, he might have learned in history class that almost a hundred years earlier, Austria, while part of the powerful Austro-Hungarian Empire, also belonged to an alliance called the German Confederation. After being kicked out of the Confederation by the great Prussian leader, Bismarck, many Austrians yearned to return to the fold, seeing Germany as a superior big brother. The decade after World War I had brought misery and deprivation, inflation and unemployment, making both Germany and Austria ripe for ultra-nationalism. In 1933, Hitler's party won control and began to re-arm and make the German economy strong. Austrian political parties jockeyed for power throughout the nineteen twenties, among them their own brand of Nazis. In 1934, the Austrian Nazis assassinated Austria's Chancellor Dollfus, paving the way for them to gain control. The country was beset by violence. One afternoon, Nazi thugs set off stink bombs in the *Staatsoper* [Opera House] while Martin sat with his grandmother watching a performance of *Hänsel und Gretel*. By 1938, Austrian democracy was in its death throes. Martin would not forget the crowds, the powerful roaring voices, the force of mob mentality, the thrill of how one man could make whole crowds shriek and swoon.

Beforehand, life in Vienna had been rather nice. Martin was born to an upper middle class family with assimilated, non-religious Jewish parents who, as many Viennese of their station, were fond of the opera, *Sachertorte* (a chocolate cake,) and fancy dress balls. His mother had been baptized and educated as a Christian, while his father, wishing Martin to have a Jewish identity, took him to the temple on high holidays. "My family lived in a sunny apartment on the banks of the Danube in the 2nd (Jewish) District of Vienna. I remember that I had a beautifully decorated room with a balcony overlooking the Danube. There was a large advertisement sign for Persil (laundry soap) across the river." When he was five, the Depression was at its worst and his father lost his job working for his grandfather. His family went to live with his maternal grandparents, where one aunt, two maids, a cook and the nanny also lived. Martin was a quiet, tidy child, even handsome, winning first prize in a beauty contest when he was three. He liked to play with his toy soldiers, his large wooden castle and his trains. Martin spoke soft Austrian German in cool, unemotional tones. (He was always quiet and unthreatening. When he grew older at Stoatley Rough the girls characterized him as sweet and he was the first of his friends to have a girlfriend.)

In 1934, six-year-old Martin started school at the *Pedagogium,* a teacher training school on the *Hegelgasse* in the 1st District. Afternoons his mother or grandfather took him to the *Stadtpark,* the big municipal park in the center of the city, where he fed the swans. He revered his grandfather, his *Opi,* a handsome man with erect bearing and handlebar moustache who, like Martin's father, had served in World War I building a railroad line across Croatia to Turkey. *Opi* remained a major in the Austrian Army Reserve Corps and a loyal monarchist despite Austria's transition to democracy. Military officers in Europe at that time had high social rank, a fact that delayed the departure of some Jewish officers under Nazism until it was too late, never believing their country would turn on them. "My *Opi* taught me to ride a bike in the Prater, Vienna's amusement park and city park, the one with the Ferris wheel that features in Orson Welles' classic movie, 'The Third Man.' He used to take me there to shoot in the shooting galleries, where I got to be pretty proficient. I learned to hit the *Watschenman,* a dummy that you hit with all your might. I had to wear a very thick mitt. We used to visit the marionette theater and also *Lilliput Stadt*, a village of tiny houses occupied by dwarves." Martin's *Grosse Omi* [Big Grandma], his father's mother, lived nearby. He liked to watch her make apple strudel on her big kitchen table. Each season the family lit real candles on the Christmas tree. The summer before he started school, Martin stayed with the parents of one of the family's maids in the country and remembers watching deer at a salt lick and the force-feeding of the goose that habitually terrorized him by snapping at his *lederhosen*. His maid read to him from his book, *Streuwelpeter* [Peter with the Disheveled Hair], about the horrific punishments meted out to naughty children, all thrillingly illustrated in bright reds, greens, blues and yellows. It had pictures of a tailor with huge scissors who cuts off a naughty girl's thumb as bright red drops of blood fall to the ground; a girl is burned to ashes for torturing cats while the cats wipe tears from their eyes with little handkerchiefs; other children are thrown into the water to drown, or are starved, bitten by a dog, or shot.

When Martin came home from the farm, he found he had a new little sister. He was only slightly disappointed that he didn't get a St. Bernard instead.

"I was nine when the ugly realities sank in as to the future of Jews in Austria. I was with my nanny one day and we joined a circle around some activity going on in the street. Brown-uniformed SA men with swastikas on their armbands had made elderly Jewish men and women kneel down and scrub the streets on which resistant groups had written slogans." Going out with his nanny was not fun any more when she made him and Lisa sit on benches in the park he knew were prohibited to Jews.

Getting Martin out of Austria was not easy. Martin's mother stood in line for hours to get the countless forms from the German bureaucracy that had quickly taken root in Vienna. Since Jews were barred from almost all legitimate work, Martin's father, formerly a manager in the family's fur business, joined forces with an "Aryan" friend to help people send money illegally out of the country, involving forgeries of documents. It was very risky, but it brought money into the family's dwindling bank accounts. Six months after the German takeover, permission came through from both England and German governments. On September 22, 1938, the family stood on the *Bahnhof* platform to see Martin on his way.

On Martin's first morning at Stoatley Rough, the school's Headmistress, Dr. Hilde Lion, was sipping her morning tea in the dining room with her best friend, confidante, and second-in-command, Dr. Emmy Wolff. (Decades later, Martin and his friends would realize that Drs. Lion and Wolff were lovers. So innocent of the realities of the world, the thought never occurred to them.) Dr. Lion did not look like a headmistress. With her roly poly figure and short stature, she was an absent-minded woman with an impressive intellect, something of the absent-minded professor who sometimes wore unmatched socks with sensible lace-up leather shoes. Renate Dorpalen [Brocksieper], one of the girls in charge of cleanup that morning, later depicted Dr. Lion as "a heavy-set short woman with sad eyes that rarely looked directly at people. Her graying hair was severely pulled back and managed to come undone during the day. Her dress was careless, clothing spotted with food or ashes from her ever-present cigarette. A nervous variety of vocal tics increased in intensity under pressure. She spoke in heavily accented English, and often left sentences unfinished. " Many former pupils have written about that vocal tic, little self-reassuring humming noises with which Dr. Lion interspersed her speech. "Everyone heard her go "*hmm, hmm, my dearchen*." Children gleefully mimicked these little hums when she was out of earshot.

Dr. Lion poured herself more tea and took a bite of toast. (She and the staff did not always eat the same fare as the children.) She was worried. The arrival of the new little boy from Vienna, Martin Friedenfeld, reminded her that her boarding school was already strained to capacity. Where would they put Martin and the others who kept arriving? Stoatley Rough was now up to sixty-two pupils, double the enrollment of last year and she feared it would soon double again. Dr. Lion was also housing temporary evacuees, English children moved out of London to safety because the country was gearing up for war with Germany. She had simply said at her last meeting of the Committee, "They have got to be taken...."

Dr. Lion had a plan. She would reveal it at the Committee meeting that very evening. Thursley Copse, a grand country house just down Farnham Lane on the other side of the street was available for rent. She'd put Martin and all the other Austrian children there. Dr. Wolff knew of the house, only half a mile or so from Stoatley Rough. It was just past what is now Woodland Trust land. Dr. Wolff had walked many times across the Heath, sometimes called the Commons, an ancient pasturage once shared by neighbors. Everybody used the Heath to get to the small town of Hindhead or as just a place to take a walk. Children sometimes played soccer at its highest point, Gibbet Hill, a beautiful site that overlooked another protected swath of far-reaching land called the Devil's Punchbowl. Dr. Wolff thought Hilde's idea a fine one, and pondered the fact that Thursley Copse stood next to a real copse of bushes through which ran a path to the tiny part of Haslemere known as Shottermill. After four years in England, the intellectually curious woman had established that the English liked to give estates names with historic weight. "Stoatley," for example, was borrowed from the nearby Great and Little Stoatley Farms, and "stoatley" was comprised of the Old English words "stott" and "leah" meaning "clearing for horses or bullocks, and not, as she had first guessed, from the English word for the little weasel-like stoat that populated the countryside.

She nodded her agreement with Dr. Lion's plan. She needed to know what was going on. Dr. Wolff placed her spoon on her plate, folded her napkin, and prepared to leave the dining area. She was as well-groomed as Dr. Lion was untidy. Like Hilde Lion, Emmy Wolff wore her red-brown hair in a bun at the nape of her neck. But unlike her friend she carried herself with dignity, erectly, her aquiline, patrician features always composed. As the two women left the dining room, Dr. Lion told her that she had already contacted Thesi von Gierke, the niece of the Anna Von Gierke, former Director of the *Jugenheim Charlottenberg*

11

in Berlin where Dr. Lion and Dr. Wolff had worked and first met. Yes, Dr. Wolff agreed, young Thesi would bring order to the new residence.

Three months later, during the coldest winter on record in England, Martin and nineteen other Austrian children moved into Thursley Copse. They would sleep there but take their main meal of the day in the main house at Stoatley Rough, an arrangement that lasted for the next two years.

Dr. Lion Remembers

With two houses filled with refugees, Dr. Lion had much to do. After four years in England, however, she felt confident she could manage. She deposited her coat in the Bungalow and prepared to return to her office, musing about her own emigration in 1934, just four years earlier, from Berlin. A rising star in those days, she had lost everything to Nazi hatred. Forty years old and out of work, how had she managed to end up in England running a school for refugee children?

Dr. Lion's childhood had played out against the extraordinary events of the war of her own generation, World War I. Born May 14, 1893, into a wealthy, non-religious Jewish merchant family of Hamburg, Hilde and her older sister grew up in a genteel and stratified society. Dr. Lion's early years, steeped in Edwardian conventionality, were not happy ones after her parents divorced. As she matured, she refused to consider any suitor for her hand and then shocked her family by declaring she would never marry. In an unpublished autobiography she described the reaction to her radical decision. "My relatives and my parents' friends regarded my intention of taking up a career as highly unsuitable, and there were rumours that my father could not be well off if he permitted me to take up teaching. …My parents were aghast when I told them that I wanted to be a teacher, be financially independent and avoid having to make a marriage of convenience."[1] Men were never to play

---

[1] Lion, Hilde, quoted by Monika Simmel Joaquin in her paper delivered at the 70th Anniversary Reunion 22-25 October 2004, Haslemere, Surrey, entitled *Background of the five Principal Refugee Teachers of Stoatley Rough School from*

any role in her personal life. Hilda doted on her sister's two sons and the half-brother that was born to her father's new wife in the ensuing years, and insecurity dogged her through life. She entered the Hamburg Social Pedagogical Institute in 1917, a year before World War I would end. There she met feminists whose goals were to advance a woman's right to economic equality with men. She joined the movement to change the rules, such as society's stricture against allowing women to work outside the home in more than just in teaching, nursing or social work. Life was slower before the first world war, less complicated, with the telephone, refrigeration and even the lowly zipper still to be invented. There were strict gender roles and women were certainly not expected to behave and think like men. But the war changed everything. Soon, social norms, the arts and even trends in fashion electrified a Continent. Picasso's Cubism came onto the scene even before the war; and by the time Hilde reached her twentieth birthday, Stravinsky's *The Rite of Spring* had stunned concert audiences. Coco Chanel's line of clothing - loose and comfortable - revolutionized women's fashion. In 1920 feminists earned women the right to vote (a year before the U.S. passed its own 19th Amendment). While other girls her age might have thought it daring to smoke in public or cut short their hair, young Hilde Lion was radicalized, taking minutes at activist meetings, writing pamphlets, planning how best to advance women's rights. But her idealism soon flagged when she understood that women would not truly share political power overnight. She entered the University of Cologne and in 1924, she earned a doctorate in social welfare, an extraordinary achievement at the time for a woman. In 1925 she began to teach at the *Jugendheim Charlottenburg* [Youth Home in the district of Charlottenburg], part of a government-funded network of facilities and services.[2] In 1929,

---

Nazi - Germany: Dr. Hilde Lion, Dr. Emmy Wolff, Eleonore Astfalck, Hanna Nacken and Dr. Luise Leven. The quotation, translated by Dr. Simmel-Joaquin, appeared in Manfred Berger's work, *Hilde Lion, in Christ und Welt* 5/1995, p. 167. "M. Berger holds several papers of many women in the history of welfare in his private "Ida Seele Institute", but he doesn't allow access to any materials."

[2] The *Jugendheim* was founded in 1898 by Anna von Giercke (1874-1943), who became Hilde's mentor and friend, who ran it largely by and for women, offering

Dr. Lion was appointed Director of another institution, the *Deutsche Akademie für Soziale und Paedagogische Frauenarbeit* [German Academy of Women's Social and Pedagogical Work], another government-funded institution established by the prominent German feminist, Dr. Alice Salomon. The Academy offered university level training of both practical and interdisciplinary value. Dr. Lion found great satisfaction in helping the impoverished victims of the Depression, mindful that women could find dignity in volunteer work. She created a program for volunteers called The Mother's Help Services for middle-class female social workers, to protect them from the "narrow-mindedness, wretchedness and early bitterness" of unemployment.

Her belief in the intrinsic value of work in Germany became a cornerstone of the governing philosophy at Stoatley Rough, where everyone shared in the work, students and staff alike. Communal work at the school provided the pupils a sense of purpose and predictability while at the same time imparting citizenship and fair play. Wrote one pupil, "The disciplines they imposed were so logical that I soon realized that resistance to them was pointless and unprofitable."[3] By requiring the children to take part in running their own school and in having a stake in it through their participation, Dr. Lion gave her displaced children a sense of purpose, of being needed. Being needed helped to save the Stoatley Rough children exactly as it had saved Depression women in Germany: they were saved from self-pity, despair and defeat.

Dr. Lion sat down heavily at her desk and picked up her calendar, remembering the worried look on young Martin Friedenfeld's face as he had wandered from the breakfast room that morning. A little lost soul. She, too, had suffered at the hands of the Nazis, back in 1933 when they took power in Germany. Almost immediate racial laws prohibited any Jew, or "non-Aryan" from leading any of the hundreds of governmental agencies and organizations. Thousands of educators, artists, scientists,

---

training to the general population in nutrition, counseling, daycare and job skills, and functioned primarily as a teacher training institution for careers for women in social work, kindergarten and child care.

3   [Rice] Weissrock, Susi, *The Story of Gabi, Susi and our Mother*, Newsletter, Issue 4, p.10.

musicians, and social workers were thrown out of work. Dr. Lion and others of her prominence began to leave the country. In 1934 alone some 60,000 people left Germany.

Dr. Lion looked forward to the Committee meeting. It would be held in London that evening. She had enormous respect for the founders of the school, and was grateful they gave her leeway to put into practice their shared values for the school. She recalled how ardently they had worked to establish Stoatley Rough School in the first place.

The idea had come from a group of British refugee workers attuned to the plight of the German Jewish children arriving in their country in 1933. These advocates for refugees wanted to teach the English language and English customs to the children to prepare them to work overseas in British colonies. Strict laws restricted the type of work available to immigrants at the time: only household occupations such as housekeeper, maid, butler, valet, etc., or farm work jobs were available even to the most brilliant emigré. Britain might be willing to accept foreigners but was not about to give up any of its good jobs to non-citizens. Members of the Quaker German Emergency Committee and the Jewish Refugee Committee, along with other concerned activists, formed a group to plan and raise money for a school. Quaker activist, Miss Bertha Bracey, who shuttled between Berlin and London on behalf of German-Jewish children, met the Dr. Lion on one of her trips to Berlin and saw just the person she had been looking for. [4] It was not long before she arranged for Dr. Lion to receive a grant from the British Federation of University Women to come to England. Dr. Lion was

---

[4] Miss Bracey found Dr. Hilde Lion through her Quaker colleagues, Corder and Gwen Catchpool, in Berlin. Not many people knew that a Berlin International Center was established after WWI to promote reconciliation between England and Germany. Bertha Bracey would be awarded the Order of the British Empire (OBE) in 1942 for her humanitarian work during World War II. Another key founder was Mrs. Anna Schwab of the Jewish Women's Committee and Chair of the Hospitality Committee of the Refugee Committee. A native of Frankfurt am Main, she had not only worked with German refugees in England during World War I, but was instrumental in converting the B'nai B'rith rooms in a building called Woburn House in London into a refugee organization that would assist the entry into England of many Stoatley Rough children during the second World War.

supposed to write about the "intellectual and emotional readjustment of children to a new environment" but Miss Bracey had bigger plans. Dr. Lion was legally forbidden to accept wages in England but her talents fit the plans of the Committee – they would take care of her. Dr. Lion moved into the University Women's club in Crosby Road, Chelsea and plunged into helping Miss Bracey and her group. Eleanore Astfalck, the school's first Matron, wrote about Dr. Lion's early activities in England. "Hilde Lion…had no money, nowhere to live, and [did not know] how to find a job or how to start her studies. In 1934 …she was only interested in finding jobs for people." [5]

Dr. Lion recalled the luck the Committee had had (fueled of course by their tireless efforts) in bringing the school into existence. Finances were the issue back then, and as far as she could tell, would always be her number one concern as Headmistress. Back in 1934 neither the Quakers nor the Jewish Women's Committee could fund the school, but the Inter-Aid Committee for Children contributed substantially, along with the Jewish Refugee Committee (£60 per annum), and the Mayor of Guildford Refugee Committee (£52 per annum). It was not enough. They turned to the very wealthy, members of the peerage, who agreed to form a temporary oversight Council to monitor the product of their largess. [6] A steering Committee (all-female) made up of the original group of founding activists would tend to the every-day business of the school.[7] Within a few months they raised around £531, in dollars roughly $2,665, some of which was a loan to be repaid within the year. Wolf Edelstein [Elston] helps us understand the relative value of the

---

[5] Eleonore Astfalck, Oral History

[6] Council members / benefactors included Miss Bertha Bracey, Miss E. Day, Sir Wyndham Deeds, Professor G. P. Gooch, Leonard Monfiore, Sir Walter Nicholson, Lady Parmoor, Lady Pentland, famous for her work with Lord Pentland, in raising money for a hospital ship for the people of Madras, and Lady Sprigge who, with her husband, worked to discredit the false science of eugenics, or race-classification.

[7] Original Committee members included Miss Bertha Bracey, Miss B. Alexander, Miss Isabel Fry, Dr. Mary E. Gilbert, Miss Mary Hayward, Ms. Omerod, and Mrs. Marjorie Vernon.

sum raised for the school. "In 1935, £5 / week was a good middle class income. £531 would have been 2-3 year's pay for an industrial worker." The Committee worked out the fee to be charged students for tuition, room and board: £100 per annum, with ongoing support to be sought for those who needed it to come from various refugee and charitable agencies. To put this fee into context, a Member of Parliament in 1934 was paid £600; a teacher at Stoatley Rough £50 per annum plus room and board.

Everything was set. The new school had a Committee, a financial Board, a Headmistress, and the financing. But where would the children live and study? At this critical juncture entered a small, self-assured, very wealthy and well-connected woman who was neither Quaker nor Jewish but rather a devout, upper class Anglican. Mrs. Marjorie Vernon owned a country estate, Stoatley Rough, lying virtually empty out in Haslemere, Surrey, forty miles southwest of London. She had inherited this lovely mansion and grounds from her father in the twenties. She now spent most of her weekends in another more elegant residence in Hampshire. She wondered if Stoatley Rough might do as a school. She checked with her husband, Roland Venables Vernon, Undersecretary in the British Colonial Office, whose family boasted baronetcies and titles of nobility dating from the twelfth century. He approved of the idea. After all, Marjorie devoted herself to charitable work and accompanied her husband in his travels and the Vernon family hardly ever went to Stoatley Rough these days now that their only child had grown up and left home.[8] In one unforgettable act of generosity, Mrs. Vernon handed over her estate lock stock and barrel.

---

[8] Mr. Vernon spent a few years after the first World War as financial advisor to the government of Iraq. Then, after a lifetime of service, he was paralyzed from the waist down after a plane crash in Palestine. He died in 1942, pre-deceasing Mrs. Vernon by almost twenty years. The couple had one adopted daughter, Sally. Mrs. Vernon, who, upon her death in June, 1961, was colorfully characterized in the local newspaper as "a bit of an autocrat and contradictory" [to which, as if to mitigate his dubious description, the writer hastens to add, "[but] generous." (Apparently she was not an infinite source of funds for the school, however. In a letter to Dr. Lion dated February 16, 1935, she writes with great cordiality, "Dear

The beautiful Stoatley Rough was instantly deemed satisfactory by the grateful Committee. Mrs. Vernon's terms were simple: the new school would retain the gardener and his wife, Mr. and Mrs. Phillips, who would continue to live in the carriage house ("The Lodge") for their lifetimes. (Mr. Phillips and his wife, who never appeared in public without her hat, lived in The Lodge for over forty years).[9] Mr. Phillips was to continue to maintain the grounds; the school would pay for all maintenance and upkeep of the property; and the gift of the house would be reexamined after three years.

Dr. Lion settled in at her desk to begin her day's work. She wondered what Miss Fry, the lady originally in charge of things while Dr. Lion acclimated herself to England, was doing in her retirement. Probably traveling. Isabel Fry, a Quaker lady who had taught school for many years had taken the helm on a temporary basis while Dr. Lion recruited staff and pupils, and had long since dropped out of sight. Dr. Lion wondered about her own future. Would she ever have the funds to travel? How long would she last at this new school? The irony was not lost on her. She who had dedicated herself to helping the impoverished and unemployed in Germany, might have been impoverished and unemployed as well if it had not been for Miss Bracey, Miss Fry, and others.

She looked up. Mr. Phillips had entered and stood awkwardly in the doorway to the tiny office. What did he want? He only delivered fresh flowers to Dr. Lion's room during the summer months. Hat in hand, he asked, Did Dr. Lion have special plans for the eastern edge of the second tennis court? He had some ideas for new shrubbery if she approved. After he left her office, Dr. Lion remembered the day Mrs. Vernon had to deliver the news to the crusty old gentleman that his sanctuary was about to be invaded. A Cockney with a green thumb and

---

Dr. Lion. Thank you for your letter. I'm afraid the income tax is yours! Also you will have to pay the tax for the 2 gardeners – I return the form, also the telephone receipt."

[9] John [Hans Obo] Obermeyer wrote that Mr. Phillips was succeeded by a "Miss Woolger who lived in his nice cottage with her big Irish Terrier dog. She was a very nice lady, always wore riding boots, and was a good horticulturist."

short temper, he was used to a quiet life at Stoatley Rough. Mrs. Vernon knew he would be fearful of little feet trampling his prized flowers. She won him over. Wolf [Edelstein] Elston recalled, "At first I was afraid of that gruff old man, especially when he grumbled about 'them bloomin' nippers, runnin' across me flower beds, Oi'll givem the shtick, Oi will!'" But Mr. Phillips was special. "To me, he epitomized the sturdy English yeoman. In England, people don't talk much about themselves and only in his obituary in the *Haslemere Herald*, years later, did I learn that Mr. Phillips had been a prominent local citizen, the respected member of boards and councils."

Mr. Phillips would have been proud to know how the pupils revered the school and its lovely grounds. The estate had been built by Mrs. Vernon's father, Mr. Arthur Leon, a stockbroker, philanthropist and wealthy civil servant, in 1898 along a ridge south of the small prosperous town of Haslemere. The seventeen acres offered a spectacular view of the forested South Downs, starting 750 feet above sea level along a promontory, then swooping 570 feet down at a steep angle to a small stream that trickled through lush farmland. Mr. Leon hired the prominent London architect, Falconer Macdonald, to design his house, intending to mirror and perhaps exceed the grandeur of the other two other Macdonald-designed houses in the neighborhood, Thursley Hall and Dunrozel, both stately and sensible residences, neither too flashy nor humble, but quietly elegant and expensive dwellings that exuded stability and prosperity with their red brick chimneys, slate roofs, many gables and large bay windows. Mr. Leon's property soon bloomed with gardens and shrubbery, two tennis courts and a winding path that led down the steep slope to the farmland.[10]

Improvements followed. Mr. and Mrs. Vernon added a gardener's cottage, stables and two small houses in the valley that they rented out to working class families. By the 1930's, however, the Vernons rarely used

---

[10] Mr. Arthur Leon moved his family from Russell Square, London, to the Haslemere house in 1889. His parcel of land on the farthest end of shady Farnham Lane was one of the prettiest sites in the county, formerly owned by a Quaker surgeon, Jonathan Hutchinson.

Stoatley Rough except to fill it with mementos of their extensive travels, allowing it to sit in splendid isolation, its fantastic view of the South Downs enjoyed only by the birds and small creatures that lived among the trees and shrubbery.[11] The view from the terrace encompassed a magnificent view: Witley Forest and the high ridge dozens of miles away known as Blackdown where once Alfred, Lord Tennyson made his home. On a clear day, one could even peer into Hampshire county.

Mrs. Vernon's gift had an extraordinary influence on its students and refugee teachers, imparting tranquility and healing to traumatized and homesick children. Edith Hubacher [Christoffel-Hubacher] wrote, "[I recall] the magnificent garden, so lovingly and competently tended by Mr Phillips...; the garden in which one could always find a lovely and quiet place to read or do one's prep. The Flowers! The age-old pine trees under whose branches one hide because they came down to the ground, forming the compact sides of a hut! The wide sweep of the path down to the tennis-court where we did our gymnastics! The Rhododendrons! The old wall below the house overgrown with wisteria, viburnum and wild roses, with the wide grassy path beneath! It's all gone, but the memories remain." Ruth Ultmann [Muessig] chose her new house in America based upon her memories of Stoatley Rough. "One reason my little house here in Connecticut attracted me right away

---

[11] Rapturous descriptions such as that of Beate Frankfurter [Planskoy] describe "high-growing bracken and yellow flowering gorse, bilberry and blackberry plants... I shall also never forget the beautiful terraced gardens with the tall mature trees, the flowering rhododendron and wisteria, and the many secret places where one could hide when in need of solitude. In the winter the branches of the trees were heavy with snow and the landscape took on the magical appearance of a Hans Anderson fairytale." "The house offered a spectacular view of many of miles of verdant countryside. The poet and Roughian Gerda Meyer [Stein] recalled, "It may need saying, for the sake of the younger reader, that the world - visually and aurally at least - was an altogether prettier and quieter place than now. But even by the standards of those days, Stoatley Rough must be reckoned to have been uniquely beautiful."

was that it faces a mountain, the Sleeping Giant, and it looks remarkably like the Surrey Downs."[12]

Dr. Lion fingered her day book. It noted that in 1921, the German government had granted women the right to vote. She smiled wistfully. So long ago, and in a place so far away, she had been a part of that great moment in history.

---

[12] In a letter to her mother dated November 20, 1936, Dr. Emmy Wolff wrote that Phillips had won ten prizes in Haslemere's vegetable and flower show that year: "…two firsts, four seconds and four thirds for the lovely vegetables (especially the English celery), pears and a rare form of chrysanthemum which he cultivates…" Translated by Katya Schaefer [Sheppard], Stoatley Rough Newsletter 8, June, 1995, p. 18.

Too Many Separations

Martin was starting to make friends with some of the children. He had barely gotten himself settled in the Thursley Copse house with the other Austrians when the school closed for the Christmas holidays and thirty-five children who could not return home were placed into the homes of English friends and supporters of the school. Martin said of his hosts that Christmas, "They spoke no German and my English was somewhere between poor and non-existent. I learned a lot of English from these kind people... For Christmas they gave me a Dinky Toy dust lorry (garbage truck) which I treasured and kept for many years." Sometimes the children landed in the homes of well-connected citizens, such as Gerhard (Gad) Wolff, who lived with a successful playwright, Miss Olive Popplewell, not only a friend of G. B. Shaw, but "a kind-hearted Quaker lady, who also got us invitations to tea parties and provided us with tickets to *Snow White*." The thirteen-year-old recalled that he had tried to convince Miss Popplewell and her friends of Hitler's war buildup but his words "were met with disbelief."13

When Martin returned to the school in January, 1939, there was a surprise in store for him. He learned that he would not attend classes with the other children his age at Stoatley Rough. Along with a few others, he was going to attend a government-run boys' school, the Shottermill County Council School. Classes in the main house at

---

13 Wolff, Gad Gerhard, *A Traveler's Tale*, Stoatley Rough Newsletter 19, August, 1999, P. 49

Stoatley Rough, then averaging from between five to ten pupils who sat around big tables, were filled to capacity.

Martin would be separated from the boys he was just starting to make friends with. And he would miss the Matron, Miss Astfalck. A very nice lady who seemed to come around to check up on him in the kindest way just when he felt most depressed. He had no choice. He would have to do as he was told. Miss Astfalck tried to assuage his fears. The youngest of the German teachers and also the kindest and hardest working, Nore Astfalck was a diminutive Mary Poppins - diligent, crisp, cheerful, and relentlessly efficient. Unlike Dr. Lion, who was only seven years her senior but something of a butterball, thirty-eight year old Nore was physically fit. Her features were finely sculpted, with clear blue eyes that had a disarmingly direct gaze, an oval face with a long, aquiline nose, and short wavy hair swept back off a high forehead. Nothing happened in the school that Miss Astfalck wasn't privy to, and the children knew it. Nobody could duck responsibility, She'd know if you didn't brush your teeth.

In some ways, Martin was lucky at Thursley Copse. At least they had enough bathrooms. Stoatley Rough had only one sink for girls, a toilet each for the girls, boys and teachers, and one boys' and one girl's bathing room. When the school was new and enrollment small, the facilities had been adequate but by 1939 the residential population had grown to over 70. Wolf recalled, "After the morning run came a rush for the toilet and the sink – the singulars are deliberate. Stoatley Rough had been a private home and there had been one indoor toilet for the family… and another in an unheated annex behind the kitchen, for the servants (now used by boys.) Mercifully, boys were allowed to use the girl's facility at night."

Martin began school that January, walking to his new school with another boy from Austria, ten-year-old Richard Gruenzweig [Green]. From Farnham Lane, they cut through the copse downhill to reach the school (which incidentally had been built as a gift to the town by Marjorie Vernon's father and original owner of Stoatley Rough, Mr. Arthur Leon in the first decade of the twentieth century). Ricky

Gruenzweig was bigger than Martin and something of a bully. Over time, the larger boy started forcing Martin into fistfights along the way, but Martin never complained. (Later Martin acquired a bike on which he flew down Farnham Lane to school at high speed in the mornings and slowly rode back up the hill on his return in the afternoons, carving out a zigzag pattern.) At Shottermill, Martin studied English, math, history and science. He especially enjoyed the woodworking and gardening. "It was a rough school. If you got out of line, you were caned and the rules were strict. We all had Victory Gardens in which we grew vegetables. We were not allowed to talk while gardening. One day, the class clown told a joke and I burst out laughing. I was caught and caned across my fingertips, whereas he escaped unpunished. It was a very painful experience."[14] Martin yearned to take classes at Stoatley Rough where no corporal punishment was tolerated. The worst punishment was to be sent to Dr. Lion for a talking to. But Martin never complained. As young as he was, he was grateful to be safe from whatever the Nazis planned to do to make Jews feel bad back in Austria.

Dr. Lion seems not to have been aware of any problems. When she wrote to the Headmaster of the all-boys' school, she merely commented, "Richard is rather a wild young fellow, and we should recommend to have an eye on him especially. Martin is a little frail, and we would appreciate it if the school doctor could see him before he begins swimming. He tells me he has been swimming since his 8th year however."[15] Dr. Lion never overlooked any free services she could extract. In a note to the same principal the following year, Dr. Lion asked if Shottermill's dentist would take care of Martin's tooth-ache "as we have very limited funds, it would mean a great help." [16]

Martin was thus consigned to living a disjointed life, sleeping at Thursley Copse, dining at Stoatley Rough, and taking classes at Shottermill. English children left the government school system of

---

14 Friedenfeld [Owens], Martin, unpublished memoir.
15 Lion, Dr. Hilde, Letter to principal of Shottermill School, Stoatley Rough Archives, LSE, Box 1/1 (ii)
16 Ibid.

basic education at fourteen, and accordingly, Martin graduated from Shottermill and joined his peers at Stoatley Rough to live and study in the same place for another two plus years. He believes today that his formal education was not harmed by attending the government school, but he suspects that his lifelong fear of separation from loved ones may stem from leaving his parents, losing the girl who looked after him (Gertrud Gans), being segregated from the other children by attending Shottermill School, and living in Thursley Copse, all of which occurred within four months of his arrival in England.

One day in the summer of 1939, Martin opened a letter from home that brought bad news. His father had been arrested for selling forged documents and had been shipped to a prison in Berlin. Martin's mother did not tell him that during this time, SS men regularly came to the apartment to harass her and to take her in for questioning, leaving his little sister screaming at the window as she was carted off. A few weeks later Martin learned from his mother that his father's partner had accepted the blame when the case came to trial. His relief turned to horror when he learned that while Martin's father was to remain in prison, the Aryan who had collaborated with a Jew was handed down the death sentence and was shot at once.[17] Months later, his mother miraculously managed to get the paperwork together to get her husband out of jail, out of Berlin, and out of the country to safety in the United States.

The adult Martin suppressed the trauma of his abrupt move from Vienna to England. Harvard-based researchers, Gerald Holton and Gerhard Sonnert, make the case that the Austrian Jews were more intensely affected than German Jews, since the *Anschluss* came so suddenly upon them. (Not necessarily a worse experience, but one felt more intensely.) In Germany, the persecution was inflicted a little bit at a time under official dicta, while in Austria, the official persecutions

---

[17] Martin's *Kleine Omi* and *Opi* also escaped, but his *Grosse Omi*, the maker of *apfelstrudel,* chose to stay behind. She died in Theresienstadt. Over the course of the war, 65,500 Austrian Jews were deported and perished as victims of the National Socialists.

and loss of status occurred to the Jewish population almost overnight. Today Martin is relatively well-adjusted, displaying only the occasional eccentricity in the form of packing for a trip several days before leaving, or having an extraordinary need to arrive at events early. He is sanguine about his eccentric habits and would agree that in part, his introspective nature, fear of abandonment and need to be ready for any emergency, seem to confirm there was an element of trauma in his experience with the events during and after the *Anschluss*. [18]

In January of 1939, while Martin was struggling to learn the tricky English verbs at Shottermill, other boys his age who would come to Stoatley Rough were still in Germany, reeling from *Kristallnacht* [the Night of the Broken Glass], which occurred on November 5/6, 1938, a month after Martin arrived at Stoatley Rough. On that night, Hitler's thugs set fire to Jewish businesses and synagogues across Germany and Austria as officials stood by. The pogrom was an unmistakable sign. Nazi hatred was out in the open. Jewish families began to search for ways to get themselves and their children to safety. Only a few children would be lucky enough to land in the welcoming lap of Stoatley Rough School.

---

[18] The researchers studied the effects of the social, psychological and economic effects of the Holocaust on Austrian Jewish children in America. They found resiliency and other abiding values, yet there were scars. "They, their families and many of their friends were suddenly considered outlaws, thrown into dreadful turmoil by the persecution, assaults, expulsion from their schools – while their parents, with some most honorable exceptions, were made to experience much worse.... The National Socialist regime and a hostile population in Austria learned in days what had taken years in Germany." The authors list possible traumas: firing of teachers; prohibition from using theaters, playgrounds, parks; exposure to assault by mobs and uniformed men; takeovers of apartments, offices, shops and other property. In April 26, 1938, the vicious newspaper, *Volkischer Beobachter*, widely read in Austria as well as Germany, even ran an article, 'How Can We Get Rid of the Jews?" While the study found that Austrian refugees did relatively well economically and led productive lives (and described positive effects of their early experience on their attitude, stating that "success was the best revenge"), others were demoralized by Nazism, became depressed in the new world, and over the years have suffered in later life anxiety, panic attacks, fear of abandonment, and suspicion of all authority.

27

One cold day in January, a boy from Berlin was assigned to Martin's table for the week, a boy his own age. Wolf Edelstein [Elston] was a big-boned, sometimes clumsy boy, with a handsome, somewhat hangdog and melancholic face. The quiet and introspective Martin soon discovered his new friend was anything but melancholic. He was an inveterate prankster who frequently indulged his impulse to utter witty, audacious or irreverent remarks, even to adults. Such bravado astonished Martin but apparently did no harm to his own standing with the powers that be. Wolf quickly became the darling of Dr. Lion and Dr. Wolff, the former a very distant cousin on his father's side. Dr. Wolff even (unwisely) tried to get Wolf to address her in the familiar "*Du*", the form of "you" Germans use for children, servants and God, instead of the appropriate formal *Sie* as in *Sprechen Sie Deutsch*? Wolf sensibly resisted being singled out. He was already wildly happy with his new life in England after having suffered at the hands of Nazi classroom martinets and was all too aware of the dangers of favoritism in school.

A Perversion of Education

While in his Berlin home, Wolfgang Edelstein often dressed in his old clothes and dashed out back in the family garden to play peg tops with his big brother Gerd. As he sat in the dirt, expertly pulled the string that set his top spinning fast, he was thinking this time he might beat Gerd. But he couldn't help but think about the day to come, his birthday. He dreaded it. First a bath! And then they would put him in a Little Lord Fauntleroy outfit and expect him to bow to grownups and little girls in frilly dresses who would come to his party. At home in Berlin in the early 1930's, the boy chafed at the fussier social conventions of his upper-middle class station. The next day unfolded as expected. Called inside, his mother told him, "Now Wolfie, here's your outfit for today. You know we have a whole party arranged for you and there will be cakes and cookies and maybe a present if you behave." She turned to the maid standing by with towels. "Maria, don't forget to scrub behind his ears – look at that boy! And please pay special attention to his fingernails." Wolf was not at all embarrassed to sit naked in the tub as Hilde scrubbed him. He loved his Mia who had cared for him as long as he could remember. His father was gone all the time doing "important work". His mother was always off curing children – and that was doing good in the world, he knew that – but sometimes he wished he could have more time with her.

In the final analysis, he was one of the few who were glad to be sent to Stoatley Rough. He was finally free of all that clicking of heels and bowing when he met someone. He did not know at the time but a notation in his personal file during his first term in 1939 at the new school under the headings "Tidiness" and "Personal Neatness" read: "Improving but not yet satisfactory." Someone else had taken a black marker to cross it out and write "BAD."

Wolf had grown up in a comfortable apartment in Grunewald, a tony neighborhood near a forest of scotch fir and birch. The forest bordered the Havel River that flowed gently into the lake that would become notorious as the site of the 1942 Wannsee Conference where the Nazis formulated their plans for the Final Solution of the Jewish Question. Wolf's mother conducted her practice in Pediatrics in their apartment, having been one of the first women in Germany to study medicine. (In the United States, at the age of 46, this remarkable woman prepared for and passed the medical boards in English; she would practice medicine in Pennsylvania into her 80's.) Wolf lived a happy-go-lucky life. It was Mia who took him to school on his first day of school, not his mother, and when Mia left service to get married, Wolf was distraught. But he was growing up anyway and no longer needed a nanny.

One day the well-to-do Edelsteins, who employed a full-time maid and cook, accepted delivery of a newfangled Frigidaire. "When my mother showed off our apartment to visitors, she'd show them the Frigidaire and make excuses for having indulged in such a luxury – 'it's to keep the children's milk cold.' Wolf later recalled, "The joke is that Gerd and I hated milk and never drank it. In those days, milk was not pasteurized. It had to be boiled and then was served warm with scum on top. Absolutely disgusting! I feel sick just thinking about it!"

Wolf started school at about the time racial laws were being enacted, in September of 1934. One day a few older boys stopped him on the street to ask, "Are you a Jew?" The scholarly Wolf said, "No, the Jews lived 5,000 years ago," puzzled by such a silly question. A few days later, his teacher asked the children to bring in a family tree with religions next to the names. It was only then that he discovered that all his grandparents were Jewish. Upon the accession of Hitler, Wolf's father, in an act of defiance, joined an underground Christian church, the Confessional Church, one that had been formed to protest the

Nazi's conglomerate of "official" Protestant churches. Indifferent to the church, Wolf drawn to the forbidden. He became enamored of the Nazi youth corps that sprang up around him. He enjoyed watching Hitler's brass bands marching in nationalistic parades, thrilling to the waving swastikas and extravagant displays of weaponry. But when he started school in 1934, he began to be the subject of bizarre and humiliating ordeals. The little boy was the only non-Aryan in his class, not such a problem for the six year old but as the years passed, he was targeted. He was too intelligent to ignore some of the more blatant excesses of the school's propaganda machine. The Reich Minister of Science, Education and Popular Culture (onetime *Gauleiter* [provincial leader] of Hanover), and unemployed schoolmaster having been dismissed in 1930 for "certain manifestations of instability of mind," Dr. Bernhard Rust, took it upon himself to pervert the entire German national educational system from top to bottom, boasting that he succeeded in "liquidating the school as an institution of intellectual acrobatics." He forced teachers and professors to take an oath to be loyal to Adolf Hitler and meddled in the curriculum with catastrophic results for German education. Wolf endured the Nazi version of religion and paganist dogma in which the teachers immersed the children. "The teachers opened each lesson with *'Heil Hitler'* as if voicing a religious incantation, and a new discipline appeared in the curriculum called *Rassenkunde* [racial studies]. "I participated in interminable flag-honoring ceremonies where teachers in SA uniforms with *"Blut und Ehre* [Blood and Honor] inscribed daggers on their belts strutted about the school yard while we sang every verse of the *'Horst Wessel Lied'* and *'Deutschland Über Alles.'* In subjects such as German literature and history, it was the Nazi doctrine that prevailed." Anti-Semitism was sanctioned by the teachers and Wolf became "the target of every bully," harassed and beaten. Children picked on Wolf almost every day for one thing or another. One day Wolf was given a moment's peace from his tormenters courtesy of an unlikely ally. A boy started to taunt him for having dark hair, but a defender rose to take Wolf's side. The defender was not just anybody but the son of the chief legal advisor to Hitler, Hans Frank, who would become Governor-General of Occupied Poland. Little Norman Frank was indignant. *"Lass' ihn doch, mein Vater und der Führer haben auch schwarze Haare."* [Leave him alone, my father and the Fuhrer have dark hair, too.] Later, Wolf could not describe the complex mix of nostalgia, revulsion and vindication that surged in his heart when he learned from the news media that Norman's father was tried and hanged at Nuremberg for the crimes he committed in Poland.

Evenings over the dinner table, the family talked about the sobering policies that were continually emanating from the Reich, such as the Nazi politicization of organizations, a totalitarian philosophy termed *Gleichschaltung* [making things equal] that put every organization such as the Protestant churches under state control. The policy that seemed to encompass every institution and practice in Germany was so politicizing that Wolf's father joked that soon the name of the forest near their home would be dubbed the "National Socialist Association of Trees." Wolf noted, "The Nazis never referred to themselves as Nazis but as National Socialists [*Nationalsozialisten*], NS for short. Motorists for example, were organized into the NSKK [*NS Kraftfahr Korps* – NS Power Vehicle Corps]. Popularly, it was said that NSKK stood for *"Nur Säufer, Keine Kämpfer* [Only boozers, no fighters]."

In August of 1938, a couple of months after Wolf's tenth birthday, Hitler closed the public schools to the *"Nichtarier"* [non-Aryan,] prompting Wolf's parents - at long last - to send him to a progressive school for non-Aryan children, the *Goldschmidtschule* in Berlin-Grunewald. During Wolf's short tenure, it simultaneously operated out of its main building in Hohenzollendamm, formerly the mansion of the steel baron Hugo Stinnes who had fallen afoul of Der Fuehrer and a subsidiary building nearby in the Kronberger-Strasse. Today a memorial plaque on the wall of an upscale Greek restaurant that now occupies the site ends with the words "1939 wurde die Schule durch die Nationalsozialisten geschlossen. [In 1939 the school was closed by the National Socialists][19]. For the first time, he found relief from his tormenters. He remembers being radiantly happy in his new school if

---

[19] Wolf Elston in an email to the author.

only for six months until the Nazis closed the school and he was sent out of the country to England. Dr. Leonore Goldschmidt (not to be confused with the great feminist, Henriette Goldschmidt, (1825-1920) founded the school in 1934 for Jewish boys and girls in an apartment building in Berlin. Like Stoatley Rough, this school forbade corporal punishment and did not tolerate abuse or fighting among the children. Male and female teachers conducted the co-ed classes in a relaxed environment free of Nazi propaganda. Wolf studied English, natural science, history, music, handicraft, and other conventional subjects that had been the fare of a pre-1933 German *Gymnasium*. Wolf learned for the first time about Judaism and sang Zionist songs.[20]

---

[20] Coincidentally, two other people at Stoatley Rough shared a common history in the Goldschmidt School. Eva Graetz was only nineteen when she was hired to teach at the Goldschmidt School, requiring Dr. Goldschmidt to give her lessons in teaching techniques. The Assistant Principal of the Goldschmidt School was Herta Lewent's uncle. Dr. Kurt Lewent, a noted scholar of medieval Provençal literature, was known to children like Wolf as *Kinderschreck* [Frightener of Children]. Wolf said, "He went around with a pained look on his face and attitude of stern discipline .... He was in fact, in constant pain, the result of wounds from his services as an officer in WWI, fighting for his Kaiser und Vaterland. Eva Graetz was so young that one day Dr. Lewent encountered the young teacher in a school hallway during classes and bawled her out (*Er hat Sie angeschnauzt*, as only a German teacher can do), mistaking her for a wayward pupil." A small group of Hitler Youth tried to attack the school in November 11, 1938 just after the *Kristallnacht* siege when one half of the male teachers were arrested. Miss' Graetz wrote "Dr. Goldschmidt called up all the women teachers begging them to come and ...let the show go on. Many of the [children's] fathers had been arrested. Everybody tried to prepare for emigration. The present and future of these children spelled danger and insecurity, but if they came to school, one part of their life would continue, business as usual. Needless to say we, the women teachers, were all glad to come. [It was characteristic of Dr. Lewent that he] insisted on completing his French class while a mob was threatening to burn down the school. Only after the closing bell did he finally lead the quaking kids to safety out of the back door, and go into hiding himself....Dr. Leonore Goldschmidt saved the school by selling it for 10 Reichsmark to Mr. Whooley, one of the British teachers [who had been hired to prepare] us for our future in an English-speaking country. That placed the school under the protection of His Britannic Majesty and the Nazis did not dare to provoke an international incident." In 1939, the

Wolf recalled that the Nazis classified one of the teachers at the Goldschmidt School as a *Mischling*, the Nazi term for the offspring of a mixed Jewish / Christian couple. "Herr Lennert, my teacher (*Klassenlehrer*) at the *Goldschmidtschule* in Berlin was a "*Mischling*." The Nazis decided he was too 'Aryan' to teach in a Jewish school and too 'non-Aryan' to teach in a public school. They solved his employment problem by drafting him into the Army. While he was fighting for the Fuehrer, his fiancée, also a teacher at the *Goldschmidtschule*, was deported and murdered. He fought at Stalingrad and was never heard from again."

On the night of November 5, *Kristallnacht*, a night of destruction and terror designed to intimidate the Jews of Germany, Wolf heard a pounding on the door. It was his grandmother's maid. The synagogue next to her house was burning to the ground. Wolf crept out of bed to listen as Wolf's father hastily packed a bag and left to hide out with Aryan friends for a few days. It didn't stop the Nazi thugs from repeatedly coming to their apartment that night and even striking his mother, giving her a concussion. After *Kirstallnach*t, the Edelsteins made plans to leave Germany. A distant cousin in England named Adolf Elston, (né Edelstein) agreed to pay for Wolf and Gerd's schooling and transport, and distant cousin Dr. Emmy Wolff arranged for them to enter Stoatley Rough. "Adolf Elston's father was the brother of my great grandfather Gustav Edelstein, born in 1833, who moved to the north of England to start a wool business, and became a British subject. His story has an interesting twist. In World War I, Adolf joined the Royal Artillery, rose to the rank of major, and changed his last name to Elston. The name Edelstein was deemed too German for an officer on His Majesty's Service. That was the time when the royal house of Hannover-Sachsen-Coburg-Gotha became the House of Windsor and the Battenbergs became Mountbattens. I'm very grateful to Adolf

SS occupied the site of the school and the students moved to Kronberger Road. Leonore Goldschmidt was unsuccessful in moving the school abroad. She escaped as Dr. Lewent stayed on to oversee the school's closing on November 30, 1939. Dr. Lewent eventually escaped the country and resumed teaching Provençal literature at the New School in New York

Elston; I don't think Gerd, I, or our parents would have survived if he and his mother had not paid our fees. I met him only once, shortly after arrival in England. I remember a portly gentleman in a double-breasted suit sitting in an alcove of the Sitting Room. He patted me on the head and told me to be a good boy."[21]

It took Wolf's parents two years to make their way to America through Unoccupied France, Spain and Portugal. "To get out of Germany and to the United States, a person had to find someone who would guarantee the U.S. Government by affidavit, $2,000 per person, equivalent today to about $40,000. The money had to be available, but was never, in fact, required. My parents got out via the wealthy financier member of the American Warburg family.[22] Acquiring a visa was a time-consuming, deliberately obscure process involving much paperwork and long lines. It was the official policy to impede and make it difficult for people to leave." One official told Wolf's father that because Bettina Warburg had guaranteed so many visas already, his and his wife's could not be authenticated. Wolf's father had the wit when appealing appeal to the clerk, understanding a German's respect for the law, "She signed a legal document, didn't she?" They got the visas. And then another German official did the family a great kindness. This time his father went to pick up a document stating they'd paid their taxes. The official slipped their paperwork to the bottom of the pile destined for rejection and issued a 'provisional' release which was enough for an exit permit. He said that he had orders to examine the file in detail and make as many difficulties as possible. He'd "get to it in about a week" after Wolf's parents arrived in New York. After the war, the Edelsteins sent him CARE packages.

Wolf arrived at Stoatley Rough late at night February 17, 1939 and was put to bed in a room with several other little boys. Just days later, Wolf was walking down Farnham Lane, happy to be heading into town

---

[21] Edelstein, [Elston] Wolf, in a note to the author.

[22] Bettina Warburg's father Paul had helped to set up the Federal Reserve for Woodrow Wilson. She and her husband Kubie co-chaired the American Psychoanalytic Association's Emergency Committee on Immigration that helped people in the medical profession leave Germany.

to buy some penny candies. He passed Thursley Copse along the way, traveled about a mile, then turned left on the road that led past the railroad station and into the little main street of town. The sun made the day unseasonably warm and as he marched along, looking forward to his candy, out of nowhere a sense of joy settled on his shoulders, enveloping him with warmth and hope. He was happy. He knew he was not going to be picked on again. He knew he should be homesick but he wasn't. He was where he should be.

The Swimming Pool

Wolf and Martin and other boys in Wolf's dormitory soon became good friends. One mid-day during the main meal in the dining room, an exciting rumor circulated. There was to be a swimming pool built on the property. A father of one of the few non-Jewish pupils at the school, a Mr. Pniower, in England for the summer, actually knew how it could be done without spending large sums of money. (Mr. Pniower would become Professor of Horticulture at the University of Berlin by 1948, in charge of restoring the *Berliner Tiergarten* (Berlin Zoo.) All the bigger children would have to work hard to make the pool a reality. Wolf was thrilled. At last he could use his *Freischweimmen* certificate, earned two summers earlier when he had practiced endlessly in order to be allowed into the deep end of the local public pool near his home. He was crushed when they not only said he couldn't take the test, being Jewish, but he was not even going to be allowed into the pool any more. Luckily that summer his family went to a resort in the Italian Dolomites where Wolf had the chance to earn the certificate. He had carefully packed it in his suitcase on the chance he might need it in England, and here was the opportunity he had dreamt of. After he had finished eating, Wolf raced up to his room, dug the certificate out of his mess of books and papers, then ran around the house until he found Miss Astfalck. She looked at it, said what a nice certificate, and turned to another child clamoring for her attention.

Mr. Pniower's plans placed the pool along the fresh water stream in the rear of the Farm at the bottom of the property. The bigger boys and adults would dig out a large cavity then line its walls with bundles of woven willow canes. It was an ancient technique (and one still used today to prevent erosion or to build temporary bridging for military use). It was backbreaking work. As the older ones toiled, the smaller children helped by hauling away the shovelfuls of the earth from the growing excavation or carried large bundles of rushes.

Dr. Lion, accompanied by Dr. Wolff, made the steep walk down the path to watch the progress of the construction. Her smile faded when she discovered that the bigger boys weren't working hard enough! Some boys were talking off to one side, one even allowing a small boy to wield his shovel. The two administrators were struck by what they perceived as a very poor attitude toward the work. What business did those boys have slinking away on long breaks while much younger children stayed at the task? The two women made the steep climb back up to the main house, feathers badly ruffled. Dr. Lion was so disturbed that she wrote about the problem in her *Rundbrief* [Round robin letter] of May in 1939, stating that the older boys "found it troublesome," to work, while the younger ones, worked "cheerfully." She had a theory about these lazy fellows, inadvertently falling into the prevailing trap of Eugenics at the time that claimed in scientific terms there were distinguishing characteristics within each "race" that could be classified, nailed down, documented. Being Jews, Dr. Lion decided, meant that these boys just had no flair for manual labor (unaware that all teenagers the world over will look to avoid hard work whenever possible). She declared that the Jewish roots of the boys negatively influenced their work habits. "As far as the non-Aryan boys are concerned, (she never used "Jewish" – it was always "Non-Aryan") going back to the land …presents a very difficult problem, because they have *neither the right physiological nor right psychological attitude, nor aptitude* [italics mine] to enjoy the 'blessing of the earth.'" She continued. "Calculating and adding up is popular [with them]." She then said that these boys avoided "theoretical knowledge via books and other possible opportunities. ..[and they lacked] "intellectual education and work technique. Just these short-comings are also very obvious in school children who today come from the German schools.... [there was an] inability to do something for themselves with initiative and so to speak, help themselves." Strong words from the head of a school dedicated to helping refugee children to cope in a new country. It seems that in 1939, Dr. Lion was just fed up with a few of her teenaged boys, one of whom perhaps had been rude to her. "Very few boys get beyond their stamp collection in their free time and few are impressed by the fairytale like gardens or the surrounding heath, impressions which could remain with them all their lives. ...The harmless enjoyment of discovering or inventing something is often missing." Dr. Lion closed her diatribe by assuring her readers that "these defects were discussed at a Teachers' Conference."[23]

Where did all this anger come from? In 1939, Dr. Lion's school was bulging at the seams. So many children were arriving. How would she find the means to feed and house them? Perhaps her outburst had more to do with stress than any deep-seated prejudices against Jewish teenaged boys. Wolf said in her defense that, "There is evidence that Dr. Lion mellowed after the war. A couple of my friends described her as motherly, which certainly was not the impression she gave in our day. In May, 1939, Dr. Lion was besieged by desperate parents wanting to bring their children to safety. Perhaps the uncharacteristic rant at the time of the swimming pool dig shows that her nerves were giving way. I wouldn't blame her if they did."[24] Her *Rundbrief* written shortly after that incident was the only time Dr. Lion expressed anything but comforting and encouraging words about her school.

When the pool was finished, Mr. Pniower routed the little brook through it. It filled with clear cold water, and the children gleefully took to it like the proverbial ducks. The pool was such a success that Dr. Lion decided to commemorate it, along with the school's summer holiday closing that year, with a gala Speech Day, just like the ones in the best British private schools which celebrated the year's end with an academic procession and the awarding of prizes. Plans for a Speech Day at Stoatley Rough were drawn up, invitations were sent out, and the

---

[23] Lion, Hilde, Round Robin Letter, Stoatley Rough Archives, Box 1/1 (i), London School of Economics

[24] Wolf Elston, in an email to the author.

Household Girls, senior girls on a special course, worked in the kitchen to prepare special treats. Someone with connections on the Board even arranged for a movie star to attend the ceremony, the blonde Elizabeth Bergner, lately of Berlin, who had been nominated for a Best Actress Oscar for her work in the British romantic drama, *Escape Me Never* (1933). Herself a Jewish refugee, the beautiful Miss Bergner went on to Hollywood, but never achieved the fame she had enjoyed in Germany and in Great Britain.

A few days before the festival, a ten-year-old boy in the little German town of Bad Salzufeln, a mineral springs resort in northern Germany, was bidding farewell to his parents. Hans Obermeyer (nicknamed Obo by the boys and later, the Ginger Nipper by Mr. Phillips) was an easy-going, red-headed boy with pale skin, a wide jocular mouth always ready with a quip, a sturdy body, and a level gaze. He loved a good joke and knew many. His father was the wealthy owner of a large hardware story that also sold milling machinery. Obo's house was the largest in the neighborhood. When his mother packed his trunk, she filled it with more than enough clothing, books and toys for two boys, and even shipped his bike with him. Like many others who came to Stoatley Rough School, Obo was destined to travel by way of the *Kindertransport* [Children's Transport], a humanitarian program that sent Jewish children to safety in England that operated between December, 1938, and September, 1939. Alone of the nations, including the United States, Britain agreed to accept 10,000 children. [25]

---

[25] The idea for a train to remove children from harm's way originated with the British Committee for the Jews of Germany, and became known world wide as the *Kindertransport*. Jews, Quakers, and Christians of many denominations helped in the courageous and heroic work, especially the Berlin Quakers, a hardy but tiny band of Friends that actually increased in numbers during the Nazi years who challenged officials time and again to right the wrongs they saw, sometimes losing their lives in their efforts to speak truth to power. England, alone among the countries of the world, agreed to accept 10,000 children. Private citizens or organizations had to guarantee to pay for each child's care, education, and eventual emigration from Britain. In return for this guarantee, the British government agreed to permit unaccompanied refugee children to enter the country on simple travel visas. The nine-month rescue operation brought

Obo's family had lived in Bad Salzufeln as far back as the 17th century, and was highly respected in the community. "The town was famous for its health spas and people would come from all over Germany to take the cure for digestive ailments and drink the nasty tasting and smelly waters which came from the salt wells in the ground. The town had a beautiful park with flowerbeds and trees and a lake with ducks, swans and rowboats," where Obo sailed his toy sailboat. Summers were pleasurable times, with candlelight festivals, concerts in the park with an orchestra or brass band that played every afternoon during the season. Obo had many friends in school in Germany, only a few of whom were Jewish. He attended the synagogue for religious instruction once a week. He received a beautiful bike for his 8th birthday in 1936, well into the era of Nazi consolidation of power, and then disaster struck. "One day, a bunch of kids came running towards me shouting, "We hate you, you dirty Jew" pushing me to the ground stomping on my bike and making my knees and hands bloody. They then ran away laughing. I was crying and pushed my broken bike home and my mother comforted me as best she could and called my father home. I asked them why this had happened and why they called me a dirty Jew? They explained to me that there were certain people in Germany who

---

about 9,000-10,000 children into the country, some 7,500 of them Jewish, from Germany, Austria, Czechoslovakia, and Poland. The last transport from Germany left in September 1939, just before World War II began, and only a few months before Obo boarded his train. The last transport from the Netherlands left on May 14, 1940, the day that country surrendered to Germany. Eighty percent of the *Kindertransport* children never saw their parents again. About half of the children (some older ones carried refugee infants placed aboard the trains by parents) ended up in the homes of foster families, some of whom immediately put the children into service as farm workers or domestics. Others treated the children as their own. Still other *Kindertransport* children stayed clustered in communal hostels and on farms throughout Britain. And some came to Stoatley Rough. Young Obo was one of the special railway wagons which would take the children on the way via Bergen, Hanover, to Hoek van Holland or Flushing, and on to Harwich in England. A committee then distributed the children at Liverpool Street Station in London. The Kindertransport Association (KITA) website, http://www.kindertransport.org/history.html, accessed November, 2007.

41

were suspicious of other people who were different from them because they believed in a different religion and that these 'different' people were out to harm them and take away their possessions.'" [26]

Obo's father was arrested during *Kristallnacht*, and held in prison for several weeks. Obo was no longer allowed to attend his regular school and his father had to sell his business at a loss. (Later, it was the Obermeyer home into which all the Jews in town were forced to move, crammed into every available room, closet and hallway until they could be deported.) Up until 1938, Obo's parents had believed that the anger and persecution would pass. After *Kristallnacht*, they realized it was time to leave Germany.

Obo left for good on July 4, 1939, secure in his parents' promise to meet him in England as soon as they could leave Germany. His father took him to the train but his mother remained at home, unable to bring herself to say goodbye.

The school's secretary, Herta Lewent, who had parents in London, met Obo at the Liverpool Street Station and took him straight to her parents' tiny flat in Hampstead. To make him feel welcome, she gave him Erich Kästner's *Emil und die Detektive*, a book which Obo probably knew well. Every German-speaking boy over eight in 1939 knew this classic tale about a little boy who solved crimes.[27] The following Sunday, Herta gathered up Obo, his new book, his bike and his belongings, and together they boarded the train to Haslemere. Obo's arrival happened to be on the day of the Festival.

That morning, the children had been allowed to sleep until 8:00. The faculty set up an exhibit of the children's art in the main house. At 3:00 the party began. First the view of the exhibit was launched,

---

[26] Obermeyer, John [Hans, Obo]. From notes of talks about his life before the Holocaust delivered over the years to schools in the Baltimore area.

[27] Erich Kästner's classic tale of a boy who falls asleep on a train and awakens to find his money gone. He enlists a gang of Berliner children to track down the thief. Written in 1929, this story is seen to attack Hitler's totalitarian regime with humor and pacifist ideals. The author also wrote *Baron Munschhausen* and several other popular tales. Books and Writers, http://www.kirjasto.sci.fi/kastner.htm, accessed June, 2003.

followed by a performance of the children's choir. The children then took up their various violins, recorders, flutes, triangles, kazoos, and a bubbling water pipe (to represent the sound of a nightingale) and cuckoo clock, and played their tongue-in-cheek performance of Haydn's "Toy Symphony." [28] Accomplished musicians among the pupils carried the melody while other children chirped, burbled, pinged, and rat-tat-tatted their parts. Wolf and a few of the boys lurked at the sidelines. Wolf didn't think the performance was all that special, not the least because Dr. Leven, who had arrived from Berlin to teach music, had kicked him out of the group just days earlier for being unable to stay with the rhythm. She had even asked him to stay away for this part of the festival. Miffed at the shabby treatment he felt Dr. Leven had unjustly given him, Wolf stole upstairs to the second floor of the main house. He planned to deposit fake love notes under the pillows of some of the girls.

The party was in full swing. Three-hundred distinguished guests, staff and children crowded the house, terrace and grounds. Obo must have been comforted to hear the familiar sound of German. Hardly anybody would have been speaking English except for the well-meaning British Committee members. When Elizabeth Bergner arrived to great fanfare, it was time for the academic awards. Elizabeth Bergner announced her gifts to the school: a pony and a ping-pong table, the

---

[28] Haydn's "Toy Symphony" was a mainstay of Stoatley Rough's musical repertoire, first performed in 1937 for Dr. Lion's birthday, when Nore Astfalck accompanied the performers on her typewriter. Peter Gaupp recalled the school performed it the following year, when Dr. Leven relented and allowed Wolf to participate. "Wolf played the nightingale using a type of water pipe with water spewing all over the place. I think I had the tambourine at one time and then was demoted to the triangle when I could not get my act together." The Toy Symphony was performed many times at the school, always tongue in cheek. Once it was a performed as surprise wakeup for Nore Astfalck's 37th birthday. The performances took place with one or two actual musicians playing the melody, while many other children played the kazoo, triangle, toy trumpet, drums, and a bubbling waterpipe that was supposed to suggest a nightingale's song. Wolf remembered that the school did one more concert in Haslemere during the war. "Dr. Leven had kicked me out the choir, without warning or explanation (as usual). I had thought my singing was just great and I'm still mad."

latter, Dr. Lion noted in one of her reports a few months later, "used almost day and night." One youngster described Miss Bergner. "She had blonde hair, a turquoise blue suit, a wine-red blouse, gloves of leather, and very nice shoes of the same color as the gloves. Her fingers were of a different red. She enjoyed herself and acted naturally and sang all the German songs with us."[29]

One of the Household Girls helped Obo take his suitcase and trunk up the stairs to Lookout, the dormitory / classroom (that later doubled as a dining room) on the third floor of the main building where Wolf and other little boys slept. Obo recalls that it was the same spot "where we later observed the dogfights between the Luftwaffe's Me 109 Messerschmitts and the RAF's Spitfires and Hurricanes as they were chasing each other through the valley below." Freshened up, Obo walked downstairs and went out to the terrace. By then the whole assemblage was winding its way down the steep path to view the new swimming pool, resplendent in the waning sun, led by Susi Horn playing the accordion, followed by the children walking two-by-two, followed by the adults. At the pool, Miss Astfalck led some of the children in a folk dance.

After the party returned for refreshments, Obo was still hanging around the main house trying to fit in, trying to find children his own age. He fatally struck up a conversation with the wrong girl. Ilse Bayer, unbeknownst to Obo, was two years older and a bully. She soon challenged Obo as to who was the stronger. They started to argue the point. Obo was determined to prove his manhood. Before he knew what was happening, they began to wrestle. Obo ended up in a struggle with Ilse on the terrace floor, thrashing about to get the upper hand in a fierce wrestling match. "I think I was probably a little eager to establish myself as some macho kid which in retrospect I certainly wasn't then or

---

[29] Kassel, Putti, "Life at Stoatley Rough," Stoatley Rough Newsletter #26, November, 2007 p. 13. Taken from a letter in German written home, translated for this book by Martin Owens. "Sie hatte blonde Haare, einte tuerquise blaues costume, eine weinrote Bluse, Handschuhe aus Wildleder und sehr huebsche Schuhe aus der selben Farbe, die Fingernaegel aber in einem anderen Rot. Sie unterhielt sich sehr nett und natuerlich und sang alle Deutschen Lieder mit."

now. She put some kind of headlock on me. I'm sure there were plenty of witnesses but I think Miss Astfalck broke it up pretty quickly."[30]

Wolf saw the whole thing. "Obo, your fight with Ilse Bayer did indeed have many witnesses; I watched from the second story window. As to what may have caused it: at one of the reunions, Ilse's older sister Ruth referred to Ilse as 'a real tomboy in those days." I remember Ilse as having had a short fuse. About the time of your fight, when the girls were not in their dorm, a bunch of us boys snuck in and left fake anonymous love notes under certain pillows." As Miss Astfalck restored order on the terrace, Wolf finished his covert mission. "Ilse correctly identified me as the author of her note and exploded in cold fury. She didn't hit me, though."

And so it was, with much fanfare and a bloody nose, ten-year-old Hans Obermeyer arrived at Stoatley Rough. Soon Obo, Wolf, and Martin, along with other ten- and eleven-year-olds, were spending many hours every day that summer in the swimming pool or tramping around on the Heath across the road. They knew that war loomed on the horizon, just across the English Channel. Yet they lived in a bubble of hope, protected by the kindness of their caretakers and the innocence of their youth.

---

[30] Obermeyer, Hans [John] in a note to the author, October, 2005.

The Calm Before the Storm

During the summer of 1939, the children at Stoatley Rough coped with the discomforts of overcrowding, continually being forced to swap rooms as others came and went. There was worrisome news on the radio that told of the Rome-Berlin Axis (May), the German occupation of Czechoslovakia (June) and Germany's move to close down all Jewish businesses (July). The younger children like Martin, Wolf, and Obo swam, hiked, went to Boy Scout meetings and were sometimes taken to the Haslemere Museum to inspect its doll's house, the miniature furniture for sale, a "poor moth-eaten bear, the huge crab spider and of course – the mummy and its exposed toes."[31] Martin's first encounter with the mummy had the unexpected consequence of giving him nightmares. Visions of those dessicated, black knobs haunted his dreams for weeks.

Dr. Lion not only educated her young charges, she had to think about preparing her older pupils for the day they would leave the school, especially those who might not have parents to come to pick them up. She had a long-standing policy of supplementing classroom studies with guest lecturers on subjects, many of them about overseas work. In addition, there were plenty of evening activities for all but the smallest of the children. Of particular interest were the nights the school's own Emmy Wolff read to the older pupils. Sometimes the children would darn stockings or work on a sewing or knitting project as they sat around the sitting room, a fire crackling in the fireplace, as she brought to life various pieces of literature. All listened aptly to her deep expressive

---

[31] Morgan [Roberts] Ruth, Stoatley Rough Newsletter Issue 9 October, 1995 p. 13.

voice. During the winter of 1939, shortly after it was published, she read *Lotte in Weimer* by Thomas Mann, a novelistic biography of Goethe and the nature of genius, a subject dear to her heart. Dr. Lion was present, sitting and smiling as her friend, her voice filled with emotion, rendered Mann's articulation of various political points of view through Charlotte, the fictional lover of Goethe.

Dr. Lion also tried to satisfy the practical needs of her older pupils. She arranged for a certain "Commissioner and Captain of Guides" to take a few groups on weekly expeditions with the objective of developing their powers of observation. "This experiment is being made with the object of extending it to refugee children generally, as part of their training for life overseas."[32] Indeed, in March of 1939, seven of her pupils left the school to live in New Zealand, Australia, Brazil, Palestine and the United States. Other lectures at the school that year covered Syria, Iraq, South America, North America, India, Iran, along with such practical topics as Kindergarten Work, Gardening, Unemployment, Quakerism, Country School Homes, and Settlement Work.

Dr. Lion had hired a Mr. S. Corfield as Farm Instructor who would oversee the ten or eleven boys who now lived in the new Farmhouse that had been built with the assistance of a grant from the local Erla Balwin Fund. A poultry farm donated 100 fertile eggs. New students in 1939 boosted the residency level to "100 people, 90 of them pupils, Farm-students and Domestic Science students".[33]

Dr. Lion found it difficult to find sponsors for her children for the few weeks she needed to close the school that summer. It was too dangerous for children to return to Germany, and she wrote in one of her reports, that if they went to an English home, most "came back too early." Some parents came to collect their children for short vacations, but she worried about the "fifty persons whose nearest relatives, father and mother are still in Germany." There was a strange air of unreality, of blithe freedom for the children at Stoatley Rough that summer while on the Continent, the forces of war gathered.

---

[32] Committee Notes, January meeting, LSE Stoatley Rough archives, 1/1 (i)
[33] Ibid.

Dr. Lion defied unwelcome thoughts of foreboding that might sneak into her schoo. Once she took sixteen of the older children for an outing in London. Dr.Wolff and two other adults also went. Their three-day excursion included the Science Museum, (where they were treated to a lecture on mineralogy followed by a picnic), Victoria and Albert Museum, an open-air performance of *Twelfth Night* in Regents Park, Westminster Abbey, the National Gallery, the Tower, and St. Paul's Cathedral. Renate Dorpalen wrote, "The last pre-war days at Stoatley Rough continued in their established rhythm of education, domestic life and recreational activities....The magnificent weather of that summer was in perfect harmony with the bucolic, peaceful, life in Haslemere, though it was the calm before the storm. Those few months allowed me a glimpse of the school's rich, broad educational programme of didactic and applied teaching. The musical and theatrical performances, the visiting lecturers from all walks of life, the imaginatively planned festivals, and the visits to near and far places for cultural exchange were only some of the events to manifest the school's aims. Such excellence was never to be reached again."[34]

There were no outings for young boys like Wolf, Martin and Obo. But they did invent a game they called "The Lands" that came to occupy many long summer hours. Using plots 5 x 12 feet given them along to the path that led down to the Farm, each boy created his own imaginary country. The boys played at The Lands during the first few years of the war.

> "Boys would build roads, forts, castles and decorate with treelike plants. The whole project took on a somewhat military character. Boys would bring their toy cars, matches to act as men, small plants for camouflage. It was a matter of pride if the layout was particularly attractive or if a road had been built that could withstand someone's weight. Competition arose

---

[34] Dorpalen, Renate [Dorpalen-Brocksieper], Stoatley Rough Newsletter Issue 6, October, 1994.

very early and with it, alliances. Pacts were drawn up, cooperative helping arrangements worked out and, as these progressed, the boys developed rules which governed the privacy of one's lands and its defenses... With all the play and the fun and the planning provided by these 'lands,' there was always a note of a war footing reflective of the atmosphere in which we were finding ourselves....The owners gave themselves names of kings or emperors who, in turn, sought the advice of the next older group, which included me. We, the older boys, then became someone's prime minister, so you had the younger boys planning and plotting as well as the older ones. There were frequent conferences between these officials. These relationships, too, provided identity and for the younger boys, a big brother."[35]

Obo called his Land Acropolis.

"We built buildings such as underground garages or defense buildings to house large armies of wooden soldiers which consisted of hundreds of used matchsticks painted with the national colours of each land. Most of us had some type of model cars, trucks or military vehicles which were mostly British made by Dinkey Toys or brought from Germany or Austria. Peter Rosenthal and Wolf Elston had a large assembly of German warship models and land vehicles. Needless to say they had to fight many wars to gain additional territory. Some made non-aggression pacts or alliances of two lands threatening to invade a third one. They printed their own money which allowed us to purchase things from each other. I remember spending many hours on my land during the darkest days of the war, probably in 1941, and I think we all acted out many fantasies as rulers of our lands."[36]

---

[35] Gaupp, Dieter, Stoatley Rough Newsletter Issue 12, October, 1996, p. 34.
[36] Obermeyer, Hans [John, Obo], Stoatley Rough Newsletter 17, June, 1998

Wolf said, "In fact, we talked a lot and built very little, but that was not the point. Here we were no longer helpless refugees from terror: we were powerful rulers whose words were law in mighty states. Our fantasies allowed us to cope with grimmer realities." A boy who joined the little gang of friends later in the year, Peter Gaupp, wrote in his diary, "I think that my nicest thing here at Stoatley Rough is my Land. Below the garden and behind a fence I own a piece of earth under a tree and there I build castles surrounded by towers (however, everything is made of sand, unfortunately!!) " Peter's older brother Dieter once found a dead bird which he buried on his plot, lined the grave with leaves, and called it Birdland." Another boy, Hans Kornberg, wrote about his propaganda minister, W. F. Kerno, and his vice-emperor for *The Bridge*, a newssheet the school published on two occasions during the war. (*The Bridge* was chock full of stories of school life, short fictional pieces written by the children, staff and alumni, liberally illustrated with sketches.) In Hans' article, he not only abolished the League of Nations, but listed the imaginative names of the territories owned by himself, Martin and Wolf in the school magazine: "*Eratoquie*,"[(no translation;] "*Rotgraben*" [Red Ditch] and "*Gelbbergen*" [Yellow Mountain].

Every summer since the school's founding, Dr. Lion held a German-English cultural exchange event. Although events on the Continent were heating up, the summer exchange took place until the war began. Great Britain declared war on Germany on September 3, 1939, ending for good the halcyon days of Stoatley Rough. Mail services were disrupted, the Red Cross had not yet developed fully its messaging service, and none of the children ever knew for certain what was happening to their parents. Now overcrowded and facing six years of rationing, the school would take a new direction.

IN THE BEGINNING

Dr. Lion slumped in her chair in her room at the University Club. It was early in 1934 and she had been in London only a few short weeks. She had thought she could speak English but found the people who actually spoke it almost incomprehensible. And speaking it was worse. There were strange words like "rural" and 'crisps" and "squirrel" she could not pronounce. She sighed, heaved herself up, and moved over to the desk in her room. Building a school from scratch involved so many things; facility, curriculum, supplies, pupils, and staff.

Where to start? Must prioritize. The first order of business was staff. The Committee had agreed that German-speakers would ease the children's transition. She brushed back a strand of coarse gray hair that had come loose from her bun. She picked up her pen. She would need a curriculum but that could come later. First, a Matron. Having little experience with children, Dr. Lion had no idea what they did for amusement or what thoughts went through their little heads. She'd need someone to take charge of the children's health, listen to their problems, and of course, keep them in line. She knew just the person for the job, Eleonore Astfalck, a former student of hers at the *Charlottenberg Jugendheim*, the federal social institution of which she herself had held the Directorship before the racial laws were passed. Dr. Lion was proud to have helped to lead the organization that first had only supplied meals and education to children of factory workers late in the last century, into an important and vast social services agency. Nore Astfalck had joined the teaching staff after her own graduation. Nore was a down-to-earth woman, a tireless worker, and she understood and loved children, especially those in need. Nore was not Jewish but Dr. Lion recalled that she had had some trouble with the Nazis recently - she might just be interested in getting out of Germany for a while. She wrote to Nore outlining the job.

Dr. Lion wished Emmy were at her side and not still in Berlin. The elegant Dr. Emmy Wolff was her best friend. Dr. Lion was profoundly lonely, always feeling out of place at the fancy parties the wealthy benefactors kept throwing. She was homesick. And Emmy was as neat and focused as she was admittedly disorganized. Emmy with her proud bearing and lovely brown eyes that sometimes reflected a private inner sorrow. Emmy knew what it was like to struggle in a man's world when education and privilege were not always enough of a shield. Dr. Lion missed their long talks about women's rights. The two had even been roommates at one point.

Dr. Emmy Wolff might need to be rescued anyway from the vile place Berlin had become, now being forced to edit and submit her articles for the popular magazine *Die Frau* [Woman] under her mother's Aryan maiden name. How long would that last? The Nazis would discover her game soon enough. Nothing escaped their attention. Dr. Wolff would enjoy England and, from Dr. Lion's point of view, she would be not only invaluable in planning the curriculum but would be a magnificent teacher of German and French Literature. And Art, too. The Committee would love her. They had already approved bringing her over. Dr. Lion pulled out sheet of stationery and wrote to her dear Emmy. When would she make up her mind about England?

Dr. Lion made herself a cup of tea on the small gas burner in her room, poured generous helpings of sugar and milk, and settled down in the small flat's threadbare armchair to re-read the brochure Committee members Miss Bracey and Miss Fearon had drafted. Her lips moved as she read the English words " ...dedicated to helping German children to prepare for an English education; provide a sound education for children of all walks of life, denominations and nationalities; develop in its pupils' character, ...responsible and useful citizens wherever they may be, etc. etc." All well and good but the real challenge was the English. The school needed English teachers. They would have to find teachers willing to live with the children after lights out, people who would take on all sorts of extracurricular jobs, wipe the noses of the young ones, get them to bed on time, that kind of thing. Since it was the Depression, there should be plenty of candidates. But one never knew.

Oh, look at the time. In an hour she was to meet Bertha Bracey for "high tea," in England - an early evening meal. The Quaker activist had come up with one solution to the English teacher problem: the well-off friends of Committee and Council members who wanted to "do something" would come to the school to conduct crash vocabulary training for the newcomers. Leave it to Miss Bracey. The indefatigable powerhouse also had put an ad in the London papers for the crucial position of live-in English teacher.

Dr. Lion deposited her cup in the small sink. She mused about the fact that there was no money for a cook or cleaning staff at the school. Thankfully everyone had already agreed that the resident staff would share in the cooking and the children would help with the cleaning. She hoped the brochure would do its job in finding pupils. Even now, news of the school was circulating in Berlin and other large cities in Germany and Austria. She sighed again. Speaking English all the time was beginning to take its toll, even if she prided herself on her stamina. All those well-meaning women and men leaning in when she spoke, as if calling attention to her German accent but too polite to ask her to repeat herself.

A week later, Nore's reply arrived. She would take the job but on one condition: the school must also hire her partner, Johanna Nacken. Dr. Lion was not surprised. She was pleased in fact, that she was getting two hard-working, fair-minded women who would bring tremendous value to her staff. Hanna was an old friend of Dr. Lion's, still working at the *Jugendheim* as crafts teacher, and like Nore, she was a sister feminist. Dr. Lion had even traveled with Emmy and Hanna to feminist rallies back when they were first at the Youth Home.

She put down Nore's letter and rubbed her eyes. She probably needed reading glasses. So much to do. She knew her instincts had been correct in selecting Nore for the critical post. Now, she not only had her new Matron but in the bargain, a new Crafts and Shop teacher. She would notify Miss Bracey first thing in the morning. She yawned. Time to get ready for bed. Dr. Lion moved to put her papers away.

If Dr. Lion was to be the head of the school, Eleonore Astfalck would be its heart.

Everybody's Substitute Parent

T he snow reflecting the alpine sun was blinding. Nore was about to hike up the mountain, skis on her shoulder, for the downhill race. Dr. Lion's letter had arrived that morning. Her mother had forwarded it from Berlin. She had read Dr. Lion's offer with interest. The job would mean a lot of work and virtually no pay. Dr. Lion was careful to point out that Nore would only earn £2 per month under Britain's stringent conditions of immigration. Nore weighed her options. Since the Gestapo wanted to see her when she returned with the Strauss family (for whom she was nanny) to Berlin, a move to England might be the most convenient way of staying out of sight until things cooled down. The Nazis wouldn't be in power forever. She re-read the letter. She liked the idea of working with needy, homeless children.

One of the school's first professional English teachers, Margaret [Dove] Faulkner, later described Nore as "short, slender and dynamic, ...everybody's substitute parent." Eleonore Astfalck would become indispensable to Dr. Lion in her ability to soothe, to make the children think that work was a game, and to inspire. Nore was one of those rare people whose compassion was almost palpable. Growing up in Nuremburg with her two older brothers, Nore had been a busy little mother, so concerned for the welfare of others that she sometimes brought dirty, impoverished children up to her family's apartment for something to eat. When she was eight, she told her parents that she wanted to marry a criminal because "when you love a person, then you love him even if he is a criminal."[1] Even at an early age, Nore brimmed over with love.

---

[1] Astfalck, Eleonore, 1990, *Oral History*, p. 1-16.

Classified as pure Aryans, Nore and her friend, JoHanna Nacken, should have had nothing to fear from the Nazi regime. But even the most casual association with the "wrong" element of society in those days could have ruinous consequences. Nore's job in Berlin had involved running classes for out-of-work young men aged eighteen through twenty-five. She held afternoon and evening workshops in money-making skills useful in the Depression such as building a bird cage, crafting small pieces of furniture, putting together artificial flowers, and bookbinding. Several of the men belonged to the Communist Party, however, a real enemy of the Nazis. One night, a Nazi thug shot at a couple of the men through one of the windows and shortly thereafter, someone broke into Nore's office and stole her records. One workbook held incriminating details about the men and an association linking Nore as a sympathizer. When she learned the Nazis were looking for her, Nore signed on to accompany the wealthy Strauss family to Switzerland.

Nore arrived in England first. (Hanna had to concoct an excuse to leave the *Jugendheim* before she could safely leave the country.) Hopping out of the car fresh from the train station, Nore tried out her halting English on the first person she met at Stoatley Rough, the Cockney gardener, Mr. Phillips. Neither could understand a word the other was saying. When Hanna arrived a few weeks later, she and Mr. Phillips launched into a lively exchange. Hanna had lived in Canada as an au pair and had the best English of the three German women at the school. The dour Mr. Phillips later declared that Hanna Nacken was the only sensible person in the house. They became great friends. The Committee soon drafted Hanna into helping with the bookkeeping. It had not taken them long to realize Dr. Lion was hopeless with money matters. She could be a bulldog when it came to collecting fees and tuitions or scrounging for a free medical exam for one of her children, but she was incapable of keeping proper records. Hanna agreed to take the job on a temporary basis until a permanent bookkeeper could be found. Six years later, Mr. Vernon said they still could not let Hanna off the hook, "given Dr. Lion's whimsical approach to fiscal management" and that Hanna was "very sound on financial principles." He added kindly (and one hopes she read his report) that she was "entirely unselfish of herself." [2]

Nore's background in child development was impressive. She studied at the *Jugendheim Charlottenburg* in Berlin in 1919, six years ahead of Hilde Lion, until she ran out of money. In 1929 she became one of its instructors. By then she had built an impressive practical background in household management and child care having participated in a work/ student program in Augsburg, and later, in a *Kinderheim* [childrens' home] for problem children in Rodaun, Austria, near Vienna. In a place where police sometimes brought in abused and neglected children, Nore managed the traumatized and unruly children without hurting them. She wrote, "It was only natural that children were punished and even spanked quite hard. In the beginning, to work in this house was very difficult, as the children would not believe that they could have a grownup who would not spank them."[3] Evidence of poverty moved her. "We had children who were criminals and bed-wetters and children who had never met their parents, although they lived quite near by."[4] She never forgot the occasion when two gypsy children were deposited at the school, full of fleas. She said the children were sewn into their clothes and that their parents never returned for them. They would be fed and sheltered. But there would never be any spankings from Nore.

Nore and Hanna began the task of converting the Vernon country manor into a residential school. The house had been filled with knickknacks from the Vernon's travels to India and China. Nore said there were more than one-hundred twenty precious objects that had to be packed up. Stoatley Rough was well suited to the needs of a boarding facility with its three stories and large rooms. One entered the house from a small parking area off Farnham Lane. Leaded windows adorned a small vestibule. A few steps up and the visitor stood in a 212-square foot "Sitting Room," splendid with wood block floors and a magnificent

---

[2] First Committee Report Stoatley Rough Archives, File 1/1 (i), London School of Economics.

[3] Astfalck, Eleonore, *Oral History*, p. 2-9.

[4] Ibid.

green-tiled William Morris fireplace. Just outside the large bay windows the panoramic view of the verdant South Downs stunned every first visitor. A large flagstone terrace ran the length of the house where children would gather in the years to come to sew, read, sort berries, talk, or study, and on wintry Saturday afternoons, consume hot cocoa. There were fireplaces in most of the rooms. Nore designated one of the larger rooms as a dorm for the anticipated small group of girls to arrive; the small boys would sleep upstairs. Nore and Hanna chose for themselves the room strategically located next to the main entrance to track comings and goings of little feet. At the other end of the Ground Floor toward the caretaker's Lodge were the kitchen, pantry, a sink, and two toilets (one for teachers, located under the stairs, and one for boys, just off the kitchen). Staircases flanked each end of the house. A rear door off the kitchen led into an open courtyard where young residents would soon be peeling the next day's potatoes. A partial lower level carved into the hill at the front of the house held yet another large common room, boiler room, pantry and several stock rooms. This area eventually became an air raid shelter.

Upstairs the First Floor had a large Music Room with an even more magnificent view of the South Downs; several smaller rooms were to become combination dormitories, classrooms and dining rooms; and on the same floor were a Girls' bath, Boys' bath, a Boys' washroom and a Girls' toilet. At the top, or Second Floor, were four rooms with dormers, three of which overlooked the terrace and countryside, and one room containing a secret passage. Hanna and Nore found enough beds for the three residential adults and the few students who were expected in late spring, but they sent out word for donations of blankets, linens, and other household items. Friends of the school duly delivered what was requested. Nore scrubbed the floors on her hands and knees and stocked the pantry, while Hanna brought out her carpentry tools and converted some of the old cupboards into wardrobes. (As the school grew, rollaway cots were purchased which the pupils folded up and tucked behind curtains along the walls by day.) Dr. Lion brought in carpenters to convert the stables at the far end of the gardener's house into a laundry room. Financial records of the spring of 1934 reveal expenses for: "sanitary closets," (toilets), towels, blankets, mattresses, bedsteads, rabbits (!), an employment bureau fee for a cook, engine repairs, cutlery, cups, plates, pails, anthracite coal, a charwoman, "medicaments," brooms, saucepans, gardener's wages, staff wages for a Miss Ryecart (who would teach English) and Cook, stationery, postage, a year's worth of insurance (costing £1.10s 0d for "accident of the children") and food. The food was for five people: Dr. Lion, Nore, Hanna, and Mr. And Mrs. Philips. In the next bill, the food item would cover thirteen people.

The School Opens its Doors

D r. Lion moved from the University Women's club in Chelsea into Stoatley Rough the spring of 1934 after a brief recruiting trip to Germany. Upon her return, she arranged for teachers of math, rudimentary science and history to supplement the work of the English teacher. Dr. Lion also scheduled German-born Mrs. List, a society lady who had given English lessons in Berlin to the brother of one of the future pupils and was now a member of the German-English circle in London. She would help teach English. The staff took turns helping out in the kitchen, with Hanna Nacken designated to put the kettle on the stove in the morning. Mr. Phillips was always up with the sun to keep her company. A local "gardener's boy" kept the furnace stoked and the fireplaces replenished.

In April of 1934, the school opened its doors. The founders had a sense of urgency; there were emigré children who needed lodging immediately. Committee member Miss Isabel Fry was elected to lead the school on a temporary basis. She was highly qualified owing to her prior experience as Headmistress of two other experimental schools. [5] She wrote in her first report, "The parents of some of these children have left Germany. One, a merchant, has gone to Africa with the rest of

---

[5]   Isabel Fry (1869-1958) was an educationist and social activist. She founded, and was headmistress of The Farmhouse School, Mayortorne Manor, Wendover, and later, Church Farm, Buckland, Aylesbury, Buckinghamshire. She came from a famous reforming Quaker background and was the daughter of Sir Edward Fry (1827-1918), jurist, and sister of (Sara) Margery Fry (1874-1958), penal reformer, and Roger Eliot Fry (1866-1934), artist and critic. http://www.ioe.ac.uk/library/archives/fy.html accessed September 24, 2007.

his family; another, who is a professor, has gone to India. One father, a younger man and a scholar, has lost all possibilities of earning anything at a university and does not know where to turn for employment of any kind. Some of the parents are still in Germany, but have to live under very changed standards of life."[6] Seven German-speaking children comprised the first coterie of students: two small boys and five teenaged girls, recruited through the network of the Berlin Quakers and Dr. Lion's former circle of friends and acquaintances at the Youth Home. The first girl, fifteen-year-old Gertrud Gans [Farnman] whose father, a dermatologist, had known Dr. Lion in Berlin, arrived a month before the school opened and helped Nore and Hanna prepare the premises. Gertrud said later the school was "not what I thought it would be," perhaps having expected a traditional, English girls' boarding school. Yet she stayed, serving as a much-loved mother-figure to young boys and girls for almost five years. Gertud briefly left the school in 1937, returned in mid-1938, then left again to live in India with her new British officer husband and her own parents, in 1939, just before the war broke out. (She and her husband later returned to England.) The first boy to enter the school was Fritz Horkheimer [Fred Hawkes], who stayed exactly one year before emigrating to Kenya with his family. He later wrote to Dr. Lion that at the ripe old age of nineteen, he had become an assistant manager of a coffee plantation, responsible for 1500 workers. He was very happy with his lot.[7]

Other early pupils were Eva Feldmann, age unknown, who stayed until November 1 the following year. Ellen Isler, nineteen, arrived in May and stayed for one year. Ayosdo and Alika Padolinsky, ages and country

---

6   Committee Report, Stoatley Rough Archives, 1/1 (i), London School of Economics

7   Fred wrote he was well paid, had his own *shamba* (land); grew spinach, lettuce, asparagus, cabbage; and had six chickens for breeding. He walked to work three miles away where he did office work and where he "engaged "or "sacked" the labourers and listened to their troubles. "I have no paper, no wireless, and am free from political worries." *The Bridge* Vol. II, 1941. (Other early agricultural students were Ernst Wilzek, who emigrated to New Zealand and became a land surveyor in 1939 before the war. Klaus Zedner was interned and sent to Canada, and later returned to England to work on a farm before the school lost track of him.)

of origin unknown (photos show them to be around six and seven), arrived on May 10 and stayed one year and seven months. Lotte Saul came in May, aged fourteen years old. It is not known when she left the school. Lilian Chasanowich whose age is unrecorded, only stayed three months, July through September, while Rosa Mazur [Hubner], fifteen, arrived from Poland in August and stayed for two years. Rounding out the enrollment up to December, 1934, was Roswilla Looman, who arrived in October of 1934 and left in November of 1935. (The pattern of unpredictable, out-of-season arrivals and departures would characterize the school through the war years, taxing the imagination and pluck of its staff to maintain academic continuity.) By word of mouth, through a modest lecture tour through Germany by Dr. Lion, and through the work of the Quakers operating in Berlin, news of the school spread. By November of its first year, the number of residential pupils reached eleven. By the end of the school year in the spring of 1935, Stoatley Rough had an enrollment of thirty-six.

The first two months of 1934 the pupils were given perfunctory instruction, but most were there to learn English, to have a place to live while their parents found a way out of their home countries. Volunteers arrived from London and local environs to talk to the children. Dr. Lion decided to do some of the teaching of history and geography. She was more comfortable with small children than with older ones but often talked over their heads. One little girl came away from one session believing that the Boer Wars involved Winston Churchill fighting wild boars with a sword in the jungle. Everyone admired Dr. Lion's intellectualism, however, and enjoyed the company of the unpretentious headmistress.

Over the summer of 1934, almost everybody returned to the Continent, giving the Committee the opportunity to focus on fund raising. Not only did the school need to repay loans, the Committee understood the problems in receiving full tuition from German families since Nazi policies made it expensive to take money out of the country. They decided to take advantage of the school's lovely locale. They would turn the place into a vacation spot, a combination country inn and cultural summer school with classes for children and adults. "We are expecting several holiday children and grown-ups to come from

Germany for a Summer School. They hope to meet English people here for a cordial exchange of views and for mutual practice in the two languages."[8] The Committee used its connections to find scholars to lecture in both English and German. Eighteen German children came for the summer school in 1934, and forty-eight visitors attended for the entire six weeks. The Committee also implemented another money-making scheme in which they offered "convalescence to specially chosen children from the East End of London. Pay by charity, 10 shillings a week."[9] The latter idea was short-lived. The Committee's Report of November 10, 1934, said (perhaps disingenuously), "Re the future of the convalescent children – it is not too wise that too many East End children should be taken, as it is not fair for the German children to hear Cockney English."[10] Meanwhile, the school also hosted "a group of Germans living in London and one English guest."[11] They came for "the rest and refreshment in the garden and the woods and especially …. the fire-side talks in the evenings.

The German-English cultural event raised local and London money by featuring music and literary readings July 28 – August 17. This cultural event became a tradition that would be repeated each summer until 1939 when it had to be suspended for the duration of the war. During the first summer exchange session, Dr. Lion was introduced to a professor Dr. Luise Leven, holder of a doctorate in Music, who had traveled from Berlin with an Aryan friend for the cultural exchange. Dr. Lion was enchanted by this lively, dark-haired woman, so sure of herself, so full of confidence. The two women became friends. Dr. Leven promised she would return the following summer.

After one final event, recorded as a "tea party" for a few dozen Haslemere residents, formal classes began in September. From the start, Stoatley Rough combined academics with healthy, outdoor extracurricular activities, an approach rooted in the late 19th century

---

8   Committee Report, First Term Report of German-English School, November 10, 1934. LSE, Stoatley Rough Archives, 1/1 (i).

9   Ibid.

10 Ibid.

11 Ibid.

progressive educational reform tradition of *Landerziehungsheime* ["countryside educational homes"]. Nore led the children every morning on a run that took them down the path past the first tennis court to the second tennis court where she conducted setting up exercises. Then it was back up to the manor to have breakfast and attend classes. The main meal was served at 1:00 p.m. Afternoons were for resting or homework but might include some sort of game or outing, music practice, or crafts. Evening meals were informal and light.

Dr. Lion's schedule was influenced by the work of the educationalists George Kerschensteiner (1854-1932) and Hermann Lietz (1868-1919), who introduced into Germany the idea of "vocational" schools, an alternative to the traditional *Gymnasium* fare of classical languages, literature, maths and science, and the value of physical exercise and recreation, respectively. Indeed, these influences can be seen in the fact that all the children at Stoatley Rough were required to work at weekly chores such as dusting, setting the table, keeping the fireplaces filled with wood, and washing and drying dishes. They worked outside at gardening and when the school acquired livestock, they cleaned the chicken coops and pigsty. Upon occasion, children helped to bring in crops. Far from being a formal school, Dr. Lion's Stoatley Rough would offer a "genial atmosphere of life in a happy, healthy environment."

The school had a pleasant, utopian quality. The Committee's first report, November, 1934, waxed lyrical about children keeping Angora rabbits to use the wool for weaving, and how each child spent a few hours at gardening, "even the youngest ones had their own little plots." It was cozy at Stoatley Rough, a family environment. The adults read aloud to the younger children after the evening meal as the older girls mended clothing or sewed. Literary fare included Sewells' *Black Beauty*; then Kipling's *The Second Jungle Book*; and Robert Louis Stevenson's *Travels with a Donkey*. The Committee was pleased with their "community in which the children have their personal relationships so that no child feels itself [sic] a pupil only, but one of a community of real friends. Simple ethical reading before bedtime is meant to help these children to find their way and to clear their opinions about eternal truths."[12]

---

[12] Ibid.

Policies, Symbols
and a Good First Year

The formal school year began in September, 1934, offering English
language instruction, arithmetic, geography and nature studies.
With so few children, Dr. Lion had the advantage of time to plan
for the larger enrollments that would materialize as word of the school
spread. What kind of a school would Stoatley Rough be? Was it to be
a real school or just a safe haven? Unable to draw on tradition, history,
or established custom, Dr. Lion and her Committee had to start from
scratch, but they all shared certain ideals: communal work by staff and
children, equality of the sexes, help for the smaller members by the larger
ones, and self-reliance. At a time when most private schools in England
practiced caning, perpetuated a rigid class system, and tolerated anti-
Semitic prejudices, the founders shared Dr. Lion's belief in creating a
school that would allow no corporal punishment whatsoever. It would
be egalitarian. It would impart tolerance for difference. And it would
be safe. Dr. Lion may not have had experience with children but she
knew instinctively that they needed to feel safe. She wrote, memorably,
that Stoatley Rough was a place "where a child could grow up quietly."

During their many planning sessions the Committee and Dr. Lion
determined that Stoatley Rough would provide traditional education
to children up to age sixteen, two years past the age the government
schools kept children in England at the time. It was a logical decision
since the school could not very well abandon otherwise homeless
children under sixteen years old to fend for themselves. A much thornier

issue had to do with the higher level of academic preparation a pupil needed to enter a university. For such a course, either the pupil had to do very well on the Cambridge School Certificate, a proof of high school completion, or alternately, had to take a stringent university entrance exam covering a wide range of subjects, informally known as the Matric (a "matriculation exam") which each university issued as its own entrance exam. A matric could roughly compare to individualized SATs (Scholastic Aptitude Test) in the United States. Since funding was forever an issue, and since the Committee sought accreditation and respectability, the Committee decided that advance preparation would be offered only to those "deemed suitable." The chance to sit for such an exam would be restricted to a few chosen ones. The Committee wrote that such a policy was good for everybody because it made sure that "students [doing] intellectual work are not cut off from practical pursuits and the opposite is true for those engaged in practical or handicraft work." [13]

Who was eligible for the matric test and who wasn't? The Committee didn't know. They left that up to Dr. Lion. She would judge a child's potential for higher learning. In hindsight, the Committee probably did not realize that it should have established criteria for the Matric. They should not have left such a decision entirely up to Dr. Lion's judgment. Dr. Lion was a feminist social worker, and not an educator of children. She had no background in elementary education or child development. With no criteria under which a child might understand his or her chances to prepare for the Matric, everything came down to Dr. Lion's opinion, something she usually formed within minutes of a first meeting. She never changed her mind, either. (She even unconsciously rubbed salt into the wounds of those she judged unfit for higher education by praising them with pronouncements such as, "This is Inge, she's good with her hands.") Later, as the school filled with many impoverished but qualified children, those not chosen to be allowed to take the Matric took this judgment bitterly and felt discriminated against. Some could not help resenting Dr. Lion's favorites who were

---

[13] Committee meeting notes, October 7, 1935. LSE, STR Archive, 1/1 (i)

blessed with her clairvoyance as suitable candidates. They privately saw these children as teacher's pets. But in 1934, these problems were non-existent, undreamed of. The school had no candidates for the Matric then. It had five young ladies already finished with their education and two young boys, nowhere near age sixteen. It all seemed quite workable.

During her first months on the job, Dr. Lion set about establishing contacts with the Shottermill and Hindhead government schools and a few of the private schools (in Britain called "public" schools) in the area, and arranged to augment her meager teaching staff with teaching volunteers and two paid instructors, the aforementioned Miss Reycart, and a Miss Postgate who came several times a week to help the children learn English. A Miss Hollick joined the teachers later in 1934. Part-time teachers Mr. Owen and Col. Hamilton were on the scene as instructors of math and science. The latter, a retired officer and known as a kind gentleman, talked so loudly that when he gave lessons at one end of the school, people at the other end of the house could clearly follow his lecture through the open windows.

Dr. Lion knew the importance of symbols. Someone – perhaps it was Dr. Lion herself - designed an official emblem, a triangle enclosing three entwined circles representing Christianity, Judaism and Islam, the symbol said to derive from the play by Gotthold Ehraim Lessing, *Nathan der Weise* [Nathan the Wise], one of the earliest pieces of literature to celebrate religious tolerance (1779). Lessing had expressed life as a pyramid (hence the triangle), the base of which represented the "foundation broad and firm enough to let each person reach his or her fullest height, or potential." Dr. Lion, ever the intellectual, wrote in one of her many messages to the school's population about Goethe's subsequent use of the symbolic triangle when he wrote to the influential Swiss thinker, Lavater: *'Ich wuenschte...! Die Pyramide meines Daseins, deren Basis mir angegeben und gegruendet ist, so hoch als moeglich in die Luft zu spitzen.'* [The pyramid of my existence, the basis of which is a given and well-grounded, I wished to reach as high as possible into the air.] Dr. Lion's allusion to Goethe reflects her passion for the power of ideas behind symbols. She knew the school needed its own spiritual, non-religious base.

One day a package arrived by post, a two-foot tall, three-dimensional wooden sign-post carved with the new emblem, showing in discs carved into the three-cornered piece bas-relief images of a girl reading, a girl at the kitchen range, and a boy with a scythe. This hand-sculpted work of art had been created by the eminent German sculptor, Mr. H. Nonnenmacher who was living in exile with his Jewish wife in London. Mr. Nonnenmacher was of such renown in Germany that the Nazis retaliated for his defection in 1934 by smashing his works from pedestals and branding his work "degenerate." The sculpted sign-post was placed at the entrance of the school. Dr. Lion later brought it inside to save it from the weather.

The Committee also endorsed a school uniform. Stoatley Rough could not begin to compete with well-endowed, established schools that housed upper class English children like the exclusive Royal School just down Farnham Lane. (Founded for daughters of naval officers in 1840 and still in operation today, it consistently rebuffed any formal contact whatsoever with Stoatley Rough.) But the young school could have a uniform. Dr. Lion decided on a simple navy skirt / trousers, white shirt and navy tie with silver stripes, to be worn on special occasions. "These colours symbolize the dark skies of our time with – in spite of it all – the still existing silver lining on the horizon." She knew uniforms would help to unify the student body in times when her ill-dressed assemblage came under public scrutiny. Perhaps a uniform also served the not-insignificant goal of impressing the school's sponsors to whom she was ever attentive.

The school' charter evolved. Various documents throughout the years show the school's changing identity. One letter to parents reflected the emphasis on the values of tolerance and strong character, e.g., "The communal life of the boarding school will be shaped in such a way as to overcome the differences of creed, nationality and language. To achieve this aim, comradeship, initiative and self determined disciplined responsibility will be fostered." One brochure stated the school's focus on English language and customs. Later the school was primarily a "safe haven" from Nazi terror. After the war, the school was "an international school." Stoatley Rough existed for refugee children in a land dotted with wealthy, entrenched independent (called "public" in England) schools. Dr. Lion was always searching to maintain a balance between educational progressivism and a proper curriculum. She made up the rules as she went along, re-defining her pedagogical vision as economic challenges forced her to make constant adjustments, yet never failing her pupils in striving for quality.

Sometime in the 1930s a school song came into being. Each of the three verses ended with the refrain, "God of the South, God of the North / God of us all, we venture forth."[14]

Stoatley Rough would always be a work in progress. In an anonymous, undated sheaf of papers (probably written in 1937 since

---

[14] Stoatley Rough School Song:

Gladly we join to sing our song
We who to Stoatley Rough belong
Proud, we display our circles three
Bound by a chain which makes us free.

God of the South, God of the North,
God of us all, we venture forth.

Many the kinds of work we do
Kitchen and farm, and classrooms too
All to the common good shall give
Learning together how to live.
God of the South, God of the North,
God of us all, we venture forth.

Silver and blue our colours are
This is the news they spread afar
Dark through the clouds of pain and fear
Silver, the ray of hope shines clear.

God of the South, God of the North,
God of us all, we venture forth.

the writer puts the school population at 42), the school is said to be "an experimental school aiming at a thorough instruction in two languages, English and German, combined with a methodical training in domestic science and handicrafts." It was also said of the school that it was a kind of "educational hostel for German refugee teachers, students and children."[15]

Miss Isabel Fry turned over the reins of the school to Dr. Lion in December of 1934. Some of the children were not sorry to see her go, having little patience with her Quaker practice of holding a period of silence every evening. Dr. Lion was expansive in her praise of the experienced pedagogue, "for her willingness to come to our aid from the very first and for staying with us for more than three months, organizing and teaching both staff and pupils. Living with us, she has been realizing an idea, and that meant more for us in this time and for the future than we can say in this short report." [16]

The school closed for two months over Christmas. The children who could not afford to travel back to Germany or who had no family to go home to were farmed out to English families. Two of the girls did housework for their host families as part of a new program Nore and Dr. Lion were launching at Stoatley Rough, the Domestic Sciences program. The school year started up again in January and by the summer closing, the pupil population was sixteen (ten girls and five boys), with one English day pupil. By December, 1935, it was up to thirty-six. The numbers did not reflect the same group of children but rather was merely a snapshot of a rapidly moving current of children

---

[15] From the biography of the interim Headmistress, the wealthy Miss Isabel Fry, by Beatrice Curtis Brown. Isabel Fry (1869-1958) was an educationist and social activist. She founded, and was headmistress of, two experimental schools: The Farmhouse School, Mayortorne Manor, Wendover, and later, Church Farm, Buckland, Aylesbury, Buckinghamshire. She came from a famous reforming Quaker background and was the daughter of Sir Edward Fry (1827-1918), jurist, and sister of (Sara) Margery Fry (1874-1958), penal reformer, and Roger Eliot Fry (1866-1934), artist and critic. http://www.ioe.ac.uk/library/archives/fy.html accessed September 24, 2007.

[16] Katharine [Meyer] Whittaker, *History of Stoatley Rough*, Stoatley Rough archives, London School of Economics, 1994.

moving in and out. Students would arrive and leave unpredictably, some staying two months, others for many years., and the original school functioned as much as a way station as an institution of learning.[17]

During the summer of 1935, travel was neither restricted within England nor prohibited abroad. Dr. Lion went back to Germany again on a recruiting tour, accompanying some of the children who would spend the summer at home. The German-English school on the hill looked after those who had nowhere to go, and the Committee continued to deal with ongoing problems.

Around the time the school reopened in the fall of 1935, a crisis presented itself. Mrs. Vernon had a potential buyer for the property. She wrote on September 29, 1935, "I have had a rather urgent letter from the people who are finally going to succeed to the house and I have promised them an answer as soon as possible."[18] Did the authorities still need the estate for their school? She might have been asking whether the sun rises from the east, since the answer was a foregone conclusion. Everyone was in love with Stoatley Rough. Dr. Lion wrote a quick response with a perfunctory listing of the school's ongoing problems of space, the water supply, and its "antiquated sewage system" but it was clear that she didn't want to leave. To her everlasting credit, Mrs. Vernon did not evict the little band of refugees. Bertha Bracey articulated the case for staying at the property, reminding the reader that the school was a haven not only for the children, but for Dr. Lion and her German cohorts. "It is only right to consider what the beauty of the garden, and the situation with

---

[17] The enrollment numbers cited in this book are approximate, gleaned from a list of students put together from the confidential files now in the London School of Economics archives. The list was created by Katharine Whitaker and Michael Johnson as a compendium to their short history of the school, *Stoatley Rough School 1934 – 1960*, (illustrated by Chris Townson) which they distributed in May, 1994, for the 60th Anniversary Reunion in England. I extrapolated milestone enrollment numbers from the ages, dates of arrival, and dates of departure noted on the Whitaker / Johnson list for each student who attended the school up to 1945. Some pupils' names are missing since some records are missing. The school lacked permanent lists and records, perhaps owing to the fluid nature of the arrival and departure of the pupils.

[18] *History of Stoatley Rough* p. 11

its beautiful views, has meant to just those people, older and younger, for whom the school was started. It has brought new hope and refreshment to many pupils, staff, casual visitors, and summer-school guests. From this angle the experience for so many is something for which we can be deeply grateful."[19] In October a new contract was drawn up for the lease of the property, "for not less than five years with permission to sublet the house in case it was no longer wanted." The terms of the lease recorded the fee of one shilling a year and reiterated the condition that Mr. Phillips and his wife would continue to live in the Lodge, employed for as long as he wished. The lease also stipulated that the internal and external repairs and maintenance would be the financial responsibility of the school. (In 1937, Articles of Association were drawn up and submitted to the Board of Trade with whom the school was registered. The school's Committee was incorporated into a Board of Governors.) At any rate, Mrs. Vernon's potential buyer was sent packing.

The Board Chair, a Miss A. R. Fearon of Haslemere (no one seems to know what her initials stood for) was especially happy. This lady of means not only worked on strategic planning and fund raising, but enjoyed being around the children, often driving small groups of them to museums and zoos. Many remember one extraordinary act of kindness from Miss Fearon during the *Blitz,* the continuous attack on London by the German *Luftwaffe* that began in September, 1940. As usual, the bell rang and the gong clanged over and over again, the signal to the children to walk quickly to the air raid shelter at the lower end of the house. But that day the throngs were diverted from entering the rear door that led downstairs, and instead were marched to the courtyard in the back where, after roll call, Mr. Phillips appeared from around the corner, grinning broadly and pushing a wagon. Its cargo? An enormous pail of ice cream, courtesy of Miss Fearon. Everyone cheered.

The indomitable Miss Fearon chaired the Committee (later known as the Board of Governors), for the entire twenty-six years of the school's existence.

---

[19] Bertha Bracey, letter to the Committee read October 7, 1935. LSE, STR Archives, 1/1 (i)

The Household Girls

When fifteen-year-old Gertrud Gans followed Nore around helping to set up the school in April of 1934, the physician's daughter knew she was finished with formal education – there would be no *Lyceum* for her in England. She was stranded, penniless, and struggling to learn the language of her new country. In their first report, the Committee conceded that "the girls who come to us have all finished their school education, though some of them much too early."[20] The five girls made the best of their situation. They understood they were marking time until they could join their families or grow up enough to work and live on their own. As the fall classes began to take shape, the two new young boys were kept busy with their studies, but the girls soon realized they had too much time on their hands. Gertrud and the others cornered Nore. Could they learn housekeeping from her? Could she train them to become real household managers? With certification, such a skill would land them good jobs – a fate preferable to ending up as an upstairs maid tucked away in some country estate evading the hands of a lecherous squire.

Why would teenaged girls from well-off families ask for such training? For one thing, it would keep them busy. For another, it might lead to a career. And finally, it had respectability. Far from being viewed as demeaning, expertise in housework had come to be perceived valuable and almost sacred, as if many 1930s-version Martha Stewarts had captured the hearts of a generation of women. A whole field of study sprang up to produce measurable standards of achievement.

---

[20] Committee meeting notes, October 7, 1935 LSE, Stoatley rough Archive 1/1 (i).

National certification in the Domestic Sciences was the foundation of a career. In her book, *Reader's Companion to US Women's History,* Mary Romero wrote, "Domestic science (also known as home economics, household administration, euthenics, and domestic economy) aimed to professionalize the status of housewife and upgrade the household arts. The new discipline …applied principles … borrowed from economics, chemistry, horticulture, and the emerging ideologies of domesticity and scientific management. Tradition, common sense, and personal taste were replaced by expert knowledge… [The goal was] to establish standards for all aspects of the domestic sphere, including cooking, child care, sewing, housecleaning, laundry, table setting, and home decorating."[21]

Dr. Lion and Nore mulled over the idea. While the school had not been designed as a trade school, perhaps such training could co-exist with an academic curriculum. Why not? Nore and Hanna, former instructors in the field, certainly could provide the expertise required. The Committee approved the idea. "We have capable teachers who give those girls instruction in everything that is necessary for the upkeep of our modern English country house…an up-to-date kitchen, laundry, and garden." [22]

As the population of the school grew, the need for girls who would be called Household Girls or "Big Girls" also grew. The girls studied hard: not only did they have the English language and literature and other academic subjects to master, but also the specific classes in "cleaning materials," "stock foods," and "house furnishing." Later, to qualify for Certification testing, a more rigorous, detailed field of topics included the economy of heating fuel, the importance of potatoes "as an energy giving food," economy in the use of vegetable waters, the strengths of starches, soaking and boiling cottons, rinsing woolens in lukewarm water, producing a good finish in ironing, and so on.

---

[21] Mary Romero *Reader's Companion to US Women's History,* http://college.hmco. com/history/readerscomp/women/html/wh_010200_domesticscience accessed October, 2004.

[22] First Committee Report, November 10, 1934, Stoatley Rough archives 1/1 (i). London School of Economics.

Soon the girls wanted to learn child care; Nore and Dr. Lion promptly added Kindergarten studies to the curriculum, the girls first practicing in neighboring child centers. As more children arrived at the school, they began to help the new younger children with their meals, their grooming, bedtimes. The girls were loving and in turn, were loved by young children lonely for their parents. The "Big Girl" in charge of them made sure they brushed their teeth, bathed (once a week!) and got to bed on time. Martin, our young man fresh from Vienna, saw his "Big Girl", Gertrud Gans [Farman], as a mother figure. Kate Lesser saw hers, Lilli Wohlgemuth [Gluecksmann.], as a source of security, having left behind "a Berlin of horror and darkness." Kate wrote, "It was to her that I brought the Red Cross letter announcing the death of my grandmother."[23] Kate was only eight years old in 1939 when she was sent off to England on the *Kindertransport*. Her arrival made her famous. Sitting in Liverpool Station in London with the other children, Kate was waiting for the next leg of her journey when she idly took out her violin. A newspaper photographer for the *Evening Standard* had been covering the arrival of a batch of children. "I was asked whether I actually played the violin, whereupon I played 'God Save the King' to prove that I did," to the delight and amazement of the photographer and crowd of bystanders.[24] The *Standard* printed the picture of the unsmiling, beautiful little refugee girl with her thick braids, legs akimbo beneath a checkered smocked dress, violin at her chin. Decades later, the enlarged photo of little Kate appeared as part of an exhibit at the National Holocaust Museum in Washington, D.C.

Household Girls helped children write to their families, an emotionally-charged, often difficult task. Nore recalled, "There were many children for years and years [who] never got mail. And some of them got regular letters and then suddenly [they] stopped, which of course for those children was more or less a terrible sign...we felt responsible. I remember we even helped them a little because younger children always say, 'Well, I don't know what to write.' I remember one

---

[23] Ibid.
[24] Lesser, Kate, in an email to the author

day [telling them to] ask them this or that.' And then one of the young boys said, 'Ask? But they are not here.' So I understood that for a child, this distance was something you can't overcome."[25] Martin never forgot the kindness of Gertrud Gans. When she left to be married in India in 1939, he felt devastated. He'd barely managed to adjust to his new surroundings, and the loss of her left a lasting mark. "I was heartbroken to lose my surrogate mother."

It didn't take long for the school to recognize the potential of a Domestic Sciences program to attract more students to the school. The pool of pupils who could pay full fare was always limited thanks to the *Reichsfluchtsteuer*, the surchage imposed by the Nazis, ten times any amount the émigré wished to have transferred from German banks into foreign countries. Only the very wealthy could fully fund their children for the several years they would be in England. Bertha Bracey noted in 1935, "The transfer of money from Germany even for the education of German children abroad is beset with difficulties and uncertainties. These are beyond our control and the most persistent and patient efforts to find a solution have only been very partially successful and in many cases have failed altogether."[26] Over time, a marriage of convenience or a Faustean bargain (depending on one's point of view) came to Stoatley Rough. The school needed labor to clean and keep the house running, and Jewish girls from less than wealthy families needed sanctuary. It was an opportunity Dr. Lion's committee could not ignore. Stoatley Rough School began to offer free tuition, room and board in exchange for work.

Of the eight girls who had come to Stoatley Rough by December, 1934 (known ages 15, 19, 14, and 15 in order of arrival and all paying full tuition), at least four of them are known to have studied Domestic Sciences. By the time Martin arrived in 1938, the school counted twelve tuition-free Household Girls among its seventy-one pupils. (The school also occasionally brought in English girls to help out, called "Helpers" who played no part in the program. There were five between 1934 and 1945; more Helpers were brought in after the war)

---

[25] Ibid.
[26] Astfalck, Nore, Oral History, November 10, 1990, Haslemere, Surrey, p. 6-8.

The school's brochure of 1938 described the fully developed program:

The Domestic Science Course (*Frauenschuljahr*) (1ˢᵗ year)

This training includes cooking, housework, laundry, handicrafts, needlework, arithmetic, bookkeeping, and the care of young children. The aim is to give an all-round knowledge of work connected with house and nursery. English, written and oral, History, German Literature, Arts, Social Studies complete this year's general education.

Household Management Course (2ⁿᵈ year)

Students continue their household work and specialize in management. This training provides the groundwork of experience in the organization of hostels and homes.

Handwork Training

The course includes dressmaking, weaving, woodwork, cardboard-work, book-binding, pottery, basket-making, repairs and gardening.

The Care of Children

The pupils are systematically trained. They get some experience with our younger children and in a neighbouring Kindergarten School. Pupils who reach a satisfactory standard in private examination in theoretical and practical subjects are given a Certificate.

Girls in the Domestic Sciences Program received fifteen hours per week of Appreciation of Literature, reading such authors as G.B. Shaw, Edith Sitwell, Robert Louis Stevenson, Joseph Conrad and D. H. Lawrence. They also wrote poetry and essays and studied shorthand, workshop, bookkeeping, and music. They learned scripture and child-psychology. Thursday mornings were reserved for theory.

A report card from the time (kindly lent by the son of Ilse Kaiser [Neibert]) shows finely parsed categories of study:

English (Pronunciation, Use of language, Reading, Spelling, Composition, and Literature)
European History
German
Shorthand
Arithmetic
Housework (Laundry, Ironing, Home Management, Odd jobbing)
Cookery & Scullery work (Applied Science, Hygiene)
Workshop (Needlework, Weaving; Woodwork and Bookbinding)
Gardening
Music
Gymnastics
Games
Condition of Health & Physical Culture (Carriage, Tidiness, Neatness, Punctuality, Attendance of lessons)
Willingness to Help
General Remarks, Hobbies and Special Courses

The Household Girls' curriculum for the winter of 1940 lists twelve Household Girls (Bauer, Bayer, Bing, Dorpalen, Kaufmann, Kaiser, Lilienthal, Klein, Neufeld L., Neufeld, T., Steinberg, and Koehler) and their curriculum: History, English, Social Geography and Songs (English and American.); their teachers were Miss Van Hollick, Miss Temple and Miss Humby. Miss Humby filed the following details:

A. Outline of American History and Civics
B. Dunkwalen's Play *Abraham Lincoln*, Shakespeare's *Hamlet*
C. Practical descriptive and imaginative composition
D. Mathematic: Frequent lists and accuracy.
E. Some practical work in Connection with housekeeping, e.g., cleaning materials, stock foods, house furnishing"[27]

---

[27] STR archives 4/13, LSE

The girls did not study higher mathematics, sciences or French. When the girls reached sixteen, the lessons ceased while the work remained.[28]

Miss Astfalck's influence on the program was enormous. Without her positive spirit and personal work ethic, it never would have flourished. She was popular and respected and she got the best work from the Household Girls through her own energy, praise, and insistence on quality. Years later, Nore liked to say that Stoatley Rough was known as a "clean house". One girl recalled Miss Astfalck's admonishment: "Whenever you have finished cleaning a room, before closing the door you must look around once more to see if the whole looks good." Not only did Nore Astfalck set an example of diligence, cheer and fairness in her own work, she assuaged the sense of social inferiority that inevitably was bound to surface. One girl said, "I minded [being a Household Girl] at the time. We were all somewhat intellectually snobbish. But I did learn a lot from Miss Astfalck, especially organizational skills that I'm grateful for today."[29] The girls took pride in their work. Ilse Kaiser [Neivert] recorded meticulous notes on the correct procedures for laundry and ironing. She used one whole page for her collection of tiny paper shirts, aprons, dishtowels, trousers folded properly and pasted to the sheet. Each is a perfectly crafted tiny creation of origami.

National certification testers came to the school in 1941 to administer exams, Nore's syllabus in hand, that stated that the "Housecraft Certificate" training at Stoatley Rough took roughly a year, with eleven two/three hour lessons per term, three mornings per week for lessons and one hour per week for theory. According to the National guidelines, each girl needed 200 hours of lessons. Nore explained to the examiners the uniqueness of the program at Stoatley Rough: that her girls were more than just pupils. "These girls run the house with the assistance on

---

28 Yet another lesson plan of 1940 lists the German literature that Dr. Wolff would teach: Summer Term: Thomas Mann, *Unordnung und fruehes Leid* [Disorder and Early Sorrow (fiction);] Schiller, Don Carlos. Winter Term: *Der Biberpelz; Gelesen und Aufgefuehrt; Bahnwaerter Thiel; Naturalismus und Realismus* [The Beaver Coat (play); read and performed; Signalman Thiel; Naturalism and Realism.

29 Rothschild [Hershkowitz], Inge, from a letter to the author dated December, 2004.

some days of the rest of the school. They do all the cooking, housework & laundrywork…[and] work in groups, so that one group learns one thing one week & the other group the same thing the next. They gain a good grasp of the essential work – because the school must be run to plan….theory is often taught whilst the cooking or laundrywork is being done for the school." The syllabus lists Miss Demuth, the school's cook, as resident "Cookery Mistress," and Miss Astfalck as resident "Laundrywork Mistress & Housewifery."[30]

The national administrators were displeased with Nore's curriculum, pointing out that her "Principles of Cookery, Cookery Methods and Kitchen Craft" were "useless – the matter overlaps and is disjointed. For example, boiling, stewing, etc. cannot be separated from retention of juices, cuts of meat, meat cookery and stoves."[31] They noted that in Laundrywork [sic], processes should be taught in conjunction with the fabric "being washed and studied. White cotton is never mentioned."[32] Nevertheless, they decided to go ahead with the exam.

The Cookery exam was especially daunting. Liesel Neumann wrote, "We did not know the recipes of all the popular English dishes by heart, and we were sure to get some of them in a test. The day before the exam one would see the Household Girls sighing over their recipe-books; but fortunately we only had to prepare some sponge and fruit pies, which are really quite simple. In spite of that the cookery was the worst part of the exam. We did not keep a careful enough eye on the pies, and the oven was not hot enough for the scones."[33] There were also problems when the girls moved to Laundry and Housewifery. "The tray cloth we had washed, starched and ironed, was not in perfect shape, and not shiny enough, [and] the metal polish was still seen in a corner of a candlestick."[34] Afterwards, the examiners commented that "…some candidates were very extravagant with heating." But it wasn't all bad. The examiner applauded the girls' knowledge of home-made

---

[30] Stoatley rough Archive 1/1 (i).

[31] Ibid.

[32] Ibid.

[33] Neumann, Liesel, *The Bridge*, 1941.

[34] Ibid.

cleaning solutions. Six girls passed. Before the examiners left they noted that more "practice in finishing finer articles and table linen would be helpful."[35]

The Household Girls always helped prepare for the traditional Christmas/Hannuka celebrations the school always held. Miss Demuth hoarded sugar and butter (during the war years) in order to bake holiday cookies and cakes, and each spring Nore always invited a few girls into her quarters to decorate Easter eggs. Inge Hamburger said, "Each child would receive one egg, a treat, which some of us 'secretly' decorated in Nore and Hanna's room. It was really enjoyable."

Thus the girls in the Domestic Sciences program were able to adjust to their special status. In some ways, they were treated like adults and reveled in the extra attention and praise they received from Nore. In other ways, they were powerless servants with little choice but to do what they were told. And like the Farm Boys (another special category of pupil,) they were learning a trade while providing essential services to the school. Unlike most of their peers, they were not on the academic track – there would never be a matric in their future. But like their peers, they were sheltered. And safe from Nazi murderers. Their goal was simply to grow up enough to get out on their own and then find work.

---

[35] Stoatley Rough Archives 1/1 (i).

The Farm Program

Although Dr. Lion did not formally articulate a Farm Program until 1938, she nurtured an idea for a training farm after well-meaning benefactors donated a few cows and poultry to the fledgling school in 1934. In some ways, the Farm Program mirrored the Domestic Sciences course of work/study, yet it was much smaller and offered fewer academic subjects. It was also less vital to the survival of the school and more fluid in concept and implementation. Before the war, having a farm allowed children to frolic with baby goats and puppies, feed geese and chickens, and tend piglets. Once the war started, however, practical considerations forced a new, focused activity, with serious crop growing and a paring down to essential livestock that could help the war effort. The farm provided milk, eggs, meat, vegetables and berries i.e., gooseberries, etc. to the table.

The original farm course consisted of one and one half years of hands-on training to prepare boys to work in "a colonial settlement." Dr. Lion still reflecting her utopian vision, wrote in 1937, "Our scheme of Small Holding is to be started on the premises. We shall have an agricultural teacher, as we wish to give the children growing up on such a beautiful estate an idea what simple country life comprises. We should like to make our boys and girls so independent that they will be encouraged to leave the Old World."[36] The seven acres of fields below the manor house were dedicated to the Farm. Boys received classes in English, carpentry, something called "Sanitary Instruction" and First Aid.

---

[36] Hilde Lion, Lecture Notes, November 24, 1937, Stoatley Rough Newsletter Issue 3, October, 1993.

A school brochure, circa 1937, describes farm training as follows, listing a Mrs. A. H. Railing as Chairman of the Department:

"In its grounds of 24 acres the School has established a special course for young people interested in agricultural and horticultural work. The object is to give the pupils, who have for the most part been educated in towns, preparatory instruction for life in an overseas settlement. At the same time the aim is to teach them independence and self-reliance and to make them familiar with the English language and with British customs and outlook."

Gardening and Elementary Agriculture
Growing various crops, vegetables, flowers.

Keeping Live-Stock:
Chicken-farming, pigs, goats, cows, calves, etc.

Carpentry, First-Aid, etc.

The school would not take anyone over age seventeen for the program and assumed pupils would be "physically and mentally fit." Participants came in to the program on a probationary status for the first three months. The school promised to utilize its connections with British overseas settlement organizations so as to facilitate the emigration of the pupils. By 1939 the Farm was fully functioning. Farm Boys did the heavier chores, while boys and girls living in the main house helped out with some of the routine chores and periodic harvestings of crops.

All the children at Stoatley Rough grew vegetables on individual parcels of land. Obo recalls, "Our plots were given to us in the winter of 1939. At first we thought it was hopeless to cultivate pieces of land – it all was just one big piece of weeds, and high grass with a lot of frogs. Well, we started to trench (which means to dig the turf underneath, leaving the soil on top). It was really a nice job but tiring. The piece of land was divided into five plots, one being an experimental one. ...We planted cabbages, kale, radishes, turnips, parsnips, mustard, cress, cauliflowers, Brussels-sprouts, beans and peas. But the cows broke through the fence and pinched many plants. We repaired the fence and the cows did not break through again. In autumn we lifted our potatoes which were of the "Red King' variety. It was a very good crop. Then we clamped them, which means that we put them on some straw on the ground and put straw all round them and then put earth on top. We left a chimney on the top to let the air out. All this was done to protect them from the frost."[37]

The pre-war Farm allowed the children access to pets such as dogs, cats, and goats, all of whom were named. Dr. Wolff recorded that Mindo had puppies, (all the females were drowned) and that the "happy" father was the "ugly brown Bobby," Mr. Phillips' dog.[38] By 1939, two breeding sows were in residence. Alexander Finkler enjoyed watching over the swine. "It is eleven o'clock of a summer night. Inside the sty we find a happy mother surrounded by her numerous progeny; all struggling for milk. But there lurks in the background a policeman in the shape of a farm boy. One is reminded of a rush-hour in a big London store; the piglets are the pushing, excited queue of buyers, and the sow is the retailer, harassed by the unreasonable demands made upon the commodity she has to offer. Finally she rises, and kicks the impatient crowd away, and they are shepherded to safety by the watching farm boy. He must stay at his post until relieved at the second watch; then up the path he climbs with a great yawn. He drops into bed, and is soon asleep and dreaming of legions of suckling pigs."[39]

Geese wandered freely. The unpredictable creatures had their favorites and those whom they disliked. One victim wrote," An aggressive goose, coming at you with neck extended and hissing, is a mean sight, resulting in bites to hands or legs if you were intimidated, but responding if one counterattacks." One day, a goose turned up

---

[37] Hans [Obo, Ginger Nipper John] Obermeyer, The Bridge, Vol. 2, August-September, 1940.

[38] Dr. Emmy Wolff, "Extracts from Letters from Emmy Wolff to her Family, August 1934-February 1939." Translated by Katya Shepard [Schaefer]. P. 8, Stoatley Rough Newsletter, Issue. 1, December, 1992.

[39] Finkler, Alexander, The Bridge Vol 2, August – September, 1940.

with a broken neck and one of the older boys on the farm decided to try to cure her. He created a small splint, wound it around her neck, and hand-fed her for a few days while she recovered. She returned to the farm as mean as ever, not favoring her savior in the slightest. Wolf commented that, "Elsewhere one might have turned such an accident into roast goose, but not here."

Ilse Kaiser was sent to live on the farm after she turned sixteen. "I did not know one end of the cow from the other, but ...I did fall in love with the two baby goats. I was put in charge of them and they started to follow me everywhere. Unfortunately Dr. Lion did not appreciate it when they followed me to the house and ran back and forth on the terrace during dinner." Miss Dove objected strenuously to the habit of Dr. Lion's of taking the smaller children down to the farm to pet the baby animals since sometimes the animals appeared later as a main course. To make her point, and to Dr. Lion's great disapproval, Miss Dove became a vegetarian.

In the 1930's and 40's, farming was more a part of community life than now. Then the people lived close to the land and more people were being born on farms than in cities. The horse was still widely in use. When automobile plants in England were converted to provide materiél for the war effort in the late thirties, horses made a comeback, deemed essential in the drive for high levels of farm production. Even Stoatley Rough had its own Black Beauty who was regularly hitched to a plow or wagon the kids called the Roman Chariot. Black Beauty hauled surplus kitchen refuse or made milk runs into town through back fields and gates. Obo recalled that the horse was temperamental, once giving him a swift kick. While the farm at Stoatley Rough was barely a real farm by most standards, it did train future farmers and provided some of the school's food.[40]

---

[40] An early participant in the Farm Program was Klaus Zedner. Klaus had left the school at 17 in 1938 with an uncertain future. He joined a program designed to train refugees to become farmers or farm managers in Australia. They were supposed to work on a real farm with eighteen other boys from Austria and Germany. They would have been sent to Australia if the war hadn't interrupted the scheme. The program attracted the attention of the press. He later wrote to

Before farm managers arrived on the scene, the administrators were seriously invested in the Farm but they proved to be rank amateurs. In 1938, Dr. Wolff wrote to her mother, "We had some chicken experts here the other day; they were delighted with everything and explained, among other things, that the fencing chosen for the coming chickens was a paradise for – foxes!"[41] A year earlier the farm's sole starter chicken met an untimely death, causing consternation among the school body. Something got into the coop and ate, as Wolf put it, "the entire stock of fowl." The culprit was never identified, but everybody except the administrators knew a fox had not breached the fence, but Mr. Phillips' own beloved Airedale, Bobby. Bobby went on to prey on a hapless moorhen who decided to nest next to the newly built swimming pool, giving rise to a wonderful irony. Again Wolf. "The Norwegian and Belgian campaigns ended in disaster, Dunkirk was evacuated, France fell, an invasion of England was expected at any moment, but the British authorities worried about protecting a moorhen. Later that summer the moorhen's gestation was terminated. It was blamed on a fox, but I suspect Bob, the fat mongrel. You may remember that the school farm was begun in 1938 with a single hen, carefully guarded by an enclosure guaranteed to protect against foxes. The moorhen was probably another victim of Bob, but no one ever knew for sure."[42]

As she worked to establish the Farm, Dr. Lion consistently preached emigration. "One boy works in the Haslemere Motor Works to get to know something about auto-engineering before he goes overseas." She was creative in garnering resources to support her goals. "Besides the English and other school lessons, a blind former County Council

---

Dr. Lion. "After some time our training farm became well-known, so much that for a fortnight or more we spent most of our time giving interviews to reporters, posing for press-photographers and answering all sorts of questions. Two sound films were made of us. Later we went to a cinema to see and hear ourselves as stars on the screen! The Bridge, Vol. I, May, 1940.

41 Dr. Emmy Wolff, "Extracts from Letters from Emmy Wolff to her Family, August 1934-February 1939. Translated by Katya Shepard [Schaefer]. P. 8, Stoatley Rough Newsletter, Issue. 1, December, 1992.

42 Edelstein, Wolf [Elston.

Agricultural Adviser comes up regularly to give farming lectures to the boys."[43] She brought in experts to lecture on colonization in Australia and India, and made contacts with local area farms. "In order to give our farm boys more experience, there were nearly only boys, they were sent for shorter or longer stays to farms in the neighbourhood and to Suffolk, where two of them had the great opportunity of being invited for ten weeks each and another one for three weeks. Besides the regular tuition, by an English farm teacher, we have enjoyed already for a month now the great help of an English builder who has been sent by Mrs. Railing. He teaches the boy in erecting sheds, incubators, in altering the laundry with kind permission of Mrs. Vernon. We have more livestock than before."[44] She reported in 1938, "We have nine little pigs from our old one; four of them have already been killed and provide the school with excellent meat."[45]

When all was said and done, three boys emigrated to Australia in 1938 to become farmers or farm managers and in 1939, one boy went to New Zealand and one to East Africa. A few others (Farm and non-Farm children) went to Palestine. After 1939, the sea lanes were closed to passenger ships. After attending supplemental lectures at the Guildford Technical Institute, a few children passed exams in poultry-keeping that were administered by the Board of Agriculture. Most in the Farm Program remained in England to work on farms until they could find other work.

---

[43] LSE Archives STR 1/1 (i) from Dr. Lion's semi-annual report, 1938.
[44] Ibid.
[45] Ibid.

Ordnung Muss Sein
[We Must Have Order]

I n 1936, Dr. Lion's friend, dear Emmy, arrived to teach and live at the school. At last. She entered an alien world and she had to struggle to adjust to a new, surprisingly unreasonable way of life. She did her best. After almost two decades in Haslemere, she left a legacy of respect for literature and art that lived long past her own lifetime.

Stoatley Rough was on its way. In its second year (1935-36) the school was a thriving little hideaway on the hill. The locals called it the German-English School. Enrollment grew steadily, reaching thirty-one pupils by December and forty, by June. Payment for the services of two new women was recorded in the Board's report: a Miss Billson, identified as a solicitor in the Board's report and a Miss Debenham, whose function is not specified. She may have been an English teacher. The Board grew to fifteen members, and its new Articles of Association expressed the hope that "one or two more Friends will consent to join the school." In late winter of 1936, the school experienced its first infectious disease with seven cases of chickenpox, a calamity that spawned five weeks of quarantine until the Medical Office of Health pronounced the "sanitary arrangements of the house" satisfactory. Someone gave the school a pottery wheel for art classes, but no one came to the rescue of the Science department. The Board claimed it was unable to spare £15 for a piece of unspecified equipment. But Dr. Lion was ever resourceful. With a captive group of pupils day and night, the school could offer a variety of informal learning opportunities within its flexible schedule:

Dr. Lion often held sessions in her own room with a few small children, discussing such subjects as "the Life and Work of Friedrich Liszt, or the German Customs Union and Development of Railways;" Nore Astfalck taught boys and girls to cook "cocoa and an egg, cutlet and fried potatoes, soup for an invalid and chamomile tisane." The curriculum now included Hebrew lessons, typing, shorthand, Arts and Crafts, Natural Science and Biology. Nature Studies took the lower forms outdoors to collect specimens and make drawings of plants. A singing teacher was on hand several times a week, and the new second-in-command, Dr. Wolff, was devoting four evenings a week to giving readings in English and German literature as the older children darned their socks. Eight visiting English speakers held regular hours of instruction several times a week. The School acquired a few large floor polishers (the children complained they were heavy and unwieldy) and established a library. Children sallied forth on educational excursions: a pottery factory, a laundry, a flower show, Arundel Castle, Windsor Castle, Eaton, Little Hampton. They also went to festivals, concerts and plays. In June, the school celebrated its year-end closing with a cultural weekend - a series of lectures followed by an evening concert of piano and violin and a children's choir – a performance held to the standards of excellence the school was becoming famous for attaining. The audience gathered on folding chairs outside on the terrace. Dr. Wolff was moved to tears when the children sang *"Der Mond is Aufgegangen"* [The Moon Has Risen] into the beautiful summer evening. The next day everyone enjoyed "a genuine English tea – toast, sandwiches and masses of cakes," following a lecture on *Romeo and Juliet*. School was out for the summer.

Neither Dr. Wolf, Leven, nor Lion was temperamentally suited to the rough and tumble world of children. In particular, Dr. Wolff had to overcome her natural aloof and cool manner. Having left behind the quiet predictability of her literary work and intellectual circle of friends, she was highly overqualified to teach literature at Stoatley Rough. She had not been prepared for communal living and moving from a world of ideas and aesthetics to the literal-minded, unpolished world of children must have been shocking. She had grown up in wealth in Berlin, trained to handle a domestic staff she was expected to govern some day. She spent her days working on her needlework and practicing the piano. Girls of her standing were not allowed to earn their living... " This dictum caused me great suffering."[46] After attending a *Lyceum* (finishing school), she took an extra year to study more foreign languages, piano, needlepoint and literature. Then she made the courageous decision that put her on the same path as Dr. Lion. She defied her tyrannical father and left home to dive head first into social work and the women's movement. Like Dr. Lion, whose sexual preference "dared not speak its name," she was determined never to marry. At the respectable age of twenty-five, she attended the *Hochschule für Frauen*, a school in Leipzig for women founded by the great feminist, Henriette Goldschmidt (1825 – 1920), and went on to undergraduate studies in Munich where she came into contact with other influential feminists such as Gertrude Bauemer (1873 – 1954). In 1922 she received her PhD from the University of Frankfurt / Main, where she and Hilde Lion became confidants and shared living quarters. Like Dr. Lion, Emmy Wolff was passionate about women's political, social and economic equality; she wanted housework to be acknowledged for its value, "even worshipped." She chose prostitution as the subject of her dissertation ("A Girls' Hostel and the Origin of its Members - A Contribution to the Problem of Female Dropouts") in which she focused on a special hostel founded by feminist Bertha Pappenheim (1859 – 1939) to help girls from Eastern countries such as Russia, Romania, and Poland who had ended up in bondage in Germany. As Assistant to Gertrud Baumer, Emmy Wolff held an important position in the feminist and literary world. She co-

---

[46] Wolff, Emmy, as quoted by Manfred Berger, excerpted in Stoatley Rough Newsletters # 13, (Feb. 1997. p. 13), and #14 (May, 1997.). Manfred Berger distinguished scholar, and founder of the Ida Seele Archive dedicated to the history of the kindergarten in Dillingen, Germany, wrote about many pioneering feminists of the Weimar era, including Johanna Goldschmidt, Alice Salomon, Luise Froeberl, Anna Warburg, Gertrud Pappenheim, Maria Montessori, and Hildegard von Gierke, among many others. The article from which this information came is in Mr. Berger's archive and was translated from the German for the newsletters by Gerda Haas.

edited *Die Frau*, [Woman], a leading women's magazine, for which she wrote dozens of articles and poems and she lectured at educational institutions on youth literature and social work, including the *Deutsche Akademie für soziale und paedagogische Frauenarbeit* [German Academy of Women's Social and Pedagogical Work] then headed by Dr. Lion. She wrote several books, including a collection of stories for children. Her formidable resume also listed the management of the Union of German Women's Associations (*Bund Deutscher Frauenvereine*) also known as BUND. After 1933, Dr. Wolff was declared "racially inferior" yet she continued to publish poems and essays in newspapers and journals under her mother's maiden name, Elisabeth Fleiss.

She always had a soft spot for children although she held a somewhat idealized view. She took children in small groups on outings, and sometimes invited them in for cocoa and a feast of freshly picked mushrooms cooked in gobs of butter and onions. When she was assigned to drive a few children to travel to Germany from Southhampton, she took a couple of their friends along. On the way back, they stopped to go rowing on the Wey, "followed by cups of chocolate in an elegant tea room."[47]

One of the hundreds of poem she wrote reflects a sentimental Victorian worldview. The childless academic depicts her subject, a sleeping child, with exquisite imagery.

Das Kind

Niemals von der Mutter Mund
Fiel ein Lied in seinem Schlaf,
Sieben Engel Sangen
Selig ueber ihm.
Flaumiges Gefieder flog,
Rauschte weis und ahnungsvoll,
Sieben Donner brummten
Unter Blitz und Schwert.

---

[47] Wolff, Gad Gerhard, Stoatley Rough Newsletter, 19, August, 1999.

Als am Regenbogenband
Sacht, so sacht die Wiege ging,
Legten sieben Leuchter
Lichtgold in sein Haar.

The Child

Never from a mother's mouth
Was a song sung as he slept,
[rather] Seven angels sang
Blessedly over him.
Downy plumage flew,
Rustling wisely and with prescience,
Seven thunders rumbled
Under lightning and sword.
As the cradle rocked gently, so gently
near the rainbow's ribbon,
Seven lanterns spread
Bright gold on his hair.

[Undated. Translated by the author.]

Dr. Wolff had never held a mop in her hand before she got to Haslemere. She had never worked in a kitchen or spoken for any length of time to a small child. In her earliest letters home, Dr. Wolff characterized Stoatley Rough as an exotic, daffy place, writing with detached amusement. "For a little while now we have been enjoying the blessings of a potato peeling machine. The thing was expensive, but it is worth it. It washes and peels enough potatoes for about fifty people in about 5-7 minutes. One boy turns the handle and then they plop into the bowl; one only has to take the eyes out."[48] During the mid-1930's the school's population was so

---

[48] Gerda Haas translated the letter into English for the Stoatley Rough Newsletter #8, June, 1995.

small that the staff was still taking turns preparing food for everybody, and that included Dr. Wolff. On the day it was Dr. Wolff's turn to cook, she took the plunge with courage. Her job was to get the main meal on the table for around 45 people by 1:00 p.m. It happened that one Monday, wash day, and helping hands were absent that otherwise should have been available to assist her. Dr. Wolff joked that her venture into the kitchen was the "Great Cooking Day." First she had the problem of not having anyone handy who knew "beefsteak;" She had to fry 140 "minced corned beef patties" (we would call them hamburgers). She put her one experienced helper to work at the stove then turned to the great amounts of red cabbage "straight from the garden" that she would have to cook with apples. Panic set in when the 100 kg of potatoes (about 220 pounds) failed to arrive early in the morning as scheduled. The delivery truck pulled up at 11:00, and she got the potatoes into the hot water she'd started bubbling in large pots on the stove. She was also in luck regarding the dessert. Yesterday's teacher on duty had prepared a fruit compote in advance. As the potatoes boiled, Dr. Wolff turned to the special requirements for the day. A certain amount of the cabbage and potatoes had to be made without salt for several "diet eaters;" she also needed to cook tomatoes instead of cabbage for one of the adults on a gallstones diet. Dr. Wolff then made a huge pot of tomato soup for the evening meal. Later she had milk brought up from the cellars for the early breakfast of the next morning that would be served to a select few early birds: the laundry girls, Mr. Phillips, his dog Bobby, several early-rising teachers, and a couple of small children whose chore for that week was to spread butter on dozens of slices of bread. Since some children were allergic to milk, apples also had to be set out. Dr. Wolff signed off with her letter to her mother with self-deprecation and a no small measure of pride at having conquered the stove. Grateful to Dr. Lion and the Board for bringing her out of Germany, she was determined to fit in.

Dr. Wolff enjoyed school life and entered into games and celebrations as happily as the children. She was playful and began to thrive in the environment of after-hours music and dance, shedding some of her natural reserve. One of her letters described several instances of dancing, including the time she led the children in a polonaise through the entire house to celebrate a fine job of cleaning. On another occasion the children danced in a conga line after refurbishing the Shed, an outbuilding down in the pasture area. The whole school attended that party with "colourful snippets of tissue paper on string ...stretched across the room in all directions." The children and teachers "wound [their] way down ... in one long chain, singing away, the Shed "booming with folk dancing." [49] And then Dr. Wolff described participating in a curious ritual whose roots went back to medieval days. "Beating the boundary" occurred when peasants marked the limits of a particular piece of land, such as a farm, manor house, or church, by pausing at certain trees, walls or hedges to exclaim, pray, or "beat" the marks with sticks of birch or willow. Dr. Wolff vividly recorded that the Stoatley Rough children ran around the lower part of the Stoatley Rough grounds that night, beating the boundary and singing with a strumming guitar, *"und so zieht der Bauer durch den Matsch, Matsch, Matsch,"* ["and so the peasant tramps through the sludge, sludge, sludge."].

From 1934 to 1938 the school functioned as a large family. Emmy Wolff recorded that there were bible readings, work days, ("Our English historian was on her knees, scrubbing the dining room parquet flooring"), literary readings (the children love anything like that and it does give them something to ...divert them a bit from their various manias") a talk on the history of the Quakers, fire drills, impromptu plays (improvised Song of the Apple – an original composition), evenings of singing and playing, a bus excursion to hear a peace lecture, and so on. Dr. Wolff wrote, "The big ones entertained us with ...an original composition which they dreamed up yesterday over the potato peeling... The little ones gave a gymnastic display, culminating in the presentation of all sorts of small gifts..."

As much as she worked at it, Dr. Wolff's patience for children was not without limits. She once wrote home about the "marvelous concert by the Busch Quarter here in the town – we were thrilled, about twenty

---

[49] STR NewsletterIssue 8, Translation by Katya Schaefer [Sheppard] Issue 8, June, 1995.

of us went. German music only, Haydn, Beethoven and Schuman. We were in quite a different world and then we swept out into a beautiful evening, clouds scudding across the sky." She concluded somberly, "Pity that up here so many different things happen to drive away the glorious impressions."[50]

In another letter home to her mother she wrote that Nore's birthday celebration was intimate and loving, a family experience. "To mark Nore's birthday we have invited Ha No (Hanna Nacken and Nore Astfalck) for supper. (Does Dr. Wolff mean a private supper with herself and Dr. Lion and the two other women, or does it imply that Nore and Hanna did not always dine with the children?). Before that there is going to be a 'Ruepeltanz' (Dance of the Louts), which doesn't need much disguise, and a dramatised fairy tale – the Swineherd – to celebrate the occasion as a dramatic opera – and a marionette play – to be performed at the same time. Every now and again there just has to be something special. We packed Nore's presents into the huge porridge bowl from which she always serves in the mornings; when she dutifully marched to the serving table, instead of the customary porridge, her ladle found a cake and other goodies to the delight of the young ones."[51]

Dr. Wolff was happiest in the classroom. Angela Galligan, a post-war pupil, remembered her as someone who believed in order, who said "*Ordnung muss sein*, [order must prevail]. "It was her insistence in drilling us in French verbs that enabled me to master them and to make real progress in the subject; her enthusiasm for French poetry and literature inspired in me a similar response."[52] Eveline Kanes concurred with the evaluation. "I liked Dr. Wolff the best; she helped me to re-learn German, and kindled my interest in German and French literature."[53] Angela Galligan wrote of Dr. Wolff's efforts to make the best of her new life. "Emmy was once in the school kitchen, with a kerchief around her head, making Swiss *muesli*. On another occasion

---

[50] Ibid.

[51] Emmy Wolff, letter to her mother dated November 13, 1936, Stoatley Rough Newsletter, Translated by Katya Schaefer [Sheppard], Issue 8, June, 1995, p. 18.

[52] Angela Galligan from Stoatley Rough Newsletter #12

[53] Eveline Kanes Stoatley Rough Newsletter Issue 18 September, 1998

she invited students to her home in Hindhead (bought in 1940 for her newly-arrived mother) where they were taking evening classes in typing and shorthand. She showed a photo of herself as a handsome young girl in leg o'mutton sleeves. She gave us a delicious home made bowl of potato soup."[54] Angela Galligan also articulated the essence of the dignified ex-patriot who never relinquished her German citizenship, in the following tribute. She said that Emmy Wolff had "all the Prussian virtues – honour, rigour, moral rectitude, orderliness and devotion to duty – without any of its vices."[55]

The peaceable kingdom that was Stoatley Rough disappeared in the early months of 1939. Emmy Wolff's feelings would be hurt, the adults would quarrel, Household Girls and Herta would be appalled, faculty would take sides, children would whisper. Private turmoil matched the public discomfort as children kept pouring into the school from the Continent to crowd the dining and class rooms and cause great shifts of sleeping quarters. Events of 1939 raised the stakes in the fight against widespread depression and fear. With Europe on the brink of war, the arrival of a prickly new music teacher did little to quell the sea change about to happen at Stoatley Rough.

---

[54] Angela Galligan [Roberts] STR Newsletter # 12 p. 9 "Not So Prussian As All That!"

[55] Ibid."

The Interloper

T he new music teacher ought to have fit right in with the other Germans on the campus: there were so many of them: Miss Demuth, Dr. Bluhm, Therese [Thesi] von Gierke, Emmy Wolff, Nore Astfalck, Hanna Nacken. But it was not to be. Dr. Leven made little effort to join the team and in fact, managed to antagonize practically everybody almost at once. Yet she stayed at the school for twenty-one years and along the way, bestowed a priceless gift on every child by raising music appreciation and performance quality to heights rarely found at any secondary school.

Dr. Lion, living in what was called "The Bungalow" with Dr. Wolff for almost a decade, nevertheless had become enchanted by one of the school's summer cultural visitors from Germany, forty-year-old Dr. Luise Leven. Dr. Leven recalled in her unpublished memoir, "In the spring of 1934, I chanced to read in Gertrud Baumer's *Die Frau* that a summer school for English and German grown-ups would be held in July, at the newly founded Stoatley Rough School in Haslemere, Surrey. I knew the name of the founder, Dr. Hilde Lion, but I had never met her. My Aryan singer friend, Marta Zillesen, and I asked for admission. For a long time we did not receive a reply; her name and the fact that I was still teaching at the *Staatliche Musiklehrerseminar* [State Music Training School] roused suspicions. Only after a...social worker supported the application were we allowed to come."[56] Like all the others before her, Dr. Leven fell in love with the locale. "At

---

[56] Dr. Luise Leven's unpublished notes on the history of Stoatley Rough, LSE, STR Box M3253

our arrival, we were overwhelmed by the beauty of the place and the spirit of its inhabitants…I repeated my visits …each year – three times with my Aryan friend, until she was denounced in the *Stürmer*," the German weekly anti-Semitic tabloid that published racist caricatures and obscene cartoons aimed to reinforce Nazi propaganda against Jews and other undesirables. Dr. Leven heeded Dr. Lion's urging to emigrate to England as soon as possible.

Luise Leven was six years younger than Dr. Lion and one year older than Matron Nore Astfalck. She was five feet tall and slight although she grew stout as she aged. She had an oval face of sharp features – sculpted lips, piercing eyes, and short, dark, wavy hair streaked with gray. In contrast to the pudding-faced Hilde Lion who was never to be termed "attractive," Luise Leven had been striking in her youth. A photo taken in the twenties shows a thin woman posing dramatically in black. Her bobbed hair is cut at sharp wedges and she stares coolly into the camera. To some, she looked mannish. The school's secretary likened her to a bird of prey, "perhaps a crow or raven." Another pupil saw a Harpo Marx quality, "he of the white hair and the zany look. … there was certainly a slightly zany gleam in the eye when she was conducting [the school's little orchestra.]"

Dr. Leven was born in 1899 in Krefeld, an ancient textile center on the Rhine near The Netherlands. Gifted in music, she studied violin, piano and music theory. In 1919 she passed an exam at the "A-level", higher than that achieved by either of the Drs. Lion and Wolff, an academic triumph that enabled her to enrol in the University in Frankfurt. Later she moved to Berlin to study science, the history of music and art and German literature. She received her doctorate in Music in 1926 and after a brief stint in Krefeld at the local conservatory, she re-located again in Berlin to give lessons in piano and theory at the *Staedtliche Konservatorium* [State-supported Conservatory]. She was a leading singer, teacher and conductor of the women's choir, heading for a career as Professor. Then the Nazis came to power. They excluded her as of April 1, 1933, from all official activities, yet, because she had been preparing music students for the Halle examination (the gold standard of exams for music teachers) the Aryan authorities asked her to stay on until her students could take the exam three years hence.[57] She returned home to become cantor in the Krefeld synagogue, but this occupation was closed to her in 1938. Six years after she had been booted out of her post in Berlin, Luise Leven ran out of choices.

The anguish she felt at separation from her home is apparent. "I could not make up my mind to leave my parents in Germany – I was their only child.... However, after my father died in 1937 and my mother received a permit to emigrate to Holland into the neighbourhood of some of her Dutch cousins and, above all, after the events of Nov. 1938 [note: she refers to *Kristallnacht*] robbed all hope of a tolerable life in Germany, (and the Synagogue, the place was destroyed), I was grateful that Hilde Lion guaranteed my maintenance in England. In March, 1939, I entered Stoatley Rough for good."[58]

Dr. Lion's ability to offer sanctuary to Dr. Leven demonstrates the wide latitude in decision-making she now had with her school Board. That they allowed her to hire a full-time music teacher when the school was in need of a science lab also speaks to their commitment to music. In fact, music appreciation was a core value of the school. Familiarity with classical music was *de rigueur* for well-bred upper middle-class families in those times. By 1937, the school employed a teacher from the town to lead a school choir and teach piano, violin, records, guitar, a huge harmonica, mouth organ and recorders.[59]

Dr. Leven's arrival in 1939 coincided with dire events on the Continent. War was imminent. The spontaneous pleasures of singing and dancing at the school ceased; music was now only to be studied and mastered. The school had always had a high percentage of talented youngsters, some who arrived with violins. Several were accomplished

---

[57] The ancient city of Halle, near Leipzig, is the home of the distinguished Protestant College for Church Music, still a respected institution.

[58] Dr. Luise Leven's unpublished notes on the history of Stoatley Rough, LSE, STR Box M3253

[59] Emmy Wolff, extracts from letters to her family, August 1936 – February 1939, trans. by Katya Sheppard [Schaefer]. Stoatley Rough Newsletter #1, p. 8, December 1992.

pianists, singers and artists. Children who expressed an interest in music (they had to pay extra fees) took music lessons from Dr. Leven. Everybody practiced seriously. People could use either of the two pianos in the house or, if they played recorder, flute or violin, various rooms and closets were occupied for practice during afternoon free time. Once Dr. Leven was in residence, music filled the house the year round. Hans [Goldy] Goldmeier, another boy who would join Martin, Obo and Wolf's circle of friends in 1941, recalled, "The large room was also used by our music students for practice sessions of violin or the piano. A grand piano graced the room near the large bay window. The students repeated over and over the difficult sections of Mozart or Beethoven sonatas, the music floating over the whole valley when the windows were open. I never resented the practicing. We always knew who was at the piano and who was playing the violin and the music students nearly always received the appropriate praise or teasing from the rest of us."[60] The musicians sometimes had to fight for practice time in the finite spaces available to them., One unidentified child wrote for *The Bridge*, "Edith with her violin victoriously practices for one and a half hours from the green bathroom," and went on to describe the day a visitor toured the school. "As we went along, the noise became worse, because we could hear the two pianos, quite distinctly. One person was playing Bach's "Italian Concerto" to the accompaniment of "The Village Green" on the other piano. A choir was rehearsing in one of the rooms, and then someone began scraping the C major scale on a violin." [61]

Controversy surrounded the new music teacher. Eveline Landau [Kanes] wrote, "Of the three, Dr. Leven was the most difficult. She recognized I was musical but was impatient and dismissive with me when she tutored me in maths because of my inability to apply concepts to problems.... She embarrassed me greatly on one occasion when the orchestra performed in the sitting room, [calling out] 'Miss Landau,

[60] Goldmeier, Hans [John, Goldy] Memoirs Part 1, pl. 51
[61] Unidentified pupil, *The Bridge*, Vol 3, September, 1941.

your G-string is flat.' At that moment I think I really hated her."[62] One could never accuse Dr. Leven of false praise. One day she was rehearsing the choir when Dr. Lion walked in, beaming. She said "Marvelous, marvelous," to which Dr. Leven retorted, "Terrible, terrible." Some children were just plain frightened by Dr. Leven. David Fielker, a post-war pupil, once played her a composition for piano he had written. Instead of praise came her response: "Nobody writes like Mozart nowadays." He later became a serious student of music with an encouraging mentor, and wrote "After years of continual discouragement," I found someone who was "actually teaching me how to write music!" and the young man went on to write plainchant and organum, masses, fugues, impromptus, and sonatas. [63] And then there was the time Dr. Leven committed an appallingly selfish act. Wolf was the injured party. "Here's my third reason for still being mad at Dr. Leven: Once a year, surplus chickens from the farm were culled and we had a glorious chicken dinner with the pieces carefully counted. Chicken was a rare treat and I couldn't wait to eat. That day, Dr. Leven was the disher-outer for one of the second-floor dining rooms and I was the server for her table. I noticed that she had set the biggest and juiciest piece aside. As the number of pieces on the serving plate diminished, I noticed with increasing anxiety that the count was short by one piece. At the end, only that big juicy piece was left but two people had not been served: Dr. L. and me. Without a word, she scarfed up that last piece for her own plate and handed me a plate of potatoes and veggies."

Dr. Leven was not without her admirers. Lilly Henschel, who had left the school in 1944 to read Medicine in Edinburgh, mentioned in a letter to Gerda Stein [Mayer] that Dr. Leven had been kind to her, especially Dr. Leven, and that she felt one could rely on her as a friend. Wolf admits Dr. Leven was "a great teacher and I learned a lot from her, especially in those voluntary Friday night sessions on the history of art

---

[62] Evelyn Landau [Kanes], *Remembering Stoatley*, Stoatley Rough Newsletter Issue 18, September, 1998, p. 51

[63] Fielker, David, p. 34 "What Did I Want to do When I Grew Up?" Stoatley Rouigh Newsletter #10, Feb. 1996.

and music. I don't think she liked children, unless they had real musical talent. Then she went all out."[64] Beate Frankfurter [Plonskoy] enjoyed her beginner's violin lessons with Dr. Leven. "Her teaching technique gave me a good foundation to build on and benefits me still; the choir singing, the recorder group and last but not least, playing the trumpet in a grand performance of Haydn's Toy Symphony."[65]

Dr. Leven babied her most talented youngsters. She would never have dreamt of stopping the car to pick up a child walking up the long steep hill to Stoatley Rough, but when her star performer needed a ride, it was different. Renate Herold [Richter] recalled, "I was to sing a Mozart cantata, the *Freimaurer*, for a concert, a complicated piece that needed a lot of practice. A few days before the event I was called to London. [to bid farewell to her brother who was leaving for Normandy]. Several days before I was due back, Dr. Leven telephoned me in a state of panic; I must go back immediately to prepare for my big solo performance. So back I went, to be met by the school car no less, an absolutely unprecedented honour, to be confronted by a near hysterical Dr. Leven who proceeded to ply me with raw eggs which were supposed to be beneficial to the vocal chords."[66]

Dr. Leven took over art appreciation, formerly taught by Dr. Wolff, sometimes catching a smart remark whispered by a bored student. Showing a superb grasp of human nature, she then made her series of Friday evening lectures on Art History the hottest place in town, by allowing attendance by invitation only. Wolf recalled, "Art history is a subject unlikely to attract teenagers but Dr. Leven used great psychology. There was no compulsion. On the contrary, attendance was by invitation, as a privilege one could earn after one's 15th birthday. Each illustrated lecture was a formal occasion, one of the few for which we had to wear school tie and blazer. I remember it so well, from Cimabue and Giotto to Gauguin and Van Gogh. Dr. Leven opened up

---

[64] Wolf Elston email
[65] Frankfurter [Plonskoy], Beate, "A Few Memries and Bits and Pieces," Stoatley Rough Newsletter 23, September, 2004, p. 5
[66] Renate Herold [Richter] email to the author.

a new world to me and I pity any child raised in a school system that regards art and music as dispensable luxuries...I really appreciated Dr. Leven's lectures years later, in New York, when I took a required college course in art appreciation from a bored professor."[67] Goldy Goldmeier concurred. "I remember with special fondness the large drawing-room with the lead-framed windows looking out over the valley, used for special events, like 'Friday Night,' a two-hour period with our Music and Art teacher who, with her projector, showed us some of the great paintings from different periods going back to the Renaissance...She also played classical music for us and explained it with the help of her wind-up phonograph."[68]

The children sometimes had trouble following Dr. Leven's rationale. She considered one of the boys, Uli Hubacher, to be very gifted, yet he received no lessons; she gave Peter Gaupp violin lessons while excluding his brother, Dieter, who'd had years of piano lessons. The younger boys did not always revere good music. They found nothing more hilarious than to apply their own words to classical tunes when Dr. Leven was out of earshot. The adults still recall the their version of "The March of the Toreadors" with its perfect cadences:

> Auf in den Kampf / Die Schwiegermutter kommt,
> Sieg – es - gewiss / Klappert ihr Gebiss...
> On to the fight / The mother-in-law comes
> Sure of victory / Her dentures clattering]. [69]

---

[67] Wolf Edelstein [Elston], email to the author

[68] Hans [Goldy, John] Goldmeier, Memoir Part 1

[69] The boys took great delight in putting words to classical music. Other entertaining versions included:

From the seduction aria from *Don Giovanni [Mozart]*:
Gieb mir die Hand, mein Leben, / Komm auf mein Schloss mit mir.
Ich will dir Bratwurst geben / Und auch ei-ein Glaessche-en Bier...

Give me your hand, my Dearest / Come to my castle with me.
I want to give you bratwurst / and a glass of beer.

When the Americans entered the war brought with them jazz and swing. The boys listened avidly to Glenn Miller's US Army Air Corps Band, electrified by the exciting new beat. They also liked a British station, *Soldaten Sender Calais,* that pretended to be broadcast from France, actually beamed out at German soldiers. The station not only delivered the straight news of the war but also Benny Goodman, Arte Shaw and other jazz stars. Dr. Leven tried to stamp out this awful stuff, this *"Jazzgedudel,"* [pronounced Yuts ga-doodle, meaning "jazz tootling"] but the kids were hooked and could be found running to the maps and geography books to find the exact locations of Chattanooga, Kalamazoo, Acheson, Topeka or Santa Fe on the map.

Something magical sometimes took hold in the hearts of the pupils, with thanks to Dr. Leven. Peter Gaupp carries lasting and specific impressions. "I have just tried to sing again "Lift Thine Eyes, Oh Lift Thine Eyes" from *Elijah.* The last time I sang this was with Goldy in about 1942-1943 when he recruited me to reluctantly sing in the Stoatley Rough choir because he felt alone. We were both sopranos. Soon after this he left the choir - asked to leave by Dr. Leven because he was no longer a boy soprano - and that left me in the lurch. Needless to say I sounded a lot better in those days - but some of the music memory remains."[70]

From Schubert's "Unfinished Symphony:"

Frieda, wo gehst Du hin, / Wo kommst du her,
Wann kehrst Du wieder…

Frieda, where are you going? / Where do you come from
When are you coming again?

From Handel's "Daughter of Zion Rejoice (from *Elijah)*

Instead of "*Tochter Zion, Freue Dich,* [Daughter of Zion Rejoice]

Doktor Lion, Freue Dich…" [Dr. Lion, Rejoice.]

[70] Peter Gaupp, email

The End of the
Peaceable Kingdom

When the day of Dr. Leven's long-awaited arrival came, Dr. Lion met Dr. Leven's train and drove her to the house next door to Stoatley Rough where she would live. She helped Dr. Leven to get settled and introduced her to the staff as soon as possible. Dr. Leven began to teach. The staff welcomed her into their small community, recognizing Dr. Lion's obvious fondness for the newcomer. And then came the all-school work day, the first Saturday of each month. Dr. Leven was nowhere to be seen. Dr. Wolff, Nore, Hanna, and the other adults toiled alongside the Household Girls supervising the children's cleaning and polishing work. But where was Dr. Leven? After dinner, Nore checked the roster, then quietly walked upstairs to the secretary's room. Had Dr. Leven's name inadvertently been left off the list? No, the secretary replied, Dr. Leven was not to be given household duties. Nore made it a point to discuss the issue with Dr. Leven. Did she understand that the morale of her Household Girls and the other children depended upon the perception that everyone was pulling her own weight? Dr. Leven was amused. What a ridiculous notion that she should have to do manual labor. She was the music teacher, not the cleaning lady. Besides, she didn't even live in the main house. It was bad enough she'd been asked to take on the Art History. There was no way she would be involved in house cleaning. Nore returned to her room that night, shaken by the insouciance of the newcomer. Over Monday morning breakfast, Hanna lost no time discussing the issue – is was a question of school morale after all - with Mr. Phillips and the Household Girls on laundry duty during their early breakfast.

Meanwhile, Dr. Lion was letting her work slip. She began to disappear from the office for long stretches at a time. One morning a call came in from one of the parents in Berlin. Secretary Herta left her office in the Bungalow after failing to find Dr. Lion still in her bedroom. She ran over to the main building and looked in the kitchen, library, and dining / sitting rooms, then out to the Terrace. She ran up and down all three floors of the main building. Next she marched across the lot, disturbing Mrs. Phillips at her morning tea. Hating the thought of the steep climb back, she nevertheless also loped down to the Farmhouse to see if by any chance, Dr. Lion had walked down to confer with the farm manager (a long shot, since Dr. Lion avoided physical exertion whenever possible). There was only one other possibility. Herta walked over to Dr. Leven's house and sure enough, there was Dr. Lion sitting close to Dr. Leven on the couch, the heads of the two women bent together, as Liszt' *Piano Concerto No. 2* played on the phonograph. In the following weeks, Herta had never seen Dr. Lion so happy. Come to think of it, she had started going around with a shy, loopy grin all the time. The next time Herta had to get a signature from Dr. Lion, she went straight to Dr. Leven's residence.

In the weeks to come things got worse. Dr. Leven sat at Dr. Lion's table every meal, while Dr. Wolff ended up on the third floor supervising a table of eight-year-olds. Evenings after lights out in the main house were now lonely in the Bungalow. Before, Dr. Lion had spent time each night talking with Emmy Wolff over a last cup of Ovaltine before bedtime. Each had a room in The Bungalow. Now the Headmistress was almost never home, invariably over across the way, sometimes not even returning to the Bungalow until the wee hours. Dr.Wolff became despondent, then angry, seeing her warm friendship with Dr. Lion coming unravelled. Before long, matters grew worse, with an escalating war of arguments and hostilities that drew Nore into the fray. Nore was on Dr. Wolff's side, resenting Dr. Leven's pull on Dr. Lion's attention. One day things exploded. It was Saturday and some of the older girls who happened to be working in the main house actually heard Nore and Dr. Leven screaming at each other, going at it for all to hear. It was a shocking turn of events. Where was Dr. Lion? How had things come to this? Herta recalled only "being partly aware of the world of grown-ups - of small power struggles and big jealousies among the elders. I had some sympathy for Emmy Wolff when Louise Leven appeared on the scene – [when she] tried to and did in fact take over in many ways."[71] The younger children, especially Martin, Wolf and the other boys who were only eleven at the time of Dr. Leven's arrival, were less aware of the schism between the Head and her Second, but not entirely spared. Late one night, Wolf was rummaging around among the books in the Library, downstairs when he should have been upstairs in bed. Unseen by the adults, he heard Dr. Leven saying something, to which replied Dr. Wolff in her deep voice. "Sie haben mir die Hilde abtruennig gemacht!!" [You have alienated Hilde's affection.] There was a pause, a muffled response, and then, each word thick and ragged, Dr. Wolff repeated, "You.. have….alienated…her affection." It was a shocking statement, punctuated by the fact that Dr. Wolff uses the formal German word for "you." Wolf sneaked back to bed, unable to get the hostile exchange out of his mind. For months an undercurrent of unease coursed through the school. The older pupils, especially the Household Girls, gave wide berth to the adult German teachers.

Dr. Wolff and Dr. Leven were very different women. The aristocratic Dr. Wolff with her warm brown eyes and aquiline nose was an impeccably groomed, elegant and intellectual woman. She always expressed herself calmly, aware she was a role model to the children. Not so with Luise Leven. She was impetuous and unfashionable and could be waspish and alternately irritated or exuberant. She didn't care who was in the room. The character of each woman showed in her attitude toward the school. Dr. Wolff had plunged into her new duties doing work she'd never have touched in Germany. Dr. Leven expressed little gratitude for her new life at Stoatley Rough and begrudged any extra duties. Her incomplete, unpublished, hand-written history of the school

---

[71] Ibid.

written in the 1950's reveals complaints just beneath the surface. "I had to coach pupils in math and had to deal with the school's finances, which involved a great deal of work and responsibility."[72]

Renate Dorpalen [Brocksieper] wrote of the effect of Dr. Leven's arrival at the school. "The institution had been changed by cliques, rivalries and favoritism. Old friendships were challenged. A rift had opened up between Dr. Lion and Dr. Wolff because of the gradual but obvious intrusion into their friendship. Dr. Lion began to isolate herself from the school's activities and withdrew into a life with Louise Leven off-campus. Dr. Wolff was spending more time taking care of her ailing mother (brought over at the outbreak of the war). Dr. Leven, a talented musician but a rather self-centred, ungiving, antagonistic woman, had a condescending attitude toward anything non-academic. She showed little inclination to share in the daily activities of the school community, and lacked rapport with the students, except a few, whom she singled out for attention in most inappropriate ways. She preferred to live outside the school complex, thus concretely separating herself from the school's life and emphasizing a conduct foreign to the basic philosophy of the school. The adults and children began to suffer badly under these new developments. It was entirely due to Nore Astfalck and Hanna Nacken who were deeply affected by the tension, that difficulties were kept to a minimum and the school continued to function relatively well. For me, the shift in relationships meant new insecurities, and I experienced the total affair as another loss, as though I were the child of newly divorced parents. Once again, the world around me was collapsing. Aunt Emmy and Uncle Lutz were dead; except for a rare-outdated Red Cross message, I was totally cut off from my parents."[73]

Dr. Lion did not ask Dr. Wolff to leave her quarters in the Bungalow, nor to abandon her post as Second-in-Command. Dr. Wolff went on teaching and performing her normal administrative duties. But at the private level, the strife took its toll. The emotionally insecure

---

[72] Emmy Wolff, letter to her mother dated November 13, 1936, Stoatley Rough Newsletter, Translated by Katya Schaefer [Sheppard], Issue 8, June, 1995, p. 18.

[73] Angela Galligan from Stoatley Rough Newsletter #12

Headmistress had a new confidante and companion. Dr. Wolff had to soldier on alone. The rift between Dr. Wolff and Dr. Lion would not heal right away. A year later, a former employee and mother of two students at Stoatley Rough wrote to ask Dr. Lion to accept her youngest, five-year-old as an evacuee from war-torn London. There ensued a flurry of correspondence among the three decision-makers: Dr. Lion, the Refugee Committee representative, and school Board member, Kathe Arndt. Who would pay for the girl? Kathe Arndt did some investigating behind the scenes, then wrote to the Refugee Committee (making sure to send a copy to Dr. Lion), that "a certain resident in one of the cottages on the school grounds might be willing to look after her. It was a sly move. The "certain resident" was certainly Dr. Wolff. The thought that Dr. Wolff might sponsor the girl right under Dr. Lion's nose galvanized Dr. Lion into taking action. She quickly agreed to admit the girl on partial scholarship. Rather than give Dr. Wolff the satisfaction of being the problem solver, Dr. Lion suddenly came up with the funding.

Dr. Wolff had lost her one friend in England. It was a blow. Herta said, "The relationship between Hilde Lion and Emmy Wolf deteriorated significantly when Luise Leven appeared on the scene. It was a hard time for Emmy Wolf, who was a slightly romantic person. ...she continued to live in the Bungalow in close quarters with Hilde. They each had her own room – but they often congregated in Hilde's room and I experienced them together there when they would give me dictation."[74] Household Girl Renate Dorpalen understood the tragic nature of the break in friendship, now seeing Dr. Wolff "awkward and distant" in the presence of children. The betrayal by Dr. Lion crushed Emmy's spirit. Renate "sensed quickly the misfortune of her [Emmy's] fate, which dislodged her from former heights of professional standing. ...I was often afraid of her suppressed anger and moodiness..."

When Emmy retired in 1960, the acrimony had softened. It is especially poignant to remember that all three women in this triangle were vulnerable by virtue of their immigrant status. When things got bad, they had nowhere else to go, no other job to apply for, no familial

---

[74] Eveline Kanes Stoatley Rough Newsletter Issue 18 September, 1998

support system from which to draw comfort. They were essentially alone, bereft of their former careers, financial security and friends. Their plight is something to be mourned on all sides.

Dr. Leven's influence on Dr. Lion is a matter for speculation. The Headmistress encountered enormous stresses in the dark days of wartime England and there is anecdotal evidence that she became less accessible, perhaps more insensitive after Dr. Leven arrived. Edith Hubacher [Hubacher-Cristoffel] tells how Dr. Lion and Dr. Leven took turns badgering her for money. Her father worked in Thailand and was unable to send her tuition until after the war. The harassment of the two women drove Edith to leave the school at 17. Desperately lonely, Edith returned to spend weekends with Nore and Hanna, sleeping on the floor in their small quarters. It was preferable to being the constant target of the older women.

By the end of the war, the rift was an accepted fact of life among those students who were old enough to notice. Decades later, former student Gerda Haas raised the question of Dr. Leven's negative influence on Dr. Lion in a piece written by Dr. Lion that she was translating for the Stoatley Rough Newsletter, Issue 12, 1996. In her only comment on the text, she pointed to Dr. Lion's use of what appears a pejorative term to describe the recently deceased Dr. Wolff. Ms. Haas wrote that she found the term, 'firebrand' to be "quite upsetting." Ms. Haas wrote, "did Dr. Leven help to word that article? A suspicion aggravating my upset!" [75] The jury will forever be out on the question of Dr. Leven's influence on Dr. Lion.

When the war ended and Nore and Hanna decided to return to Germany, they were sent packing without a farewell party or public words of gratitude from the headmistress. The Matron who had worked tirelessly to manage the day-to-day functions of the school and whose spirit had healed countless lost children for ten years had no bitterness. Nore wrote, "We had told Dr. Lion a long time ago that we were prepared to go back as soon as ever possible, to this bombed

---

[75] Angela Galligan [Roberts] STR Newsletter # 12 p. 9 "Not So Prussian As All That!"

and destroyed and hungry country which was our country. But things turned out quite different. As you know, one of those other German schools closed down [she refers to Bunce Court] and there were a few people who were ready to come to Stoatley Rough. And so they gave us the 'sack' without much ...talk about it. They said, 'Well, there are some people who can take your place, so we think you should make arrangements to leave.'"[76] Herta said, "Hilde Lion treated Nore Astfalck and Hannah Nacken incredibly shabbily after the war..." One gets the sense that Nore was meant to feel like a traitor for wanting to return to Germany. It is hard to imagine how Hilde Lion could have behaved so badly before the arrival of Luise Leven. Without Nore's tireless work, loving attention to detail, and leadership, the school literally could never have functioned and Dr. Lion knew this. Margaret Dove wrote about Nore and Hanna, "the two of them really gave the school its unique quality and I cannot imagine what it was like without them when they returned to Germany after the war. I often wonder if Dr. Lion realized how much she owed the two of them. She herself was not practical person and did not always understand the everyday problems that the rest of the German staff had to cope with."

Dr. Leven neglected to mention Nore and Hanna by name in her unpublished "history," of Stoatley Rough, recounting the school's story as if the two women had never existed. Dr. Leven wrote, "A crisis developed immediately after the end of the war. The staff, especially the domestic ones who had been glad to live in a safe place during the bombing of the large [undecipherable] started to move. Some returned to Germany..."[77] Although certainly some omissions in her history can be chalked up to a poor memory or lack of interest, Dr. Leven must be called to task for failing to give Nore her due. The only reference Dr. Leven made to the uproar that began with her arrival at the school in 1939 was a passing reference to the relationship between the Jews and the Christians. "There was never the slightest friction...though

---

[76] Ibid."

[77] Dr. Luise Leven's unpublished notes on the history of Stoatley Rough, LSE, STR Box M3253

there were many frictions of a different kind especially among the grown-ups."[78]

Dr. Leven stayed on in her rental quarters until the deaths of Mr. and Mrs. Phillips and departure of Mr. Phillips' successor, Miss Woolger. Then she took possession of The Lodge. Dr. Wolff retired in 1956, ceding to Dr. Leven at long last, the official mantle of "Second-in-Command."

What was it that had attracted Hilde Lion to the dynamic Dr. Leven? Perhaps it was her self-confidence, coupled with a kind of glamour that the short, shy headmistress was missing. Perhaps Dr. Lion needed someone strong to help her make decisions. Four years into life at Stoatley Rough, bereft of family and friends, her school bursting at the seams, war about to break out, Dr. Leven offered strength at just the time she needed it.

Dr. Lion must not be judged by her personal relationships alone. Having absorbed plenty of educational theory in her professional life in Germany, Dr. Lion built her school around the needs of the child, at the time a novel idea, and that ideal never faded. There is no doubt she liked children. She instituted communal work by staff and children, equality of the sexes, and an ethic of self-reliance. That Dr. Lion was impractical, unorthodox, quixotic and sometimes dictatorial was beside

---

[78] Wolf Edelstein [Elston] explains: "*Der Stuermer* was a viciously anti-Semitic paper published by Julius Streicher, the corrupt and sadistic *Gauleiter* (Nazi Party Governor) of Nurernberg. He was so notorious that even a lot of Nazis were disgusted by him but he retained Hitler's confidence in return for total loyalty. He had been at Hitler's side during the failed 1923 uprising in Munich. Streicher was one of the defendants at the original 1946 Nuremberg Trial, convicted and hanged. *Der Stuermer was* displayed all over Berlin (and other towns, I imagine) in framed public bulletin boards called *Stuermerkasten* (Kasten=box) (not many solid citizens would have wanted to be seen buying a copy at a news stand). As it combined anti-Semitism with pornography, it was very popular with *Gymnasium* (secondary schools for boys) students; the kind who waylaid me on my way home from the *Goldschmidt-Schule*. For this reason, I had to avoid one corner of a city square, the Elsterplatz. The *Stuermerkasten* at that corner faced a Jewish *Altersheim* (Old Age Home). Today the building has a plaque in memory of its staff and residents, who were deported and murdered in 1942."

the point. Her secretary, Herta Lewent Loeser, said Dr. Lion "didn't even know if the children wore stockings or underpants." Yet Dr. Lion steered her school through twenty-six years of extraordinary political turmoil and social change.

Renate Dorpalen [Dorpalen-Brocksieper] calls attention to the extraordinary contribution made by Drs. Lion and Wolff, and to the same degree, Eleonore Astfalck and JoHanna Nacken, hired with "great wisdom and foresight," that their work is relevant to today's complex problems in the area of social services. "This was the generation of the feminist and suffrage movements who worked for social reform and human rights."[79] She points out that their philosophies were very much in line with those developed by the earlier feminists, Alice Salomon, founder and director of the first school for social work in Germany in 1908, Hildegard von Gierke, director of the *Jugendheim*, and Hedwig Heyl, its founder, all friends of Renate's mother. She points to the great tragedy of Dr. Lion and the others who were dislodged suddenly from their prominent academic and writing careers, never to regain such status in their adopted occupations, in which they felt ill at ease and poorly prepared for. Yet they created in Stoatley Rough a living example of the great feminist principles forged by a generation earlier by forever maintaining the founding principles, in spite of personal strife.

All three holders of PhDs - Lion, Wolff and Leven - brought high standards of literary and artistic excellence to the school. The two who supplied the emotional support to the children, Nore Astfalck and Hanna Nacken, gave the school its stability and sheltering atmosphere. The distinguished British poet, Gerda Stein [Mayer], wrote a poem about the learned women (whom some wag post-war dubbed as the "three Prussians.") The poem reveals as much about Gerda's happiness while she was at Stoatley Rough as about the personalities of Dr. Lion, Dr. Wolff and Dr. Leven. Ms. Mayer wrote the poem thirty years after she left the school.[80]

---

[79] The ancient city of Halle, near Leipzig, is the home of the distinguished Protestant College for Church Music, still a respected institution.

[80] Dr. Luise Leven's unpublished notes on the history of Stoatley Rough, LSE, STR Box M3253

A Lion, a Wolf and a Fox
Gerda Stein [Mayer], Haslemere, 1942-1944

I went to school in a forest where I was taught
By a lion, a wolf and a fox.
How the lion shone! As he paced across the sky
We grew brown-limbed in his warmth and among the green leaves.

The fox was a musician. O cunning magician you lured
A small stream from its course with your *Forellenlied*,
Teaching it Schubert; and made the children's voices
All sound like early morning and auguries for a fine day.

Now the wolf was a poet and somewhat grey and reserved,
Something of a lone wolf – thoughts were his pack;
There was a garden in that forest, walled with climbing roses,
Where we would sit or lie and hear the wolf recite.

And sometimes we would listen, and sometimes the voice
Would turn into sunlight on the wall or into a butterfly
Over the grass. It was the garden of poetry and so
Words would turn into flowers and trees into verse.

This morning I received the grey pelt of a wolf,
And the fox and the lion write they are growing old;
That forest lies many years back, but we were in luck
To pass for a spell through that sunny and musical land.

PART 3

THE CHILD WORKERS

The girl with a slender, athletic body, piquant face, and mounds of thick curly hair sat quietly, respectfully. Dr. Wolff saw at once in this applicant a lively, strong girl, one unafraid of work. That she was also intellectually curious and smart also became apparent to the second-in-command.

"Herta, what are your favorite things to do when you aren't studying?"

Herta sat up straight. "I used to play tennis and only three years ago I was mad because they stopped letting us non-Aryans play sports. Before then I rowed and played *schlagball*."

"Is that a team sport?"

"Yes, it's really fun."

Dr. Wolff picked up a few documents, frowning as she read to herself. It was the summer of 1936 – the Nazis in their third year in power - and already they had denied this girl German sports programs and had forced her out of her school. She flushed with sudden anger. These outrageous laws the National Socialist government kept passing. Would no one stop them? How could this country of Goethe and Schiller - of Beethoven, Haydn and Wagner - sink to such madness? No one was safe any more. Dr. Wolff reminded herself to step up her efforts to get her mother, now staying with friends in Belgium, into England as quickly as humanly possible. Dr. Wolff looked up and spoke in English, her low, well-modulated voice kindly. "I see that you have a fluency in English and also that you know English shorthand. Those are remarkable skills in one so young – you are only sixteen, is that right?"

"Yes, ma'am, I like to keep busy and when they kicked me out school, I wanted to keep on learning. I also studied home economics but I am more interested in secretarial work than household management. And I'd like to visit England. It would be fun." Dr. Wolff knew this was the girl she would hire – there was a sweetness and honesty, a directness that Dr. Wolff knew Hilde would admire. Dr. Wolff rose to her feet and switching back to German, asked Herta to bring her father into the room so that the three could discuss the conditions of the job.

Mr. Lewent listened attentively. There would be no salary, of course - British laws were strict about paying aliens. Only those who worked a farm or became a domestic worker such as maid, butler or housekeeper could receive wages in Great Britain during the Depression. Dr. Wolff hastened to add the good news. Herta would receive free room and board for the simple tasks of handling Dr. Lion's correspondence and filing and answering the telephone. Mr. Lewent sat back in his chair. He did not want his little girl to be overworked. Dr. Wolff assured him that Herta would get time off and she should fit in nicely with the other children her age at the school. Mr. Lewent, an engineer at AGFA said he and his wife, an economist, were trying to relocate in England as well. Their son, Helmut, planned to apply for Stoatley Rough's Farm Program. The two adults and Herta concluded their meeting with handshakes all around.

At the door, Herta turned back, her curls incongruent with the look of grave concern in her face. "Dr. Wolff, please, just one more question"

"Of course my dear."

"May I bring my canary with me?"

The adults laughed heartily.

Herta packed a large steamer trunk for her journey, bade farewell to her mother and brother, and kissed her canary goodbye. She and her father set off for England. It was on March 6, 1937. They arrived on the 7th and took a cab up to the school on Farnham Lane. The car pulled into the courtyard and Herta hopped out of the car and ran over to look at the view. She saw the second tennis court just below the main house. Two people were engaged in a fast volley. She couldn't tell for sure but they seemed to be a teacher and a teen-age boy. "A grass tennis court!…I made a vow to myself that before the day was over I didn't care what else I did, but I wanted to play tennis with that boy. And I did." The boy was Hans Loeser, destined to be her future husband.

The Young Secretary

D r. Wolff had been in Berlin a year earlier, the summer of 1936 just before Dr. Lion was to join her on the Continent for a six-week marathon of recruiting and interviewing prospective pupils. She was greatly disturbed by the ugly prejudice now openly expressed in Berlin. In her talks with the parents of prospective pupils, she learned of the damage the Nuremberg Laws were inflicting on the Jews in every day ways – park benches restricted to "Aryans," public places such as swimming pools and theaters closed to Jews, Jews being depicted with leering, evil faces in the pornographic and virulently anti-Semitic tabloid *Der Stuermer* [The Stormer] whose ugly political cartoons drew curious crowds along the urban streets.

In England, Herta, a trusting and fearless girl, was ready for adventure. She would not know that her story would be unique, not just because she was the first secretary of Stoatley Rough School, but because her tenure of four years spanned both the pre-war period and the early wartime years at the school. She arrived when the founders had little trouble maintaining the original child-centered concept of education, when the children had plenty of wholesome food and access to diversions across the English countryside, when Stoatley Rough still retained its halcyon quality. Once the war began, she witnessed the hardships that the war would bring to England and how Stoatley Rough coped. Without family and childhood homes to comfort them, the children at Stoatley Rough (like millions of British citizens), faced physical deprivations and restrictions that forced the school community into uncharted territory.

Herta was born in 1921. She grew up with her parents and younger brother in an apartment in Berlin, happy to watch the streetcars and the occasional horse-drawn carriage from the balcony. Her assimilated, non-religious family attended services only on high holidays, if at all. Herta had a pleasant childhood and was happy to spend summer vacations with her family in the mountains. Her father, an accomplished amateur photographer, would amble about taking pictures wearing his Loden coat, his baggy knickerbockers and special knee socks he wore only on holiday. Her mother was more conventional in her dress but Herta, too, liked to wear her short socks called *Wadenstrumpfe* which she had explained to Dr. Wolff, were socks that "just went up to your calf."

Herta had been slated to enter the rough equivalent of 11th grade in an American high school. The German educational system started children at six, offering four years of primary school. At ten, boys typically went on to the *Gymnasium* while girls entered the *Lyceum*. Everybody went through *Sexta, Quinta, Quarta,* [Sixth Fifth, and Fourth forms], then *Untertertia, Obertertia* and *Untersecunda.* [Under-Third, Over-Third, Under-Second, Over-Second, and so on, meaning first and second semesters of each year.] At sixteen, some children entered vocational training called *Berufschule*. (Informally, the training was called the"*Einjähriges*" [One year], a military term.) Boys destined for a university education (and in rare cases, girls), took a stringent exam commonly called the *"Abitur"*.

Herta needed a trade. Her family sent her to learn home economics at a Jewish school (near the future site of the Sachsenhausen-Oranienburg concentration camp built in 1938, thirty-five kilometers from Berlin, whose Commandant would be hanged for the shooting, hanging and marching hundreds to death by war's end.) Herta's father knew she would need something practical and transferable in the event they needed to leave the country – there were few jobs in Depression-era Germany, regardless of an applicant's ethnicity. Herta had studied English for six years at school, and while her aural comprehension was less than proficient, the plucky girl decided to take on English shorthand. She had no particular objective in mind. It was enough for Herta that it was challenging.

After her father left to return to Berlin, Herta moved into the room she would share with another girl her age, Baerbel Guerstenburg (Prasse). She unpacked her things and quickly made friends.

The boy on the tennis court was sixteen-year-old Hans Loeser, a tall, good-looking boy with a shock of thick dark hair and an unspoiled and generous personality. Although he knew why he had had to leave Germany, he had cried the night before his departure, afraid he'd never be able to make the quips and jokes in English for which he was famous among his friends. He was afraid he'd lose his very identity in the new country. His family had owned a big department store in Kassel, a bustling city in the center of Germany and once home to the brothers Jakob and Wilhelm Grimm. With a population of 180,000, Kassel had a thousand-year history. During WWII, the inner city of Kassel was reduced to rubble. Before 1933, Hans remembers standing at his bedroom's balcony watching the ubiquitous streetcars that clanged past the building with comfortable regularity. With the election of the National Socialist party, however, the scene now included gangs of warring political parties engaging in hand to hand combat in the street, "Nazis, Social Democrats, Communists, and right wing German nationalists led by Prussian Junker families and ex-officers."[1] His parents did not keep a kosher kitchen, and celebrated Easter and Christmas. It was a cultured family. His parents spoke French when they didn't want Hans and his big sister, Elisabeth (Fontana), to understand them. On the high holidays, his father dipped his silk top hat as the family strolled to the temple to take their inherited seats. Herr Loeser played the violin and sang, a true son of the Gilded Age, and made sure Hans received violin lessons in spite of Hans' self-acknowledged lack of musical talent. It did not matter - children of his class always played an instrument. Hans was thirteen in April of 1933 when the storm troopers arrived at his father's department store and started telling the shoppers to leave, calling the Loeser family, obscenely, *Scheissjude* or *Stinkjude*. [shit Jews,

---

[1] *Hans History* p.50

stinking Jews.] They used black, white and red paint to write '*Jude*' [Jew] on the plate glass.

One of the ironies of being a child in an oppressive state is the lure of the oppressor's culture. When his classmates became members of the youngest of the Hitler Youth groups, "*Jungvolk* [Young people], Hans and other Jewish boys wanted to join. The Hitler Youth wore black, very short corduroy shorts, and brown shirts with a black kerchief held in place by a Nazi swastika ring at the neck. The Jewish boys imitated the costume, wearing their own very short corduroy pants with knee socks. "My military belt had a more neutral buckle than the *Jungvolk's* swastika. But I have little doubt that, had we been allowed to join, we would have."[2] Hans recalls that at first, the anti-Semitism at school was "good-natured" but after 1933, when it became mandatory to greet teachers with a raised right arm and a "*Heil Hitler*," the six Jews in Hans' class of twenty-six children stood but were not allowed to salute. He recalled the small packs of Hitler Youth waiting to attack and beat up the unwary child who rode a bicycle. His teachers became scornful and insulting. Birthday parties came to an end and neighbors began to look away when they met the Loesers on the street. At his violin lessons, his teacher greeted him with "*Heil Hitler*" to make him feel uncomfortable. After the collapse of his business, Hans' father became depressed then rallied, as if exclusion from German activities heightened his sense of Jewish identity. The family began to observe the traditional Friday night ceremony of welcoming the Sabbath, lighting candles and saying *Kiddush* over bread and wine. They attended high quality lectures for Jews sponsored by the newly-formed civic organization, the *JüdischerKulturbund*, because they were now barred from attending the opera and other cultural events. Some of Hans' uncles began to quietly transfer assets abroad and to nurture foreign business connections. In 1935, Hans' parents sent Elisabeth to boarding school in Northern Italy, and Hans followed, in 1936, to a boarding school near Nyon on Lake Geneva. His father sold the business. Within days, the 75-year old business of Ferdinand Loeser and Company re-opened under an

---

[2]   Ibid. p. 53

Aryan name and customers flooded back. Five years later the store was bombed to the ground.

Like Martin and many others, Hans traveled by train, boat, and train to London and somehow, with only two years of English (and failing utterly to understand any English he heard in the Paddington station), managed to find the train to Haslemere, arriving at the school in April, 1937. He took his violin in its shockproof case and his luggage to the school. "Haslemere taxi drivers had learned by then that people with little or no English had to be taken to Stoatley Rough.[3] Miss Astfalck and others received him warmly at the school. He recalled, "God what a relief it was to be back in a comfortable German atmosphere."[4]

Herta and Hans made friends with other children their age, especially Klaus Zedner, a boy who had arrived in September of 1935 and Barbara Gerstenberg who had arrived in August of 1936. Roommates Hans and Klaus slept in The Tin, a room at the end of a long corridor behind the kitchen, a relatively isolated den with its own entrance from the outside. "One could slip in and out day and night unobserved and without having to account to anybody."[5] The boys explored the house together and then Hans noticed a most intriguing thing, the trap door in the ceiling of their very own room. They found a way to get up and through the trap door, landing in a hidden room under the eaves. The room, in turn, led to myriad crawl spaces connecting to other parts of the house. The excited boys soon pulled up mattresses, pillows and other items and proceeded to hold night parties in their ceiling lair they dubbed Klingsburg" [*Burg* for "castle," the meaning of *Klings* long forgotten.] There they would spend long hours discussing the mysteries of life with friends. It didn't take Miss Astfalck long to find out about the hideaway. "She raised some hell over the unauthorized disappearance of useful things, but she also expressed admiration for our inventiveness and decorating skills. When we offered a deal, namely that she would be invited to our next party,

---

[3] Ibid. p.72
[4] Ibid.
[5] Ibid. p. 74

she accepted -- and did come. The extra pleasure of secrecy was now gone, but a new, conspiratorial bond had been established with Miss Astfalck which felt very good."[6] Klaus and Hans must have discussed girls although Hans claims their talk was always respectful. But the fact was, Klaus Zedner and Baerbel Gerstenberg became a couple. They took walks together and when he gave her a wooden box he made in shop class, she vowed to keep it forever. But their love was not to be. Before long, Baerbel dropped Klaus for Hans. Their love was not to be either. In July of 1938, Baerbel left for the United States.[7] By now Herta had been at the school for over a year, rooming with Baerbel until she left. Summer of 1937 arrived. There was a whole world to be explored. Hans and Herta were ready for adventure.

Both teenagers developed a special bonding with Nore Astfalck who tolerated the penchant of some of the older residents for roaming the countryside far beyond the boundaries of the Stoatley Rough community. Miss Dove was a young English teacher who arrived in the fall of 1937. She wrote about the times: "The older pupils were given a great deal of freedom, or perhaps they just took it, I am not sure which. ...On Sundays sometimes the older ones were given permission to go hiking all day since walking in the country had been very popular in Germany during the Weimar Republic. In actual fact, the pupils often hitch-hiked all over the south of England, usually two by two, a boy and girl together – and no one came to any harm."[8] Ilse Feldstein [Bauer] actually hitch hiked to Edinborough with Katya Schaefer

6 Ibid. p. 77

7 Stoatley Rough was a powerful influence in her life, as it was for so many of its pupils. Not only did Baerbel save the little wooden box, but she carried the imprint of William Blake's majestic old standard, "Jerusalem," learned while at Stoatley Rough, deep within her soul. "There was a big event to which patrons and supporters of the school came and we had all learned to sing it. Several years ago, the movie *Chariots of Fire* used it in its closing scenes, with the schoolboys amassed in the chapel and the organ booming. It stirred some very deep memories as I viewed it in the theater. I could still remember all the words to it." Living in Connecticut, she remains friends with Hans and Herta, in Cambridge, Massachusetts, to this day.

8 Margaret Dove Faulkner, Reminiscences, February, 1991, Boston, MA

[Sheppard] to visit Lilly Henschel who was a medical student there. The authorities allowed the older children to travel to London on their own. On December 11, 1936, a few Roughians, one wearing her Girl Guide uniform, stood most of the night outside Buckingham Palace to be in a good spot when the parade swept by bearing the Cinderella carriage of the new king, George VI, the father of Elizabeth II, who would be crowned May 12, 1937.

Sometimes the children went on picnics to nearby Waggoners Wells and Gibbet Hill. Laurie Halls, an English child somehow deposited in the School, described how many Roughian children tramped together over the heath, carrying their picnic, and singing, '*Wir haben hunger, hunger, / hunger haben wir,* etc.' [We are hungry, hungry, / hungry are we]. (This impoverished eight-year-old Laurie was a British citizen, plucked from his home by one of the well-meaning Board members to live with the pupils at Stoatley Rough in order to help them learn English, an arrangement Laurie found perfectly satisfactory during the two years he was there.) The Roughians were well ahead of their time in matters of environmental protection. They meticulously removed all their trash after their picnics and carted it back home.

In the summers of 1937 and 1938, Herta and Hans hitchhiked around southern England, sometimes with others, sometimes just with each other. Matron Nore felt the experience was healthy. When she had been a teenager, Nore had been part of an informal movement in Germany known as *Wandervogel* (Ramblers), groups of young people who went for walks in the woods equipped with rucksacks, guitars and cooking pots. In those days before World War I, Nore's own Sunday outings caused tongues to wag since there were usually more boys than girls, but Nore's mother was progressive and dismissed the gossip. Nore credited *Wandervogel* for giving her independence, self-confidence and enthusiasm for life. The experience was more than just walking around with other children carrying a guitar: "We started...something quite new...it was not only an organization for young people who wanted to be out of the towns and to live in the woods and meadows. It was much more than that. It was a beginning; the aim was to start a new way of life in more freedom, not to follow the rules but to think of new rules, to create our own young life."[9] Herta and Hans benefited from Nore's liberal attitudes. They always reported their escapes after the fact, telling Miss Astfalck that they had gone "beyond Liphook" (a village near Haslemere) as code for going far afield. "And [Nore] would know very well that we had been to the beach or some other fun place." Herta loved Nore for her tolerance and trust in never knowing that the couple may have hitchhiked to Brighton Beach for a bracing swim in the ocean. As long as they were back in time for evening meal, the outings were tolerated. Nobody even thought of the possibility that killers might be out to kidnap innocent youngsters. It was the war, not fear of strangers, that would put an end to the fun. After September, 1939, Roughians were not allowed to venture near the coastal regions newly- designated as "protected areas." Such high-security places were forbidden to aliens.

Drs. Lion and Wolff were still housed in the main building, as were Herta, Nore, and Hanna. But at the end of 1936, good news arrived for the two senior women on the staff. The Board approved £550 to build a new building, to be called the Bungalow. It would have a bedroom each for Drs. Lion and Wolff, one bathroom and a room for sick children. Almost as an afterthought, it would also have a tiny office for Herta with a window that looked out toward the main house and Farnham Lane. Herta would spend a great deal of time in that room, would see to the school's official business there, and would witness the turbulent personal affairs that erupted when the new music teacher arrived in 1939.

[9]   Eleonore Astfalck, *Oral History of Nore Astfalck on her 90th Birthday*, p. 5-14.

Halcyon Days

In 1936, school offices were primitive compared to today's electronic operational centers. Herta had to type everything in duplicate using carbon paper, correcting her typos twice with a special eraser. Not even the machine that bridged the manual typewriter with the computer, IBM's Selectric, had been invented yet. Herta also sent out bills, sorted mail, filed correspondence and reports, answered the telephone and ran errands. She typed official notices - the school did not get a duplicating machine until 1941. (People in the United States over sixty will remember seeing the boxy contraption in the school office, the teacher cranking away as the big drum churned out stenciled announcements for the children to carry home the next day. Herta called the school's own duplicator a "Gestetner multiplying monster" that got ink all over her hands). Herta itemized her duties in an article she wrote for the school newspaper, *The Bridge*, in 1941:[10]

"Passports and Registration Certificates need constant watching as they might want renewal. Lectures and Visits must be arranged and sometimes people who have left long ago want a testimonial...The card-index has to be kept up-to-date. Books are to be written for from various libraries and the days of return must not be forgotten. Timetables and lists of any kind are just another "source" for work. And in between the telephone rings." Herta typed each pupil's report at the end of each term and issued circulars regarding holidays and travel. During the war she cut out and organized food and clothing coupons from over one

---

[10] All quotations in this section appeared as part of Herta's article, *A Glimpse in the Office*, The Bridge, Vol. 1, p. 10 May 14, 15, 1940.

hundred ration books; she saved stamps for the children's hospital and recycled paper for "wrapping up parcels."

Peak work periods, such as the end of a semester, kept Herta up all night with worry. "This sounds rather a scrappy account, but that is just what a day in the office is like. There are so many little things to be thought of and so many people to be hunted after, because I must ask them one or the other question. But it can be very exciting too, if important messages and news have to be given out in time." Looking back at all the work it seems that Herta ran the place single-handedly.

While grateful to be safe in England, Herta felt thwarted, frustrated not being able to further her education, especially since Hans, Baerbel and Klaus were allowed to waltz off to class every day. She grew to resent Dr. Lion's power over her future. "Instead of taking the school certificate [matric] which is what everybody took to enable you to go to the university, I had to take something that qualified you for English. I was really mad at them because I probably could have managed to attend school even if it had taken longer. .... Dr. Lion was narrow-minded in that she pigeonholed you. Once I went to take some sewing classes and she said 'No, that is not for you. Sometimes I just went to classes and the telephone would ring. ... And Dr. Lion would have to go chasing after me and I'd have to drop what I was doing. 'You can't take any classes. We've been looking all over for you.' So I was exploited a lot. I had no money. They weren't really allowed to pay. All I got was a tiny, tiny pocket money." The immigrant adults eventually received some form of salary. Herta never did.

Like the older Household Girls, Herta dwelled in an interim place at the school between pupil and staff, preferring to socialize with girls and boys her own age, yet technically a member of the staff. When she entered the teacher's lounge for a morning break, only Nore and Miss Dove welcomed her. "We didn't have any money to pay so I couldn't go to school. I was as mad as a hatter. I wasn't right away mad, I was glad to be out, but I had to work for the headmistress."

Herta had a tough time with some of her work. "I was told on the first day to keep all information confidential. And I certainly kept to it. I had access to the confidential files on all the kids, and I really wasn't any older than most of them. So that was a huge burden, because whenever anybody asked me anything I always had to say, "I don't know," so everybody had to think I was an idiot. But it taught me a lot about confidentiality." Her office was a small space partitioned into the Bungalow. "My office was cold, tiny and had a window looking out on the path to the main building. I could see who arrived and when, and who left. When it was cold I could use a little electric fire which roasted me in the back and left my fingers frozen and full of chilblains."[11]

Herta and Hans and others in the mid teens felt confident they could wander around at night after "lights out," in what came to be known as going on "Night Walks." Everybody sneaked out. They climbed out of windows, tiptoed down hallways past snores coming from behind closed doors, and ran across Farnham Lane to the Heath. The key was not to get caught. Children speaking German-accented English were not favored in an England mistrustful of anything German. The situation worsened when curfew was law. Dr. Lion was intensely opposed to night walking not only because she feared unwanted pregnancies, but she wanted to protect the reputation of her school with the locals. She feared backlash, and rightly so, for any sign of disrespect for English law. But only once did she deliver the ultimate punishment – expulsion – and it was for someone who had been caught. Her usual reaction was to give the child (or children) a good talking to, and if the truant was female, to assign her to sleeping quarters well-guarded against future escape.

Many anecdotes concern the subject of night walking. In 1941 Dieter Gaupp went out walking with his friends to enjoy the fresh air on the heath, look at the stars, and watch the wartime searchlights in the distance over London as they painted their pale swaths of light across the black skies. A few of the boys lit up cigarettes, officially banned to children. On their return, they suddenly ran into Dr. Lion and another teacher. "One of the guys jerked the cigarette from his mouth, sank it into his jacket pocket, and gave it a quick pat." After a brief greeting,

---

[11] Chilblains is a condition that causes hands and feet to swell painfully, itch, and produce purple or green sores. Some treated chilblains with applications of iodine.

Dr. Lion said, "Carry on smoking." Out came the cigarettes, passed all around, and Dr. Lion took one offered by one of the boys. (Dr. Lion, a notorious chain smoker, was known to cadge a cigarette shamelessly from anyone who offered it, even taking a second one for later.) They all had a little chat as they smoked. Then everyone went off to bed.

Herta returned to her full time duties when classes resumed in the fall of 1937 and Hans went back to his studies. Some of the older students left the school for weaving school, engineering evening school, and apprenticeships in a carpenter's workshop. Two girls left for India and Palestine. Miss Margaret Dove settled in, and a Mr. Basil Grimshaw and Miss Hetherington joined the teaching staff. There were many excellent teachers at Stoatley Rough throughout the years, but a few, like Miss Dove, would occupy a special place in the hearts of its pupils. Although her tenure lasted only two years at Stoatley Rough, Miss Dove, a tall slim lady, "of upright carriage," was always polite, spoke in a soft voice, doled out kindness to all, and treated the children with sensitivity.

Herta passed her government English proficiency exam in 1938. By then, Hans had finished school and passed his university qualifying exams, the Matric. He went off to work for Gimbel's Department Store in London, hitchhiking back and forth to the school on weekends. When London became unsafe during the Blitz, Dr. Lion, who was fond of Hans, took him back and gave him a job as resident handyman. Herta likes to say that Hans worked for her personally as her office boy. "We had a bell system that went from the main house to Dr. Lion's bungalow. Hans had to fix the bell and I remember him, we had an attic above my little office, and he was sitting up there fixing the bell and taking an awful long time. He and I became very friendly in the course of his working for me, and he also became the school's driver, so that he was always allowed to take the car."

To her credit, Herta made the most of life in the sun of her adolescence – she knew how to have fun and to take life head on. In 1937, she and Hans fell in love. She is frank about their relationship. "I lived in a room called The Woods, above the kitchen. Just outside it had a very nice lightening rod. Hans would come in through the window. The Headmistress had an absolute thing about boys and girls. In retrospect it is totally un-understandable to us why somebody didn't get pregnant. I mean, she had such a phobia about it all. Usually when you are so worried, it happens. She never quite knew what went on."[12] Only one other couple married who first met at the school: Lilly Wohlgemuth and Peter Gluecksmann. Like that of Hans and Herta, theirs was a lifelong union.

Herta and Hans understood that when a child was admitted to the school, he or she was escaping the Nazis. They did not know about death camps yet but they knew, through Herta's access to Dr. Lion's correspondence, that the situation on the Continent was deadly for Jews. Hans and Herta began actively to help children escape from Germany. Rescuing children was grown-up work and they were aware they were doing something important. "By then it was becoming quite clear that things were getting worse and worse in Germany, and we took any kids that we could get into England and out of Germany and Austria. By that time there were some committees in London that paid the school fees if the parents could not. We had very good connections to them, and the headmistress, I told you, wasn't a very practical lady. So Hans and I figured out a way to get more children out. We were only seventeen and seventeen-and-a-half ourselves, but we made friends by mail with a British Consul in Berlin, and we worked out a system with him. If we could get any semblance of an affidavit from an English person who would say they would pay for a child….we would send the guarantee to this British consul, and he would immediately give the visa to get into England. …That way we must have gotten out something like twenty to thirty kids who wouldn't have gotten out otherwise. Our Headmistress was not very gifted for this kind of thing. We got it by writing. The Headmistress probably helped with that, and we had daily contact with the refugee committees and got guarantees from them. But we were very imaginative about it all, and it was very exciting because we knew every time we got one of those letters off, we had another child out of danger."[13] Herta approached this work with an adolescent's *joie de*

---

[12] Herta Lewent, Oral History 2.10

[13] Ibid.

vivre. "There was a mailbox, halfway down Farnham Lane, and if we couldn't catch the mail going out that night then a whole day would be missed. So we got permission to use the school car so we could mail our letters at the post office in Haslemere. We almost always managed to miss the mail pickup on Farnham Lane, as you can imagine, and we had a very good time going down to the little town. It was very exhilarating. ...This was the one time that Hans ever had an accident, not a very serious one, because he was driving with his arm around me....We had to go home like two sheep and confess."[14]

Hans and Herta sat down to the Christmas/Chanukah party in December, 1939. It was a special breakfast with apples and lighted candles in front of every place setting, and each child feasted on hot chocolate and spice cake. In the middle of the table stood a pyramid of fretwork animals someone had made in the woodworking shop. It had become a tradition to have such a party and even in the worst days of the war, the school celebrated the two holidays jointly. Later that evening, Hans had news for Herta. He had learned his visa had come through and he would go to America with his family. In the two and a half years they had been together at the school, Hans and Herta developed a bond that became more than a passing infatuation. Hans at nineteen, Herta a half-ear younger, were almost grown up. Like millions of others at that point in history, they were captive to the larger events swirling around them. Like the lovers who would become famous in *Casablanca* a few years hence, personal plans were not "worth a hill of beans" to these two Stoatley Rough teenagers. Neither questioned the fact that they would be separated, although they had told their respective parents they wanted to get married (to which came the scoffing reply: it's just puppy love). Just before Hans was scheduled to sail, Herta landed in the hospital for a tonsillectomy. "Hans came to visit me and I think he brought me a present. He was always a little embarrassed when he gave you a present, so he tossed me something, and it was a very nice fountain pen." And then he left. Separated by a continent and a war, they had no idea if they would ever meet again.

---

[14] Ibid.

Workers and Scholars

One of Herta's best friends at school was Inge Hamburger [Pavlowsky], a talented artist who arrived as a Household Girl in February, 1938, at age seventeen. Nore tried to fit the duties to each Household Girl's abilities and inclinations and along with regular cleaning duties, Inge's lot was to weave cloth and help Mr. Obee, the school's handyman, with his repair jobs. Later, Nore promoted Inge to be Hanna's assistant in the shop, where she taught younger children crafts and woodworking on her own, working as a regular teacher. She found time to paint a decorative border around the shop ceiling. Like Herta, Inge and the other Household Girls had no real choices as to their duties, schedules or level of exertion required to perform their duties. No one escaped the hardest chores and some of the work was difficult, as Ilse Kaiser [Neivert] indicated, especially "polishing floors with heavy polishing brushes, which one was pushing back and forth between stretched out legs."

Once a month the Household Girls led the general cleanup morning. Children might help Mr. Phillips in the gardens or work under the direction of Miss Astfalck in the main house. Dr. Lion wrote, "The whole school, including the teachers, have to do something practical; the little ones brush mats and clean the silver, the older ones look to the electric lamps."[15] Standards were high. Maria Goldwater [Danziger] recalled that after leaving furniture polish on the wood around the knocker she was cleaning one Saturday, Dr. Lion chastised her. "Na ja my dear, not even the poorest housemaid would do that!" Yet it was the

---

[15] Hilde Lion, "Dr. Lion's Lecture", *Stoatley Rough Newsletter* #3, p. 7.

Household Girls who did heavy cleaning every Saturday, rain or shine. Young Renate Dorpalen [Dorpalen-Brocksieper], described with great cheer, a typical Saturday morning.[16]

> "Saturday morning! 'Don't come through here! The other way round, please.' Through the whole house you can hear this shouting of people who do not want to be disturbed while they clean the house. ....One only can hear the running of water, the rushing through the house of household people, the rattling and clashing of pails. Beginning on the Third Floor and ending in the nursery they sweep and scrub, they dust and polish bathrooms, floors and lavatories. Nevertheless you must sing and think of something nice – what it would be like to sit in the sun and to read a book. Don't dream too much otherwise you may be blamed for forgetting something! Work begins. The first thing is to get enough pails to scrub with, otherwise you must start with a fight! Secondly if you need your neighbour's polishing brush, you go to her, ask for the brush, and say how nicely the floor is done, and that it looks awfully good and so on and then you have a chance of getting the brush. That is the way we fight over our work! In the cellars there are several larders, like dairy. There is one for food, of course, and one for soap and wax and Pulvo [a laundry power]. Nothing else is allowed in these cellars except one big trunk, which cannot go anywhere else. In this so-called 'soap-cellar', you can find everything you need and on Saturdays it is a very useful place. Now the trouble is that you cannot go into the house when they are cleaning and you are not

---

[16] *The Bridge,* entitled, "Work of the Domestic Science Group." Vol. 1, No. 1, May, 1940. Renate omits the fact that once a month general cleaning was undertaken by the whole school.

allowed even to walk through without a big struggle with the household people. They clean the entrance, they close the door, and in the school room there are lessons, sometimes you can rush through the kitchen without further ado. At least at one o'clock we have finished cleaning, the house looks tidy and nice for Sunday, you can almost skate in the sitting room, the floor is so shiny. Hardly anyone can believe that the cleaning is done only by the household girls."

Like Herta, the Household Girls were not quite staff, not quite pupil. Their average age was fifteen. While they all did cleaning chores, they had specialties such as caring for the youngest children or taking over the kitchen every Tuesday, Cook's day off. One of the more arduous tasks, reserved to older girls and performed rain or shine, every week in the year, was laundry. They washed clothing, sheets and towels for the entire Stoatley Rough population (which grew to over 100 in 1940). Washing clothes was primitive by our standards. There were no synthetic, drip dry, stretch or wrinkle-free fabrics. The girls washed woolens, linens and silks in cold water and they washed cottons in boiling water laced with lye. There was no Woolite®, fabric softener or packaged stain remover to help the homemaker; there were no colorfast dyes, pre-shrunk cottons, or fleece. And of course, Stoatley Rough had no electric washing machines or dryers.

While it is natural to imagine their work as drudgery, once again, the girls with laundry duty seem to have enjoyed the camaraderie and the sense of accomplishment the hard work yielded. They felt privileged to share breakfast tea and bread with Mr. Phillips, Miss Astfalck and other early risers, happy to sit in the cozy kitchen with others who worked while the rest of the household slept.

The process was well-understood. The girls sorted on Mondays then washed the actual laundry on Tuesdays. Halfway through breakfast, one girl would leave the group and let herself into the laundry area near the kitchen door. Her task was to light the fire under the tubs, an unpleasant task during the cold, dark winter months. When the others arrived, they began to separate the woolens and silks from the cottons; then the large items from the small. Socks went into a special lidded tub with a handle that rotated four wooden blades in the water. After stirring the socks around for awhile in the hot water, the girls had to fish them out, turn them inside out, then return them to the soapy water for further agitation. Then they transferred the socks to a clear-water tub to be rinsed. The sheets (having been soaking overnight in cold water and soda) were wrung out between the rollers of the hand-cranked mangle then put into water that had been brought to a boil in enormous tubs over a wood fire. The girls had to use wooden sticks to extract the sheets from the burning hot water before plunging them into tubs filled with cold running water, stirring them around, then passing them through the mangle. They hung everything on clotheslines to dry, after passing selected items through another tub of starched-infused water. Some winter days the clothing froze to the lines. Every other week the girls alternated between washing whites (mostly sheets and towels); and colored items. Lacking rubber gloves, their hands would be red by the end of the washing cycle and they would laugh as they applied lotion in the evening. They managed what grew to be an enormous volume of bedding by an ingenious method: children transferred their top sheets to the bottom of their beds once a week and received a clean sheet for the top. (Fitted sheets had not been invented yet.)

It took almost a week to do a complete cycle of laundry. After the clothing and sheets were dry, everything had to be ironed. The girls placed heavy padding across a large table and worked with hot irons as other irons heated up on the coal-burning stove. They used sprinkling bottles of water to wet down the fabric. When her iron cooled, a girl would simply place it back on top of the stove and pick up another one, using a pot holder since the handles were as hot as the irons themselves. When an inspector once asked why Stoatley Rough didn't use ironing boards (they did not have any) Edith Hubacher [Christoffel] piped up. "It would be easier using ironing boards, but we don't have enough room." Nore whispered, to her immense gratification, "Good answer."

After ironing, the girls folded each piece to specification. Familiar with the clothing of everyone, Nore would help the girls place items labeled with the students' names in the correct cubby holes.

The program that had begun as technical training, an experiment, inevitably led to a class system at the school. (The other large German-English school, Anna Essinger's Bunce Court in Kent, never asked its scholarship students to assume this type of work, or tried to solve its domestic labor problem so "creatively.") The Household Girls were not always invited to events open to other children such as special outings or evening lectures, and along with the Farm Boys, were at the bottom of the implicit social hierarchy. Renate Dorpalen said "the designation carried a rather negative connotation among the student body and teachers, and it did little to strengthen my already fragile self-image. ..." Helmet Lewent (Herta's brother), a Farm boy in 1938 / 39, wrote (without rancor): "There was always some rivalry between the farming department and the rest of the school. We farm lads were somewhat looked down upon, nevertheless we were still good enough to have English lessons by that indomitable Miss Dove and to enjoy Sunday breakfasts with real cornflakes and boiled eggs in the school dining room." (Farm boys only studied one single academic subject: English.) This sense of difference must have been particularly galling to the children, most of whom had come from upper middle-class families. Renate Dorpalen wrote of class sensitivities in her own Jewish family when she described playing a role in *Der Biberpelz* [The Beaver Fur Coat]. 'For once I had sanction to use Berlin slang, which fitted the character. In my family the use of slang had not been allowed, especially if it had any resemblance to Yiddish, which in the Berlin dialect was not uncommon."

The Domestic Sciences program begs the question as to how much work each day would have been fair. How hard were the girls working? Did they have choices as to what work they did? Did each work the same number of hours? Did older girls work more hours than younger ones? What were the labor laws of the time and who was monitoring the school? Over its ten years of operation, approximately forty European girls participated in the Domestic Sciences program at Stoatley Rough, their ages ranging from thirteen to nineteen. The school maintained a ratio of one girl to every six students; as more students arrived, there were always proportionately more Household Girls. Yet who was looking out for the girls' interests? Child labor laws in England at the time (holdovers from the Industrial Revolution) dealt only with the knitting mills, where children were limited to twelve hours, and to no night work.

The well-meaning Committee always put a positive spin on the Domestic Sciences program, reporting the work of the girls in terms of a learning experience rather than as a contribution to the school. Referring to the experiment (never-repeated) of bringing convalescent children to the school from London in the summer of 1934, the Committee wrote that the incident provided "excellent practical experience in the care of the children for some of the older girls." When two girls were sent to do housework for English families one Christmas holiday (receiving room and board and relieving the school's responsibility for their care), the Committee reported that the girls "were improving their English and [gaining] experience managing an English household."

Sometimes the Household Girls and Herta performed as real servants. For example, the school's secretary who, like the Household Girls, received no pay for five years of on-demand service, had the duty of awakening Dr. Lion each morning by drawing the curtain in her bedroom. Girls cleaned not only the rooms in the Headmistress' Bungalow, but traveled to Hindhead to clean the house of Dr. Wolff's mother. The Household Girls were called upon to serve meals to important visitors, at which times they wore a servant's apron. A little note was posted in the kitchen dated the spring of 1940, admonishing, "These aprons are only to be worn on special occasions. They belong to the school and when you leave you are requested to give them back." Sometimes the girls were sent to work for important benefactors. Ruth Bayer [Tuckman] even became cook for a week. "On my arrival at Miss Fearon's house, she told me that her maid and gardener were also away on holiday and that a girl and boy from the local Bernardo home (a Mission

House for homeless urchins) were taking their places. She explained that as cook, I was in a status above the maid and the gardener. I was to sit at the top of the table at meal times and socialize with them as little as possible, an attitude that I not only found extremely strange, but utterly alien to the way I had been brought up. Although I obediently sat at the top of the table, I found both of them good company." She finishes her story with "Most importantly, by the end of the week I was paid...and for now I could buy the soap and toothpaste for my sister and me. ..The less said about my cooking, the better."[17]

It speaks to the quality of the leadership of Nore Astfalck and Hanna Nacken that any resentment on the part of the girls was tempered by a spirit of optimism and pride in work. Former Household Girls have claimed general satisfaction and immense gratitude for the program, and unlike Herta, have not written they felt exploited, probably because they were under Nore's tutelage (whereas Herta was virtually on her own and reported to the emotionally distant Dr. Lion). There is no question that the motives of the school's Committee and administration were honorable, even heroic. They admitted Jewish girls and boys who otherwise may not have been able to leave the Continent. The program saved lives. Yet the school benefited greatly in receiving inexpensive services that otherwise would have had to have been done by salaried adults.

The School blurred the lines between expediency and socially acceptable pedagogy. We turn to the girls themselves for the last word on the program. As adults, some former Household Girls uniformly recognize a modicum of unfairness in their fate yet they recall having felt satisfaction and pride in their work. The young and idealistic Margot Silverbach [Kogut]] expressed a youthful joy at being given responsibility and receiving praise for a job well done, of belonging to a social structure in which their place was honored. "I must see that everything is O.K. This includes such things as seeing where a table

---

[17] Ruth Bayer [Tuckman], Memories, *Stoatley Rough Newsletter* 7, February 1995, p. 12

cover needs cleaning and replacing. ..."[18] Margot also saw herself as liberated. "So I am now a real 'housewife." She was proud of learning handicraft "so that I can do running repairs. I also enjoy the lessons in nutrition...that have to do with chemistry and biology." Referring to two new girls, she said, "The expressions on their faces seem to say, 'well, a modern girl has to know how to do this but later, in real life, it's going to be done by servants;' but one has to be a modern educated girl, knowledgeable in household tasks..." Her words reveal the radiant influence of Nore. "Yesterday I managed to do the whole house with only minimal help, in three hours. And so well that I got praised."

Like the administrators themselves, the Household Girls had grown up with nannies and cooks and cleaning women, never having to do the duties they were now asked to perform. Yet they didn't complain. Ilse Kaiser wrote with pride and humor about her work: "I got to get up early on Tuesdays to help with the laundry. Mr. Phillips' cups of early morning tea were wonderful. Someone always had to run down to the farm when the water tank ran over. I got my turn at cleaning Dr. Lion's bungalow once a week. It was too bad that she did not appreciate my changing the position of her little wooden figure she used for sketching. In fact, I got into some sort of trouble with Dr. Lion. I cut Lilly Wohlgemuth's long beautiful hair, much to Dr. Lion's disapproval. Most of all, I did not manage to catch the mouse that had decided to run around the bungalow and the mouse turned up in her bed."[19] Renate Dorpalen wrote to her mother cheerfully about "...dishes, knives, forks, spoons, pots and pans. I do the washing and three or four other students do the drying. A person has to be quick and well-organized to keep everyone busy, and to get the job done as pleasantly and as fast as possible. Sometimes the work is accompanied by singing or good conversation." Inge Hamburger [Pavlowsky] said, "I came to Stoatley Rough as a "Household Girl" which in my mind is

---

[18] Margot Kogut, "Letters Home," (from a letter she wrote home on April 1, 1935), *Stoatley Rough Newsletter* 3, October. 1993, p. 29.

[19] Ilse Kaiser [Neivert], "Reminiscences of Stoatley Rough," *Stoatley Rough Newsletter* 21, October, 2002, p. 43.

really a name of a low level, and in any case is much more interesting and valuable than it sounds... What we learned was rather up to each person. But the possibility of feeling responsible for the work we did in order to make the school a new home for all the children - a place which was beautiful and agreeable, where the food was good, and where everybody had a task to play - was our mission."[20] Miss Astfalck's spirit lives in Inge's words. Today, former Household Girls who have stayed in touch reflect with pride on their role, noting with satisfaction that the academic-tracked students also had to work. "Peeling potatoes, doing the washing-up, sweeping the floor, laying the table, etc. was the work of all of us, students included, and [duties] changed once a week...So it was not only the work of the Household Girls, as though they were the servants."

Dr. Lion made every effort to place the girls in good jobs after they left the school. She maintained a warm correspondence with them. Although some girls found the means to a university education after the war, almost none did so right away. First jobs for the Household Girls were more of the kindergarten teacher or "lady cook" variety. One issue of *The Bridge,* listed the occupations of former pupils under categories such as "Farm Work," "Higher Education," etc. Dr. Wolff, the editor, chose to fold "Domestic Work" into the broader category she titled "Teaching – Social Work – Domestic Work," thereby granting the field a professional standing. Of eleven pre-war girls who responded, four had "nurse/teaching' jobs; two were kindergarten teachers, one worked at the St. Bernardo Home for orphans, and one, in Buenos Aires, became a handicraft teacher (while finding time to be a "champion javelin thrower"). One young woman administered a center for mentally-defective children, following directly in the footsteps of her mentor, Nore Astfalck. One was taking classes in sewing and clothing design. And the feisty Ursela Selo was working toward a certificate in Domestic Science; but they "kicked her out for lack of room because of the war," and she only got a "Housewife's Certificate" instead of the "Housekeeper's." Finding herself taking a class in shorthand, she wrote,

---

[20] Inge Hamburger [Pavlowsky] from a letter to the author dated November, 2004.

"Don't worry,' I am not going into business as a typist or something equally horrid." (The War effort apparently interfered with her plans; she signed up for Red Cross lectures in first aid and home nursing and was about to join a Voluntary Aid Detachment. She later became a nun known as Sister Mary Ester.)

Today the Domestic Sciences Program raises the question of fairness. Renate Dorpalen wrote, The program "..was supposed to combine theory and practice, and to include general academic subjects. In reality, the major responsibility of carrying out the household duties for the school rested on these young girls and adjunct staff. This programme offered little in the way of academic enrichment or systematic training. The workload was very heavy and the hours extraordinarily long, without remuneration except room and board."[21]

The Household Girls played a crucial role in the history of a struggling school. Dr. Lion's role in approving this work program must be viewed in the larger context. She managed a school over twenty-six years against a backdrop of constantly changing conditions and a never-ending quest for funds. It probably never occurred to her that the Domestic Sciences program was exploitive. She saw it as a way to admit scores of refugee children, and her legacy, on the whole, is viewed favorably by the Household Girls, burnished by the luminous leadership of the indefatigable Nore. And Nore's role must be equally adjudged to be without blame. As the last to bed and the first to rise every day, she worked tirelessly and only asked the same of her Household Girls. In 2006, Renate Dorpalen said, "I think without [the school] I would not have made it. The work and life was very hard and perhaps not always understood by me, who was too young to understand how the school served us all." Later she wrote, "This community and its functions were created by great sorrow and misery …Many children who had to leave their parents have found their new home here in the house I love....." She then refers to her role as Household Girl. "It is work which has the power of bestowing on the people in this house some kind of peace,

---

[21] Renate Dorpalen [Dorpalen-Brocksieper], Stoatley Rough Newsletter issue 7, February, 1995, p. 15.

and which in spite of the unquiet time, can give to all of us a certain inner content."[22]

The Domestic Sciences program at Stoatley Rough died toward the end of the war. No new Household Girls can be identified in the school's records after 1943. Letters from desperate parents had ceased to jam the mailbox; children had begun to leave. Post-war, Dr. Lion hired English girls for the larger cleaning jobs and she instituted a benevolent prefect system that gave older children administrative tasks, e.g., managing the duty roster. Children may have continued to have weekly chores after then, but no child was ever expected to do the school's laundry, help with the cooking, care for younger children, or polish the floors.

---

[22] Renate Dorpalen [Brocksieper] from "The House I Love" *The Bridge*, Vol. II, 1941.

PART 4

THEIR OWN FINEST HOUR

isiting day at Stoatley Rough dawned gray and windy. Goldy's mother, who had flown with Goldy to London and found work as a maid, drew her coat around her neck as she walked the two miles up the hill from the train station. Goldy waited for her in the Sitting Room dressed in his blue wool jacket. Obo, as usual, had followed him up from the Hut. Obo hung back as Goldy greeted his mother. No. He wasn't jealous of Goldy. Not at all. Some kids just had parents in England and Goldy was one of the lucky ones. Soon Mrs. Goldmeier was urging Obo to come along with them – they were going to a restaurant in Hindhead for the mid-day meal. Every month it was the same. Obo never planned to horn into Goldy's time yet he was unable to help himself. That day he ordered a plate of bubble and squeak, a cabbage and potato dish. *Sauerkraut mit Schupfnudeln.*

Returning from the Pickwick, once again they took the muddy trek back across the heath. Goldy and his mother began an earnest conversation while Obo lagged behind, kicking at clods of earth along the way. Goldy leaned in toward his mother and put his arm around her. The sight unleashed a wave of yearning in Obo. Swept up in memories of his own mother, Obo stumbled on a root in the path, and fell, scratching his palm. He picked himself up, brushed off his pants and caught up with the Goldmeiers who walked on, oblivious to his tears. By the time they crossed Farnham Lane, Obo had recovered. Bidding goodbye to Mrs. Goldmeier, Obo promised to follow her advice about treating his painful chilblains. And how did you get that scratch on your hand? she had said.

The boys went their separate ways, and Obo found himself in the main house. He would write his parents another letter. It had been a couple of weeks since their last postcard had arrived from Luxemburg. He hated the swastika covering the stamp of the tiny country. The odor of cooking onions drifted up from the kitchen and he heard boys from the Farm arguing about something – probably latrine duty. Someone was scraping away at a violin – probably Kate Lesser. Obo had learned to ignore extraneous noise. He fetched one of the squares of pastel papers they were supposed to write on, drew up a chair at the desk in the main living room and picked up a pencil. He could use up to twenty-five words. It was funny. By the time he got through the Dear Mother and Father and the Love, Hans, there was not much room for news. He would not tell them about his near-disaster last week. He'd been revving up the ancient flywheel with the crank handle and almost broken his arm when the engine backfired. Nor would he speak about the boil on his neck that wouldn't heal, or of his chilblains that had started to color one of his fingers green. Obo decided to report on the trip he'd made to his distant relatives in Glagow. While Dr. Lion never let him ride out very far on his bike, for some reason she had let him take the train to Scotland all by himself. *"Liebe Eltern, Danke für Nachricht. Besuchte Gumprich in Ferien. Sehr schön. Haben Kaninchen hier. Mir gehts gut. ... Arbeite viel Farm. Lese viel. Küsse, Hans."* [Dear Mom and Dad, Thanks for the news. I visited the Gumprichs on my holiday. Very nice. We have rabbits. I am fine. I work a lot on the Farm. I read a lot. Kisses, Hans.]"

He would give the note to Miss Astfalck who would pass it to Herta to transcribe it onto the official Red Cross form for posting. His parents should get it in a few weeks. He put down his pencil. The sun had almost set, sending a single white ray into the darkening room to land on a green tile in the fireplace and turning it to brilliant emerald. Obo stared, heedless of the squawking violin, the running feet on the terrace, the thudding of doors. Someone outside said, "Has the gong gone yet?" He scraped back his chair, tucked the note in his pocket and walked outside. He needed to find someone to fool around with until it was time to eat.

He would give Miss Astfalck the note who would pass it to Herta to transcribe it onto the official Red Cross form for posting. His parents should get it in a few weeks. He put down his pencil. The sun had almost set. A few wispy rays stole into the darkening room to reach a small patch of fireplace tile to create a brilliant emerald out of one of the tiles. Obo stared at emerald heedless of the squawking violin, the running feet on the terrace, the thudding of doors. Someone outside said, "Has the gong gone yet?" He scraped back his chair, tucked the note in his pocket and walked outside. He needed to find someone to fool around with until it was time to eat.

The Calm Before the Storm

A sense of unease hung in the air at Stoatley Rough throughout the summer of 1939. Wolf was especially unhappy, although it had nothing to do with the impending war. For no reason at all, Nore had made him move from the Hut and back to the top floor of the main house into Lookout, the room for younger boys. Once again his routines would be supervised. There wasn't much to do. Everybody knew war was going to happen. They just didn't know when. England declared war on Germany in September of that year: for the next eight months both countries built up their war machines and arsenals avoiding serious conflict until May of 1940 when Germany attacked France and the low countries.

Wolf recalls those dog days. "During the summer, a group of us used to meet in secret and plot forbidden things. For example, we pooled our meager cash and decided to buy a tin of pineapple (about sixpence in those days.) How we expected to do this is beyond me, as we eleven-year olds were never allowed to go to Haslemere on our own. Nevertheless, the deed was somehow accomplished. Defiance of Authority added sweetness to the pineapple. Another mystery: How did we open the tin?"

In August, Dr. Lion called the children back from their scouting trips and excursions. She fretted when two of her pupils, Beate Maier and Juergen Wolffson, left England for Holland and Germany. Obo's brother, who had been working in England, also left for Holland, planning just a short trip to visit his parents. None would return, caught and sent to their deaths by the Nazis. Renate Pniower also returned with her father who was called back to Germany to enter the draft. Miraculously her Aryan father and Jewish mother survived the war.

Juergen had been a roommate of Wolf's that summer. He had left behind his ticket and passport when he departed; it was discovered and someone from the school chased him down with the forgotten documents en route, enabling him to board. The loss of the twelve-year-old was especially hard on Dr. Lion. Juergen Wolffson had hailed from her own hometown, Hamburg, and she had known the distinguished family. Juergen was the grandson of one of the noted authors of the *Buergerliches Gesetzbuch* (BGB), the basic German legal code. Notwithstanding the predations of the Nazis on the German legal system, Wolf said it had "stood the test of time since its origin in the 1890's and even in New York, my father kept a copy of the BGB at his bedside and revered it the way Americans revere the Declaration and Constitution." Yet Juergen Wolffson ran out of luck even before his final voyage home. He had somehow been sent to safety in England only to be placed in one of Dr. Bernardo's homes according to Wolf, "famous for the pedigree of their occupants: abandoned children whom the British in those days regarded as half-breeds, unwanted offspring of dark-skinned sailors from distant corners of the then –British empire and English waterfront whores." Nobody ever knew how this well-born German boy had managed to land in an English orphanage.

In 1937 a new building had been built on the campus next to Dr. Lion and Dr. Wolff's Bungalow. It was called, simply, The Hut. It housed boys between twelve and fifteen years old. (Girls stayed tucked safely in the mansion on the upper floors.) The Hut was anything but luxurious. Dieter described it as "a flimsy wood-and-corrugated iron barracks building left over from World War I, painted green with rooms for five and three boys, respectively." The five-person room (named "Cornwall") had folding beds – like rollaway cots – which one pushed under a shelf with a curtain and when unfolded allowed just enough space to get in and out of bed. The other room ("Mark") had regular twin beds. Dr. Lion named Cornwall for the location of the boy scout camping trip that summer, and Mark for the portrait of Frederick II The Great that someone had hung on its wall. "Mark" was universally understood by Germans as the territory known as the March of Brandenburg. Wolf explained. "The portrait of the great man was symbolic of the loyalty that still bound many Roughians to their German Fatherland in spite of persecution and exile. Some kid (I don't know who) carried [the portrait] into exile." The Hut's quarters were cramped. According to Wolf, "Between the two boys' rooms was a teacher's room so narrow that the adult could sit at a desk at night and pound on both walls without getting up." The Hut's external walls were paper-thin. Wolf remembers hearing agonized cries of despair when Household Girls, who lived in an extension of the Hut (called the 'New Hut',) heard of the retreat of the 8th Army after the surrender of Tobruk on their radio. There was a bathroom with shower off the entry corridor, and a furnace room in a small basement. A gong that could be heard all over the property summoned the boys to the morning run and meals hung nearby.

Nore and Dr. Lion were always shuffling the children around. (When they reached sixteen, Stoatley Rough pupils, boy and girl alike, were sent to the Farmhouse unless they were still taking classes and preparing for the matric.) But for the younger boys like Martin, Wolf, Obo and Peter, to be promoted to the Hut was a rite of passage, a highly prized escape from the clutches of the Household Girls. Wolf said, "A bathroom and a toilet all to ourselves were real luxuries, but they were our only luxuries. In the ... rooms, the wind howled through the gaps between walls and ceiling. Winters were a perpetual battle between freezing cold and a temperamental coal-fired furnace. Each room was dimly lit with a naked 30-watt bulb. I loved it!" That summer Dr. Lion had placed the eleven-year-old Wolf temporarily in the Hut to share quarters with thirteen and fourteen year old boys, "much older and more mature than I. They were in the throes of puberty, had heard of S.E.X. (which officially did not exist at Stoatley Rough) and had girlfriends (which was frowned upon)."

Within a year, Wolf, Martin and all their friends were promoted to the Hut. The Hut provided fertile grounds for bonding and occasional good-natured conflicts. Austrians referred to the boys from Berlin as "Piefkes," meaning a city smart alecks, and the German boys retaliated by calling the Austrian snobs "Juenkes," whose meaning is lost to history but was intended to be equally insulting. An occasional argument or wrestling match flaired up over such weighty topics as failure to pick up one's clothes from the floor. When Martin and newcomer Peter Gaupp discovered they had been born on the same day of the same year, each claimed seniority. To settle the question, each sat down and wrote his mother requesting the exact hour of his birth.

Peter's first day was harrowing. He was sleeping in the Schoolroom, close to the kitchen in the main building. He recorded in his diary his "Day of Great Disasters." One of my roommates threw a pile of thirteen plates on the floor; and another one broke the wall in our bedroom. Not satisfied with this, he also broke my bed so that I had to sleep on the floor but it was not cold since I got my mattress."[1] Obo once had a loud argument with Felix Schiller, a relative latecomer to the school, "a gentle, polite, neat chap, a bit of a dreamer with a great sense of humor." That day, however, both boys engaged in an angry dispute, so thrilling to the onlookers that they insisted the boys settle it mano a mano. Obo recalled, "It was a prospect neither one wanted but when it seemed unavoidable. So we talked about it and decided we would give them their fight. We rehearsed a staged showdown that would be

---

[1] Peter Gaupp, Stoatley Rough Newsletter # 22, December, 2003, from his diary an entry dated January 9, 1941.

the least painful, and then performed. I don't remember whether our room mates bought it."

Informal social rules obtained in The Hut. Dieter Gaupp wrote, "Grouping by threes has never been a good idea and we found that frequently there were arguments or disputes pitting one against two. [But] overall the comradeship was close...Each room had its own rules, arrived at by consensus...For example, it [was] the norm to attack anyone's edible contributions received in the mail. Thus, a bar of chocolate was first tasted, courtesy of the recipient; followed by the rule that the 'corners had to be cut,' until there were no corners left, all despite the useless protestations of the owner." The boys always shared packages of food from the U.S. - cocoa, canned fruit or candy. Wolf recalled receiving a can of Ovaltine: nobody had heard of it but they knew it was edible. They produced spoons and ate it dry. Dieter continued:

"Once someone received a large tin of peaches. This was a novelty and it presented a serious practical problem. How do you open such a tin in your bedroom without a can opener? We finally managed to mutilate the tin enough so that it reluctantly yielded its contents... Someone else once received a coconut, which was a complete mystery to all but one of us. The enlightened one (we think it was Felix) had heard that one needed to punch a hole in the nut, drink the milk and then break it up and eat the insides. Oh, how carefully we opened up that coconut and divided up the pieces. Someone saved the shell and tried to make something of it in the workshop. Another such rule concerned the neatness of the room. Everyone made his own bed and put up his clothes ...One of us had the weekly assignment of cleaning the room. It was never stated at what time the room had to be finished [yet] clothing not picked up on time was found hanging from the trees outside the window where they had been flung to clear the room, a sight greeting you as you ambled back from the main building. Retrieving those clothes and not tearing them (clothing was also rationed) was a chore. There was no recourse; it was one of those rules. Arguments and anger might result but the behavior stuck."[2]

Mail was always welcomed. Sometimes what arrived was more than simply the mail. According to Wolf, his hutmate, Hans Kornberg, "used to receive a newspaper from Berlin – the Berliner Illustrirte [spelled without an 'e' before the 'i,' the magazine's snobbish way of letting people know that it had existed before German spelling was standardized in the nineteenth century]. Hans would take the paper to his cot and carefully unroll it. Pressed between the sheets of paper would be valuable stamps, an ingenious way to get money out of the country, which he would sell. Hans' parents took a terrible risk in smuggling those stamps out of Germany."[3]

Most resident teachers had to take on a tour of duty in the Hut. Martin recalled that Miss Humby knew how to keep order. Obo's favorite was Miss Eva Graetz, "a gentle person, very sensitive, who tried to keep us under control but was overwhelmed." (Miss Barnes, a Canadian woman who was not known for her physical beauty, took charge of the girls housed at the adjunct quarters called Rowallan for a time and was known to tell her fascinated female charges the details of her various dates with Canadian soldiers). Mr. Victor May,

---

2   Dieter Gaupp, Stoatley Rough Newsletter (source unknown yet)
3   Hans [John] Obermeyer, in an email to the author.

also took a turn in the Hut until he was called up. A Mr. Taylor was at the school for a very short time.

The teachers had their hands full. Miss Eva Graetz, according to Obo, "although technically was supposed to be in charge of us, had to take a fair amount of abuse from us adolescents whose hormones were raging at that time. ...I recall her wind-up portable phonograph and a wonderful collection of 78 classical records. I well remember her evening concerts in Cornwall. What a treat they were! Tom asked for the Fledermaus "Overture" over and over again. Miss G was reluctant to comply, not wanting to wear out her record. Anyway, that's what she said. But Tom suspected that she didn't want Strauss' music to overly arouse his adolescent testosterone." Peter said, "She induced us to wash and go to bed in an orderly manner with the promise that if we did she would play a record for us. The one that stayed with me was the Rosenkavalier. I still think of her playing that for us with all of us sitting on our beds in pajamas. Amazing how much of an impression something like that can have on a child."

Miss Joan Humby was a thirty-something Oxford-educated woman who had spent a year in Germany on a farm program, and was perhaps the only native English speaker on the staff who knew German. Wishing to learn German in the 1930's, she had naively signed up for the Reicharbeitsdienst, the compulsory Nazi labor service, although she never converted to the cause. She took her Hut duty at Stoatley Rough seriously:

"One night I [Dieter] and another of my roommates had been visiting in the other room after 'lights out.' Miss H. asked for silence. We could have sneaked back to our quarters but the visit was too important, and we stayed and kept talking, in low tones. The wall was patted, then knocked, and finally Miss H. gave a last warning, followed by her coming from her room and telling us to stop forthwith. We hid under the beds, Miss H. returned to her room, and after a moment, we resumed our conversations; eight whispering boys just asking for it. Miss H. filled the doorframe once again and declared that she was going to stand there until it was completely quiet and we were all asleep. Snickers did not amuse her and the room finally did become quiet: six plus two sets of lungs breathing as normally as possible. Those in their beds could even go to sleep; those of us under the bed, couldn't. Miss H. stayed. We thought she would never leave. She never intimated if she knew we were there, [but] after that interminable night, ...we never did that again."[4]

Dieter Gaupp had recently arrived at Stoatley Rough, along with his brother, Peter, by way of Italy, having spent four years in the sun after moving from his birthplace, Berlin. Dieter was small framed, wiry and tough, with sturdy shoulders and a long, mournful face that masked an understated, folksy sense of humor. He was independent, decisive, and morally and physically courageous. Peter was quiet, a beautiful child with poster-boy Aryan looks -a shock of light brown hair, even features, wide, sensual mouth, and big eyes that often reflected, in his early years at Stoatley Rough his timidity, as if to ask what else was he going to have to face without his parents. The two boys spoke Italian together; Peter having almost completely forgotten his German. He was used to following Dieter's lead but soon developed independence. The family was living in Florence when the boys learned they would go to England. Dieter usually spoke German with his parents, but by then, he was not only fluent in Italian, the language of his school, but he also knew passable French. Was there room in his head for one more language? Shortly after the decision, the family sat in the sunny kitchen of their villa. His mother opened a book. She was going to help Dieter

---

4   Dieter Gaupp – TBD

get started with English. Now this word, she said, pointing to the word "one" – is pronounced "wun." Dieter took one look at the book his mother held out to him, then said, "The heck it is," and slammed the book shut. Peter, hovering at his mother's elbow, was thrilled to learn a new language. Believing that "eau de cologne" was an English word, he ran outside to ride around the neighborhood on his bike, showing off his mastery of English. "Eau de cologne," "eau de cologne" he proclaimed to anybody he met.

The family had lived in an apartment in Berlin in the wealthy borough of Steglitz. The boys' mother was a stay-at-home woman, whose emergency training as a bookbinder landed her a job when she reached the U.S. She was of Sephardic descent. Their father, not Jewish, was an editor at Ullstein, one of the largest publishing houses in Germany. His father was involved in getting his company to publish Erich Maria Remarque's internationally acclaimed novel, *All Quiet on the Western Front*. (Later banned by the Nazis, it was one of the books they publicly burned.) Soon after 1933 when nine-year old Dieter showed his eagerness to join the Hitler Youth, his parents shipped him off to friends in Italy to "recover from appendicitis." Left behind, five-year-old Peter was exposed to Nazi theatrics. "In 1933 and 1934 I remember there being more and more loud parades along the *Mariendorfer Strasse* at the end of our block, with lots of loud band music and people in Nazi uniform." The parents warned their sons. "We had instructions to never open the door at night if we heard noises outside. We understood that if the Nazis were hauling away a neighbor and we saw them do it, we would also get hauled away…We were told that someone might rush us or break in if we opened the door., and we should never repeat outside the house what our parents talked about - especially not at school."

His parents registered Peter in school as non-religious, inadvertently causing the boy no end of discomfort. He stood outside his classroom once a week as religion class was taught. "Very embarrassing!" Herr Gaupp tried to start a political opposition to the Nazis but since his publisher did not support the Nazis in the elections, his name ended up in the Nazi's "little book," prompting the family to leave for a permanent vacation in Italy in October, 1935. Peter remembered the interrogation his Jewish mother underwent at the police station trying to get travel permits. "Even at that age I knew that this was dangerous stuff." He mourned having to give away his toys, "for a seven-year old that was more important than issues of political preference."

The family moved into a villa in Chiavari on the Italian Riviera where the boys spent the next four years in the sunshine, virtually unmolested in school. Every six months Herr Gaup, who remained on the payroll at Ullstein and worked long distance, returned to Berlin to renew visas; on his return he sometimes toted an expensive camera to sell. "These trips were obviously dangerous and Dieter and I were aware that my mother would be very worried when he made them, but our parents shielded us from much of this reality."

The Fascist government of Mussolini (in power since 1922) did not intrude in the daily life of the Gaupp family. The only harassment the boys experienced was the day they ran into some Italian toughs. "I quickly learned not only formal Italian but also the street language and street gestures - of which there are many. Coming home from a good movie one day a bunch of boys threatened us and Dieter suggested that we quickly walk away from them. I was inspired and turned around and tried out a number of the most insulting gestures on those boys. Dieter was appalled! He yelled 'Run for it!' and we did with those boys in hot pursuit."

The family moved to Florence in 1938. One day Hitler made a state visit, starting with Florence. The authorities rounded up prominent Germans in the area as hostages to guarantee his safety. Herr Gaupp claimed that he "met some of the nicest people in prison," one of whom offered him a teaching job in America. By 1939 the family were making plans to leave. The children would go first to England, to be joined by their parents, and then they would all sail to New York. But war has a way of ruining even the best-laid plans. Just after the boys arrived, England closed its borders and the senior Gaupps managed to get the last train to Switzerland where they waited out the war.

The Gaupps were well-connected. A distant relative by marriage sponsored the boys in England, Dr. George Peabody Gooch (1873-1968), a distinguished British historian, political journalist, and liberal Member of Parliament from 1906 – 1910. During his brief political career Gooch criticized the policy that led to the South African War, ironically having been good friends while at Oxford with none other than Jan Smuts who became the Prime Minister of South Africa in 1919.

Peter's trip to England was punctuated by one terrible scare, not from harassment by Nazis but because of Dieter's brazen stand against them. The boys' train had stopped at the Italian / French border. Peter recalled, "Dieter announced with alarm that his bicycle was being taken off the train! He told me to stay put and ran off. My worst fears were coming true. Dieter, as always, was going to desert me... There he was on the platform arguing with a bunch of train officials who would not let his bike through. I cared nothing about that bike. If only he would get back on the train. The French authorities evidently wanted to impose import duties on the bike, and since that was higher than the value of the bike, he objected. The Italian and French authorities argued with each other over the bike, and then the train started to move - just to the other side of the station, namely across the border....and Dieter was not with me!! It stopped again and after a while it started up again and we were off - without Dieter!!" The hair-raising finale to this drama (coming on the heels of his tearful separation from his parents) did little to put Peter at ease. As the train started to move, Peter sat frozen in his seat. Then big brother Dieter opened the door to his compartment and came sauntering in. His bike was back on board, untaxed.

The boys spent the remainder of the summer at a boarding school in Watford, a town near London, before they would move to Stoatley Rough in the fall. It was then that they learned how it felt to be a German in England. They were in the Headmaster's living room listening to the news of the German invasion of Poland on the radio (September 1, 1939, two days before Great Britain declared war on Germany). The Headmaster translated the words into French, which Dieter translated into Italian for Peter. The boys sat in shocked silence, stunned by the news they had dreaded. A shooting war was the least of it. Peter said, "Suddenly the Germans were 'they' and we did not have an identity."

The boys fit right in at Stoatley Rough. Dieter went immediately into the Hut, and Peter to the top floor of the main house with other boys his age, who would later give him a name they created - "Squink" - because, "Someone (not me) said we really ought to have nick names, ...'cowboy' names, as they did in the movies, and this name seemed to have a real Western flair to it."

War

Germany's invasion of Poland forced her treaty partners, Great Britain and France, to declare war. It happened on September 3, 1939. The news spread around the school. Herta was in her office when she heard the news. "There was a little window that looked out on the path that led to the main building...One day this horrible smirky little face appeared at my window and it said, "War's broken out" sort of triumphantly....We had all been waiting for it, but it was such a yucky way of telling you; I mean he almost sounded full of glee. He was an awful twerp." Dr. Lion turned on her radio in the Bungalow and, as if they were gathering round to listen to fairy tales instead of the details of the coming storm, children clustered under her window. Wolf and his friends learned the news later that evening. "It was school policy to give us as little news from the real world as possible. I don't know why. Nevertheless, we heard about Danzig and the Ribbentrop-Molotov pact and knew that war was very near. On Sunday, September 3, 1939, some of us boys (Peter Lassow, a non-Jewish boy from Munich, admitted for the summer program, possibly Hans Kornberg, along with Obo, Martin, Francis LeMesurier and Peter Rosenthal) sat in a clearing in the woods above the farm and watched the RAF fly in the direction of France. We were too depressed to play. I had temporarily been transferred from The Hut back to" Lookout" to my unhappiness. That night Miss Astfalck came in, sat on a bed, and told us with a sad and tired voice that war had been declared. Her entire family was in Germany, as were my parents. We had to hang blackout curtains on all windows. In the valley below, the lights of Haslemere disappeared and would not be seen again for five and a half years."[5]

The day war was declared, a German U-30 submarine sank the British liner *Athenia* en route to America, killing 112 of her 1,400 passengers. Then they sank the merchant ship *SS Rio Claro*. U-boats sank the aircraft carrier *Courageous* and in October, the battle ship *Royal Oak,* inside the main British naval base of Scapa Flow. After that, nothing much happened except for a few isolated incidents. So few skirmishes took place between the two countries in the next seven months that the newspapers began to say Britain was in a "Phony War" and commentators joked about the "*Sitzkrieg*" or "Bore War." As the nations went about building up their war machines, an unnatural calm settled in at Stoatley Rough. New rules were quietly implemented such as a restriction on travel from the school to within a five-mile radius. The school's single car was demobilized for a few days. The constabulary confiscated the school's wireless sets and all the cameras only to return them within a few weeks. In October, twenty-seven Stoatley Rough students, all sixteen or older, joined the entire German staff and Dr. Lion to go to the Guildford Aliens' Tribunal where they were examined and then classified as category "C" Friendly Aliens. Thereafter, each time a pupil turned sixteen, he or she was required to be evaluated for security trustworthiness. Renate Dorpalen recalled, "I had to appear before such a tribunal in Guildford (in 1940) [but] Dr. Lion's extensive connections to all levels of government, to refugee organizations, and to prominent, influential individuals, helped the school to remain intact. None of us was interned." Christmas came and went and there were sporadic skirmishes. When Germany invaded France and the low countries on May 10, 1940, the "Phony War" was over and the real one began in earnest.

Mr. May joined up to become Lieutenant May, and Mr. Taylor arrived, a pacifist raised in China by missionary parents, who was assigned to Hut duty. Wolf said of him, "Mr. Taylor went swimming in the dead of winter, insisted we keep all windows open on cold nights,

---

[5] Wolf Edelstein [Elston] *Reminiscences*

tried to teach us Chinese, and was gone by the end of the year." There were advantages to knowing two languages. The boys talked about Mr. Taylor in his presence, confident he knew no German, but he finally noticed a certain word kept popping up in their conversation: "*Schneider*" [Tailor], thinking perhaps they were discussing the pre-war Schneider Trophy seaplane races. When he asked about the word, the boys had, according to Wolf, "instant amnesia." One more male teacher came to teach for a short while according to Wolf, a married man who tried to ogle the girls in their baths. Soon he "was seen no more." From that time on, all teachers were women, with the exception of Mr. Hughes, the new Farm Manager. The Farm's staff over the years included Mr. Corfield, Mr. Pniower (inventor, landscape architect and father of one of the pupils), Mrs. Charlotte Weissrock (Farm Matron for a brief time), Mr. Edward Hughes, a Mr. Bibbe, and in 1944, the last manager, a former Farm Boy, Fritz [Fred] Dreschler.

In London, barrage balloons went up in parks (over 3,000 of them throughout the duration of the war), and anti-aircraft batteries appeared in Hyde Park, Windsor Great Park and Green Park. At Stoatley Rough, Herta and Nore passed out tan, square cardboard boxes with string handles containing gas masks, one for each child. They were a minor sensation but within a few weeks, the children stopped carrying them around. (Wolf reported that at war's end, they were supposed to turn them in. He carried his now useless gas mask, rubber parts brittle, falling apart, to the ship in Scotland he would board for America. "I left it with a pile of gas masks on the dock; nobody paid the slightest attention.") Household Girls sewed blackout curtains from old quilts and other bedding and the chore of hanging them nightly appeared on the duty roster. Inge Hamburger [Pavlowsky] helped to design a particularly decorative curtain with big appliquéd stars. People learned to navigate through a black night, absolutely devoid of light when the moon was new. One girl recalled how dark it was to stumble about at night with no light to guide. She once bumped into a "soft thing," after which came a "pardon me" and she went upon her way.

The school maintained a steady-as-you-go course. As new clothing and shoes became scarce, the school made every effort to become self-sufficient. Self-sufficiency was dear to the hearts of Nore and Hanna, who thrived on challenges as a matter of course. Even Dr. Lion, who frankly enjoyed the few luxuries afforded her (such as the occasional special meal or the opportunity to arrange the flowers Mr. Phillips brought her daily in season), embraced sacrifice. Uneasy with great wealth and aware of the need for sacrifice, she once expressed her distaste for living on "millionaires' lane." Reprising their *Jugendheim* days, Nore and Hanna began to teach the children bookbinding and other practical crafts. Children learned how to cut bowls and buttons from coconut shells left over from care packages sent to some of the children by American friends and relatives. The school would not neglect the arts, not even for a war. Miss Sileezinski was brought in to give instruction in painting flowers and later a Miss Kaethe Wilcynski came in to teach oil painting. She was an artist from Berlin who had come to England for an exhibition of her work, having won the Rome Prize of the *Akademie fuer bildende Kuenste* when Max Liebermann was its president. Later she was known as an illustrator of children's books. (Once again, the school benefited from overqualified teachers!)

Appropriately, the administrators brought in a cobbler to teach the Household Girls how to repair shoes. Ilse Kaiser wrote about the project for *The Bridge*:

> "Eighty children! That means quite a lot of shoes to be repaired, ...our workshop was too small for us [and so] we moved to the so-called 'nursery' with our shelves and cupboards. ... The children themselves are very interested in the work and keep on asking: 'How do you do this?" and 'Why do you do that?' Even our little Walter [at five, the youngest resident who lived at Stoatley Rough for five years], is really anxious to know all we do. The boys know all about the work 'of course' and should a girl dare to ask about the soling

of shoes, the boys are disgusted and give a long lecture. 'Put a sheet of paper on the shoe and file round it, and you get the exact shape you have to cut out of leather. Be very careful in cutting; firstly it is War-time and we have to save every bit of leather. Secondly the knives are quite sharp and our fingers do not like to be cut. The pail with water is not there to splash other people, but to soak your piece of leather. Later you stick and nail it on the shoe after having taken off the old pieces. The very small pieces are really given to us to play with, but generally our shoemaker thinks it is worth keeping it. So we have to believe it. File the edges smooth and lastly polish all round.' Then our little Walter is again given the job of taking the shoes to their owner. Our boys really know it perfectly, and if they go on like this in practice too, we will have many good shoemakers in this school."[6]

There were formal personnel changes that fall: a Mrs. List started giving English lessons once a week and Martin's own Gertrud Gans left the school for good, the action breaking his heart. She had fallen in love and gone with her parents to India to marry a British officer and wait out the war. (She later wrote to Dr. Lion about her difficulties in training her new all-Indian household staff.) Miss Dove announced she would leave to get married in December in Dundee, Scotland.

That month, Stoatley Rough had its first air raid – a siren sounded in the valley below in Haslemere that prompted a steady ringing of a bell at the school alternated with a bell. It happened early in the morning. Everyone filed down into the lower basement of the large house into the large room called the "Schoolroom" in various states of dress - pajamas, robes, hastily thrown on clothes. Some tried on their gas masks. Marianne Gluecksmann, wrote, "I felt for the first time the great

---

[6] Ilse Kaiser, 'Shoe Repairing," *The Bridge*, Vol. 1, No. 2, August – September, 1941. p. 18.

responsibility which had fallen on Dr. Li. and all the other teachers. In the first week we had every evening some silent minutes in memory of all those people who must suffer during the war. ....We all felt a great unity. Correspondence with Germany is becoming increasingly difficult. One loses touch with one's relations. This makes for a growing community-spirit. We have come closer to each other. Thus we try to make our life a little easier in these hard times. We don't forget the silver ray on the dark horizon."

The experience was "curious and sometimes even amusing," according to one blasé seventeen year old identified as HP (probably Hans or Heinrich Pachmeyr) who described for *The Bridge* how the Household Girls lugged mattresses and cushions into the basement shelter:

"During the late summer the regular night raids on London began and we had an alarm almost every day between 8 and 9 o'clock in the evening, until 3 or 4 o'clock in the morning. People started early with getting ready for the night.... Everybody is provided with a book or some needlework. In the laundry cellar and in the box room the light is switched off at 9 o'clock and everybody is supposed to sleep. Many do, some don't. In the passage the light is kept on. A part of the staff and some of the older pupils are out here on chairs or improvised mattresses. They darn stockings, knit, read, or write letters on their knees. After two hours or so, Dr. L. provides the awake people with a water biscuit. Then everybody tries to sleep a little until one of the guards in the stoke-room brings the news: ALL CLEAR! Rather drowsily you take your blanket and go to bed to sleep until 8 o'clock – Breakfast has been postponed after night alarms."[7]

---

7   H.P (Hans or Heinrich Pachmayr) *The Bridge*, August / September, 1941.

During the Battle of Britain, August – September, 1940, daylight raids were common. Otherwise, alarms rarely occurred during the day. "If they did, lessons were continued in the basement. You could hear mathematics from the box room, handicraft theory (as a substitute for an underground workshop) from the laundry cellar, while Shakespeare's plays were read in the passage." The administrators tried to keep the children from being frightened. HP continued:

> "For about a fortnight the siren was sounded almost daily at one of our mealtimes: Miss A. rings the bell and sounds the gong and, after having grumbled at the disturbance, we go down into the cellar, quickly swallowing another mouthful of bread and butter. In the cellar every available room is occupied. Some people even sit on the stairs. The box room has become an air raid shelter for most of the smaller ones under the supervision of Dr. W., and staying there became an envied thing for its German readings. In the same room Miss R., as long as she was here, used to play very exciting games with the children which were sometimes connected with so much noise that the roaring airplanes overhead were not to be heard. Outside the stoke room door two pails filled with water are put up with a stirrup pump next to them. Three or four people walk about there enjoying the sunshine – they are supposed to watch but generally the planes are far enough away not to be dangerous." [8]

Wolf confirms that there evolved at the school a certain jauntiness, a business-as-usual attitude toward the air raids. "In the next nine months we had air-raid alerts almost every night and, at first, several times a day. I tried to count the number of alerts but they mounted into hundreds. We saw little of the fighting except for twisted contrails high in the sky. Sometimes,

---

[8]   Ibid.

spent bullets and cartridges clattered on the corrugated iron roof of the Hut. We put pillows over our heads when we ran for our supposed shelter in the main building. After nights spent on mattresses jammed on cellar floors, we would march back to the Hut at dawn, singing, 'Heigh-ho, heigh-ho, it's off to work we go,' or 'Good morning, good morning, we danced the whole night through.' and other hits of the day.")[9]

The school rigorously followed wartime rules regarding rationing and the extinguishing of light at night. HP wrote with great sincerity, "We always look carefully to see that nothing is wasted in the house and that nobody is taking too much of the rationed food. All paper is put together and collected once a week."[10]

That Christmas of 1939, the well-to-do Miss Fearon took it upon herself to invite some of the children to a special tea in her home. Dieter Gaupp, relatively new to the school, recalled the event for the utter generosity of the woman. "She set beautiful tables in her large living room…with pretty napkins and glasses, a variety of cookies and cakes (again, remember this was a war time with rationing) and hot chocolate."[11] She never mentioned the misunderstanding that must have been costly for her in what ensued during the meal. "We admired the decorations on the table, small replicas of ancient galleons, carved in wood, handled them and played with them during tea. Somehow we gained the impression that these were for us to keep and many of us took them home…Someone later pointed out that we were probably mistaken in our assumption; we felt bad but as far as I remember, we kept the ships." [12]

---

[9] Both American songs were featured in movies, the first from *Snow White and the Seven Dwarfs* released in 1937. Modern audiences associate the other song with the 1952 movie *Singin' in the Rain*, yet it was first sung by Judy Garland (her co-starred was Mickey Rooney), in the movie *Babes in Arms* in 1939. "Heigh-ho" was composed by Frank Churchill with lyrics by Larry Morey. "Singing in the Rain" was written by Nacio Herb Brown, lyrics by Arthur Freed.

[10] Op. Cit.

[11] Dieter Gaupp "Reminiscences," *Stoatley Rough Newsletter* 10, February, 1996, p. 12.

[12] Ibid.

Loveable Misfit

I n May, 1940, Dr. Lion's refuge was about to endure great strains as the war began in earnest. The event known as Dunkirk was an eye opener for British citizens that Germany was dangerous. Furthermore, it opened up to the British the possibility that the enemy lived among them. British and French soldiers who comprised The British Expeditionary Force (BEF), not only had been powerless to stop Germany's invasion of Norway, northern France, Belgium, Luxembourg and the Netherlands, but had been forced into a small pocket of land at the little French port town, Dunquerque, their backs to the sea. A massive naval response from the British merchant and private sector managed to evacuate over 335,000 troops, including 100,000 French. People saw for the first time the effect of fighting the invincible and cruel Germans: wounded young men, some of them disfigured, appeared in public covered in bandages and walking on crutches.

Rumors swept the nation. German paratroopers might be silently dropping into England by night to invade the towns and cities aided by unseen supporters – spies, secret agents - already lurking in Britain: a Fifth Column. Great Britain moved swiftly and without hesitation to root out the evil in its midst. It suspended the practice of Tribunals and locked up all aliens over the age of sixteen without the usual loyalty hearings. Six children – two Household Girls and four boys from Stoatley Rough, including Dieter - were swept up by this precautionary measure.

At about this time, Tom Wongtschowsky entered the school. He was a charming and intelligent boy dominated by his overbearing and brilliant father and traumatized by the earlier death of his mother. Tom's neuroses were little understood by the adults. In today's world he may have been diagnosed and helped to live a satisfying life. While some children arrived at the school hurt by external events, others arrived damaged, like Tom. Yet Tom was beloved by the other children. The twelve-year-old arrived in May 1940, from another school in England, a dyed-in-the-wool Berliner who refused to speak English. From the day he showed up, Tom entertained the boys in the Hut with his thrilling disregard for authority. The other boys marveled at what they perceived as courage, but in truth, were the actions of a boy who felt he had nothing left to lose. The well-bred and polite boys who were raised in intact homes had no concept of the psychological basis of Tom's behavior. They didn't know what to make of someone who could get into trouble on a regular basis. Tom was never insolent or sullen. His anger was always directed toward himself. Dieter Gaupp said he was "very lonesome, unattached to any adult, basically hurt."

Tom was fearless. When he read somewhere about the properties of conductivity in wood, water, and metals, Tom decided to run his own experiment. One night he drew up a chair under one of the ceiling lights in the Hut, placed a rubber mat on it and set about to test the insulating properties of rubber. As others stood watching, he proceeded to unscrew the light bulb and put his finger in the socket. The current blew him across the room, leaving him with a burnt finger (but miraculously, alive). Another time while talking to a friend, Tom absently put an open safety pin in his mouth and accidentally swallowed it. He landed in the Haslemere hospital, his bodily functions about to go under intense scrutiny until the doctors were sure he would not need surgical intervention. (For Christmas that year, the Hut Boys gave Tom a nicely wrapped box of rusty nails and pieces of metal with a little card offering him a hand-picked midnight snack.) It did not take Tom long to discover the space in the main house between the exterior and interior walls (the same gap discovered by Hans Loeser in 1937). Tom saw the possibilities at once, figuring he could find his way to the ceiling above one of the girls' rooms. Great place for peeping! Just before bedtime when the girls would be undressing, Tom wound his way to the room and began to inch across the fragile flooring. He made it halfway across when the supports gave way, chunks of plasterboard raining down. One of his legs suddenly broke through, Tom hanging on for dear life above, to the astonishment of the girls.

More than most, Tom suffered from chilblains during the cold, damp English winters. He once almost blew up the school to bring in more heat. Obo recalled, "I was put in charge of supplying the "big boiler." It was located next to the "Schoolroom" a large room on the Lower Level. This work was under Mr. Phillips' jurisdiction and as soon as I was strong enough to carry the heavy steel coal buckets from the coal cellar underneath the kitchen, ... to the boiler room, that job fell under my job description. Sometimes some of the other kids helped me "schlep" the buckets. He also showed me where all the main hot water valves and other devices were located and I guess I got what would today be considered a basic boiler operator's license at the advanced age of 15.. ...At any rate, one day Tom Wongtshowski wanted more heat and without permission, shoveled in more rationed coal than what was safe. He cranked up the lever in the main furnace room. The temperature got so high that it set off the safety valve and almost blew up the furnace. After that they installed an industrial grade padlock on the door." (The boys used the Boiler Room as a refuge for the nefarious practice of smoking. Tom had introduced cigarettes to the boys, according to Goldy, Woodbines, "the cheapest" and also the smelliest. Obo also lay the blame squarely on Tom's shoulders for "persuading us to 'at least try it,' getting us hooked very early.")

Tom's bed was always unmade, his clothes strewn about, and his things, like his life, were in disarray. Later on the Farm, some of the boys got so exasperated with him that they moved his bed into the feed room next to the pigsty. Tom's fear of water (Wolf called it "*wasserscheu*") was legendary. While the other boys could not get in enough swimming time, Tom refused to go near the pool. One day Miss Astfalck had had enough. She insisted he go swimming in the fresh water, probably thinking a good dunking would do him good. Tom's flair for the dramatic surfaced. He went through the house collecting every hot water bottle he could find– four or five of them– and filled them with hot water. He then tied them to his body, venturing into the pool decked out like a Michelin tire man.

Tom was connoisseur of classical music. Renate [Herold] Richter wrote, "I remember Tom as an enthusiastic and gifted piano player, his favourite composer being Chopin. Once he drew up an alternative board game to "Monopoly", where the fields weren't street and road names, stations and hotels and houses, but names of _composers._ ...The last, most precious field, instead of 'Mayfair' ['Boardwalk' in the American version] was 'Chopin!' What he used instead of houses and hotels and other value-increasing objects for his game, I just don't remember. But I learnt about a lot more composers playing the game than I had heard of before from Dr. Leven; names like Glinka, Moussorgsky, Borodin, Mascagni, Donizetti, Leoncavallo, Respighi, and of the "lighter" muses like Adam, Franz v. Suppé, Lortzing, Offenbach, Auber, Reznicek. These were Tom's Boardwalk properties."

Tom's father was often invited to give violin concerts at the school, but Tom never performed with him, complaining that his thick short fingers held him back. He played the piano to entertain himself and sometimes accompanied Renate Herold when she sang.

Tom liked girls and girls liked Tom. Obo remembered, "One girl, Ruth Deutsch, a Viennese girl with long pigtails, became the object of his affection. Tom told us he was able to kiss her after presenting her with a bar of Cadbury chocolate, a rationed treat that we all treasured dearly. It was just one more act that we would have liked to carry out ourselves but didn't have the guts to do." Renate Herold claimed she loved Tom madly until she caught his attention and then she moved on to another conquest. Gerda Stein [Mayer] was a steadfast friend of Tom's, remaining in contact with him for many years. The distinguished poet was surely thinking of Tom when she wrote the following:

Chopin's Minute Waltz[13]

First love
who played it
with learner fingers
slow ten
der notes drif
ting in
to the garden…

Wolf recalled, "Tom had the most complex love life, with not one but two girlfriends. He'd keep Obo and me awake at night, talking about it. One of the two actually kissed him (or he, her.)" Tom always spoke in German and could be crude. He had a particular proclivity to talk on and on until nobody answered, on the verge of sleep. Tom would pause in his monologue for a moment, and then say, *"Arschloch?"* [Asshole] as if addressing one of the drowsy room mates. Whoever answered, of course, would pay the price. Wolf says Obo was the one who always answered, *"Wer?"* [Who?], to which Tom would retort in triumph, *"Du!"* [You!] Wolf claims, "Obo fell for it several times until he caught on." Obo disputes the story.

Tom's humor was almost always self-deprecating. Long after he had left Stoatley Rough he wrote from London to Wolf, by then living in Albuquerque, New Mexico, about a female pen pal he had acquired who lived in West Africa. Her letters to Tom had begun with formal pleasantries, but as the months went on, she became more and more friendly, going from "Dear Mr. Warner" to "Dear Thomas," then "Tom," "Tommy," "Dearest Tommy," "Tommy, Darling," etc." Then one day she announced she was coming to England to meet him. The fateful day arrived and they met at a restaurant. Tom concluded his letter with the outcome. "She took one look at me and disappeared."

---

[13] From *TIME WATCHING,* Hearing Eye, 1995. First published in DANCING THE TIGHTROPE, The women's Press, 1987.

It was not unusual for Stoatley Rough pupils to be related to each other. Several in the Stoatley Rough community were connected. Wolf was related, through his maternal grandmother, to Dr. Wolff's father. A true nephew of Dr. Wolff also attended Stoatley Rough, Gerhard Wolff, who ended up living in Israel. (One of Wolf's aunts, Tante Erna, was a well-off lady who dismissed her maid in Berlin, escaped to England and entered Mrs. Marjorie Vernon's household as a maid herself. After the war she came to America and died shortly after her hundredth birthday.) Renate Dorpalen's father, a physician, had delivered Gina Schaefer's little brother. There were siblings, cousins, and in Tom's case, second cousins at Stoatley Rough.

Tom's geneology carries special pathos. The grandfather of one of the Household Girls, Ilse Kaiser, had married a sister of Tom's grandfather, Dr. Adolf Wongtschowski. A Berlin transvestite enters the story at this point. In 1955, one Charlotte von Mahlsdorf, a German transvestite who had survived the Nazis and the post-war East German Secret Police, the Stasi, published *I Am My Own Woman*. [14] The man, born Lothar Berfelde, had grown up in Berlin. He became estranged from his abusive father in the early 1940's, just as the Nazis were rounding up Jews in earnest. Lothar left home and began dressing as a woman, calling herself Charlotte. She lived hand to mouth in the streets in war-racked Berlin. (She confessed in her memoir, perhaps spuriously, that she killed her father and hid his body, never to be brought to trial for the crime.) At the height of the deportations, the young vagrant was hired by the Nazis to go to the empty houses of Jews who had been deported and report back on the contents of the homes. (Later, this slight, unassuming man who always wore plain housedresses, built a collection of furniture and decorative objects from the *Grunderzeit* period (1850 to 1914) which, after the war, she made into a museum in Denmark where she lived out her days.) In her book she describes her grisly work for the Nazis. One day she entered the Adolf Wongtschowski apartment in Berlin and found evidence of a swift departure. On the floor were two

---

[14] The book was later made famous with the Pulitzer Prize-winning play in 2004, *I Am My Own Wife,* by Doug Wright.

items: an autograph book and a World War I medallion, lying there as if their owners had considered taking them and then abandoned them at the last minute. The book's handwritten contents identified the owner of the house as one Dr. Adolf Wongtschowski.

Ilse Kaiser's son, Peter Neivert in America, whose mother had been Tom's cousin at Stoatley Rough, read Charlotte's book in 2004. Astonished to see the name of his mother's great uncle mentioned in the book, Peter corresponded with Charlotte in Denmark, identifying himself as Adolf Wongtschowski's sister's great grandson. He learned that Charlotte had also corresponded with Tom Wongtschowski's father, Karl, in England when the dentist was in his seventies. "Charlotte wrote in one of her letters to me that she sent the diary and medallion to Karl, Adolf's son, and Tom's father, in London. It was not really a diary, but a 'Poesie Album' in which family members or friends would write short poems and then sign them. It's really more of a signature booklet." In her book Charlotte recorded her emotions upon reading the name of this particular victim, noting, "Over and over you heard the harmless phrase, 'called for.' The words sprang readily to the mouths of neighbors, as if the Wongtschowskis had been called for and taken to a little party by dear friends. Only this time, they had been 'called for' to be murdered." Adolf Wongtschowski and his wife, Blanca Pniower Wongtschowski, died in Theresienstadt in 1943. Charlotte von Mahlsdorf died in Denmark in 2000. [15]

Tom's stay at Stoatley Rough ended on a sad note. In 1945, Dr. Lion expelled him, an almost unheard of punishment. He'd gone on a prohibited night walk with Eddie Behrendt, one of the younger Hut Boys, and one of the girls. Eddie Behrendt said, "We got picked up in the middle of the night in Hindhead by one of the local watchmen. He thought he had caught a bunch of 'German spies' from 'that foreign school' and treated us accordingly." The arresting officer "made a big fuss and thought of himself as a real hero. He called Dr. Lion from the phone box and woke her in the middle of the night. We were carted

---

[15] This anecdote was related to the author by Peter Neivert, Ilse Kaiser's son, who contacted Charlotte after reading her biography.

back to school and met by Dr. Lion who was furious. Furious because we were outside, furious because she had been routed out of bed in the middle of the night, and above all, furious because she said we were ruining the STR reputation with the locals. It was right there and then when she told us about having to expel Tom to make an example." (Dr. Leven expressed regret for the decision many years later.)

Only sixteen, Tom was sent packing. Refusing financial help from his wealthy father, he found odd jobs until he graduated to zipper salesman. In 1988, forty-four years after he had left the school, Gerda Stein Mayer, who had been at the school at the same time as he and the Hut Boys, invited him to a dinner party at her home because Wolf and his wife, Lorraine, were in town from America. Tom brought to the party his partner, a blowsy woman eighteen years his senior. He also had with him a book to return to Wolf, *Immensee*, that he had borrowed from Wolf in 1943. It had been a gift to Wolf for his 15th birthday form Dr. Emmy Wolff and Wolf had never had a chance to read it. It turned out to be a frustrating if happy reunion for all. A few months after the dinner party Tom suffered a fatal stroke. His elegant companion not only failed to notify Gerda Stein Mayer of his death until after the funeral had taken place, but was purported to have missed a chance to save his life in her delayed call for help. All who had known Tom mourned. Tom's estranged father's grief was so profound that the writer of his obituary, upon the old man's death a few years later, recorded in the paper that Dr. Wongtschowsky had never recovered from his son's untimely passing. Gerda Stein Meyer wrote an unpublished poem about her maverick friend shortly after his death.

School Casanova

The school – Casanova.
All the little girls who loved you
grew up
long before you did.

At twenty already
too adolescent:
(I say! – he's the same
old Tom.)

Then plain girls and
the plainly awful;
girls with problems
alighted, departed.
Wifeless, childless,
jobless, penurious
you died
a juvenile sixty.

Old flame,
dear chump, my
almost-brother,
I cry…

How handsome your
teenage photographs;
how silly your
teenage letters;

How suddenly recent
youth.

Interned on the Isle of Man

I n the spring of 1940, several children turned sixteen, an event that normally involved a routine trip to the Haslemere police station for a perfunctory Tribunal. Eleven days after Dieter's sixteenth birthday, Dr. Lion summoned him and three other boys to her office. They were to be interned and they needed to pack. This time there would be no Tribunal. Every German alien (who had not already been cleared in a Tribunal) was classified as "Category C" or "enemy alien" and was to be locked up. The boys left her office and next she called in two more sixteen-year-olds, Household Girls, Ilse Kaiser and Liesel Neufeld. Inexplicably, she failed to tell them to pack, and merely directed them to report to the Haslemere police station. This act, whether because of absent-mindedness or miscommunication, turned out to be a spectacular gaffe. The girls walked into town in their summer dresses and were immediately carted away. It was a dark day for the school when people learned of the forced internments, according to Margaret Dove, It was "the saddest time when the staff had to help some of the pupils through the double trauma of being persecuted as Jews in Germany and as Germans in Britain, while gradually many of them came to realize that they might never see their parents again."[16]

The boys were taken to nearby Guildford, issued blankets, and were placed in a school under guard by British soldiers. Over a hundred other men and boys were milling about. Dieter and the other three boys did not know what to make of their predicament. "I encountered

---

[16] Margaret Dove Faulkner, "Where School was Home," AJR Journal, 1990, [issue unknown.]

for the first time in my life Orthodox Jews who practiced their rituals at appointed times daily [and] men obviously fearful and nervous, others who considered the whole experience a joke. Some …wanted to be helpful with us boys; others wanted to impress us… No one could know whether there was any stopping the enemy and to some, the thought of a German invasion of England produced talk of suicide. On the other hand, it never occurred [to me] that England could lose the war and [even though] we were non-British subjects, we hung on every word spoken by Winston Churchill."[17] A week later, the internees were transferred during a rainstorm to Huyton, a suburb of Liverpool, where the boys shared a tent for two more weeks. "Everyone was interrogated with the result that some were taken away, including the colorful Captain von Rintelen, a German agent of World War I vintage, whose nefarious work resulted in many Allied merchant ships being burned in mid-ocean.[18] Then they were shipped to the Isle of Man, a crown dependency of 221 square miles in the Irish Sea, and assigned rooms in hotels encircled by barbed wire in Douglas, the main city.

Meanwhile, the two Household Girls were driven to a boxing ring in Reading, and after spending the night on the floor with a few hundred women and crying children, were immediately ferried out to the Isle of Man. The girls threw their Identity Cards into a large wicker basket, and were assigned a room in a hotel, each with a double bed and washstand.

Boredom was the biggest problem for girls used to heavy work schedules. Ilse wrote to Dr. Lion, "Two weeks ago we have left. You

---

[17] Dieter Gaupp, Stoatley Rough Newsletter, Issue 15, October, 1997

[18] This former officer of the Imperial German Navy had developed a small cigar-shaped incendiary, composed of two chemicals that when fused, provided an intense fire, which could easily be smuggled among the cargo being loaded in the U.S. He wrote a book about his espionage, *Dark Invader*, which Germany refused to publish or sanction. He turned against his former country, went to live in England, befriended one "Blinker" Hall, his former captor, and asked if he could don a British uniform and join the fight against Germany in World War II. He was widely respected by the British. Editorial review of *Dark Invader*, amazon. com; http://www.amazon.ca/exec/obidos/ASIN/0714647926/702-3183931-0806431, accessed June 18, 2006.

really can't imagine what it means for me to be unable to do anything. We just sit around and have no possibility of work...could you please send something to work. ...some recipes and how to crub [sic] the floor for instance. I'm afraid I will forget otherwise....Our washstand was our salvation. We washed our clothes in the evening and hoped they would dry by morning. When our clothes were still wet we could not go to the dining room for breakfast. Sometimes we had enough dry things for one of us to go, so that one would try sneaking some food to the room for the other."[19] Three weeks later clothing arrived. "Dear Dr. Lion. Thanks very much for the suitcase, unfortunately s6.4d had to be paid, so we borrowed the money. We'll have to give it back as soon as possible. So if you would kindly send it on quickly, and you might even be so kind as to send us a little more, as we have no money at all (for stamps, shoesoles, etc.). May I ask you for something else? Poor Ilse [she coyly refers to herself] didn't get any underwear nor socks or *bathingkostuem* [her German-English word for bathing suit] and dresses. Would you please send this and more dresses and shorts for both of us, in a parcel (cost 6d or 1s.) We are very well but wish we were back in school."[20]

Dieter's quarters were on the opposite end of the island from the women's barracks. The men and boys of each house were shown how to make their bed and fold blankets and towels according to army regulations. Each house appointed a leader and chief cook and in this one detail, Dieter was lucky - his cook had once been a chef of the Ritz Hotel in Paris. Among his housing cohorts were a former German chess champion "who played with us frequently" and an elderly man who taught the boys Ju Jitsu. "This made us physically very fit...We worked to build up our abdominal muscles and learn the art of falling on.... mattresses on the floor. ...Our instructor demonstrated his firmness by letting us punch him as hard as we could into his stomach, which resounded like a hollow drum ...To practice with knives or guns we used sticks or rubber knives, learning to parry, unbalance and throw our opponents, pin them to the ground, disarm them, render them

---

[19] Ilse Kaiser's letters, collection belonging to her son, Peter Nievert, Providence, R. I.
[20] Ibid.

harmless, and so on. …We learned to dive, tumble and somersault on piles of mattresses, on our own."[21] After a few weeks, Dieter sank into depression. He wrote Dr. Gooch, his patron. He wanted to join up. At least fighting Germans would get him off the island. "I was hoping I might be able to train as a fighter pilot and shoot some of those Germans down." But the only avenue open to aliens was the Pioneer Corp, an option Dieter rejected because British nationality was not given to its volunteers and "moreover, the uniforms were baggy." The Corp engaged mainly in road building and other manual tasks, were not issued arms, and worked under the direction of officers unwanted in the regular army. [22]

Tensions were high. Men talked about their wives interned on the island and discussed endlessly what would happen to them if the Germans invaded England. One man had been in a concentration camp. "He had his face slashed from one eye to his mouth, with his face muscles pulled to one side and a resulting speech impediment. He also walked with a limp. He spoke forcefully, saying he would rather take his life than wait for the Germans, and several agreed with him. To him, the invasion was imminent and once the Germans were on English soil their advance would not be stopped. It was a sobering assessment though most of us never believed for a moment that England would fall or that we would lose the war. Was it faith, deep conviction, or were we avoiding reality?"[23]

Among those interned on Man was the German sculptor, Hermann Nonnenmacher who had carved the beautiful wooden sign donated

---

[21] Dieter Gaupp, *Reminiscences*, Stoatley Rough Newsletter, Issue 15, October, 1997.
[22] Originally formed in 1917, this group performed jobs such as engineering, road clearing, and other manual tasks for the British military. They were later known as the Royal Pioneer Corps. "Some six 'alien' pioneer companies were set up in the 1939/40; they were not issued arms but expected to engage in road construction work, setting up Nissen huts and other such works…The officers appointed… were those unwanted in other parts of the army. Their camps were miserable…. They were not given British nationality upon enlisting, which meant that they would have no protection if they were taken prisoners of war. Walter Laqueuer, *Generation Exodus* p. 74.
[23] Dieter Gaupp, *Reminiscences*, Stoatley Rough Newsletter 14, May, 1997.

to Stoatley Rough in its early days.[24] The best part of the day for Dieter was after dinner when a couple of the prisoners gave impromptu concerts with accordion or violin accompaniment. "The tenor's voice was, indeed, wonderful. His favourite song was Romberg's 'Be My Love...'" "We all cheered and asked for more. What was most memorable was the fact that on the other side of the fence stood the British in a large group, taking it all in, joining us in the applause. Sometimes the British were already waiting when the musicians arrived. It was an odd feeling that we should all be on the same side ...but here we were separated by tall fences of barbed wire."[25]

One day a large white ship showed up in the harbor. The authorities told Dieter and the other Stoatley Rough boys to get on board. They were going to Canada. As they were unpacking in their cabin, word came through the ship's loudspeaker that only a thousand passengers would fit on the ship; two hundred would have to stay behind. The passengers would choose. Two boys chose almost immediately to go on, afraid of the coming invasion of England. Perhaps in Canada they could enroll in the service. (Klaus Zedner, out of school but also interned at the same time, chose to go to Canada. He later returned to England to work on a farm.) "Eddie, [Eduard Roussel] the third guy, and I

---

[24] In *Yealm*, Sheila Lahr relates that her father was a friend of Nonnenmacher, and was also interned. There were many artists on Mann who found themselves bereft of tools and art supplies. Ms. Lahr tells the story of how the many interned artists improvised their art supplies. They used "oil paint made from crushed minerals, dyes abstracted from food rations mixed with oil from sardine tins, paint brushes from Samson Schames' strong and wiry beard." She names various artists and their scrounging activities: 'While artists Dachinger and Nessler collected gelatine from boiled-out bones and mixed it with flour and leaves to size newspapers, and so made paper on which to draw with burnt twigs for charcoal. The artists of Onchan used also the reverse side of wallpaper, and having stripped one room completely, formed a human chain along the walls with each artist drawing a portrait of his neighbour on the bare wall, to form a continuous frieze. Lino from corridors and kitchens was used for linocuts. And Weissenborn manufactured an enduring printing ink by mixing crushed graphite from lead pencils with margarine. Kurt Schwitters made use of ceiling squares of a composite material to paint portraits and landscapes.)

[25] Dieter Gaupp, Stoatley Rough Newsletter Issue 14, May, 1997.

were ambivalent. The discussion went back and forth. I had Peter in England, my parents were in Switzerland and the prospect of additional separation did not sound good. There was also the possible danger from U-boats on the high seas. … Ironic enough, the fact that clinched it was that Eddie and I had combined our packing into one duffel bag, and had to stay together, or so we thought. So we stayed." [26] The next morning the white ship carried away two of the boys from Stoatley Rough while Dieter and Eddie returned to a joyous welcome from their former housemates. A week later Dieter received his identity papers, a train ticket and some cash and was shipped back to the mainland. From London, Dieter boarded the train to Guildford, where he planned to transfer to the Haslemere train. Halfway along the route, he stayed in the wrong car when an engine was added and cars were switched. By nightfall, the exhausted teenager was stranded at the end of the line in Aldershott, the site of England's largest military training establishment. It was a Saturday night. Dieter was in a real pickle. An alien with a German accent surrounded by drunken and boisterous military men should not be in Aldershott. He crept along the streets looking for a room. Eventually a policeman rescued him, and gave him one of the maximum-security cells for the night. After breakfast, Dieter boarded the right train to Haslemere and walked the two miles back to the school.

Ilse and Liesel were released after two months of internment, receiving their identity papers and fare to London. Ilse used her lucky shilling to get to the school. "My friend told me: 'Put it in your shoe and it will bring you luck.' My friend had joined the British forces and was killed. His shilling, however, was enough to get me back to Haslemere."[27]

The internment of the six pupils received scant notice in the October minutes of the Board meeting; it neither named those interned nor offered an explanation. "Then came the first internments, but thanks

---

[26] Ibid.

[27] Ilse Kaiser, conversation with Ian Holmby, unpublished article, "In Search of Kurt Deutscher."

to the great effort of some of you here, we have now got all our pupils back except for two, who have been shipped off to Canada before news of their release could reach them."[28] The two boys who opted to go to Canada were interned once again. One disappeared into the Canadian wilderness and the other committed suicide after the war upon learning his mother had died in a concentration camp.

Wolf Edelstein [Elston] offers his thoughts. "At age fourteen we were issued Alien Registration Cards which identified us as 'enemy aliens.' They were an ironic counterpart to our German passports, which had been stamped with a big scarlet letter J. Regardless of our official classification, the people of Britain and of Haslemere in particular, continued to treat us with remarkable understanding and consideration throughout the war. I learned to admire their innate sense of decency and fair play." During the war, about 8,000 people were interned in Britain, many on the Isle of Man.

Why were the Stoatley Rough children allowed to be scooped up by the authorities? The tribunals were orderly hearings for which Dr. Lion had always supplied documentation attesting to the children's security fitness; she'd always had time to prepare adequate documentation. According to Herta, Dr. Lion was afraid of authority, "a very Germanic thing." She believes Dr. Lion's fear rendered her unable to push the right buttons to protect her children from the "C" classification of "unfriendly alien." Renate Dorpalen [Dorpalen-Brocksieper] also wonders. "Why did not Dr. Lion intervene, or the governing body of the school? I cannot imagine they did not care, but perhaps they did not care enough. The school was not without connections to prominent, influential figures."[29] In her defense, Dr. Lion had plenty on her plate in the spring of 1940. As long as the war lasted, she would have been highly protective of public opinion toward her Germanic "family." It may have been that she simply did not understand what would happen to the

---

[28] Board meeting October 6, 1940, Stoatley Rough archives, London School of Economics. 1/1 (i).

[29] Renate Dorpalen [Dorpalen [Brocksieper] Stoatley Rough Newsletter Issue 14, May, 1997, p. 8.

children, or that she did not have the resources to get the paperwork together on time. Wolf remarked that after the fall of France, Churchill was so busy that when asked what to do about the refugees, he merely said, "Round "em all up." The matter was raised in the House of Lords but eventually the refugees were released. Wolf points out that even in America, he had to get permission from the District Attorney's office to travel more than fifty miles, and that the Canadians were even more paranoid – upon landing in Halifax in April, 1945, "we were put on a train and guarded by soldiers with fixed bayonets."

The children who returned to Stoatley Rough tried to pick up their lives where they left off. All three, Dieter and the two Household Girls, Ilse and Liesel, were sent to live on the Farm. Worse, they learned they would not be allowed to continue taking classes. Dr. Lion would not allow Dieter to prepare for the matric. By her decision, one that would not change in spite of the intercession of Dieter's sponsor, a member of her own Board, the esteemed Dr. Gooch, Dieter was deemed unsuitable for a university education. "This was the only time …that I remember being truly angry but discussions with Dr. Lion, Dr. Wolff and others made no difference. I was stunned…"[30]

The consequences of the Board's decision to give Dr. Lion unilateral sway over the fate of her children were felt by many others besides Dieter over the years. A child could never recover or move up in her estimation. Hans Loeser recalled, "I liked her. It also didn't take long for me to find out that I was one of the favored ones. She was a strong, commanding woman, with powerful ability and desire to do good. That quality was dominant, but she was also able to make life hard for those whom she didn't like for some reason or - more often - those whom she had wrongly pigeonholed as, say, potential farmers, or not suited - or only suited - for academic work, etc. Once one became classified in her mind, it was hard to break out even though the classification didn't fit." Inge Hamburger once wrote about dining table assignments, always posted for the children to read, and never to be altered. "Some children often

---

[30] Dieter Gaupp, Stoatley Rough Newsletter Issue 16, February, 1998 p. 20.

sat with Dr. Lion, but others were never given the privilege, and what made it worse is that I felt I deserved to be disliked."[31]

Dieter, devastated, moved his belongings from the Hut into the Farmhouse. Was it his fate to become a farm laborer?

---

[31] Inge Hamburger [Pavlowsky] Reminiscences, 1990. At the Stoatley Rough reunion in England in 1990, Inge learned that her tablemate at one of the meals felt she had suffered a similar fate from Dr. Lion. Inge said with a smile, "So it was not me, after all."

Banished to the Farm

T here were two jobs Dieter hated more than anything - hosing the manure from the cowshed and slopping the portable toilets. "While the floors were concrete and we had big rubber boots on our feet, the hosed manure had to be swept toward a tank in the ground which was teeming with worms. It turned my stomach."[32] On the first morning of his stay on the Farm he saw he had been assigned toilet bucket duty. He and his teammate, one of the Farm boys, decided to get it over with first thing. The Farm boy handed him the two poles that would be used to carry the waste containers. They had to slip the poles through the handles of buckets the size of a small oil drum, then move them one at a time to the manure pile. One of the boys would climb the manure pile and then, both boys striving to keep the bucket from sliding down toward the one on the lower plane, together they would overturn the contents. The trick was to get the bucket to the manure heap without letting it slide. It was warm on Dieter's first time he had this job, but in winter he knew there was the risk of slipping on the ice. The manure heap was several feet high, a stinking hill laced with straw mucked from the cowshed. "It was teamwork, and the close calls were many." (During the war, the system changed and human waste was dumped into a large hole on the premises.) Finding the silver lining in this cloud, Dieter had one good thing to say about the general plumbing setup on the Farm. "The toilets were certainly of a higher standard than many rural outhouses." But, he continued, using the toilets at night without any light was iffy. Sometimes the boys just "opened the

---

[32] Dieter Gaupp, Stoatley Rough Newsletter Issue 16, February, 1988 p. 22.

window in the hall." Wolf recalled that once the girls who also had to carry their buckets as well. "One of them tripped one night outside the open window of the boys' room, and the bucket spilled." Phew-eee!"

Sixteen-year old pupils not preparing for the Matric were sent to live in the farm house. With the school's population at its all time high, there was no room in the main manse. There were now one hundred people living and working at Stoatley Rough: "61 school children including 2 non-resident [day] pupils; nine Household Girls, seven helpers, (girls paid to come in and work during the day); ten farm pupils, two evacuees and eleven teachers."[33] Within a few months in 1940 the school took an additional seventeen children from the New Herrlingen School at Bunce Court who had been evacuated from their Kent home owing to its proximity to London. No one could see the farm house from the main house but since everyone got together every day for the main meal, those from below had to make the arduous ascent once a day. Going back to the farm, according to Dieter, was a breeze. "We negotiated the shortcut at a good speed, knowing when to brake or skirt a tree without losing the rhythm of the run, somewhat like a skier on a slalom run. The walk up took several minutes, the run down took less than one. Once, I was galloping down the trail while enemy planes overhead were being pursued by fighters. Suddenly one dived out of the sky towards the farm. …I was distracted just as I was about to make a tight turn around a tree. I crashed but wasn't hurt. Another time I almost reached the bottom when I caught my foot on a rock and went sailing through the air [doing] a complete flip, landing on my feet below the steps."[34]

Dieter described his new home. "It was probably a converted army hut, which included a kitchen, a living room, a bathroom and two toilets. Central heating of steam heat, generated by electricity…[kept] the outer parts of the room much warmer than the central areas, … a

---

[33] Board of Governors meeting, October 6, 1940. Stoatley Rough Archives 1/1 (i) London School of Economics. That year a list was kept of the Farm boys: Heinz Pachmyr, Fritz Drechsler, Franz Otto Ernst, Heinz Guggenheim, Goetz Houser, Hans Heinz, Helmut Lewent (Herta's brother), Peter Rosenfeld, and Ernst Roussal.

[34] Dieter Gaupp, Stoatley Rough Newsletter Issue 16, February, 1998. P. 20.

good [arrangement,] since our beds were against the walls....The toilets were primitive seats on portable drums which had to be cleaned daily. The walls were made of some kind of particle board which in damp weather assumed the consistency of cardboard; in both damp and freezing [weather] it could also become brittle, causing cracks, bulges and breaks."[35] There were several feed and animal sheds nearby, and near the end of the path, an old fashioned generator, a primitive one-cylinder diesel engine, dating from 1896, with an enormous flywheel that provided water to the main house.

In the summer of 1940, the Household Girls did their daily work, but most children had little to do. Foot travel across the heath was constrained because of the radar towers that would provide decisive defense against air strikes by the German Luftwaffe in the coming months. Dr. Lion continued her practice of bringing in guest speakers for Friday evening lectures: "Weather in the Making " was met with great success, and a Mr. Kewley (whose wife would help prepare the Household Girls for the King's College Housecraft exam in 1941) came in to give travel talks. Some of the Farm and Household workers passed the national poultry certificate examination that summer after attending poultry lectures at Surrey County Council at Guilford Technical Institute. Among them was one girl who had only taken the training in order to improve her English. The school sold sixteen pigs to the government.

In the fall, classes started again and Nore moved the children in the big house from the upper floors into lower rooms where windows were taped to prevent flying glass. Residents of the Farmhouse apparently never used the air raid shelter they had worked hard to dig into the side of the hill early in the war. In October the school was recognized as "efficient" by the Board of Education, a rating most welcomed by Dr. Lion and her Board. The School was now accredited.

Dieter and three of the full-paying academic boys lived in the Farmhouse, alongside six boys, most of them tuition free, who were training to be farmers. Caring for livestock and tilling and harvesting of

---

[35] Ibid.

fields gave everybody plenty to do. The school kept livestock now only if it was practical, e.g., a flock of ducks who refused to lay went under the knife. The pet goats and their kids (with one exception) disappeared. The Shetland pony was also sold. Animals remaining on the farm were "Black Beauty" or, according to some, "Betty", the horse that hauled a cart into town on a regular basis to fetch pig food or to take away trash; two milk cows named "Suzi" and "Hannah;" two heifers and a calf; a pony; a goat; four sows with "innumerable piglets;" fifty Rhode Island Red and Light Sussex Breeder chickens; and a pair of geese. There were also puppies from Fred Dreschler's long-haired mutt, Betty, sired by Hanna Nacken's Welsh terrier, Keedah, who dug under the chicken wire to get at her when she came into heat. Miss Nacken tried to deny that her dog would do such a thing, but one of the litter, a little thing who was the spitting image of Keedah, became Keedah's best friend in the ensuing months.

Sometimes someone would refuse to do a chore. After a series of farm managers, young Mr. Edward Hughes from Wales was in charge by 1940, and he was a man who did not countenance rebellion. He tried to head off resistance with "Don't argue with me," but usually both parties stormed up the hill to Dr. Lion's office for resolution. Edward Hughes spoke with a broad accent and possessed, to Dieter, "a strong physique and stubborn mentality,"[36] but he provided a vital masculine role model. Dieter wrote, "Sometimes the farm boys played soccer with Mr. Hughes on an uneven pasture staked out with improvised goals and sidelines. Competition was fierce. There were no set teams, but whoever played against Mr. Hughes relished the chance to beat him or outfox him. They took the risk of fierce physical contact and many a time Mr. Hughes and one of the big boys would find themselves in a shoving match that, in turn, sometimes degenerated into animosity. Such an instance would be cause for intense discussion later among the boys. Lacking fathers, they found in Mr. Hughes the much-needed strength against which to test themselves. Good sportsmanship was the rule, and the games provided a necessary outlet."[37]

---

[36] Ibid.
[37] Ibid. p. 20

Mr. Hughes had a sense of humor, luckily for Wolf. One summer day Wolf had the audacity to push Mr. Hughes into the swimming pool. Mr. Hughes, who had been wearing his swimming trunks, nevertheless emerged unsmiling from the water and grabbed Wolf by the scruff of his neck, marched him to the changing booth. Wolf reports that Mr. Hughes "stood by me with his hand raised in a threatening manner while I changed back into my swim trunks, marched me back to the pool and chucked me in" to the delight of the onlookers. There was never rancor between them over the incident, and Wolf admired the man. Like others, Wolf could produce an excellent imitation of Mr. Hughes' heavy Welch accent when the instructor was out of earshot. Rolling his "r's" and broadening his "a's," Wolf went around chanting, "the r-r-rahbbits, the r-r-rahts, and cahterpillars have bahdly dahmaged the cahbbages").

The boys on the farm were known to have daily rounds of what could be called amiable fighting with each other. Alexander Finkler made light of the almost daily combat in his ironical commentary on school life pegged to the alphabet. "A - America seems to be a glorious country and it is so exciting to have a visa to the United States;…E – Education. The manners of the farm boys are said to be atrocious. Efforts have been made to improve them. Now everybody has to feed the pigs in evening dress;… I – Imagination. Our milkman dreams that he is the dairy owner." When he gets to "U," he targets the roughhousing on the Farm. "U – Unity under the farm boys is excellent. Every day is a fight and some people feel that the walls will soon look like Swiss cheese."[38]

In 1940 the school acquired a tractor from a wealthy gentleman who had an "iron horse" to spare. An unidentified farm boy wrote about the gift in *The Bridge*. "Imagine, a tractor as a present! It was brought over in a butcher's van. I do not know whether you can call it amusement or disappointment which the boys felt…The tractor had firstly only two wheels, secondly [could get] only 8 h.p., and third, it [was so small that it] could enter the horse-stable and still leave room for the horse! The

---

[38] Alexander Finkler, *The Bridge*, Vol. 1, 1940.

engine was probably the greatest attraction and [at the same time a] bother. It was pretty strong and difficult to handle once it worked. I say 'once it worked' because it was often a long time before it worked."[39] In 1941 another tractor arrived. Dr. Lion said, "The greatest surprise for everybody was the present of a real tractor worth a hundred pounds or more. It was given to us by a personally unknown friend of our cause, after we have been struggling for some time." Wolf remembered that he earned three pence per hour for weighting down the bouncing mowing machine that Mr. Hughes pulled with the tractor over a hummocky pasture, giving him a sore bottom. Dr. Lion also wrote that "the first real Land Army girl, [Miss Woolgar] a girl who really wants to do farming and is going to take it up as her career, has arrived recently and does her pioneer work quite bravely."[40]

Mr. Hughes maintained a farm diary, filling it with rich details about the farm which by then had become though small, a productive entity with a serious purpose. Pages from his farm diary show that he collected wild bees with "a smoker," a skep [wicker beehive], a white sheet and a short knife; he took a crossbred (Guernsey-Shorthorn) bull calf and a sow and five pigs to market; he was pleased that the ordinary and "not a pedigree" Red Poll cow, "frequently milked by different milkers often inexperienced" was yielding 3 – 4 gallons daily." In the spring he noted that carrots, swedes (rutabagas), peas, onions, leeks, sugarbeet, beans and potatoes [were] all in the ground. He also noted in midsummer that the workers were gathering hay into stacks."[41]

Birgitte Heinsheimer, the girl who took poultry classes to improve her English pronunciation, was an enthusiastic worker. "We have an incubator where, I hope, we shall very soon rear some more chickens. All our birds are kept out-of-doors and the ducks enjoy a nice pond

---

[39] Author unknown, from *The Bridge*, Vol 2, August – September, 1940.

[40] Dr. Lion, *Rundbrief*, dated May 20, 1941. Stoatley Rough archives, file 1/1 (ii) London School of Economics. Women who took over men's jobs on farms during the war were part of the Women's Land Army (WLA) and widely known as "Land Girls."

[41] Edward Hughes, Portions of his farm diary reproduced in *The Bridge*, Vol. 2, August – September, 1941.

next to the swimming pool which was made by the boys last year. Now for the cheese. I do not know, how many sorts of cheese there are, and from white cheese to gorgonzola every country has her own secret way of production. The white cheese [cottage cheese] is the simplest to make; it is the sort which we had last summer and which we saw on the tables in the evening. How we did like it! It tasted so good and is so easy to make; pour the sour milk into a thin cloth, hang it up and let the milk water drain away, and mix what remains with salt, with cream, if you have it, and with caraway seeds."[42]

Farm work was strenuous. Weekly duties consisted of preparing breakfast, cleaning the building, and emptying the toilet tanks; children had to bring in the cows in the morning and milk them, feed them, clean the sheds, sties and chicken coops. Dieter liked caring for the hogs, although the less experienced children had to be careful not to get caught between a hog and the wall of the pen. One night Dieter stayed up with another boy to tend to a sow who was about to have a litter. She gave birth to one pig after another, frequently standing up to count them, and then dropping back on her belly to continue the process. He wrote that the boys had to rescue piglets that might otherwise have been squashed by her ponderous body. The boys made their own swill in a large iron kettle over an open fire fed with wood that they'd chopped earlier. "We used all leftovers and trimmings of vegetables from the kitchen, vegetables that were not fit for the kitchen, and special potatoes purchased for hog consumption only. The odour from the cooking was as from the best of stews..."[43]

The worst job was harvesting cabbages in the winter that were destined to be cow feed. "The cabbage heads were frozen and wet and we had to cut them from the stem with the cold seeping through my gloves."[44] Dieter also hated cleaning out the chicken coop, the odor clinging to his body and clothes which he imagined was not always cleansed away with a shower. Another unpopular job was to attempt to

---

[42] Bridgitte Heinsheimer [Pring-Mill] *The Bridge*, 1940.
[43] Dieter Gaupp, *Stoatley Rough Newsletter* Issue 16, February, 1998 p. 23.
[44] Ibid.

exterminate mice and rats who invaded the feed shed, rodents entirely at ease with two cats who spent their time dozing in languorous comfort inside the farm house. It became ongoing sport. The boys tried inserting an air rifle into one of the holes then shooting, but they never hit anything. They couldn't use poison because it might affect the feed, so they began to set traps. Freeing and re-setting the traps became one of those rotating assignments that nobody wanted.

Farm people ate breakfast and supper on the Farm. "Breakfast duty had its hazards. First of all, farm schedules are strict: cows need to be milked at the same time daily, without exceptions. School begins for certain people at a given time, …and food had to be on the table and ready on time. …There was [always] the risk that the porridge might not be ready because the fire would not burn or it became burned on the bottom of the big iron pot., giving rise to grumbles and complaints. We laid the fire for the next day's breakfast the evening before. The wood had to be chopped, the paper and matches available, the pots and pans ready. …It was strictly wood burning fire and one always hoped that the wood was dry enough to burn, hard enough to last, and of sufficient quantity. …The tables had to be set, the milk had to be filtered by those taking care of the cows…Once the porridge was on the fire it needed frequent stirring. We were about 15-20 persons at the table, all hungry and hard working, all critical if not satisfied….I always felt the horde's restlessness close behind."[45]

Taking advantage of the use of the kitchen, Dieter and his friends developed what they called Our Weekly Meal plan, OWM for short, for their weekly special meal when they would cook up something the rest of the school's population did not have in the main house. One summer day they made an egg custard by using eggs and milk from the farm, unrationed custard powder, and blueberries from the surrounding woods. They put the blueberries into the hot yellow custard and let it stand overnight in the cold pantry. In the morning

---

[45] Ibid. P. 24

they eagerly fetched their treat and discovered the gelatinous treat had turned "richly-green."[46]

Everything was recycled. Manure and chicken droppings became fertilizer; Mr. Hughes, the only one strong enough to work behind the horse pulling a heavy, one bladed plough, churned crop remains back into the ground. Weeding, cultivating and digging out produce was done by hand, a challenge in the thin soil strewn with rocks. Dieter said, "We'd set aside the rocks we had dug up, the following season there were just as many as before."

Later in the war years, Dr. Lion suggested that Mr. Hughes might grow sugar beets. It sounded like a great idea. By producing their own sugar, the school could supplement their rationed allotment and satisfy the children's constant craving for sweets. In the spring he duly put in a crop of beet plants. They grew to maturity and then were harvested (with great difficulty, since they grow with multiple roots and cannot be pulled up like carrots) and mashed. The farm boys set up a large cauldron to boil down the pulp. Upon tasting the outcome, there was disappointment. Unfortunately, they had made an "inedible concoction with a bitter aftertaste." Determined not to waste food, the authorities instructed Miss Demuth to serve some of the mash to the children. Nobody touched it. Undeterred, the cook then stored the bitter syrup derived from the mash in a large barrel in the kitchen, ostensibly for cooking. Nobody recalls that it was ever used.

Mr. Hughes left Stoatley Rough in 1941 to continue his training at Culham Training College in Arlingdon, Berkshire. He was replaced by a Mr.Bibbe. Mr. Hughes wrote to Dr. Lion September 18, 1941, that he was "learning, even though it is the toughest clay I have ever met with," and he included a recommendation that Dr. Lion not sell the old sow. She seemed, in his opinion, "fit for another season." He concluded with words of gratitude. "I often think of you all and shall never forget how much you did to make a very lonely man very comfortable. I only hope that when I have completed my training here, that I shall secure a good appointment with as happy a home as I found at Stoatley Rough."

---

[46] Ibid.

The Droning of Bombers

The spring of 1940 was brightened with the arrival of the duplicating, or mimeograph machine that Herta dubbed the "Gestetner multiplying monster." Dr. Wolff set about reprising her former job as editor of Die Frau. She produced a cheerful newsletter called The Bridge which she called a "magazine." With the exception of Mr. Obee and Mr. Phillips, practically everyone contributed. In her article, "A Glimpse in the Office," Herta explained that now the school had time to publish a magazine since mail deliveries were down to one delivery per day. And besides she said, "Something good must come out of the war," unconsciously channeling the words of her adult bosses. Herta typed the nearly forty single-spaced pages of Volume I, and Dr. Wolff put the pages together with the artwork that some of the talented youngsters at the school like Inge Hamburger [Pavlowsky] and Lili [Putti] Kassel [Wronker] had produced. Charming drawings of ducks, shoes being repaired, and children diving into the pool, dancing, waiting for a haircut or studying adorned the pages. Dr. Wolff fed the masters into the big drum, Herta turned the handle, and out came the freshly-inked copies. Only two editions of The Bridge saw the light of day, Vol. I, issued on the 14th – 15th of May, 1940, and Vol. II, numbers 1 and 2, issued in August / September of 1941, but they offer a window into school life in their German or English articles, almost each page bearing some kind of pen and ink illustration.

Dr. Lion, now in her seventh year in England and forty-seven years old, addressed the war in the first issue with eloquence and passion. She recalled having been a teenager during the First World War, and offered the benefit of her experience. "We knew our own lives were unimportant at a time when masses were suffering. But we were quite confident, because we felt that we had run into the path of a new wind, which – although it sometimes blew against us – would in the long run, help us on our way." She then referred to a picture, famous in its day, that she had mounted in the school library. It was Max Liebermann's (1847 - 1935) 'Netzflickerinnen' [The Net Menders], a portrayal of women mending huge piles of brown fishing nets under a cloudy blue sky. "It expresses what I want to say. 'Wonder is the beginning of worship.' And Stoatley Rough was a wonder for all of us, coming after the darkest days of our lives. It has kept its overwhelming beauty, not only on this exceptional spring Sunday on which I write, but on every day in the year…We have not lost a single of our old friends since war broke out and of that we are glad because we have had to fight still harder for our existence and for the welfare of our younger children. Many of them are entirely separated from their relatives and it is still more important for us to provide the 'home' where they can be quietly growing up."

On other pages, children wrote about trips to the museum, working in the garden, baking cookies. One poignant section was devoted entirely to essays about homes left behind. And of course, they wrote about the war.

The following piece by Inge Schleimer [Wurm], fourteen, appeared in *The Bridge*. She had been inspired by the newly fallen Christmas snow that covered "not only the houses, mountains and all the other concrete things, but also the evil of all living creatures. I sat at the window and looked at the white town thinking of that which belonged to the past and to that which was to follow. My thoughts presented themselves to me as a great question-mark. There was a sound like soft music as if chimes rang. Without noticing it I closed my eyes, and then everything became light and I saw one image after the other passing by. There was the ship which was to carry us to America, and when at last we stood on American ground, our father met us. Naturally we had much to tell each other after such a long separation...and we went by car to our simple but pretty little house...Then I passed over many years and saw myself going for a walk with my children followed by a small puppy. I saw how I kept the house, cooked for my family and prepared surprises on Christmas Eve, lit the candles and...everything vanished. Through thinking of Christmas I was brought back into the tangible present."[47]

Hitler had decided to invade Great Britain by way of the English Channel in "Operation Sea Lion," first launching a massive effort to cripple the Royal Air Force. While the German air force bombed British air fields, factories and cities in what was known as The Battle of Britain, it began to concentrate on London in what would be called "The Blitz." [Lightening (strike)] a determined, sustained campaign of night time bombing that lasted from late summer, 1940 until May of 1941. Luftwaffe Chief of Air Staff, Hans Jeschonnek, rashly predicted the invasion of Britain would take about six or seven weeks, but Commander of the Luftwaffe, Hermann. Goering, knew better. "An Englishman is like a wounded bull, he is most dangerous when he is injured."[48]

---

[47] Inge Schleimer, "The Past – Music", *The Bridge*, Vol. II, 1 and 2, August, September, 1941, p. 54

[48] The Battle of Britain Historical Society, The Chronology, p. 23 http/www. battleofbritain.net/0023.html, accessed May, 2005.

What relative peace the pupils may have enjoyed in the summer of 1940 was over. Only forty miles from London and located along a major flight path, the school provided a front row seat to the action. Renate Dorpalen recalled, "We heard a buzzing as if from innumerable bees in the sky above. It was the sound of squadron after squadron of Spitfires and Hurricanes taking to the air and flying towards the English Channel. Searchlights probed the sky for Nazi bombers droning overhead until, finally, an All Clear was sounded and we emerged from the cellars....The German bombers came seldom in bad weather but were certain to show up in full moonlight. Standing on the heath near the school we could see the stars and watch the searchlights crisscrossing the sky in a frantic hunt for bombers. We could hear the approaching roar of enemy planes and then see their flares. First would come the lead plane, which set flares at four points to mark the target zone, followed by the squadrons. Their incendiary bombs lit up the area in the distance. We could watch the bombs falling and, moments later, hear the faint sound as they hit. Occasionally there would be aerial dogfights. Each time a German plane was shot down we cheered, and mourned the loss of an RAF plane."[49]

During the Blitz, children at Stoatley Rough saw flames in the horizon nightly as whole neighborhoods in London lit up with incendiary bombs. The bombardment lasted over fifty-seven straight nights. Articles written for The Bridge during this time show that the response to the drama the children were witnessing was varied, ranging from indifference to amusement to fear. According to Eyewitness to History.com, the Germans committed 348 German bombers escorted by 648 fighters on the first day alone, blasting London for about seventeen hours.

Creature comforts came to an end as a steady flow
of refugee children came and left, children constantly
moving into the shelter each night to sleep in a mad

---

[49] Renate Dorpalen [Dorpalen-Brocksieper] Stoatley Rough Newsletter, Issue 7 p. 22

game of musical beds. They were constantly alerted by the school's air raid signal, a sustained bong-bong, ding- ding-ding of gong and bell. Wolf wrote, "Before the war, girls slept in rooms on the second floor (circa 1938) and boys on the third, but when the war came it was deemed safer to move girls to the ground floor and boys to the basement next to the "Schoolroom".[50] Children slept on mattresses on the floor packed in like sardines, and also on the shelves normally used for sorted laundry. Renate Dorpalen recalls that she moved nine times during her six-year stay at Stoatley Rough. Air raids became routine.

The younger boys found the Blitz exciting, especially the dogfights. After the sound of planes faded into the distance, they would run outside to pick up spent cartridges which they traded with each other. A trip to London yielded other treasures: pieces of molten land mines, shrapnel from bomb casings, and shreds of silk parachutes. Obo said, "We used to look for and PICK UP exploded smoke bombs and what might have been anti personnel bombs that had been dropped on the Heath, not realizing what mortal danger we put ourselves in. When I think about this now I can only say that someone was looking out for us."

With the exception of Peter Gaupp who, true to his gentle nature, lacked interest in fast-moving machines as a matter of principle, the other boys became intensely involved with airplanes. They educated themselves with official pictures and small metal cast models of airplanes and warships. Dieter wrote, "The plane models, made by Dinky-Toy, were very good scale models and augmented our avid interest in plane identification. Some models were harder to obtain than others. Sometimes we would project the images of these planes on a wall in a dark room with a flashlight and have the other person guess what we were showing. The models of warships came from boys

---

[50] Wolf Elston *On the Occasion of Nore Astfalck's 90th Birthday,*

who had brought them from Germany. While we had no occasion to see warships, we could talk authoritatively about them when they were reported on the evening news or in the newspapers.[51]

The boys had plenty of chances to identify the planes. Over the five years of war, the boys learned to recognize each type and version of British, German and later, American aircraft in the sky. Sometimes their experience with the planes and their pilots was weirdly intimate. Goldy recalled, "The view into the valley (from the manor house) was beautiful and our strategic position high up above the valley enabled us to look down into the cockpits of passing fighter planes when they flew low. None could go faster than about 400 miles per hour. When the pilots were taking a training flight through the valley we could usually wave to them and they would sometimes wave back."[52] The German air force was divided into *Gruppen* [groups] much like the RAF with its Fighter, Bomber, Coastal, and Training Squadrons, Groups and Commands.[53] The boys could distinguish one from another. Today they easily detect errors in old World War II movies where directors have substituted aerial footage. Wolf avers, "I'm appalled by the sloppy way *The History Channel* makes up collages of alleged events in the air war in WWII and to my surprise, P-51's suddenly morph into Spitfires, B-24's into Lancasters, etc."

The boys saw so many airplanes because not only was Haslemere situated between Portsmouth and London, it was also close to the two largest air force bases in England: Biggin Hill and Croyden. The first, the "aerodrome" Biggin Hill, in northern Kent, 20 miles southeast

---

[51] Dieter Gaupp, Stoatley Rough Newsletter, Issue 12, October, 1996. p. 35.

[52] Hans [John Goldy] Goldmeier unpublished *Memoirs*, Part 1, p. 49.

[53] At first, the British planes were no match for the Messerschmitt Bf 109 and 110 fighters, and later the Focke-Wulfs. British aircraft developed during the 30s such as the Bristol Bulldog, the Hawker series and the Gloster Gladiator (including some old biplanes), initially slow and cumbersome, were soon upgraded. Airplanes began to roll off the assembly lines: The Boulton-Paul "Defiant" (1936), the Bristol Blenheim (1938), the Hawker Hurricane (1936) and the Supermarine Spitfire (1938,) the Bristol Beaufighter (1939), and the DeHavilland Mosquito (1942) along with constant upgrades of the others.After 1941, the Americans filled the skies with Corsair, Tomahawk, and Mustang airplanes.

of Central London, was supposed to protect London. Its hangers, workshops, mess halls, shelters and married quarters were made ready by 1938. Biggin Hill was to be one of the most important bases during the Battle of Britain.[54] The other major British airbase was Croydon, fifteen miles south of London. Imperial Airways was founded at Croydon in 1924 and many aviators started or completed flights there, including Charles Lindbergh, who landed the Spirit of St. Louis at Croydon amidst a crowd of 100,000 people in May, 1927.

The Hut boys lost their soccer, kick-the-can and hiking grounds (parts of Hindhead Common and Gibbet Hill) when the RAF cordoned the areas off with barbed wire to build lookout stations. Radar was a potential target of the German air force, a potentially powerful technology. It more than proved its worth during the Blitz in its ability to warn of incoming planes, allowing the RAF to be ready when the German planes appeared on the horizon.[55] Even closer was the RAF Experimental Station at Farnborough, enclosed by a thick hedge to protect top-secret designs from prying eyes. Wolf recalls that there were gaps in the hedge and the boys would slow down their bikes, hoping to get a glimpse.

As the Hut boys grew older, the school expected them to honor the custom of helping the younger children, a duty that sometimes involved the simple act of giving comfort. One day, Nore asked Goldy to leave the Hut on a temporary basis to sleep with a roomful of small boys in the manor house. Goldy recalled, "The German planes [sometimes] came closer to Haslemere than usual and there was some anti-aircraft fire and concussions from bombs which made the birds chirp even at night. (Bombs can sound just like thunder, especially when far away, but

---

[54] After the war, Biggin Hill became an RAF hiring center and, until 1992, the site of an annual air show on Battle of Britain Day, 15 September. Today the site houses a small civilian airport and is owned by Formula One magnate Bernie Ecclestone. Http://Answers.com; accessed May25, 2005.

[55] While British radar technology was superb, the country recognized early on that its supply source was inadequate. In 1940 the British made an informal arrangement with top U.S. military and industrial leaders to share their technology for mass production processes supplied by the Americans. The agreement saved the day.

apparently there are differences in the atmospheric pressure that make birds chirp when there are bombs but not when there is thunder.) One night the bombs seemed louder than usual, and one of the boys came into my little room as if to ask me to stop it all. He was afraid too and asked to stay... I remember getting his mattress and putting it on the floor next to me, holding his hand from my bed until he fell asleep."[56] The boys also remember some close calls. Dieter was lying in bed on the Farm one summer night when an air raid sounded. As usual, the Farm kids hadn't bothered to put up the blackout curtains and the windows were open. Dieter was lying in the dark watching the searchlights of London sweep the sky. Then came the sound of an airplane. A single bomber was approaching Haslemere. Dieter saw a big flash of light over the sleeping town followed by the burst of a bomb. The flimsy farm building shook and his bed shook. Then there was an awful quiet. The next day, he learned that a German bomber under pursuit had jettisoned its bomb while trying to hit the railway yards. Instead, he had scored a near miss on the little Haslemere museum. There were no casualties. Another time, a bomb fell into the courtyard of the Haslemere Hospital and did not explode. Later, it was exhibited during a war bond drive.

The maintenance man and general factotum, Mr. Obee, was an official airplane spotter. He came to the school a few times each week to do the odd job and was much admired by Dr. Lion for scrounging parts to keep things running. The boys admired him because he belonged to the Royal Observer Corps, i.e., he was a spotter for enemy aircraft. Wolf recalled, "We all read his copies of the *Aeroplane Spotter* avidly and all of us became expert spotters." Obo said that, "when Mr. Obee brought us our copy of the weekly *Aeroplane Spotter* tabloid, we would first turn to the quiz on the back page to see who first could identify the Friend or Foe partial plane views. Renate Dorpalen described the little handyman with fine detail. He was "a friendly talkative handyman

---

[56] Hans [Goldy, John] Goldmeier, *Memoires Part 1*. Wolf later wrote that the noise came mostly from the British defensive planes. "After the 1940-41 Blitz, there were "little Blitzes" in the springs of 1943 and 1944. Bythat time, Briths AA defenses were formidable. That's where most of the noise came from. Then, in 1944, shortly after D-Day, came the V-1s and (later) V-2s."

with ill-fitting dentures and a Cockney accent, who lived in a nearby town. [He] consumed quantities of tea before contemplating [any] task as did his ever-present dog who was provided with a special saucer near his master. The genius of this man lay in his ability to make any repairs presently, which usually meant some time, often never. He seemed to be as puzzled about us as we were about him. Later, however, he proved to be a vital resource when things got scarce during the war, for he always had a friend who just happened to have what some of us needed."[57] He was famously known for the following line regarding his dentures: "Somebody asked me if they were my own teeth. I told 'em: 'they jolly well ought to be, I paid fifteen quid for 'em!'"

In his youth, Mr. Obee had traveled the world as a soldier and evangelical missionary, but what the boys liked about him was his ancient Vauxhall, a rattletrap that somehow he'd been allowed to keep. (It was rare to have a car since gas was rationed.) Dieter marveled, "the fact that it functioned at all often seemed like a miracle to us, though we knew nothing about cars. First of all, it looked old, of a bygone vintage. Secondly, it sounded old. It put-putted. At times it roared. It had squeaks. Most remarkable was its ignition system. I am not sure if I have the sequence correct, but it seems that to start the car (if it did not turn over the first time), the hood had to be raised, the radio turned on, the windshield wipers activated, followed by a lunge to a location under the hood (bonnet) to catch the spark which would start the engine. Given that Mr Obee usually wore a jacket, the added sight of coat tails flying made the performance all the more fascinating."[58]

August 13, 1940 was a day Wolf would never forget, since it was not only his twelfth birthday but also *"Adlertag"* [Eagle Day], the official opening of the Battle of Britain and the prelude to invasion.

> "[We were] awakened about 6:00 a.m. by the throbbing of many aircraft engines. It was some time

---

[57] Renate Dorpalen [Dorpalen-Brocksieper] Stoatley Rough Newsletter, Issue 5, June, 1994, p. 41.

[58] Peter Gaupp, Stoatley Rough Newsletter, Issue 10, February, 1996, p. 10.

before we spotted dozens of silvery dots, high in the sky and in neat geometrical formations. A few moments later, a pair of Hurricanes swooped over our heads and climbed out of sight. We heard distant machine-gun fire and thuds. Only then did the sirens of Haslemere sound the alert, followed by the school alarm signal, the alternate sounding of a gong and ringing of a bell. We dashed over to the main building and were told to take shelter in the coal cellar, probably the most unsafe place around. Someone remembered that it was my birthday and everybody sang 'Happy Birthday to You' and *'Hoch Soll Ehr Leben'* ['High Should He Live,' the German equivalent of 'For He's a Jolly Good Fellow']. I thanked Hermann Goering for providing fireworks for my birthday party. Later…Miss Evans took us to Frensham Pond which was being drained because it was a landmark for German bombers. We splashed and crawled through the mud of the remaining puddles, collecting fresh-water mussels and minnows. Mr. Obee had agreed to pick us up in his ancient car. Instead, he took one look and said, "Oh no! Not in my car you don't!" After we had scraped off most of the mud, he allowed us to stand on the running boards all the way back to school."[59]

Mr. Obee will be remembered most for having once faced down the British army. Dieter tells the story:

"Mr Obee had to go to Hindhead from time to time which entailed crossing the dirt road across the 'heath.' The actual distance was probably no more than five miles, but the trip was slow. Frequently the road sank between two banks to a point where it could not

---

[59] Wolf Edelstein [Elston] Memories of Stoatley Rough, 1990, p. 8.

be seen. On one side of the road was the expanse of heath, on the other, a rolling slope. Tanks for practice runs and manoeuvres frequently used the site. On this particular day, Mr Obee was returning from Hindhead and had reached the sunken part of the road when, up ahead, a column of tanks was advancing in the opposite direction. For each this was a one way road. Mr Obee had been in World War I – he had fought in Gallipoli among other places (where he said he spent much of his time on his stomach overlooking the harbor, according to Wolf) – and perhaps because of this experience, he was not impressed. I believe that a certain British pride may have motivated him. He continued on his appointed route. He could have done little else, other than retreat until there was sufficient space to leave the road, but he didn't. The car was rocking along, slowly, hitting boulders and rocks as it went, emitting its usual range of sounds. The tank leader soon realised that there was no solution available, other than to reverse. Thus the entire tank column, some six or more vehicles, put their caterpillar tracks in reverse and retreated in the face of Mr Obee's relentless progress! Whether greetings were exchanged, I don't know; Mr Obee never stopped."[60]

From August 24 to September 6 the Germans sent over an average of a thousand planes a day. On September 15, 1940, the British RAF intercepted, diverted or shot down seventy-six bombers, escorted by three times as many fighters, and routed a second wave of 200 more. Historians write that Goering's bombing of London extended the time for Britain to manufacture armaments and planes for future warfare on the Continent. But the attack exacted an immense toll. Intense bombing

---

[60] Op. cit. Wolf Edelstein [Elston] adds that the army was probably the Canadian army, the 2nd Canadian Armoured Brigade had its HQ in Hindhead and would become famous after the Normandy D-Day.

lasted until May of 1941, leaving 375,000 Londoners homeless. Hitler's bomber losses over England had been so severe that the Luftwaffe never fully recovered from the blow it received in the skies over Britain that late summer and fall. The Battle of Britain was effectively over (although the Blitz continued). Damage had been inflicted on Buckingham Palace, Westminster Abbey, and the Chamber of the House of Commons. After June, 1941, air raids became sporadic as the *Luftwaffe* turned its attention to the Soviet Union and the Mediterranean. The schoolchildren at Stoatley Rough were left to deal with the psychological consequences of the German's attacks. For the rest of their lives, they would not forget they had witnessed Britain's "finest hour."

Coping with Fear

W hile plane spotting may have been exciting, fear lurked beneath the surface of daily life at Stoatley Rough School.[61] Dorit Bader Whiteman stated that Jewish refugee children suffered, no matter where they had been during the war.[62] Not only were the children at Stoatley Rough uncertain whether their parents were alive, they also thought they might be attacked: a German plane might drop a bomb or paratroopers might land on the heath bordering the school. And then there was the insurmountable problem of nationality: they were, after all, Germans and Austrians, the enemy. Finally, some of the children had been in London when the first serious bombing began. The school was still on holiday and quite a few children had gone to London when Dr. Lion called them back. Wolf recalls, it was "too late for some of the younger ones – they would have screaming nightmares for a long time." Fear might have destroyed the slender thread of courage that sustained the children but for the discipline of hard work and shared responsibilities that Nore and the others imposed on the children each day. Hope and hard work kept everyone going, regardless of realities. Typical was Ernst Wohlgemuth, a young boy from Germany, who said

---

[61] Wolf believes that although the children were frightened on a regular basis, they were not "continually on the edge of our seats, worrying about bombs, safety, being taken for spies, etc." He wrote, "The wonder is how normal our lives were in the midst of horror. That was the school's principal achievement."

[62] Dorit Baden Whiteman, *The Uprooted: a Hitler Legacy*, Insight Books, Plenum Press, 1993.

many years later that he "wrote to his mother every day since he first had come to Stoatley Rough and never saw her again.[63]

Renate Dorpalen, at seventeen, arrived from Berlin in May, 1939, typifying many Roughians as a child of privilege who suffered a wrenching loss of family. Renate's wealthy family had lived in the Charlottenburg district of Berlin, the same area where Dr. Lion and her German staff had lived. Her father was a gynecologist; her mother sat on several charitable boards of directors, including one of the three Pestalozzi-Froebel Houses in Berlin through which she came to know Dr. Lion, who had spent time there as a teacher. In that capacity, Renate's mother introduced young Renate to several leading feminists of the time: Dr. Lion (who had been in her home), Alice Salomon, and in particular, Hildegard von Gierke, the great educator and a close friend of Renate's mother. The family was assimilated and staunchly patriotic, with banking money on Renate's mother's side, law and commerce on her father's. Another key member of this close-knit family was the housekeeper whom they called "Mürt," who also lived in the spacious apartment with the family and a few domestic staff. Mürt, A.K.A. Martha Grams was a fair-haired woman with grayish eyes and a long braid, a poster-woman for the healthy Germanic Aryan.

Everybody in Renate's family played an instrument and spoke fluent French. Unlike many Jewish children who were schooled in the public system, Renate did not experience harassment at her post-primary school, a Huguenot school, the *Hohenzollern Oberlyceum* in Berlin-Weilmersdorf, where everybody spoke French. During *Kristallnacht* her father fled to the country home of an Aryan patient. During that long night young Renate watched Mürt politely admit the Nazi police into the house several times to allow them to search the premises. (Owing to Mürt's age at the time, 57, the Aryan servant had been allowed to remain in service to the Jewish Dorpalens.) After *Kristallnacht* the family broke up. One brother was sent to the U.S. to live with an uncle; another to England into British military service; the third ended up starting a business in South America. Renate would go to Stoatley

---

[63] .Margaret Dove [Faulkner], in a letter to Herta Lewent [Loeser], March 31, 1990.

Rough and her parents would stay in Berlin to wait for visas to the U.S. On May 28, 1939, Renate's father accompanied her to Hamburg where she would start her journey to England. They stayed in the best hotel in town. She was surprised to see him wearing his Iron Cross pin in his lapel in an effort to ward off suspicions. By then, Nazi bullies were openly arresting Jews right off the street, night and day. Renate's trepidation about the impending voyage took away her appetite and she found it difficult to converse with her father that night. When they said goodbye the next morning, her father told her she was loved no matter if they ever saw each other again, and when her bus pulled away, he waved his handkerchief at her according to the custom of the day. She arrived in Haslemere the next day. Dr. Lion received her warmly. At first she went to work typing for Dr. Wolff, but Renate soon tired of the isolation of the job and became a Household Girl, welcoming the long hours of hard work. From then on she kept to herself, plunging into work and studies without forming attachments, finding solace in the many letters from home and her brothers who were now scattered in various parts of the world.

Like Renate, the children at Stoatley Rough seldom talked about their fears with the brisk and sensible adults who marched them through their daily routine. Goldy wrote, "Denial was the main psychological mechanism used by the children. Some had not heard from their parents for months, even years; others received a card through the Red Cross from parents pretending that all was well. It was already known that the Germans were killing people but the children whose parents were in danger seemed to totally ignore this. As for how all this applied to me, I still find it hard to understand how I could watch in the distance the red clouds over London, the result of flames from the air-raids, without it occurring to me that Mother or Ralph would be in the thick of this. I was too occupied watching as the searchlights tried to pick out the German airplanes and wondering how many would be shot down." [64] Wolf remembered the school's response was something between "Prussian discipline and the British stiff upper lip. Boys had

---

[64] Hans [John, Goldy] Goldmeier, Memoirs, Part 1, January 2000, p. 55.

been taught to keep their emotions to themselves. Any show of emotion was met with *"Stell' dich nicht so an!"* [Don't make a fuss!] He concludes, "When I reached age sixty, I decided I'd earned the right to make a fuss (or to 'stell' mich an')."

Sometime in the spring of 1942, the messages from Renate's mother stopped coming. Unknown to Renate, her parents had been deported to Theresienstadt, a "model" concentration camp designed to house privileged Jews from Czechoslovakia, Austria and Germany. A year later, in August, 1943, Műrt, who had remained in Berlin, wrote: "My beloved child, news from Alice [Renate's mother]. Deeply saddened: Georg [Renate's father] died on December 13.God be with her and us."[65] After the war, Renate held in her hand the postcard her mother had sent to Műrt from Theresienstadt about her husband's death. She noted "A reply to the card could be sent only via the *Reichsvereinigung der Juden* [State Association of Jews] in Germany, Berlin-Charlottenburg 2, Kantstrasse 158 – not very far from where we used to live. My mother's message was written in pencil, almost illegible and with spelling errors." Her mother had addressed Műrt with the familiar "du," an act that profoundly upset Renate, remembering the strict relationship once maintained between the mistress of the house and her servant. Renate reflected on the situation:

> "It was truly symbolic of Nazi aims and left me in a quandary about my mother's feelings, almost more so than about any other deprivation or degradation she had suffered. I grieved for the woman she no longer was... Mail had [been] a tangible sign of their presence in our separation. Separation allowed for hope, my struggle between hope and despair was present at all times. And now my father had been dead for almost a year when I thought him alive. How does one mourn such a loss, hidden beneath the fragile hope of a reunion? What

---

[65] Renate Dorpalen [Dorpalen-Brocksieper] Stoatley Rough Newsletter, Issue 9, October, 1995, p. 30.

had happened to him? And what about my mother? To picture her apart from my father was inconceivable. I did not want to think what life was to be without my parents. In reality I had been alone for more than four years."

Renate soldiered on with her household chores and her studies, refusing to give in to despair. She articulates her uncertainty, dread, and lack of control over events at the time. "But the tears did not come and life at Stoatley Rough continued in its daily rhythm of hard work and the caring for others. By year's end a clamouring for change grew slowly in my mind but uncertainty about my mother held me in check. As long as she knew where I was, I thought we had a chance to be reunited.... Was this uncertainty a disguised fear of the unknown and had I become totally dependent on Stoatley Rough? More likely mental depression was the ultimate cause."[66]

Renate began to horde her weekly ration of one small Cadbury chocolate bar and her clothing coupons. She was saving them to give to her mother.

The authorities at the school ignored or suppressed self-pity and despair, wisely. They, themselves, had much to grieve for. After an initial attempt to suppress news of the war, they allowed the children access to world news. Before each dinner hour, radio broadcasts from the BBC informed the assembled children and teachers about "the numbers of dead and injured soldiers and civilians...the military advances and losses, the sunken ships, and the never-ending reports of how many tons of bombs were dropped on our cities and elsewhere" (and of course, the bracing rhetoric from the great Winston Churchill.)[67]

During the Blitz, the Household Girls noted an increase in laundry chores, the result of bedwetting by transient children recently evacuated from London. Hard work helped but depression was contagious. Renate

---

[66] Ibid. p. 32.

[67] Renate Dorpalen [Dorpalen – Brocksieper] Stoatley Rough Remembered, *Stoatley Rough Newsletter*, Issue 6, October, 1994, p. 35.

recalled, "Most of the children experienced separation with intense longing and sadness. Often they did not understand the reason for the breakup of their families. I remember a young couple whose small children [at Stoatley Rough] …were soon informed of their mother's death. Such devastating news affected all of us."[68] Some children found resiliency, their spirits braced by the no-nonsense leadership of Nore Astfalck who whisked away doubt and worry. Martin recalled, "The Matron and Headmistress never pitied or comforted the children. We all dealt with our loneliness alone, although the Household Girls in charge of the younger ones provided selective comfort. I think that they felt that if they had shown any sympathy, the children would never have been able to endure the separation from their parents."[69]

Renate confirms Nore's healing influence. "Routinely we spent our nights in the cellars, where the small children were bedded down in safe corners. Thanks to Nore Astfalck's extraordinary organizational skills and reassuring manner, there was never panic or overt anxiety about the real danger of a direct hit by bombs on the school. Somehow that likelihood was blocked out of our minds in spite of the daily reports about disastrous bombing effects all around us. Perhaps the fact that the older pupils were responsible for the younger ones strengthened our ability to master our own worries and thus extend comfort to our charges."

The older the child, the greater the fear. Seventeen-year-old Inge Rothschild and her friend Edith Hubacher (still friends, sixty-eight years later), were on the heath "ablaze with purple fragrant heather, our favorite place for walking." Inge was worried. She had not received mail from her mother for two weeks. She recalled breaking off the conversation at the point when Edith asked, what are you afraid of? Her response was one of silence. Unable to articulate her fear, Inge recalled, "I couldn't go on."

While the chances were slim that a German paratrooper would land anywhere near Haslemere, the possibility existed. In 1943, with

---

[68] Ibid.
[69] Martin Owens, unpublished memoirs.

Martin and Goldy now fifteen and old enough to be appointed Air Raid Messengers, they never knew who might be hiding in the dark blackout of night. Martin recalled, "We took turns usually at night, getting up when the air raid siren announced the beginning of a raid. We wheeled our bikes through the dark gardens to a neighbor's house while the searchlights probed the sky and sometimes, anti-aircraft guns boomed. Our job was to run messages down Farnham Lane on our bikes in case the Germans knocked out communications. The neighbor was the Air Raid Warden, and we remained at his house until the 'All Clear' sounded. It was scary. The thought of an enemy soldier lurking behind the bushes was never far from our minds. Thank goodness I never had to run a message down the lane."[70] One time Goldy was taking a bath when "there was a terrific explosion…I crouched almost below the water level, ..[then] after awhile I put on my clothes and with soapy hair, put on my steel helmet to report to my civil defense station. I was a fire-bomb messenger and had to be ready to get on my bicycle to call the fire engines if telephone connections were cut. We later learned that a German plane with a full bomb load had crashed into Hindhead across the heath."[71]

Children feared not only the parachutist lurking just beyond the hedges, but injury from an exploding bomb. When Goldy was put in charge of the blackout curtains for the large dormitory in the main building, "that meant that I had to climb on the window sills of the long bay windows to fasten the curtains which were always open to allow for fresh air. If a bomb would have dropped at the moment I was standing there so exposed, it could have been serious because of flying glass. I was afraid to do this chore but gathered up my courage when I had to do it."[72]

There were times of intense excitement at Stoatley Rough, times when spectacular events captured everyone's attention. Haslemere lay along the flight path between London and the naval base in Portsmouth.

---

[70] Ibid.
[71] Hans [Goldy, John] Goldmeier, *Memoirs* Part 1, p. 59.
[72] Ibid.

An American bomber, a B-24, had crashed in the streets of Haslemere, one of its engines plowing through the roof of the Rex Cinema during a matinee show and setting fire to the theater. Large parts of the engine burned outside on the street. Two groups came to the rescue: Canadian soldiers from their barracks in Hindhead, three miles form Haslemere, and the Haslemere fire brigade. The Canadians rushed to unleash carbon tetrachloride on the smoldering debris from their side, while the Brits feverishly ran out their hoses on the other side. It wasn't long before the Canadians mistakenly gassed some of the English firefighters in the process. There were no casualties in either group of first-responders.

All British children were taught to put out fires with buckets and stirrup pumps, owing to the German habit of dropping incendiary bombs as beacons for navigation. When the school's notorious pump house with its 19th century flywheel caught fire in 1945, the drill turned out to be of real use at the school. The children knew exactly what to do, their efforts to be especially vital since the site was almost impossible for the Haslemere Fire Department to reach. Hanno Pilatz said, "As regards the fire we did completely extinguish it before the fire brigade could get there and what a fire it was. At the end Dr. Lion had got more or less the whole school to the blaze and organised a chain of buckets to supply us with water from the swimming pool. Of course as a result of that fire all the main fuses for the farm including our Black Hut [an outbuilding near the farm house that became a dwelling for some of the pupils toward the end of the war] were destroyed and it took a few months for the current to be restored." [73] Uli Hubacher added, "We successfully fought the fire in the pump house on the farm, and practically extinguished the actual fire before the fire brigade, with no proper access road in the farm valley, reached the site."[74] The fire chief later praised the children in the local newspaper. Earlier the children

---

[73] Hanno Pilartz, in an email. The Black Hut was one of the sheds on the farm. Hanno and Uli were allowed to live in this shed after the war and apparently, it had also been commandeered as a getaway for some of the teachers at the school.

[74] Uli recalled that Dr. Lion was pleased that the local newspaper reported the quick action of the boys. The Haslemere Fire Department later gave formal commendation to Dr. Lion.

had fought a large brush fire on Hindhead Commons just outside the school's gates. They fought with "buckets, brooms, anything handy" according to Wolf, who said "we speculated that it could have been set by German bombers – to light a beacon or destroy the Gibbet Hill radar station.

There were times of genuine panic. One day a six-year old walked into the dining room carrying an unexploded 20 mm shell exclaiming, "Look what I found." With such events, it's hard to imagine the steadiness these conditions demanded of the adults. Common sense usually prevailed. One girl remembered watching a dogfight overhead. "We watched the first dogfight between a German plane and a Spitfire in bright daylight, until somebody rushed us inside.[75] Each of the Hut Boys remembered watching various air battles between planes until being hustled into the house, sometimes cheering as a German plane went down in flames. On one such occasion – a night time occurrence - one of the adults gently admonished Wolf with the sobering thought that "the pilot might very well have been a former neighbor of yours." Wolf later wrote, referring to the puzzling complexities of their situation, "we weren't pampered or spoiled or spared much. Not at all."

In spite of all the chaos, the Hut Boys seized upon every opportunity to have fun. Wolf recalled one prank. "We found an empty smoke bomb on Hindhead Common, probably left behind from a Canadian Army exercise. We got some black paint (where?) and wrote on it something like *Achtung! Nicht Anfassen!* [Attention! Don't touch!"] Then we planted it--I can't remember whether it was on the path outside The Hut or The Bungalow. At any rate, our teachers were not amused."

One day the dinnertime was interrupted by a particularly horrific event. The mealtime had started out perfectly well, with everybody enjoying at least two items that were standard fare during wartime – potatoes, always part of the main course, and sometimes stewed prunes for dessert, considered a treat. (Canned prunes in syrup would have been a luxury.) Wolf was at Dr. Lion's table, and he recalls "Dr. Lion had the habit of looking around to see what the rest of us were eating

---

75 Inge Wurm [Sloan-Schleimer], 1990 Reminiscences.

and, if she liked it, would consume a generous portion on top of her diet (I'll try just a little bit')." On that day, Dr. Lion contemplated the prune pits in her bowl for a moment, then turned to Wolf. "Hmm, *Kinder*, I have an idea. I want you to collect all prune pits today and from now on, and use them for paving the muddy path that leads to the Bungalow and beyond, to the Hut." Wolf stopped eating, mid-bite. "My immediate reaction was a vision of a forest of plum trees sprouting out of the path. I did some quick mental order-of-magnitude arithmetic: Assuming that 100 people consume five prunes each fifty times a year and that each prune pit occupied one square centimeter. Of a path fifty meters long and one meter wide, how long would it take to collect the required pits? The answer: twenty years (check it out)." Wolf did not collect any pits that day and went about his business. A few days passed, then Dr. Lion mentioned the project to Wolf once more. He mumbled some response, intending to do nothing about the pits. It was to his great relief afterwards that either Dr. Lion came to her senses or she forgot all about it. At any rate, the prune project died.

That day at dinner something else happened - the war paid them a direct visit. While some ate in the Sitting Room or smaller adjutant rooms, Dr. Lion and Wolf were seated in Lookout that day, the big dormitory on the second floor where the little boys were placed when they first arrived at Stoatley Rough. Lookout had an enormous picture window that gave a panoramic view of the South Downs, a dazzling vista of forests and hilly lands stretching before the eye at great distances. As everyone was finishing dessert, a noise from outside penetrated the quiet hubbub of conversation. Diners turned toward the window to see what was the matter. Barreling straight at them was an American bomber, a B-25, with propellers churning on its distinctive gull wings. The bomber was traveling about 300 mph, having failed to lift up to avoid the promontory upon which Stoatley Rough perched. Everyone stopped talking. At the last minute, the plane veered up and flew over the house in a tremendous roar of its engines, pulling out just in time. Nobody could finish their dessert of canned prunes that day.

Nore Astfalck could not ever completely assuage all the children's fears, nor could anyone change the fact that they were Germans in an England at war with their motherland. In 1941, as if the reality of the situation suddenly scared the authorities, the school adopted the questionable policy that the pupils should shed all vestiges of their Germanic heritage. No longer would the school overtly cherish its Germanic roots. Children were instructed to throw away all their letters from home and thenceforth, to speak only English. (Many defied this directive and kept their letters.) At last they were supposed to become English. The German teachers started exhorting the children more forcefully to "*Sprecht Englisch!*" Subdued, the children took care not to speak loudly or often when they ventured into town, fearful that their accents would give them away as aliens, but among themselves, still spoke German until 1942 or so. But those children old enough to understand the implications of both a possible invasion and hostility from the town folk were now confused. Renate recalled the situation. "The school told us to destroy all letters and items linking us with our German past… I was puzzled to know how our pronounced accents could be hidden. And accents we all had, some of which were acquired from the extraordinary pronunciations of the German staff. The atmosphere in the school remained predominantly German, with German customs and traditions, and with the German language as the chief mode of communication, particularly among the German educators. This was, in some small way, comforting in my transitional phase. But acclimatization was far more difficult."[76] Renate tried to become English overnight. "I frantically learned to knit and eat 'the English way', and very conscientiously counted in English. …Each night I repacked a small suitcase in preparation for sudden flight to whereabouts unknown. But my decision about what was most important to me – and it changed every day – led eventually to the awareness that nothing really mattered. Finally, I did not pack at all."[77]

[76] Renate Dorpalen [Dorpalen-Brocksieper], Stoatley Rough Remembered, *Stoatley Rough Newsletter*, Issue 7, p. 18, February, 1995.

[77] Ibid. Wolf Edelstein [Elston] has no memory of being told to destroy letters.

Digging In – the Hardships of 1941

Almost two years into the war, the material deprivations, the overcrowding, and the constant fear of attack settled around Stoatley Rough like the thickest London fog. Misery permeated every activity, threatening to blot out expectations for the future. Early on, Germany had blockaded shipping lanes with their U-boats, making it difficult for England to import, among other goods, food, wool, cotton and oil. (By cutting off Atlantic travel, not only could Germany prevent America from entering the war but force Britain toward surrender.) In January, 1940, Britain began to ration basic foodstuffs (meat, eggs, butter, sugar, tea, milk, cheese, jam). In 1941, clothes were rationed. In 1942, sweets and chocolate, along with gas [petrol] joined the list. In a letter to her mother, Renate Dorpalen [Dorpalen-Brocksieper] described how rationing worked at Stoatley Rough. Each pupil received "... eight ounces of sugar, four of butter, four of tea, two of bacon and one shilling and ten pence worth of meat per person per week."[78] Later that meat ration was cut to two pence worth of Argentine corned beef. Imported fruits became a thing of the past. Eggs, according to the boys, rationed as "one egg per person per week perhaps" were preserved in waterglas (sodium silicate) brine for the winter months. Even hot water became scarce. The bathtub was to contain no more than five inches of "tepid" water. The pre-war porridge (in German, according to Wolf, known as the off-putting *Haferschleimgruetze,)* [gruel groats][79] seemed a veritable

---

[78] Renate Dorpalen [Dorpalen-Brocksieper] Stoatley Rough Remembered, *Stoatley Rough Newsletter* Issue 7, February, 1995.

[79] Components of this word mean roughly grain, soft mass, and cereal.

luxury now that it was no longer available. Now the children were eating "boiled oats intended for animal feed" for breakfast. On Sundays, the former treat of corn flakes was replaced with puffed barley, a food so strange to the boys that they called it *Ammeisen* [ants] since the grains were oblong in shape. Gone was the newfangled delicacy of corn flakes, once described to parents as *gequetschter und gebackener Mais* [squashed and baked corn], unknown on the Continent. Yet all was not lost. Under the new rationing, Miss Demuth kept finding creative ways to please the children, her "yeast balls" a perennial favorite.

Wolf recalled:

> The remarkable thing: rationing was never unpopular during the war (that changed when it continued for years after the war.) Lord Woolton, Minister of Food, was very popular. Much of this probably had to do with the pre-war class system. The upper classes were, by European standards, grossly overfed, drawing food from all over the empire and the world. The working class had a notoriously poor diet – chips with everything, no fruits, veggies, an aversion to things green. The German name for rickets (Vitamin D deficiency) is *Englische Krankheit* – English disease. The war brought on a social revolution – a great leveling experience. His Lordship got the same rations as his scullery maid. With lots of government propaganda, working class diet improved. Full employment helped. Of course, the rich still ate better, especially if they had access to Scottish salmon streams, etc., or could afford to pay £7 6d ($1.50) for one hothouse peach, pre-inflation,) about $15.00 today.
>
> More about the rationing system. In addition to fixed rations, there was a points scheme (a much more generous version existed in America.) thirty-two points per person per month. A pound of beans might be

two points, a can of salmon or peaches in heavy syrup sixteen points (that's why we never got canned fruit). I remember seeing a big sign in a department store in late 1944: New – Americans love it! Peanut butter, only 6 points for 8 ounces! Try it!"

Along with the bombing, the air raids, the blackout curtains and animal feed for breakfast, the students endured poorly heated rooms and illness. Peter Gaupp recorded in his diary at the time that he was "forever being dragged out by Miss Humby to go on walks when I wanted to be inside where it was warm." He also noted that the school was quarantined around January 20, and that the "cold water pipes froze and some big boys came and thawed them out."[80]

The older girls noticed that some children received more attention than others, that the sense of fairness and equality formerly paramount at the school was diminished. Renate Dorpalen wrote, "Many of the children were highly gifted and came from educated professional families. Those of lesser endowment, or lack of competencies, or coming from more modest family backgrounds adapted less successfully to the new environment. Though the children were tolerated, they were rarely rewarded with deep human relationships or recognition. They suffered silently and their symptomatic behaviour often worsened their vulnerable position. Perhaps there was a certain harshness towards psychological difficulties on behalf of the school. Could it be that no-one was able to face and deal with the enormous emotional reactions produced by the reasons for the school's existence? Expectations were for excellence, acceleration and proficiency at all cost. The adults, as substitutes for the lost parental figures, were hard pressed to meet all the children's needs in addition to coping with their own problems."[81]

The school carried on. In the annual report of February, 1941, the school's population was listed as holding "fairly even" with eighty-seven

---

[80] Peter Gaupp, Notes from a Diary, 1941 – 1942, *Stoatley Rough Newsletter*, issue 22, December, 2003, p. 37.

[81] Renate Dorpalen [Dorpalen-Brocksieper] Stoatley Rough Remembered, from family correspondence, *Stoatley Rough Newsletter*, Issue 5, p. 38, June, 1994.

permanent residents, two day pupils, two visiting teachers. Of the seventy-four pupils, including the Domestic Science group and a few helpers, there were six farm pupils and two London evacuees. Six of the children were attending elementary schools in Haslemere.[82] In September, the school relinquished its lease on Thursley Copse and the Austrians moved back into the main house. Martin was glad to be able to live with his friends in the Hut. Some of the older girls moved into a few rooms at another nearby house, Rowallen. A new German teacher arrived in 1941, holder of a PhD in Mathematics, former *Direktorin* [principal] of a large girls' secondary school or Lyceum, *Oberstudienrätin* Bluhm, who became the Mathematics and Science Mistress. Dieter recalls, "Dr. Bluhm had been a professor of some sort in Germany. I would guess she was in her late forties-early fifties when she came. She did speak English quite well, with less of an accent than some of the other leaders. She made the subject interesting and challenging, making you think and being supportive rather than intimidating." Science was problematic for the school, since it required expensive facilities. Dr. Lion notes, "The need of a small laboratory is felt ever more, and we are trying to collect some funds for it."[83] Dr. Bluhm converted Dieter's fear of all things mathematical to "fascination." That year Dr. Lion also engaged a retired professor in Haslemere to give a few weeks of practical instruction in Chemistry and physics. A small group of older boys including Dieter and the Pachmayr twins walked into town a couple of times a week to experiment with litmus paper. They mixed chemicals to produce intense heat and performed other wonderful experiments. When Dieter went on to college in the United States, he found that his academic preparation at Stoatley Rough had been more than adequate with just one exception: true biology.

General Rommel began to consolidate his *Afrika Korps*, while in Haslemere, the children continued to follow the war with their maps and pins. Yet there was always anxiety. Wolf Edelstein worried about his

---

[82] Annual Meeting of School Board, 26/2/1941, held in London. London School of Economics, Stoatley Rough archives, 1/1 (ii).

[83] Ibid.

parents. "The *Luftwaffe* robbed us of sleep during that winter of 1940-41, the RAF was keeping my parents awake in Berlin. Like so many at Stoatley Rough, I watched daily for the little red Royal Mail van with the G VI R cipher."[84] Early in the war, a few letters originating in Germany or Austria penetrated censorship, those forwarded by friends in Sweden and Holland. After Norway and Holland fell, children received (rarely) the twenty-five word Red Cross messages from their parents, many coming in weeks old. Months of silence was the norm. One day in March, 1941, a telegram from Spain arrived unexpectedly for Wolf. Miraculously, his parents were on their way to America by way of Occupied France, unoccupied Spain, and Portugal. Wolf knew he was among the lucky ones. Worse news awaited some of the children. According to Nore Astfalck, "there was one famous saying in these Red Cross letters, '*Morgen muessen wir verreisen*' [tomorrow we have to take a trip] ...and everybody knew what it meant."[85]

Because of the volume and frequency of correspondence to and from Stoatley Rough, the school became a "Bureau" of the Red Cross Message Scheme in February 1941.[86] Messages went from the school to Red Cross headquarters in Geneva for distribution. Dr. Lion's responsibilities now included passing along Red Cross updates to letter-writers in the community at large, the steady stream of official notices that were continuously citing new rules as the war raged through Europe and elsewhere. One early Red Cross dispatch forbade anyone to write information about a member of the armed services, e.g., rank, number, address, regiment, etc. Another came along to amend the preceding rule: "Senders of messages may state the <u>county</u> [in England] in which they or any friend or relative are living but not special part of the county (e.g., North or South.)" Lists of allowed languages were distributed and updated. As of October the Red Cross started to accept letters written in Finnish.

---

[84] The embossment G IV R stood for George IV Rex. It could also be found on other governmental property such as mail boxes.

[85] Eleonore Astfalck, Oral History.

[86] The material that follows was found in Stoatley Rough Archives M3207 Box 2, London School of Economics & Politics.

To conserve paper, the pupils wrote on scraps of very thin paper, some colored pale blue or yellow. Even Dr. Lion used thirds or half pieces of paper, neatly trimmed, for her correspondence. The children's messages were copied onto the official forms and sent through a clearinghouse to be reviewed by the British censors before being sent across the Channel for delivery. The Red Cross asked for brevity on July 30, 1941. "You may write up to 25 words on purely personal and family matters on the back of the enclosed Red Cross message form." The school kept a file of a subgroup of missives entitled "ENQUIRY FOR MISSING RELATIVES," something probably unofficial, for Dr. Lion's eyes only.

The tone of the Red Cross notices was businesslike, disconcertingly neutral. One dated November 19, 1942 (after the Allied landings in French North Africa and when the Germans occupied all of France that had previously been unoccupied), stated: "…all postal communications with Vichy France have now ceased, and we can therefore extend the Red Cross Message Scheme to what was 'Unoccupied France.' You can now dispatch messages to the whole of France, including Corsica and Monaco." Another dated April 24, 1945, said, "In view of persistent rumours that the internees have been moved elsewhere and of the uncertainty of communication, we very much regret that we consider it is now useless to accept any further messages for the Theresienstadt camp. Moreover, we are unable at the present time to institute enquiries for persons known or believed to be in Theresienstadt."[87]

The school collected small sums of money to help the war effort, including the Red Cross Penny-a-Week Fund to which it sent in January, 1942 £19.0s 31/2d. Later that year the school sent roughly £3 to the Red Cross & St. John Fund, for which it received this response: "On behalf of the Duke of Gloucester, I acknowledge with grateful thanks your contribution to the above fund."[88] The school also once received a gracious letter from HRM the Queen.

---

[87] Stoatley Rough Archives M3207 Box 2.
[88] Ibid.

Dr. Lion asked the Red Cross if the children might fill out the forms in their own handwriting. She knew what it would mean to the parents and family. The request was denied. Dr. Lion saved these small scraps of paper, dozens of bits of yellow, white and pale blue paper covered in a scrawling child's script, most in German. Sometimes the address is longer than the message itself. Some messages reflect yearning or fear, but most are childlike, simple, blithe recitations of activities, a poignant display of innocence.

"Liebe Muttile, Brief erhalten. Nett beschenkt würden. Alle gesun.[sic] *Roma grüsst. Wohne nähe ihr. Geburtstagsglückwunsche. Grüsst alle, Küsse. Hannele"* [Dear Mommy, Letter received. Everybody's fine. Roma sends greetings. I live near her. Happy birthday. Greetings to all, kisses, little Hanna.]

"Lange nichts gehört. Hoffe alle gesund. Ruth macht Examen fur Krankenschwester im Mai. Schreibt bald. Küsse." [Long time that I haven't heard from you. I hope everyone is well. Ruth will take the exam for nursing in May. Write soon. Kisses.]

"Liebe Eltern, Ich gehe Anfang Sept. auf eine Fröbeltagung, habe 14 Tage Ferien hoffe Korri Lisa zu sehen. Heute freier Sontag, darum besonders herzlichen grüss." [Dear Parents, I am going away for a Froebel Conference at the beginning of Sept. I have 14 free days I hope to see Korri Lisa. Today is a free Sunday, with especially warm regards.] This message is from one of the Household Girls, who would learn about the deaths of her parents from a couple of strangers. After being imprisoned in Theresienstadt, a severely malnourished man and his wife had managed to get to England via Switzerland after the war. They traveled by train to Haslemere in order to tell the girl in person about their friendship with her parents and the circumstances of their deaths. As free Europe slowly shut down, the news worsened. One day the Red Cross wrote: "We have decided that the time has now come to stop Red Cross messages to those parts of enemy and enemy-occupied Europe that still remain under German control. This is in view of the rapidly

changing war situation and the extreme difficulty of the I.R.C.C. at Geneva maintaining communication with these territories."[89]

The sporadic nature of communications was unsettling for the children whose parents were still on the Continent. Inge Hershkowitz, whose father had been forced to continue to manage his factory in Germany for the war effort, recalled "..for two weeks I had not heard from home. My mother always wrote twice or three times a week. Not to have a letter made me feel out of touch with my family. I was very upset. When another week went by without a word from home I became frantic. What could have happened?...For no one to get in touch with me must mean something happened to all three of them. I feared the worst." She comforted herself by mentally walking through the rooms of her former home in Cologne. "In the music room I touched our Bechstein piano. I looked out of the bay windows at the tree-lined street below...in the living room I lingered over our mahogany book cases, opened one of the glass doors, and soothed herself by reciting Goethe's poem: *Dem Schnee, Dem Regen, / Dem Wind entgegen...*" [The snow, the rain / Against the wind...]"[90]

The bombing of London continued through May of 1941. Then it stopped. Germany turned its attention to the East, to the Soviet Union. While the intense attacks on London ceased, the war was by no means over. Occasional night raids, Little Blitzes, that the children witnessed were to continue through 1944. The fear of an internal Fifth Column grew, causing no end to Dr. Lion's worry that her little German-speaking community could stoke the embers of anti-German sentiment that understandably smoldered in Haslemere. This concern grew as the war dragged on. As early as 1936, night walks had been forbidden the children, and not just for their safety or out of fears of sexual activity. Dr. Lion was trying to protect her community. One day

---

[89] Archives, M3027, Box 2.

[90] Inge Hershkowitz, Stoatley Rough Newsletter Issue 22, December, 2003, p. 11. Her parents survived the Nazis, primarily because her father was allowed to continue manufacturing a compound he had devised that was equal to crude rubber, of vital importance in the war to the Nazis.) The poem she quotes is from "Restless Love" by Johann Wolfgang von Goethe (1749-1832).

someone finally came under suspicion of the Haslemere constabulary. It was not a pupil, but none other than the second-in-command herself. Wolf recalls, "Emmy Wolff (who, you remember, had a deep voice and a heavy German accent) went to visit her mother in Hindhead, bundled up against the cold in a heavy coat, hat and muffler. At a bus stop apparently she spoke to someone, and immediately was suspected of being an infiltrator. She was surrounded by a muttering crowd when the policeman came by to tell the crowd, 'It's ok, they've caught him.' A German bomber had been shot down the previous night, the crew had bailed out and and one of them had not yet been accounted for." On another occasion, again it was part of the staff and not one of the children, who was caught outdoors at night. Joan Humby was questioned after discovered wandering around Hindhead Common clad in her black velvet dressing gown.

Summer arrived easing some of the hardships. (The alumni of the school refuse to admit to "suffering," determined to draw a distinction between their plight and that of concentration camp victims). The pupils exhibited their homemade arts and crafts in a nice show - cotton shirts, picture frames, table-mats - a myriad of useful things, all made by the pupils. Ilse Kaiser, something of a beauty and the object of several boys' attentions, presented a shirt to Dieter Gaupp, who, a couple of years earlier had struggled to close the top button on a dress shirt that he had received from America. Younger than Ilse by two years, Dieter was stunned by the unexpected gift.

Since no one could emigrate from England to join family on another continent, or go home to German-dominated Europe, Stoatley Rough became everyone's year-round home the summer of 1941. Dr. Lion realized she could no longer farm out an entire schoolful of children. A new challenge arose. How were the children to spend their summer days? Since idle hands are the Devil's playground, Dr. Lion came up with an idea. The children would take up hobbies. Gina Schäfer [MacKenzie] in *The Bridge,* wrote, "Miss Astfalck passed around a big sheet of paper which went around each classroom and everyone put down a choice of hobby, be it pottery, kitchen, farming, or weaving." The thirteen-year-old girl then added wistfully, "I think it is a pity swimming is not a hobby, but perhaps it is a good thing, or our swimming-pool would be overcrowded." [91] Another (unidentified) child wrote that "bookbinding is also a nice hobby and there is about half of our library to be repaired." The scheme died out pretty quickly, but some took up pottery and worked in the shop over the summer. Then the good news arrived that the Free French and British took Syria on July 14. But the evil of Hitler's regime was in its fullest bloom: as the children in Haslemere labored over their woodworking and sewing projects, Hermann Goering was instructing Reinhard Heydrich to prepare for the Final Solution (July 31). On September 1, the Nazis ordered Jews to wear yellow stars on all outer clothing.

Dr. Lion sought to raise flagging spirits during the dark days of 1941, quick to report on the successes of her pupils, to praise those who received School Certificates or who passed the Board of Agriculture's poultry-keeping examination. She reported the news that "best of all, one farm-pupil has passed the Royal Horticultural Society's Examination as the seventh out of 130 candidates."[92] She maintained cheer and praise for her community. In her *Rundbrief* [Letter for general distribution] of late 1941 she expressed her gratitude for "the life we are allowed to live here, ...for the vegetable garden and farm, the use of the piano (fought over for practicing time), and the handwork departments which are continuing to supply us with furniture either new or repaired." She ends on an upbeat note. "A home-made armchair with weaving out of old stockings has been given me at Christmas, thought I am afraid it has disappeared now since some farm-boys sat on the arms instead of in the chair!"

Thus was life at its lowest point at Stoatley Rough during the war years. While children dealt with their fears of attack from invaders from Germany as best they could, it is interesting to note that for some, there was no fear at all. The fear of attack in Britain paled in comparison to what they had experienced while in Germany at the hands of their

---

[91] Gina Schaefer [MacKenzie] The Bridge, 1941.
[92] Dr. Lion, in an article written about the school's status in *The Bridge* Vol II.

hate-filled schoolmates and teachers. Wolf remembered "I was never in fear of attack. None of this compared with what we had experienced in Germany." He concludes, revealing the true extent of the children's ordeal at the hands of their countrymen, by stating, "In Britain, we were in the same boat as everybody else."

Hard Landings

N ot every child came directly to Stoatley Rough from the Continent. Some first bounced around among sponsoring families, government institutions and other schools. Gerda Stein [Meyer] for example, was eleven when she left her family in Czechoslovakia for safety. For five years she lived in an English preparatory school, then a Council school, then a traditional boarding school and Stoatley Rough. Gerda was one of the 669 Czech children saved by Nicholas Winton, the young stockbroker who had been summoned to Prague by his friend, Martin Blake ("don't bother bringing your skis") to help save Czech Jewish children not eligible for *Kindertransport*. Other children of Stoatley Rough known to have been saved by Winton were Laura Selo, born in Berlin, but living in 1939 in Prague, and Rosemary Gumpel[93]

---

[93] Along with private school instructor, Trevor Chadwick, the three well-heeled men set up a rescue organization for the thousands of Czech children they had discovered not eligible for *Kindertransport*, working night and day to save them. Great Britain would only admit children for whom homes were found and guarantors deposited - £50 for each child - an enormous sum. Raising money, cutting through the red tape, even forging Home Office entry permits, Winton and his helpers succeeded in getting the first transport by airplane out of Prague in March of 1939 with several trainloads in the works. The effort was short lived. The last trainload of children left on August 2, 1939 while one month later, a large transport of children was shut down when Hitler invaded Poland and closed the borders. Winton returned to England, married, and carried on, never mentioning this part of his life, even to his wife. In 1988, almost fifty years after the fact, she came across a scrapbook dated 1939 in their attic, with the Jewish children's photos and names and he was honored by the world. Honors included those from Yad Vashem (Holocaust Martyrs' and Heroes' Remembrance Authority, located

Ten-year-old Hans [Goldy] Goldmeier was not a Winton child yet he, too, came to Stoatley Rough via a circuitous route, faring badly during his first months in England. His story provides a window into the trauma experienced by many refugee children who were denied safe landings, whose residence with English families was marked by disappointment, exploitation and sometimes abuse. (Even children at Stoatley Rough were not entirely safe from exploitation in homes opened to them for holiday breaks. Baerbel Guerstenberg [Prasse] was farmed out to a British family for Christmas, 1936, into a family that made her work for her keep. "It was not a happy experience. ... I had to get up early, start the fires in the kitchen and living room, start the breakfast and was kept busy working most of the time. My bedroom was cold, and I got a terrible cough." Hans Loeser came to her rescue after an impromptu visit. He rushed back to the school and located an elderly couple on the southern coast of England who would take her. Baerbel lived with them in a residential hotel for the duration of the holiday.)

Goldy was the last of the Hut Boys to arrive at the school. His story was one of trauma followed by rescue followed by trauma followed by sanctuary. Goldy, a tall boy with a slender build, prominent nose, soft brown eyes and thick wavy hair, was considered cautious, studious, passive. He was also kind to the bone, a gifted raconteur, and enormously popular for his clever, understated wit, and ability to deliver a funny story. He was the one who paid for the *Sunday Express* on the boys'

---

in Israel) who named him a Righteous Citizen of the World; he was made an Honorary Citizen of Prague; received the MBE (Member of the British Empire); was awarded the Order of T.G. Masaryk by the Czech Republic; and in 2002, was knighted by Queen Elizabeth II.." Winton's story is the subject of two films by Czech filmmaker Matej Mináč: *All My Loved Ones* and the award-winning *Nicholas Winton: The Power of Good*. Today, Sir Nicholas Winton, age 97, lives at his home in Maidenhead, Great Britain. A ring given him by some of the children he saved is inscribed with a line from the Talmud, the book of Jewish law: "Save one life, save the world. Nicholas Winton, The Power of Good website, http://www.powerofgood.net/story.php accessed November 10, 2006. Laura Selo attended Sir Nicholas' 95th birthday party hosted by the Czech Embassy. BBC History, WW2 People's War, *Three Lives in Transit* (Miss Selo's book) www.bbc.co.uk/ww2peopleswar/stories/82/a6988882.shtml, accessed October 24, 2007.

weekly forays to the Hindhead Corner shop. Goldy might have been a comedian with his witty views and killer delivery had he not been raised so strictly, to mind his manners, to behave, to avoid risk. His mother admonished him that Please, Thank you and Excuse me were the most important English phrases he needed to survive in England. He and his older brother, Ralph, arrived, extraordinarily, by airplane from the Frankfurt airport late in 1938. Upon learning how difficult it was to book passage by sea, his grandmother sensibly bought two tickets on fledgling Sabena Belgian airlines for her two grandsons. Off they went, flying low in the two-prop plane, "making the countryside and ships in the channel visible like a toyland."[94] Goldy recalled the cunning with which his mother prepared for his trip. "Jews were forbidden to take more than the equivalent of about $5.00 out of the country and that was all the money in our pockets when we left. However, the Germans probably overlooked that one could…take a bicycle and an unlimited supply of clothing as long as it was not 'new.' Because we all realized that buying clothes in England as we grew out of what we had would not be possible, mother took us on shopping sprees for every item of clothing imaginable. Both Ralph and I had two sizes in our luggage, and the clothing was carefully marked with labels that said HG1 and HG2 for Hans, and RG1 and RG2 for Ralph.….Mother planned this so carefully that I needed no new clothing the whole six years in England. To hide the fact that we did buy new clothes, tags were taken off, creases made, and my job was to rub dirt from the garden on the shoes."[95] (The senior Goldmeiers also emigrated to England. Goldy's mother joined the ranks of those immigrants who dismissed their own maids in Germany and became maids themselves in England. Goldy's father failed miserably at his own job as valet and died from a heart broken before the war ended.)

The boys landed at the Croydon airport, London's major civilian airport, took the train into London, then changed trains for the small town of Sunderland in County Durham. Friends of their cousin had guaranteed their visas. The new hosts were Rosie Wolfson, a Jewish

---

[94] Hans [Goldy, John] Goldmeier, Memoir Part 1, Columbia Maryland, p. 25
[95] Ibid. p. 26.

schoolteacher and her husband George. Goldy had been stimulated by the flight and train ride, but when he arrived at the Wolfson's, the "full impact of our separation from our parents and the uncertainty of what was to happen next ...hit me like a proverbial ton of bricks."[96] The row house was filled with many relatives. "Not long after we took our coats off and were introduced, Ralph and I were told that we would be separated, that I would be staying with George's parents, the older Wolfsons." Goldy continues. "I felt a sense of betrayal. We had been told in Germany...that we would stay together. However, remembering Mother's admonitions that I should always be appreciative for what people were doing for me, I said nothing. Still, I could not stop the tears that started coming down and so as not to embarrass myself I excused myself to go to the bathroom. There I really burst out crying. After a while people knocked on the door and asked what was the matter. I was quiet, hoping my tears would just dry. They did not, and when I emerged, I think I did admit that I was unhappy about the unexpected separation from Ralph. ...After a few minutes of conversation – it seemed the whole idea must have been concocted on the spur of the moment – the subject of our going to different homes was dropped and my sadness lifted."[97] After five months, the Wolfson family was notified they would need to evacuate the "danger area" by the British government. They had falsified their address by making it seem they were inside one of the targeted areas unsafe for children, seizing the opportunity to get rid of Goldy and Ralph. "We obviously were not part of their evacuation plans. That said, I must hasten to add that the Wolfsons did not desert us and, in fact, kept in touch with us. I also cannot blame them for perhaps being intimidated by the likelihood that what at first may have looked like a temporary stay while we were waiting to go to America could turn into something much longer."[98]

Refugee officers placed the Goldmeier brothers on a farm in Bellerby near Leyborn, in North Yorkshire with a kind family named Scott where

[96] Ibid.
[97] Ibid
[98] Ibid

they would remain for the next two years. Goldy and Ralph attended the government school and participated in healthy summer farm work. They would always be grateful to the Scotts. But they did not forget the Wolfsons. "When we were evacuated to Yorkshire, they [the Wolfsons] regularly sent us pocket-money, enough to go to a movie now and then and buy our two ounces of candy rations allotted to each child every week."[99] That the Wolfsons belatedly realized that they weren't equipped to keep two German boys is instructive. Well-intentioned English families did not always know what they were getting into when they offered to take refugee children. There were plenty of stories of a darker nature during these times of escape "into the arms of strangers", of people who used refugee children as unpaid labor and worse. The Wolfsons illustrate that the families who took in children did make a tremendous sacrifice of time and money that could last for years.

Goldy had started school in Frankfurt, the *Farntrappschule*, the city in which he lived until he was ten. "I remember arriving at the school on my first day with a '*Zuckertuete*' as was the custom, a paper bag of elliptical shape which was filled with candy that we all shared. I was about five years old at the time but I was immediately aware of changes, like being required to remove the old red-white-and-black flag of the old Germany which had decorated our balcony on national holidays. Our parents were not about to display a flag with the swastika that everyone else, except the Jews, began to hang out. One day a Jewish boy told me that Jews were no longer German citizens. I asked him what that meant, but he couldn't tell me."[100] (Regarding the flag of the old Weimar Republic, it was symbolic of the loyalty to that period. Wolf himself never saw the official flag as well. His family, too, preferred to display only the one of the empire.)

For Goldy, travel to school became dangerous. "There might be an innocent question by some Nazi who would stop us, like did we get enough to eat. If you did not answer this question correctly, ….someone [might come] to the house to arrest a parent for black marketing or

[99] Ibid. p. 35.
[100] Ibid.

other trumped-up charges. We were taught what to say: never volunteer anything and always be non-committal. Bands of Hitler Youth boys could also beat one up if provoked or for no reason at all. There was no winning these fights because if one defended oneself, the boy could complain to his father who might make things disagreeable." [101] Goldy became wily, spotting the hooligans before they spotted him and ignoring their shouts of abuse. "Our parents said name calling didn't really hurt us, and they felt they could nullify ignorant or abusive statements, but irrevocable injuries were hard to reverse. They always said it was the mean boys who had the problem, not us."[102]

Goldy was happy to sing *"Deutschland über Alles* in the mornings at school. In 1935, the official Nazi Horst Wessel song was added, and as in Wolf's school, the children had to hold up their arms in the Nazi salute, "not easy when one is only seven. When I finished first grade, my grades were nearly all "Cs." I received "B's for religious studies which were offered during regular class hours by Jewish religious teachers who already taught us Hebrew at that early age. Christian children received Christian instruction as there was no separation of church and state. All Jewish children received C's because the teachers were ordered to give C's in reading, writing and arithmetic."[103] Goldy's parents raised no objections as long as their children were learning.

Then the teachers decided to segregate the Jewish children, prompting Goldy's parents to send him to a new "Jews-only" school, the *Philantropin,* located on the other side of town. During his last year when he was nine, a group of boys ambushed him while he was riding his grand *"Adler"* ["Eagle"] bike home from school, a normal ride of thirty-five minutes. "I had no escape route, I was stopped and my bicycle was vandalized. The boys threw the valves of the tires into the bushes and they wanted me to go find them. I knew instinctively that it would be asking for trouble if I did this as I could be more easily attacked there. The boys, however, had so much fun doing it

---

[101] Ibid.
[102] Ibid.
[103] Ibid.

that they let me go, throwing curses at me and then stones...I wheeled my bicycle away as fast as I could. The principle of Don't provoke had worked again. I found my Uncle Jakob's house where I was soothed and collected by my mother."[104] Arbitrary indignities abounded. Goldy recalled seeing a crowd gathered in the *Opernplatz*, the central square of Frankfurt. "Always curious, I investigated and found ordinary people laughing hilariously. Then I heard abusive names hurled at a number of Jewish men who must have been stopped on the street a little earlier and then given toothbrushes with which to clean the sidewalk. When I saw what was happening, I crept away as unobtrusively as possible lest someone would pick on me."[105]

The hardships of 1941 did not curtail the opportunity for religious instruction for children at Stoatley Rough. Christian children were allowed to attend services in Haslemere and to prepare for confirmation and although the school was formally secular, Dr. Lion never abandoned her Jewish roots nor did she ignore those of her pupils. Periodically she arranged for each crop of boys to be prepared for bar mitzvah. When Martin, Goldy, and Obo turned thirteen in 1941, they were scheduled for lessons with Dr. Stein, who came twice a month by train from Oxford to teach the basic ritual prayers a year prior to the actual event. Dr. Stein was a German Jewish refugee who earned a PhD from University College, London in 1963. Besides preparing boys for their bar mitzvahs, the rabbi taught religion to fifth formers. Gerda Mayer [Stein] – no relation to the rabbi] remembered him for teaching "at a far higher standard than required by the modest demands of the School Certificate."[106] Dr. Stein only ate Kosher meals, requiring Wolf or another to fetch eggs from the farm. Goldy (the future rabbi in Dr. Lyon's mind) received special, more arduous private lessons.

It was perhaps logical for Dr. Lion to point Goldy to the rabbinate, but not entirely justified. Goldy had simply come from a traditional

---

[104] Ibid. p. 21

[105] Ibid.

[106] Gerda Meyer [Stein], "Professor Siegfried Stein", Stoatley Rough Newsletter, Issue 9, October, 0995,p. 20.

and religious family and he tried to follow the rules. After the death of his father in England, Goldy believed he should join a group of ten men and say Kaddish every day for eleven months, although it is not clear whether his mother instructed him to do so or whether Goldy was trying to follow the Hebraic laws on his own. Saying Kaddish every day for eleven months was impossible. "For a while that was OK, but then, in the normal course of 'grief work' I forgot more and more often. This started me thinking about ritual and what else there was to religion."[107] Goldy made sacrifices for his beliefs, on one occasion refusing the rare opportunity to attend a show at the Rex Theater of recently released *Pygmalion*, starring Leslie Howard and Wendy Hiller. Such entertainment was not allowed in the year of mourning. Goldy became proficient in Hebrew. One day Dr. Leven handed him a transliterated Hebrew text to sing for a recital for which the chorus was practicing. He handed it back to her, to her great surprise, saying he could pronounce the Hebrew text with no problem.

Goldy mused on his Jewish identity many years later. "When I went with a non-Jewish girl [after the war in New York] she was generally ready to convert to Judaism even though I was not necessarily close to proposing marriage. However it must have been clear that I was giving out signals that religion was important to me even though I was not a very observant Jew. At the point where the girl was willing to convert I would often flee." He entered psychoanalysis, searching for reasons he was not finding a suitable mate. He wrote, although "it might have seemed logical that my experiences as a child, growing up in Germany and England at a difficult time, would leave some effect on my sense of identity as a Jew," they never did. "I was more interested in the present...."[108]

Nineteen-forty-one came to a close, bringing the moment of Martin's and Obo's bar mitzvah. Goldy had his own bar mitzvah at another time and place, with his mother and his older brother in attendance.

---

[107] Hans Goldmeier "Religion at Stoatley Rough" p. 31, Stoatley Rough Newsletter, Issue 18, September, 1998.
[108] Hans [Goldy, John] Goldmeier, Memoirs, Part 1, p. 101.

For Martin and Obo, there would be no family. The date was set for Saturday morning December 13, 1941 at St. John's Wood Synagogue on Abbey Road in Hampstead in northwestern London. Although the boys recognized the solemnity of the occasion, Obo reminds us they were also, first and foremost, males in their adolescent years. "...After the ceremony Dr. Lion, who accompanied us by train to London, took us to a beautiful private home of a Jewish family I think nearby, where we had a luncheon with some St.R. people and others and I especially remember Marianne Glücksman [a Household Girl] whom I especially asked to be there, because she always took very good care of me at school and besides I had a mad crush on her."[109]

---

[109] Hans [Obo, Ginger Nipper, John] Obermeyer, email to author.

When They Were Sick

When he arrived at the school, Goldy was immediately accepted by Wolf, Martin, Obo and Peter, along with other boys. He quickly became one of the gang. But conditions at the school were deteriorating in the winter of 1941. A rash of infectious diseases tore through Stoatley Rough. The school existed in a kind of frozen cocoon, remote from daily English life, and even the milder weather below their aerie above the town. Snow and ice might blanket the grounds at Stoatley Rough, while in Haslemere, it had turned to slush.

The United States declared war on Germany on December 11, news that the school received with joy. Yet fever, coughing and vomiting dulled the full impact of the event. The crowding, cold, and wartime diet were taking their toll. One girl inexplicably put herself on a strict vegetable diet and became so weakened that she had to be institutionalized. The children did not have the luxury of galoshes or boots and after a walk outside in the snow or rain, their shoes became soaked. Even socks failed to dry overnight in the chilly dormitories. The furnace often went on strike in the Hut, and heating in the main house was so minimal that many children began to suffer the ugly purple and green sores of chilblains, ulcerations of the fingers and toes that produced painful itching. (It was not the only time the children were cold. The winter of 1939 had been the coldest in Europe in forty-six years.) Children coped as best they could. Renate Dorpalen sometimes wrote her letters to her family huddling under a pile of blankets. One night, the water in her rubber water bottle turned to ice overnight. Renate's father forwarded to her brothers her account of a day in the life of a Household Girl, written in the third person. "Her day from early morning until nightfall is filled with work. Then back...to her unheated little room, half the size of Martha's [their housekeeper.] The kerosene stove, adored by Renate and her roommate, is used to heat water for the hot-water bottles. Attired in thick pajamas, a bed jacket, a bathrobe, stockings and gloves, she sits in bed to maintain her correspondence."[110] In 1941 at least two-thirds of the pupils and several teachers contracted a nasty intestinal flu. Wolf Edelstein [Elston] recalled, "To this day I don't know which was worse: being sick or working as a member of the mop-and-bucket brigade. The epidemic soon passed. The relentless *Wehrmacht* [German Army] finally ground to a halt in Russian snow and African sand. Better yet, America entered the war. Our health improved as the sun returned and as rare lend-lease delicacies like Spam occasionally appeared on the menu."

Wolf described the school's nostrums. "The stock preventative against all ills was a daily dose of cod liver oil-in-malt (Ugh!!) and the stock remedy for feeling unwell was to put us to bed for 24 hours, with only dry toast and chamomile tea at mealtimes. Very effective for curing tummy-aches, diarrhea, or straightforward malingering. (To this day, Martin will not go within sniffing distance of chamomile tea.) The children suffered from boils as well. Wolf had some on the back of his neck, Martin also had one on his arm "which one of the matrons squeezed, popping the pus sky high."[111]

The children received regular dental care at Stoatley Rough from a visiting dentist. Martin said, "The dentist was always pulling my teeth. I have my wisdom teeth but a couple of molars are gone. He used

---

[110] Renate Dorpalen [Dorpalen-Brocksieper] Stoatley Rough Newsleter Issue 6, October, 1994, p. 35. from a letter written November 24, 1939, by her father to her brother.

[111] Stoatley Rough children fared better than their counterparts in Bunce Court, in Kent, at least in its early years. In 1933, the school's first year in England, the crowded living conditions at Bunce Court gave rise to a few cases of diphtheria and scarlet fever. That terrible year, one boy even died from polio, placing the entire school into isolation for weeks, forcing tradespeople to leave provisions at the gates and restricting short meetings with parents or relatives to the open November air. Quaker Refugee Projects from We Bring History to Life, http://www.traces.org/quakerrefugeeprojects.html accessed January, 2005.

laughing gas. One time I woke up and I was crying." The drill was something just short of a medieval torture instrument. "This was in the days before sophisticated electric equipment and unfortunately I had one or two cavities at the time. A treadle drove the drill. As [the dentist] stepped on the pedal and activated the belt which drove the drill, he also had to bend over me and apply the drill where needed. …The speed of the drill surged and waned with each stroke of the pedal, as did the accompanying hum of the drill which at times became quite hot, and then got …cooling from a squirt of water."[112] Household Girl Ilse Kaiser wrote for *The Bridge* her experiences with corralling the children for the dentist's visits. Note her barely concealed *Schadenfreude.*

> "It is sad to look at the children's faces when the drilling machine has to be fetched across! Now all is ready and we are only waiting for the dentist to arrive. We hear the noise of his car. He is here! With all his drills and tools he goes over and now he can start. The worst part is the waiting outside and hearing the groans from within. Poor dentist! We aren't easy patients. Glad, because a small boy's tooth has been pulled out without any tears, he throws it into the pail. But now the boy starts to cry terribly. The dentist looks at him in surprise. 'What is the matter? It can't hurt now.' 'No,' says the little boy, 'It doesn't hurt, but my mother wants to keep my tooth and you threw it away.' So our dentist has to recover the tooth and with contented smile the boy puts it into his pocket and goes off. 'Next one, please!' This patient sits down and looks only at the drilling machine. There is still the hope that nothing need be done. But alas! He has a big hole. Then: 'Can't you fill the hole without any drilling?' Poor dentist. But the next one is a little girl. He looks at her mouth. He thinks, he will be very kind to her and tells her that nothing need be done.

---

[112] Dieter Gaupp, Str Newsletter Issue 12, p. 31

But that is the wrong thing too. The drill machine is
just the thing she likes. Poor, poor dentist. He will never
get it right. And this is what always happens when the
dentist comes."[113]

The administrators minimized pain and distress as much as they could
but their limited funds made them err on the conservative side when it
came to actually taking a child to the doctor. Gut-wrenching stories of
suffering are all the more poignant in the light of the child's forgiving
nature. "Once I had a terrible toothache and even a fever. So. Dr. Lion
and Dr. Leven plus the matron at that time were worried. They took
me for a walk on the Hindhead Common hoping to alleviate the awful
pain. I was also given aspirins. ...And so we walked up and down til
finally the pain got better. The next day I was sent to an ear, nose and
throat specialist and it transpired that I had an abscess on the eyetooth
and my eustacean tubes were closed. The treatment I got was most
unpleasant. I fainted in the doctor's office but he also cleared my sinuses
and voilà, I was better." She adds with perhaps intended irony, "Both
Leven and Lion were delighted and said the walk helped and cured
me!"[114] At least one pupil is not so forgiving of the school's leaders.
Post-war pupil, Jan Schneider, wrote that the "doctor-ladies" [referring
to Drs. Lion and Leven] raced past in their car the time he was walking
his sick sister up Farnham Lane on a return trip from the doctor's
office in Haslemere, at least a two mile walk. "The Austin climbed the
hill, drew alongside, and passed us without a glance from the doctors.
Clearly there was no room in the car for a small sick child."[115] He reports
not without irony that later that season he had been walking along the
same road, this time hand in hand with a blonde pig-tailed girl from his
class. Again Dr. Lion happened by in the Austin. This time she stopped
the car and rescued the girl, insisting on driving the maiden back to the
school without further discussion.

---

[113] Ilse Kaiser, The Dentist is Coming, *The Bridge*, Vol. II, no. 1 and 2, August-
September, 1941.

[114] Rosemarie Gumpel, letter, *Stoatley Rough Newsletter* Issue 21, October, 2002. p. 21.

[115] Jan Schneider, 1945 – 1947, Stoatley Rough Newsletter Issue 5, June, 1994

While the years brought chicken pox, impetigo, and the need for delousing at regular intervals, Eddie Behrendt recalled that certain diseases landed children into quarantine. "As for the mumps, it was the usual story of multi cases of an illness where kids gather closely together. There were one or two new cases almost daily. Those with mumps isolated from anyone else. We didn't have much supervision, so that it could have been fun. However they put real greasy stuff on your neck which stunk and felt awful and then covered that with a couple of layers of woolen scarves or similar materials. Ugh! No one was anxious to "pretend" to have the mumps."[116] Susi Weissrock was only five years old when she joined the ranks of the ill. "I was one of the mumps children, and have vivid memories of several of us sitting in our beds, with wool scarves wrapped round our faces and tied on top of our heads to hold sickly-sweet hot poultices in place against our swollen cheeks, looking rather like comic-book caricatures of people with toothache! In the night, there was an air-raid siren, and we all crowded along the window-sill to get a ringside view of the action from the neighbouring airforce base - searchlights picking out the passing enemy bombers, and the glimmering flack from their anti-aircraft fire. During my time in isolation, I discovered that blue paint was nice and sweet. After eating my way through a whole paint box I had found on the floor; I also discovered that chamomile tea was horrid, but very effective for dealing with the sickness brought on by eating blue paint."[117]

In mid-July, 1941, there was an outbreak of whooping cough. This time the children were put into a section of the ground floor of the manse. Liselotte Kauffman wrote, "We live in a sort of protected area. That means a place where there is one string behind which we stand, and then there comes another string, where all the others stand. In the middle of these two strings, there is nothing. Our life is not so bad, first of all, we have a very nice room which is called the 'Tin." It is very airy. Of course we have no proper drawers, so all our things have to be put where there is enough room, the books on any chest-of-drawers, our

---

[116] Eddie Behrendt in an email to author May 13, 2005
[117] Susi Weissrock [Rice], Since Then.

dishes on the window, covered with a clean dish-cloth, our bathing-tub behind the bed, also covered. We have everything we want, even too much. We have four injections, one every second day, and we hope that it helps a lot."[118] During the darkest days of the war, many children were discovered to have head lice. Eddie Behrendt wrote, "As for the lice, well that affected only the girls. The longer the hair, the more lice. All the hair on a girl's head would be cut short and greasy stuff was put all over her head. The difference was that with mumps we were more or less together and yet isolated. With the lice, once the hair was cut short and greased, the girls had to run all over school that way and continue to try to live more or less normal lives."[119]

Even when the children were healthy, clashes occurred within the boarding environment, where living in close quarters sometimes provoked quarreling. There were differences of opinion among the staff too, petty grievances about privilege and belonging. And as we have seen, sometimes the boys on the farm had fist fights. Miss Dove, who left in 1939, reported on "many weaknesses at Stoatley Rough." Although she praised the School as a safe place, and admired "...a belief in the importance of art, of thorough scholarship and solid hard work," she was critical of the "lack of balance" at the School, referring to the children from London's East End who found temporary refuge at the school, whereby the School mixed "highly-intelligent German-Jewish children with a handful of British ones of a completely different level." She discerned "a certain hardness towards emotional and psychological difficulties," on the part of Dr. Lion and she criticized the policy of selective opportunities to take the Matric,

---

[118] H.W. and B. L., twelve and thirteen years old, Our Whooping-Cough Isolation, *The Bridge*, Vol. 1, no. 1, May-June, 1940.

[119] Email from Eddie to the author.

"the unnecessary pride which allowed no one to sit an external examination without a ninety-nine percent chance of passing." Also she noted the physical hardship in having, "growing teenagers trying to study late at night without so much as a warm drink to help them along."[120]

Christmas of 1941 inspired the children to patriotic acts. Instead of making presents for each other, Dr. Lion recorded that "the children and grown-ups prepared parcels with garments (sewn and knitted) and toys (for the larger part home-made) for bombed-out people and evacuees." Dr. Lion then told a story of sweet unselfishness. "The nicest gift came together with the following letter. 'Dear Dr. Lion, Here is a contribution of 3s6d for the Red X Fund. It has been collected from members of an organization called the "Secret Help." This particular organization was founded in order to aid people who are in need of help. We kindly request you not to investigate or try not to find out who we are, because we want to keep matters secret. Yours faithfully, "Secret Help."'[121]

---

[120] Margaret Dove [Faulkner], Since Then, 1971. p. 16

[121] Dr. Lion, Old Roughians, *The Bridge*, Vol. II, No. 1 and 2, August – September, 1941.

Remainders Pie

P reparing appetizing meals at Stoatley Rough was a challenge for Miss Demuth but to her credit, the Hut Boys claim they never went hungry. She had help from some of the older girls, who, either indulging a nurturing instinct or simply watching their weight, often scraped their shares onto the boys' plates. After dinner leftovers never went to waste. During the earlier years, the Household Girls used to hand out "bread and dripping" after meals to their friends, who in turn, fed scraps to small children waiting just outside the kitchen door. Sometimes the whole school population went on excursions to pick wild blueberries, blackberries or other wild fruit, the bounty of which would become the object of steamy canning sessions for the Household Girls. Sometimes the children just ate what they found outdoors. Susi Weissrock [Rice] reported eating "sour yellow blossoms and sweet red berries of forbidden yew trees; bilberries, black berries, beechnuts and sour clay [sic.] meaning "*Sauer Klee*, an edible wild plant that looks like clover – every walk was primarily a search for edible experiences."

While the farm supplied milk, eggs, and some meat and poultry, most of the food consumed at Stoatley Rough was delivered to the kitchen by truck (lorry). One day Inge Hamburger [Pavlowsky] overheard Miss Demuth ordering in her accented English "tepid water," a phrase the person on the other end of the line kept asking her to repeat. "God knows what she did mean, but at least it's an indication that food was ordered by phone." Some foods became so scarce as to become treasured, horded, relished. Rarely a treat might arrive from relatives in the U.S. They took months to cross the ocean and there

243

would never be fresh fruit but this fact did not stop children from dreaming. Once Wolf overheard Dr. Bluhm conversing loudly at a nearby table about pineapple, in German, and stating with authority that one "must peel the tough skin." Since any pineapple served at Stoatley Rough came from a can, the image of a fresh pineapple was one of overwhelming richness to the growing boy. Wolf recalled, "the chances of encountering a pineapple in wartime Britain were about as likely as meeting a visitation of angels."

Eggs were doled out at one egg once or twice a year per child during the war. Months after the war had ended, Wolf, now living in America, had not yet become accustomed to the bounty of his new country, post-war. One day some friends took him and his brother Gerd on a picnic by the banks of the Hudson River. When they unpacked the food, one of the hard-boiled eggs in the basket was discovered to have a crack in it. Their friend held the egg for a moment, frowned, then hurled the offending egg into the river. Speak of culture shock! Wolf and Gerd stared at each other, speechless. "If the man had flung a diamond ring into the river, we wouldn't have been more surprised."

Eggs were served to each child at the annual Easter breakfast. Although there was no acknowledgement of Easter's link to Christianity, the staff made a great effort to make a special Easter breakfast every year, reading the *Oster Spaziergang* [Easter Walk] from Goethe's *Faust*], a piece of literature that celebrated the resurrection of the Lord, a truly ecumenical gesture as well as a reminder of the richness of the German culture. Goldy recalled, "There had to be one continuous table and we were all to sit at it. I am sure that the littlest ones did not participate at this time but otherwise all of us were there. It was incredible how crowded we sat together, our elbows in our laps and our hands barely able to reach our plates. Why this practice I don't know.[122] The tables were always cheerfully decorated with "egg trees" (sets of parallel/horizontal rods on a pedestal) from which were hanging hand-painted Easter eggs, usually empty shells blown out by the kitchen helpers and painted by hand by various artists. In addition to the hard-boiled egg,

---

[122] Hans [Goldy, John] Goldmeier, Memoir Part 1

each child received toast and jam and perhaps a slice of coffee cake. Peter Gaupp recorded when he was eleven that the Easter breakfast also included a piece of matzo. The best part for him was the session of games held after the feast.

> "The whole school met at the tennis court. Miss Astfalck explained that everyone must participate in running an obstacle course. Everyone who won got a prize [in 1939 it was Cadbury's crème-filled chocolate eggs] as well as those who did not win. It was very exciting. One had to summersault. Then one had to crawl under a board, then one had to jump over a rope. Then one had to bind a shawl around someone else. Then one had to run through a swinging rope and jump on a table. On this table was a ladder on which one had to climb and jump down into a sand pit. Then one had to run between sticks with a bucket full of water. Then one had to sit down at a table and write out on a piece of paper one's name and address. After that, one had to creep under a structure, step into a sack and hop. Then one had to try and throw a soccer ball into a net. Then, as quickly as possible, one had to run around a special place and jump over a bench. Then came the winning post. I was once first, once third. After that there were egg races. I was fourth."[123]

Standard meals at Stoatley Rough were neither sumptuous nor elegant but always filling. Porridge evoked strong feelings. Some, like Wolf, found the smell sickening. Others, like Edith Hubacher loved porridge.

"I loved its rich oaty taste and smell. That is, I loved it when it happened to have turned out well; as it was, there were innumerable contingencies that had to be thought of by the distressed porridge cook, there were innumerable hazards that could lead to failure, there were

---

[123] Stoatley Rough Newsletter Issue 22, December 2003, p. 39.

multiple variations of making that nutritious dish unpalatable. And so our morning porridge was, more often than not, either too thick or too thin, there was either too much salt in it or none at all, it was either raw or – and that was always a negative climax, - the taste and smell of the burnt crust at the bottom of the cooking pot pervaded the whole lot and forty or eighty pupils and teachers had to eat it willy-nilly. Just think how difficult it was for the house girl on breakfast duty to prepare the enormous quantity of porridge needed every day. The pot required was huge and, filled to the brim, was really too heavy to lift for the slighter editions of 17-year olds. When the mixture of rolled oats, water and salt reached a certain temperature, it had to be stirred continuously to prevent burning; that was heavy work. At the same time the coal fire under the pot had to be kept up, and all the other preparations for breakfast had to be tended to. And so of course it was a rare stroke of luck if the result of all these exertions was neither too thin nor too thick, neither too salty nor…"

Others disliked the porridge. Herta said, "I know that at my first breakfast I nearly fainted because we all got porridge, slimy, wet porridge with brown sugar. And I hated every spoonful of it." Martin liked its taste well enough but was unable to eat it if it was lumpy, in fact, claiming that the lumps made him gag. During the war years, the Hut Boys started saying, "Porridge really isn't as bad as it tastes" (Another comment made the rounds at the same time: "Hindemith's music isn't as bad as it sounds.") The brown sugar topping was of course never refused, and was never enough for Peter. He recalled that when Wolf had the job of ladling it out, passing it around in an aluminum bowl under the teacher's watchful eye – one heaping teaspoon per person - he was sure he would get more. "I thought oh good, I know this guy is going to treat me well." It did not happen.

All the cooking for the main meal was done on the huge coal-filled range and an electric range in the kitchen. Edith recalled, "Mr. Phillips, our wonderful gardener, came early every morning to get a fire going, and I will never forget how once he swore at " that bloomin' teaspoon" of a coal shovel which was really much too small for a decent portion of anthracite lumps." She also remembered that Mr. Phillips' dog Bobby sometimes got into the groceries. Wolf corroborates, "On at least two occasions, our rations were shortened by Mr. Phillips' dog Bobby, who discovered that food deliveries were sometimes left outside the back door of the kitchen. One time, he made off with a beef roast intended for Christmas dinner. On another occasion, a large fish mysteriously disappeared until I found its chewed-up remains in the bushes."

Drs. Leven and Lion ate a somewhat different menu than that of the children. The blackboard in the kitchen always listed the day's menu and at the bottom, the notation for the two women's food was always marked with "Dr. L²." Peter was once sitting next to Dr. Leven who was eating toast spread with marmite, a dark-brown spread made from yeast, something akin to peanut butter.[124] He recalls he was always hungry for more bread, but was put off by the looks and smell of the spread. "I never could make up my mind whether to be envious or disgusted at what she was served."

Wolf took spectacular risks with his pranks, even risking Dr. Lion's displeasure in dining. "One day I found a stone in the garden that looked remarkably like a small steak. By current wisdom, it was probably a piece of calcite (white, like fat) with reddish-brown stains (hermatite, lean meat). When it was my turn to serve, I carefully put it on a plate and added potatoes and veggies. Dr. Lion's countenance lit up; "Ah, steak!" (a rare delicacy, even for the privileged). It turned to dismay when she tried to cut it. Luckily for me, she joined in the gales of laughter at her table. It was my first successful geologic experiment." She was quite tolerant. On one occasion, one boy decided to improve upon the table service by installing a small electric train on tracks that ran around the table. They used the device to send the salt and pepper and other condiments on a little car that sped around on its tracks for a few days until everybody tired of the novelty.

---

[124] Marmite has a strong, slightly salty flavor and is loaded with vitamins B2, Folic Acid and B12. A love-it-or-hate-it type of food, it has an addictive quality. Children in Britain are fed it from the time they are weaned.

Once the authorities went too far in their belt-tightening. Wolf recalled, "There was no refrigeration and in summer our carefully hoarded butter ration was rancid by the end of the week. One hot summer day, a pig from the farm was slaughtered and some of the meat spoiled. It was served anyway; its offensive smell sickened even those of us who had not been raised in kosher homes. Complaints were met with reminders about the starving children of China. We laughed about that (how could our eating of stinking meat help the children of China?) but in our hearts we knew we were really were privileged." Goldy balked. Raised in a kosher household, he proclaimed he could not eat any of the pork, rancid or not. One of the teachers insisted that he take a bite. He resisted, was pressured, and he gave in. No sooner had he swallowed than he immediately vomited. Nobody ever tried to make him eat anything he didn't want to eat again.

The children especially disliked the infamous "remainders pie" (in America it would be "leftover pie"). Such a dish had been a staple of the Stoatley Rough kitchen since earliest days and before the war, was a tasty treat. In 1938, Emmy Wolff wrote, [*"Unser Betrieb ist trotz Erschwerungen recht gut belaufen. Jeder strengt sich eben ganz vergnueglich an. Diesen Dienstag habe ich zum Abendessen von uebriggebliebenen Kartoffeln, die ich stampfte, 3 Riesenbadewannen Kartoffelauflauf gebacken – mit Milch, Eiern, geriebenem Kaese und etwas kartoffelmehl, dazu Tomatensosse. Alle nahmen 2mal davon."*] Our establishment in spite of aggravations is running along smoothly. Everyone is trying hard. On Tuesday I baked supper from leftover potatoes which I mashed and filled three giant washtubs - with milk, eggs, grated cheese and a bit of potato flour and tomato sauce. Everybody had two helpings."[125] But during wartime, remainders pie (missing the eggs and cheese) was less palatable. The boys called such a dish (which apparently could contain any item served the prior week) *gedraengte Wochenuebersicht* [condensed review of the week.] They sometimes also pronounced it "Remainder *Spei* [*Spei* – spit, *spien* – to spit out, vomit.]. Wolf described

---

[125] Emmy Wolff, *Wir Lebten in Stoatley Rough*, p. 12 letter dated March 25, 1938. translation by the author.

one such offering. "It had an appetizing crust, which turned out to be mashed potatoes browned in the oven. Underneath was a gloppy mixture of porridge or worse, boiled barley, mixed with spinach. The entire mess was called 'remainders pie.' The poor children of wherever would probably upchuck at the sight of it."

Lest we feel too sorry for the children of Stoatley Rough, one of them who spent time at a boarding school in Ware before arriving in Haslemere, claims the food was pretty good by comparison. Andreas Pilartz (known as "Hanno" to the boys), remarked upon one difference between Stoatley Rough and the boarding schools he'd experienced. "One of the most incredible differences for me was the food. In St. E[dmund's] the cooking was very English and did not agree with me at all. Every term I spent at least ten days in the infirmary and that meant ten missed classes. In Stoatley Rough I had no trouble. The cooking was continental and really excellent."

Game with teachers, 1935

1937 Wash Day

Boy in Shop

Household girl at stove, porridge

Inge Hamburger with child

Kate Lesser

The Library

Branches to line the swimming pool

Martin ten years old

Martin, Wolf, Goldy prepared for an air raid

255

School seen from rear path to tennis courts

Sixtieth birthday reunion of Hut Boys Martin Owens,
Peter Gaupp, John Obermeier, Wolf Elston

PART 5

WE'LL MEET AGAIN

Martin was all set to sail to America. Alternating currents of foreboding and excitement coursed through his body, confusing and exhausting him. First he'd feel disappointed at not being able to take the Cambridge matric to enter University, then he'd feel relieved. He looked forward to seeing his family in New York but was afraid of losing his independence. He loved England and its rules and propriety and Americans were said to be rude. (And they spoke atrocious English.) England was poor yet Americans had big cars and fresh fruit, eggs and meat. And don't forget Benny Goodman.

He was supposed to go on a night walk with Odette once last time. It was all so hopeless. He felt dizzy as he left the breakfast table, his porridge untouched. He pawed through his clothes wondering if he could take everything, then spent a few hours in the shop. He skipped the main meal, took a nap back in the Farmhouse, and still with no appetite, also skipped evening tea. When he caught up with Odette that night, the itching on his chest was starting to burn and he had a sore throat. Damn, he couldn't even touch her, let along kiss her goodbye. Her parting words to him were Go see Miss Astfalck. He traipsed back up to Miss Astfalck's room. She knew at once what was wrong. Several of the third formers were down, too. Martin had chicken pox. He was not going anywhere – not to the dining table where he could contaminate others, not on a night walk with Odette. And certainly not to America.

* * * *

Wolf peeked in on Martin the day before their ship was to sail – Wolf had been booked for the same passage. Martin roused himself to promise to meet as soon as he made it to New York. Wolf backed out from the Farmhouse and climbed up the hill for a last goodbye with Dr. Lion. A stillness settled over the Farmhouse, the kind of quiet that a windless, spring day brings when the world starts to wake from hibernation. Martin lay in his bed and watched the ray of sunshine slowly move across his blanket, oblivious to the cackle of a hen pecking around outside. He was trying not to scratch at his sores. He'd long gotten used to farm sounds, (and to its ripe odors of dung and feed). Martin fingered the frayed edges of his blanket, releasing a faint scent of mothballs. Up close, the gray fibers were thick and hoary in the ray of sun, silvery bristles, pretty. He struggled not to scratch at his chest. Miss Astfalck had told him to apply cool wet compresses every few hours but it wasn't working. He hurt. He hoped she would come down again to the farmhouse with some Calamine lotion.

Martin sighed, raised an arm to make sure his glasses were still tucked behind his pillow, and pondered his future in New York. His sister Lisa would be eleven now. He hadn't met his new stepfather but Henry Owens (ne Oppenheimer) was planning to adopt both of them and make them citizens. Martin would have to change his name to Martin Field-Owens. What would that feel like? What would it be like to see his mother again? He dreaded her tears. He fought against feeling sorry for himself, all alone in the empty dormitory. When they first put him in quarantine, he'd felt like a prisoner. But he was getting better – a stirring of something deep inside began to radiate little tics of strength outward to his limbs, and lying there in the sunlight, new possibilities streamed into his head, sparking dreams of a new adventure.

He exhaled loudly and picked up his airplane magazine. At least he wouldn't have to muck the pig sty while he was sick. Nor, come to think of it, when he went to America.

Kinder, Sprecht Englisch!
[Children, speak English!]

Ich bin in den Mud gefallen!" ["mud" in German is *Schlamm*]. This mixture of German and English was likely to reverberate around the school well into 1941 and then, with anti-German sentiment in England threatening the very existence of the school, Dr. Lion had, at last, put her foot down. From now on children were to speak only English. Although English had always been the top priority ("Our most important task is to teach our German children good English...,")[1] for much of the school's existence, German had echoed through the house night and day, with the adults the worst offenders, speaking German most of the time together, often shutting out the English teachers from conversation and information. Their English was heavily-accented and poorly enunciated. One day, a Miss Krohn (a refugee temporarily housed at the school) was struggling with some containers in the kitchen and she shockingly asked Wolf to "help me empty my bowls," pronouncing the last word to rhyme with "owls." It amused the children to hear their betters constantly hectoring them to *"Sprecht Englisch!"*

A key strength of Stoatley Rough had always been its Germanic linguistic and cultural environment; offering a great measure of security for the children who had lost everything else. As Dr. Lion wrote for a lecture dated November 24, 1937, "We consider it our foremost duty

---

[1] Taken from an early brochure, cited by Katherine Whitaker, History of Stoatley Rough, p. 24 from her research; Adenda, File 6/117, Stoatley Rough Archives, London School of Economics & Political Science.

towards these children to cherish and preserve ....all the good and great essentials of the German culture whilst teaching them to recognize, appreciate and accept those of their foster country. "[2] The children read German classics in Dr. Wolff's class and had to recite from memory passages of classic German poetry, even those few English children who had no idea what they were saying. The multicultural experience was reinforced through the English teachers' contributions as well, who allowed the boys not to click their heels when being introduced, and the girls to desist from curtsying. The children learned to eat with the fork upside down, never to say "bloody," and so on.

Some found the school too Germanic and, with sufficient resources, fled. Hans Kornberg left at age eleven after only a year. "Even if one does not want to forget one's German origins, one does not want always to be reminded of them – and the still-German atmosphere, with German customs and German language as the common modicum of communication – became burdensome to me."[3] Renate Solmitz [Frankenstein] also stayed for only one year because she "had some feeling I ought to really become part of the English culture, language, etc. At Stoatley Rough everyone did talk with an accent (and I still do!)[4] While Edith Hubacher [Cristoffel] also recognized the liability of speaking German, she was financially unable to move to another school. So she did the second-best thing. She befriended a refugee who had spent a year at a traditional English girls' boarding school, newcomer Katya Schaefer. Hearing Katya's beautiful English had made her aware of her own strong accent. It was not long before Katya was giving weekly

---

[2] Dr. Lion, Dr. Lion's Lecture, Notes of a lecture given by Hilde Lion on November 24, 1937, *Stoatley Rough Newsletter,* Issue 3, October, 1993, p. 8.

[3] Sir Hans Kornberg, from "Since Then." P. 49 His English schooling served him well. After working for one year in the biochemistry laboratory of Sir Hans Krebs (1945-46),Hans graduated from the University of Sheffield (UK), received his PhD, and conducted research at, among other institutions, Yale in the U.S. and University of Oxford. He headed up the Biochemistry department at the University of Cambridge, became Master of Christ's College at Cambridge and was knighted by Queen Elizabeth II, in 1978, "for services to Science."

[4] Renate Solmitz Frankenstein, *Since Then,* p. 87

lessons in correct pronunciation to the grateful Edith. After a few years working in England, Edith returned to her native Zurich, armed with the soothing English of the educated classes. Hans Loeser doesn't regret his accent. "Nothing would have made me give up voluntarily the warmth, the feeling of comfort and home that Stoatley Rough meant to me. As it turned out, I traded a life-long accent in speaking English for a home at a crucial time in my development. I think I got the better end of the bargain."[5] Herta Lewent [Loeser] concurs. "One reason ...we have our accents, (I, even more than Hans, because later he lost some of his in the army] [is that] most of the people in the school with very few exceptions were refugees themselves. .....Since we were in that school way up on the top of the hill, we really did not get to meet many native people from Haslemere.... We would go into the village, but basically we were exposed to bad English spoken by people who spoke it only a little bit. That's really the reason why we never lost our accents."[6]

Martin and any who entered the Haslemere public school system such as the Shottermill School also escaped the burden of a lifelong German accent. The occasional Britishism, however, escapes his lips. He might say, "learnt" instead of "learned," or call his wife, "Love," instead of the more common (American) term of endearment, "Dear." But he can pronounce a word containing the deadly "th" with the best of them. Not so with his friends. Peter Gaupp, highly educated, refined and intelligent, speaks a delightful Texan English overlaid with a German accent. Or is it a German-accented English spoken with a drawl?

How did the children manage the shift to English? They arrived speaking German and they left the school speaking correct, if accented English, well versed not only in English literature, but in grammar and they received strong writing training rooted in the ability to form a précis of any paragraph. The new arrivals at Stoatley Rough always first excelled in listening comprehension, the easiest of the four general categories of mastering a new language (listening comprehension,

---

[5] Hans Loeser, his Memoires, *Hans History*.
[6] Herta Loeser, "Oral History Recorded During the Winter of 1988 between Herta and Tom Loeser" Cambridge, MA, 1988.

reading comprehension, writing and finally speaking, in that order.) Miss Fearon bragged in her first term report on the school in 1934 that the children "after a bare three months for most, and less for some, - all the children understand any English conversation, even those who did not know a single word when they came."[7] The more active speaking and writing skills would have taken them longer to acquire, somewhat complicated by the fact that they had learned to write using a German script called "Sutterlin, a script based on a centuries-old "Fraktur" or broken script, so-called for its ornamental serifs, that was taught in German and Austrian (or Polish, Czech, etc., where German was spoken) schools during their era (although some had started to learn Roman script in their English classes). This meant that the children had first to learn to reproduce the slightly different Roman alphabet, both as print and cursive. In September of 1938, one of the part-time English teachers noted in her monthly report, "The handwriting of the children is a mixture of script and flowing hand. Much practice is needed."

Wolf Elston muses on the subject of speaking English. "It must have been about 1941-42 that English became our language of choice [but] in 1939, German was commonly used in the Hut. Mr. May, who [having joined up and] had been assigned to a West African unit, wrote back to Stoatley Rough that his new charges in the army were much like his old at Stoatley Rough; he had to admonish them to speak English."

In the thirties and forties, language training largely depended on dictionary-aided translation and rote memorization. At Stoatley Rough, children were simply thrown into English: they were assigned to read age-appropriate literature. They were put through vocabulary drills, assigned writing papers (which were then corrected) and encouraged to perform in numerous plays and skits. Dr. Lion's approach was progressive in a way. She wrote, (unconsciously assigning "child" the genderless "it" as it is in German, "das Kind") "we do not believe in teaching language chiefly through ...grammar, but ...through doing a thing, as they pick up colloquial English more quickly in that manner....It is a very delicate job to teach a child a foreign language when it has lost its home, so as

---

[7]   Miss Fearon, Archive STR 1/1 (i), London School of Economics & Politics

not to also give it the impression of being deprived of the possibilities of expressing itself in its own mother-tongue...".[8] Dr. Lion explained how English was taught at the school. "... The children began by using English at the table, at washing and dressing, and...at games.... "Of course slang expressions are most captivating and it is a real fascination for them to repeat (You lazybones!"). She also mentions that some of her pupils had received in other schools the French 'Globule' [or cobweb] method, and the use of Beacon readers." Some children arrived learning phonetic reading and insisted on knowing the sound of each letter. "Jessie, eight, distinguishes the eight different types of the German alphabet and the English one with its different pronunciation, as well as reading and writing in both languages. Those children who had already mastered the rudiments of reading in Germany are capable of reading and writing English nicely after some months."

In the early days of the school, thoughtful British volunteers, while untrained in pedagogy, did their best. Cesia Rothbart recalled a Miss Pelmare who would walk around the grounds pointing to things, naming them and having her repeat the words, then phrases and sentences. Miss Pelmare "never scolded for mispronunciation and always encouraged us for words remembered. Crumbs of kindness very much appreciated."[9] Dr. Lion was not to know that not every effort was successful. Beate Frankfurter recalled a Miss Bewley, "a thin elderly woman, with brown eyes, a deeply lined, brown face, graying brown hair [who,] dressed in brown tweeds and sensible shoes, took us for nature walks in the countryside. She had a mousy looking lady assistant whose name I can't recall. The pair were not on the staff of the school but, I think may have had some connection with the Quakers, and in teaching us were doing their bit for refugee children. I remember that Dr. Lion enjoined us to be especially well behaved and polite on these walks, implying that these two ladies were doing us a favor. In any event, they appeared to be very

---

[8]   Dr. Hilde Lion, "Dr. Lion's Lecture" Stoatley Rough Newsletter Issue 3, October, 1993, pp. 9 – 11. The quotations in the remainder of this section come from this paper.

[9]   Cesia Rothbart [Szajnzicht], I Remember, *Stoatley Rough Newsletter* #17 June, 1998, p. 12.

knowledgeable about the area and about plants and animals and took a great deal of trouble to teach us, but as I knew no English most of what they said passed me by. In order to hide this fact and not cause offence by looking bored, I learned to keep a fixed, polite smile on my face, an expression that came in useful on many other similar occasions in the classroom during the next few months where I was equally at sea."[10]

Curriculum notes from 1940 refer to a teaching manual at the school that recommends various exercises such as pointing to items and asking the students to name them, but there is no evidence of any formal speech / language methodologies at play. In fact, the teachers like Miss Dove had arrived at the school ready to teach literature and grammar, not language, and they were forced to devise their own methods to reach children at the start of a semester who had no English at all. It was a process that depended on a child's innate ability to learn quickly, a cumulative process that might allow Miss Dove within a few weeks to ask the children to describe a circular staircase without using their hands. Alternately, the pupil would just listen in class until he or she could pick up a few words. Ruth Bayer [Tuckman] wrote in 1990 to her former English teacher, Miss Dove, mentioning not only her lack of English but a politically horrific episode to the newcomer. She said," You may not recall a slight, thirteen-year old with black hair and very dark eyes whose knowledge of English was non-existent. I never uttered a word in your lesson and was incapable of writing an essay. But indelibly imprinted in my memory is one of my early History lessons in which you spoke most disparagingly, to the point of derision, about the Hanovarian kings. Having just come from an educational system that had nothing but praise for the rulers of Prussia in general and for Fredrich the Great in particular, I feared for your safety.; You cannot imagine my relief when you, kind and cheerful Miss Dove, appeared unscathed at supper time." [11][Later the school created ever

---

[10]   Beate Frankfurter [Planskoy], A Few Memories and Bits and Pieces Related to My Time at Stoatley Rough School (1939 – 44), *Stoatley Rough Newsletter* # 23 p. 6

[11]   Ruth Bayer Tuckman, letter to Margaret Dove Faulkner, March 26, 1990 from her home in Israel.

shifting English classes to conform to the language ability of its newer pupils, and an eleven-year-old newcomer like Peter Gaupp could end up in a class with six and eight-year-olds until his grasp of English had sufficiently matured. The Hut Boys joked about the funny new words they were learning. Goldy came up with a few definitions: "Icicle" is a bicycle with one wheel. A "public conveyance" was a toilet. The older students helped the newcomers, even in language learning. Ilse Feldstein remembered when Hans Loeser spent time at Thursley Copse to teach English. "I have never forgotten your vivid explanation of English plurals: tooth-teeth, goose-geese, you said exasperatedly, "but look, it is just like in German - - *der Fuss, die Fiess.*" [12] [The joke is that the plural of the German word for "foot" is *Füsse,* while *Fiess* is a common dialect.]

While the children were reading Goldsmith's *She Stoops to Conquer* or, for the younger ones, Kipling for homework, they preferred German books in their free time. Many girls devoured the popular *Nesthakchen* book series. The *Nesthakchen* or "baby of the family or pet" was a slim, golden-haired girl named Annemarie Braun who, over the course of several books, grew up and took a job while not forfeiting marriage and children. She was a breathtakingly modern role model and the books are still read today. The series was written by a young aristocrat, Else Ury (1877-1943), who would die in Auschwitz.[13]

---

[12] Ilse Feldstein "Since Then"

[13] The Ury series is still popular in Germany. Else Ury's *Nesthäkchen* is a Berlin doctor's daughter, Annemarie Braun, a slim, golden blond, quintessential German girl. The ten book series follows Annemarie from infancy (*Nesthäkchen* and Her Dolls) to old age and grandchildren (*Nesthäkchen* with White Hair). The first was published in 1906. *Nesthäkchen* and the World War, the fourth volume in the series, is the tale of a pre-adolescent girl growing up in Berlin at the outbreak of World War I. A recent survey of German women revealed that 55% had read Else Ury's *Nesthäkchen* books. Even more had heard them read over the radio or had seen the television serialization, and feminists at the beginning of the 20th century had even read them, finding inspiration in the bold idea that Annemarie could have it all, get a degree and marry. http://stevenlehrer.com/nesthaekchen. htm Accessed January 4, 2007.

The boys read Karl May books, a German author (1842-1912) whose stories were (and still are) wildly popular in all of Europe.[14] Based on *The Last of the Mohicans,* James Fennimore Cooper's masterpiece, (known to the Hut Boys as *Der Letze Mohikaner,*) May's hero was a German do-gooder named Old Shatterhand who had a sidekick, an Indian named Winnetau. Old Shatterhand was so called because he "knocked out a bruiser with one blow." Although May had never been to America, his books perpetuated a mystique of the old west that had fascinated Europeans since Cooper introduced Hawk-eye and his cohorts to the world in 1862.[15]

As the Stoatley Rough boys grew older, they were happy to switch to reading in English primarily because they discovered penny dreadfuls. Wolf tells us that, "By the summer of 1940, monthly magazines for boys, like *Adventure* and *Hotspur*, began to displace Karl May." These cheap publications provided serialized escapist stories of superheroes, the more fantastic the better. George Orwell explained in an essay of

---

[14] The works of Karl May (1842-1912) have thus far sold over 100 million copies across the globe, his 60 novels having been translated into over 30 languages, including a recent series in Chinese. Born into a poor family in Hohenstein-Ernstthal, while imprisoned for petty theft, May began to write his books most likely inspired by *The Last of the Mohicans*. From "The Strange Life and Legacy" by Danica Tutush. http://www.cowboysindians.com/articles/archives/0999/karl_may.html. Accessed May, 2005.

[15] Wolf Elston, a resident of Albuquerque, New Mexico, for most of his life in America, sets us straight about Old Shatterhand. "Karl May didn't get all his American geography and ethnology right. Winnetou's home was supposed to be a pueblo on the Pecos, near the present Roswell (famous crash site of space aliens). There were no pueblos on the Pecos and, anyway, the Apaches were nomads who didn't live in pueblos. However, an Apache band, the Mescaleros, live in the vicinity to this day. They own much of the resort area in the mountains around Ruidoso, NM. This is where Texans come in droves to do all the things that at home are either impossible (like skiing on 12,000-ft Sierra Blanca) or illegal, like playing the horses at Ruidoso Downs or gambling and boozing at the Inn of the Mountain Gods, the fanciest (and most expensive) resort in New Mexico. Recently the Apaches voted to offer their reservation as a site for a nuclear waste dump. What would Old Shatterhand say to that?"

1940 that "boys at certain ages find it necessary to read about Martians, death-rays, grizzly bears and gangsters."[16]

The magazines gave the boys inspiration, escape from uncertainty and loss, and feelings of helplessness. Again, Orwell, captures the lure of the cover illustrations: "On one a cowboy is clinging by his toes to the wing of an aeroplane in mid-air and shooting down another aeroplane with his revolver. On another a Chinese is swimming for his life down a sewer with a swarm of ravenous rats swimming after him. On another an engineer is lighting a stick of dynamite while a steel robot feels for him with its claws. On yet another a man in airman's costume is fighting barehanded against a rat somewhat larger than a donkey!' This character is intended as a superman, whose usual method of solving any problem is a sock on the jaw." Orwell nails the salutary effect of these stories for the boys in the following conclusion: "At the same time the scenes of violence in nearly all these stories are remarkably harmless and unconvincing."[17]

By 1942 the preferred reading of the Hut Boys was in English. Wolf said that "only a die-hard Berliner like Tom Wongtschowsky would insist on speaking German." Of course the school authorities frowned on the penny dreadfuls, and assigned only approved age-appropriate classics of English and German literature. Wolf recalls that "Our teachers regarded penny dreadfuls as trashy literature which, of course, made them all the more attractive."

At any rate, roughly two years into the war, the children at Stoatley Rough began to speak English with regularity. Wolf said, "It is… difficult to remember when my private thoughts and dreams switched from German to English; most probably it happened about age fourteen (1942.)" Wolf had had to work hard at his English. "To overcome my heavy German accent, I was put in special speech class taught by a prim English lady whose name I have forgotten (Miss West?) But to

---

[16] From "Boys' Weeklies" written by George Orwell for *Horizon*, March, 1940. Essays and Journalism, http://www.netcharles.com/orwell/essays/boysweeklies2. htm Accessed February, 2005.

[17] Ibid.

whom I am very grateful. She made us repeat words like 'hyacinths' and 'chrysanthemums' endlessly, saying, 'You'll pronounce it correctly, or you shan't have any tea.' In England, tea is not just a beverage but the principal meal of the day, which made this a very serious threat to a growing boy. Without her perseverance, I would today probably sound like Henry Kissinger."[18] But Wolf's real trial in his acquired language was yet to be faced when he began life in New York. "I had arrived at Stoatley Rough as a German in language and thought. On leaving, I was not exactly an Englishman but had acquired fluency in the English language and a lasting understanding of British ways. Americanization followed gradually. Upon enrolling at the City College of New York in 1945, I was required to read aloud from *The New York Times* to demonstrate proficiency in English. My statement that "aircrahft were sheduled to fly to Schenectahdy" landed me in Remedial English, along with natives of Brooklyn and the Bronx. This came as a shock, as I had regarded myself as the only one in the place who actually spoke English!"[19]

Newcomers sometimes got into trouble not knowing English. Ilse Steinberg took newcomer Wolf into town to get haircut after he had just arrived. While walking across Hindhead Common, Ilse entertained him, in German of course, with a blow-by-blow account of an exciting book she was reading for English class, *Tom Sawyer*. They arrived at the barbershop and Wolf was seated in the chair. The barber started in with pleasant small talk, asking Wolf questions as he trimmed this side and that, turning him in the chair, snipping away. Wolf tried to be pleasant by answering "Yes" each time the barber paused.

The barber said, "Did you bring your comb?"

Wolf answered, "Yes."

"Well, where is it?"

"Yes."

"I said, where's your comb?"

"Yes."

---

[18] Wolf Elston, upon the occasion of Nore Astfalck's 90th birthday.
[19] Ibid.

"Are you trying to be a smart aleck with me?"

"Yes."

At that point, Ilse woke up, put down her book, and broke into the exchange to explain to the barber Wolf hadn't the slightest idea what he was saying. The barber finished the haircut in silence.

Household Girls were sometimes assigned special work on the Farm, such as helping to paint a room or bring in a harvest. Birgitte Heinsheimer [Pring-Mills] had just arrived from Germany. "I was sent to work on the farm (perhaps because I had grown up in the country?) to help with the building of a stable. The instructor had a most beautiful singing voice. [She refers to Mr. Hughes, the Welsh Farm Manager who succeeded Mr. Corfield, and who spoke no German.] And the picture I remember is of both of us hammering laths onto the roof, and my asking whether he would teach me a special song. He did. I thought it was beautiful, and fifty years on I still think so. I learnt it, and next day, on kitchen duty with Lizzi Loebl, I tried it out on her and asked what my pronunciation of English was like. "Can't tell," was the sobering answer, 'You are singing it in Welsh.' I have now forgotten the Welsh text, but the song was "All Through the Night."[20]

Goldy, who was ever alert to propriety, said about learning English, "There was teasing at times when we mispronounced certain words, but people really tried to help us master the language, especially the "r" and the "th" sounds. One tricky aspect of learning a new language, mainly from other twelve-year-old boys, was to discriminate acceptable from unacceptable words, like swear words, which should not be repeated at home."[21]

The children performed often in plays. The students cite many instances in which they successfully played roles. Dieter said, "On one occasion I was cast in the part of the Miser (L'Avare) in the play of the

---

[20] Birgitte Pring-Mills nee Heinsheimer [in 1990 *Reminiscences*]. "All Through the Night" is an ancient Welsh song, "Ar Hyd Y Nos," the most popular version in English by Harold Boulton that begins with, "Sleep my love, and peace attend thee / All through the night." Folk Songs of England, Ireland, Scotland and Wales. Accessed October, 2006. http://www.contemplator.com/wales/allnight2.html

[21] John Goldmeier, "Memoires."

same name by Moliere. This was in the original French. I don't know how many people who watched it understood us but I imagine most people had been briefed beforehand and we all enjoyed it."[22] He liked the period piece in which he played a German lord. "I had only a few lines...I was drunk most of the time and what I had to say came out accordingly. It brought a lot of laughter. ...When I left the school Dr. Lion gave me a letter of recommendation in which she mentioned my stage activity, saying she thought I was quite gifted. I don't know what a prospective employer was to do with that."[23] He once had the occasion in which familiarity with Shakespeare provided an amusing moment in class. English teacher Mr. Taylor had arrived late to class that day, so late that the children were out of their seats, running around and talking loudly, doing what children do when the teacher is late. Mr. Taylor soon restored order but one child remained behind a curtain in the room, creating great suspense. "We wondered how things would develop. Mr. Taylor, generally ... a friendly but also controlling schoolmaster, made some comments which led him to talk about *Hamlet,* the play in which there was a scene where Polonius, hidden behind a curtain, was stabbed while trying to hide....The missing student emerged, much to everyone's amusement."[24]

---

[22] Dieter Gaupp, "Reminiscences," Stoatley Rough Newsletter #12, October, 1996, p. 36.

[23] Ibid.

[24] Dieter Gaupp, "Reminiscences 1990 Reunion" The following plays have been mentioned by various students as having been performed over the years at Stoatley Rough. This information appeared in newsletter accounts, interviews, and articles in *The Bridge. Julius Ceasar* (excerpt) was apparently performed in parody. An unidentified child wrote "Since I have been in Stoatley Rough, I have seen in the summer of 1940, two plays on the same day. It was on Dr. Li's birthday. One of them a gay, bright play of a stolen princess was acted by Group V on the second tennis-court with Miss Evans as producer. The other was a somewhat odd parody of *Julius Caesar* performed by older boys and girls. Other Shakespearean efforts included scenes from *Hamlet,* (excerpt) and *Henry VIII,* both performed by the farm boys and directed by Miss Humby. When the farm boys played a scene from *Richard II,* it was reported in *The Bridge,* unkindly, that "they had trouble pronouncing their W's, K's, O's and R's." For the production of *Midsummer Night's Dream,* Peter Gaupp played Oberon, Uli Hubacher was in

There is at least one instance when it is clear how difficult the nuances of spoken English must have been for the German children. Wolf was only eleven or twelve and had walked down to the Farm to watch the older Farm boys dig out the side of the hill to make an air raid shelter (which apparently they never used). The boys were hard at work on it, hacking at the earth with various tools. "Someone called to the digging crew: 'Have you got any picks here on the farm?' The answer by one of the Farm boys: 'Ve haff two big sows and a dozen little picks.'"

---

charge of props, and Wolf Elston was Bottom, who wore the ass' head. Wolf says the kids commented that he didn't need a fake head to play the part. Wolf also appeared in *Richard II*, and Martin Friedenfeld (Owens) was Sir Tobey Belch while Felix Schiller played Sir Andrew Aguecheek in *King Henry IV, Part 1*, (subplot). The children also performed scenes from Dickens' *Nicholas Nickelby* and *Captain Scuttleboom's Treasure*, the later only interesting in that its playwright, Ronald Gow (1897 – 1993) was married for 56 years to Wendy Hiller, the star of the original *"Pygmalion"* film. The children performed *Turandot* for which, as reported in *The Bridge*, "wings were painted and many a young man's head popped up on the wall. The performance would have been excellent except for the laughs certain actors had to give at their own dramatic speech." Students performed the comedy *Tovarich* in English. Yet another play is mentioned by Baerbel Prasse, *"Victoria Regina*, in which she played the queen in a role that made Helen Hayes famous. The children also performed two other plays that we know of: *Le Voyage de Monsieur Perrichon*; performed in French, to which apparently the students initially objected, putting up a "strong and vigorous protest." Miss Humby, producer, director-stage-manager-dress-maker-arranger" persuaded them to tackle it, which the reporter claims was great fun to rehearse, and a play entitled *Der Biberpelz*, [The Beaver Coat] a comedy performed in German.

Confessions of an Army Cadet

I n September of 1942, Dieter left the school. He had turned eighteen in May and it was time for him to find work. Gerd Edelstein [Elston] knew of an opening in the optical factory where he was working, in Offenham in Worcestershire, about a hundred miles north west of London. Soon Dieter was making spectacle frames from plastic. His building was used for Home Guard practice raids and he recalls times when he would look up from his workbench to see troops slinking along the wall outside. He often joined his friend Gerd to go to concerts while there. In 1944, Dieter joined the Home Guard himself, "feeling we needed to do something tangible for the war effort...We were issued real rifles, though I don't know if they had firing pins in them...Our rifles were made for giants, were longer and heavier than regular rifles – I can't imagine what their initial purpose had been. They were obviously not wanted by the regular army. We drilled with them, specially marching and cleaning. That's as far as it went as we ordered uniforms which never came because in a week or two after that the Home Guard was disbanded." While he was at the factory, Dieter received a scholarship to a Youth Leadership course in 1946 at the University of Bristol for starting (with the help of Gerd and Miss Jenks, a local schoolteacher), a youth club.

Dieter's departure gave brother Peter, still at Stoatley Rough, pause to consider his own status. When his friend, Michael Strauss, proposed they transfer to a "real" English school, Peter agreed. With Dieter gone, he had nothing to lose. The two fourteen-year-olds enrolled in Shoreham Grammar School, an independent school in Shoreham-by-Sea, on the

273

south coast. [25] Peter left Haslemere thinking he would become more self-sufficient away from the warm nest of Stoatley Rough and in a very real sense, he got his way.

For the first time in his life, Peter experienced the cruelty that boarding children are capable of inflicting on outsiders. Peter was German – that was bad enough. Worse, Peter was also a Jew but not really, because worst of all, he wasn't even a real Jew but a *Mischling*, the product of a marriage between a Jew and a Gentile. [26] Peter found himself thrown into an elegant purgatory, mired in the finely tuned nastiness of prejudice that was prevalent in public schools then. His situation was exacerbated by the existence of what was known as the prefect system. Supposed to build character, the prefect system conferred privileges and responsibilities on upper classmen and heaped punishment and humiliation on the younger set. The prefect, a privileged senior boy was allowed to wear clothing that would distinguish him from the rest of the boys and had the power to bully lower classmen (sometimes called

---

[25] The school was relocated to Liphook, Hampshire, close to Haslemere, during the war. Afterwards, the school became Shoreham College, relocated in Shoreham-by-Sea, a small coastal community near Brighton West Sussex.

[26] Peter found a book that describes *Mischlings* that also contained information about his family name. "This morning I had a surprise phone call from Ralph Gomar (formerly Goldmeier), Goldy's older brother. Sounded just like Goldy to me! He had read a book (Bryan Mark Rigg, *Hitler's Jewish Soldiers*, University Press of Kansas) which describes the treatment of "*Mischlinge*" (i.e. part Jewish) who were in the German army during WWII. Somewhere in there is a photo of one Peter Gaupp, "*Soldat*", and I gather there are several other mentions of this person who was interviewed. He must have been about 10 years older than I was. He wanted to make sure it was not me (and remembered that he had met me at Stoatley Rough when he visited with his mother) and to see if I knew anything about him. So far I have found references to twenty Peter Gaupp's in my family tree collection, the earliest going back to the 1500's. So, it was a fairly well used name. There are also references to intermarriages with Jewish spouses. My father used to say that probably all "Gaupp's" are interrelated somehow, and I am inclined to agree. Of course the relationship could go back a few hundred years!" email to the author, June, 2005.

"fags") and even to consign them to canings administered by teachers.[27] "I was harassed badly by the other kids as a 'Nazi,' and since I was such a shy character did nothing about it."

Shoreham's system of rewards and punishments brings into sharp focus the benevolent atmosphere that Peter had abandoned. Stoatley Rough fostered, if nothing else, a relaxed environment of non-competitive, positive encouragement. Discipline at Stoatley Rough consisted of sending children to bed early or remanding them to Dr. Lion for a stern talking to. Roughian children certainly were capable of mischief; they could be rude to their teachers; they were known to steal food, fight with each other and break rules such as taking a night walk. But as long as Miss Astfalck reigned, physical punishment was unimaginable.

Peter himself became a prefect in his last year at the school but there seems to be an element of sadomasochism in the attitude taken by his elders. "Caning was a part of the school principal's options. It did not happen very often, but I was caned the evening of the day I was made a prefect. The boys in my dorm room decided to have a pillow fight at night, in which I was really not interested, when Mr. Bruder opened the door just as I finally sailed a pillow in his direction. I know he thought it was funny in a way, but invited me to his study for a caning anyway. After all, I was supposed to set an example…or something like that." Peter continues with more graphic examples. "There were always rumors that he 'chalked' his cane, even though that was never proved. Chalking the cane was a barbaric system which assured that one hit the identical spot over and over again, inflicting maximum punishment. It was a widely held belief in British schools that principals did this. I was never certain whether mine did or did not. I suspect that since he was basically a rather decent fellow, that he did not -- but the myth

---

[27] In many British public schools, prefects, usually sixth formers, have considerable power. They effectively run the school outside the classroom. Corporal punishment administered by a prefect is now abolished in the UK. There may be a senior prefect known as the *Head of School* (colloquially, *Head Boy* or *Head Girl*) who carries some responsibilities, but gone is the ability to inflict bodily punishment on younger classmates.

prevailed. The trouble is that while one is bending over, it is hard to look behind to make sure! And afterwards most kids don't really want their peers to examine the injured article."

The educational systems in the United States sanctioned corporal punishment in the 1930s and 40s, but "caning" (as opposed to spanking with a hand or ruler) conveys an approach to punishment that employs humiliation and fear. Peter recalled that he was frightened by the mere presence of a cane at his elementary school in Germany. "The male teacher always walked around with a cane under his arm, a clear suggestion that he would use it if we misbehaved. I never saw him use it and my parents said that he was actually a very nice man -- but I was awed!" Wolf's teacher also used a cane but Goldy, Obo nor Martin have no memory of caning punishments.

Andreás [Hanno] Pilartz's first school was St. Edmund's College, Old Hall, in Ware, the oldest Catholic boarding school in England. "We played cricket and rugby, had boxing, and luckily I was very good at that, which allowed me not to be pestered by the others. There were Prefects (upper classmen) who could punish you by giving you lines to write say forty or eighty times, 'I must not do this or that, etc.,' they could also send you up, which meant that you had to report to your House Master after supper. So after supper you went up to your House Master's rooms, there were usually three or four others waiting and that, in a way, was the worst moment - the actual waiting and maybe hearing somebody else being caned. Eventually it was your turn to go so either you were told off or you got it. There was a big armchair and you had to put your knees on one arm and bend over to put your hands on the other arm. There were different thickness of canes, normally there were three strokes but some times there were six. You could have it with your trousers down or up. Six is the maximum I ever had, but apparently in the not so distant past, twelve strokes and even in one case there had been twenty-four strokes, and that in public. Of course when you came out of the room one had to have a smile on one's face." Hanno concludes, "They told my mother that they thought it might be better for me to change schools... Of course my first impression was what a curious place, no discipline; no real punishment. I soon got used to it, and in the end I got so much more out of Stoatley Rough than I would have done in St. Edmund's." David King, a post-war pupil, testified to the existence of sadistic behaviour in his English school before he arrived at Stoatley Rough. His poem, "Six Whacks with an Old Gymshoe," described a teacher who inflicted pain "like six lightening sparks" on children's behinds. The teacher "Always had the same ones up to beat / He made them think it was a special treat." [28]

Another post-war Stoatley Rough pupil, Franceska Amerikaner [Rapkin], started out her British education at the exclusive Polam Hall School (Darlington, Durham) a place distinguished by the fact that the fathers of most of the girls were still in the armed services. She learned early that she was "the enemy, if not because I was German, then because I was Jewish and the Jews had killed Christ, hadn't they?" She was "taunted and tugged, pulled and shouted at." This refugee child suffered for two years, coming home to her mother, "dirty and dishevelled, with so many detentions and bad reports," and "never invited to parties." She was asked to leave after she had inexplicably stolen a hockey stick from one of the other girls. She reports about the goodness of Stoatley Rough, "The school may not have been known for its academic achievements, but my goodness, it prepared us for life and taught us decency and I will be ever grateful for the opportunity that I was given. ... to leave my traumas behind me and to develop my potential as a human being." [29]

Peter persevered. He would see the last three years of World War II at Shoreham. He joined the school's branch of what was called the Army Cadets, a program roughly comparable to the U.S. Army's Junior Reserve Officers Training Corps (ROTC). No mere play-act, Army Cadets were expected to be a rear-guard deterrent to a real enemy should it appear on English soil. Michael Strauss, who seems to have led Peter

---

[28] David King, "Six Whacks with an old Gymshoe", Stoatley Rough Newsletter Issue 9, October, 1995, p. 27.

[29] Franceska Rapkin [Amerikaner], "How I Came to Stoatley Rough," Stoatley Rough Newsletter issue 7, February, 1995. p. 26.

off the straight and narrow path again and again, had volunteered for the Cadet program and become a Quartermaster with the rank of Sergeant. He arranged for Peter to become his assistant. "I was promoted to the rank of Company Quartermaster Corporal – a rank which actually did not exist. I was told that it was especially created for me. Then I found out that there WAS one other person with such rank: he was in charge of the queen's horses at Buckingham Palace!" The following is a verbatim account of Peter Gaupp's adventures as a Cadet.

"My British Army career in the Cadets during World War II was a little like being around the Keystone Cops. To all intents and purposes we were the Home Guard for the area while living at the Shoreham Grammar School. One day the great General in Charge of the Southern Command (i.e., all of Southern England) came by to inspect our company. There was a formal inspection in which we looked all polished up and stood forever in the broiling sun for the great man to come. I was the company "spotter" which means I was the one in a position around which the rest of them organized the straight ranks, etc. It was hot! With my friend the Quartermaster I had scavenged beautiful Canadian uniforms for us which were designed for arctic conditions. Great in the winter, but in the summer…After standing at attention for what seemed like hours waiting for the great man, he finally turned up and started walking along the ranks until he came close to me when I fainted in front of him. Some impression!

> We were told that the German invasion seemed to be imminent. Then the General stood on top of a high cliff in the Liphook area and pointed towards the broad valley below it and said something to the effect that if the Germans came through there we were in charge of seeing that they were stopped. One has to remember that we were a bunch of teenagers with long Enfield rifles from the Boer War, with no rifling left and no firing pins. During the deadly silence which followed he added that our principal role would be to

be artillery spotters in that event. Otherwise we would be in charge of field communications. Perhaps that was because we could do semaphore? We had antiquated battery operated field telephones from WWI which required wires to be laid out in order to connect them. I suspect that had we ever been required to do this, we would have had a high casualty rate just from the accidents we used to have laying that wire!

Every now and then we went on maneuvers preparing ourselves for the great invasion. One time I found myself sitting in a small forest at night in charge of a platoon. Word came that German parachutists with evil intent were thought to have dropped in the area. One of my "men" came to me and whispered that there were people moving around on the other side of the broad meadow. So, what does one do? One captures the parachutists...with Long Lee Enfield rifles! Talk about terror. I ordered my men to sneak carefully towards that area and then I shouted "charge!" What we found as we broke into the clearing was a herd of cows, placidly moving through the field. We won the battle of the cow. But, I think some of us died on the way there. I don't remember reporting this story to my commander.

One day, in the middle of classes, the principal, who was also our Company commander, told us to quit school and get into our uniforms and be ready to board lorries in thirty minutes. Now, there is excitement. We boarded and rolled out in what seemed like an endless, very bumpy trip towards Western England. At night we drove into a large British Army camp while the Army rolled out in a long row of trucks and tanks. We were told that we were in charge of the camp. Every morning the Germans were said to send over a small spotter plane to take pictures and it was our job to make it look like we were the busy army still occupying the camp. Most of my time that night was spent peeling an endless supply of potatoes while my friends stood guard around the camp. When I was really sleepy, I was told to take my turn as a sentry and once again we were told that there were rumors of German parachutists in the area and to keep a sharp look out. I don't remember the details but still have a vivid memory of being told that those parachutists could be real mean and slit your throat without your knowing it had happened. Next morning we were all over the camp looking "busy" while the army rolled towards the coast and "D" Day" was on. Next day we marched around and I remember going past a farmer's field with lots of tanks and airplanes on it. We looked at them up close. They were made of plywood and painted very realistically. Again, the object was to deceive that spotter plane. (This was one of many fields, also described in Ken Follet's book *The Eye of the Needle*.) We really did not know why we were asked to do this strange and demanding thing until quite some time later.

> Our Company took its obligation to stop the [German] invasion very seriously, except that we really had nothing much to fight with. Our original uniforms were Boer War uniforms with puttees to wrap around the legs and other strange things which were totally obsolete. My genius friend, the Quartermaster, concluded that it was up to us to outfit the company since nobody else would do it. He dreamed up the idea of visiting the various army camps which surrounded us, an English one, a Canadian one, and an American one. He would secure beer and we would carry it to the Quartermasters in those camps who, to my amazement, would tell us to take whatever we wanted! That's how we got those uniforms. Then we started collecting weapons and ammunition and grenades of all kinds. It was amazing how easy it was. Then we had everyone train with these wonderful modern things and, like teenagers, we did very silly and dangerous things with the explosives. One

day we decided to carry out a beautiful, large Bren Gun [a light machine gun] plus wonderful heavy Canadian Ross rifles. The MPs stopped us. The next thing I knew that our principal had been called and we returned very sheepishly. He had accepted all we brought home in the past, including a gorgeous Canadian uniform for him and had never questioned it! Now we were in really hot water with him. But, as I remember it, all the stuff we had scrounged in the past we kept throughout the war and were possibly the best equipped Home Guard unit in the region. Certainly, the inspecting General was impressed but evidently did not ask how we got all that stuff. In the midst of war there is always some idiocy?"[30]

---

[30] The entire story "Confessions of an Army Cadet" appeared in the Stoatley Rough Newsletter Issue 23, September, 2004.

The Birds and the Bees

I n the halcyon days of the school when there were far fewer pupils than during the war, Herta said that policies regarding sexual contact were "relaxed to non-existent." According to Hans, "Dr. Lion…had fears, and we sensed them and even respected them (largely by way of caution), but at least at our time there were dances in the School Room attended by Astfalck and many coed parties which were well known to Astfalck . Dr. Lion's stricter code emerged only when the student population swelled and she no longer had the close contact with each student she had formerly enjoyed." Since there is no record of any unwanted pregnancies (with the exception of a rumor that one precocious upper-level pupil had a liaison with a soldier during the war and had to be sent away, which Wolf debunks as having been started by a notorious liar), Dr. Lion had success with her approach.

After 1939, the prospect of large numbers of adolescents of both sexes growing up together in her school caused Dr. Lion no end of anxiety. She was determined nobody would get pregnant on her watch. In part because the nineteen forties fostered a general atmosphere of naivete and censorship (everyone knew that sexual activity could lead to pregnancy and ruined reputations), but more because she herself did not have any experience with adolescents, she sensibly created an environment least conducive to romance. She would not countenance public displays of affection, prohibited dancing (except for conga-line or folk dancing), and maintained constant vigilance. She was known to save more than one girl from a fate worse than death. Driving along Farnham, if she spotted a boy and girl from her school walking along holding hands, she would screech to a half, ordered the girl into the car and whisk her back to safety.

But children are curious and will learn about sex by hook or by crook. Tom Wongtschowski, although no more curious than the rest of the Hut Boys, was the boldest. Even as a little boy in the Schoolroom in the manse (a large room holding rows of beds for the boys), he was not above peeping. There was one screened-off corner of the room where the Household Girl in charge had to sleep and keep her clothes and belongings. Wolf said, "The screen had more or less conspicuous holes, and the curtains on the doorway tended to leave a small gap when closed, which gave little boys an opportunity to ogle big girls undressing. One night Tom Wongtschowski hit the jackpot by getting a good glimpse of one of the older girl's pubic hair."

Renate Dorpalen [Dorpalen-Brocksieper] reported that when she stumbled upon a source of forbidden knowledge, Dr. Lion nipped it in the bud. She loved cleaning Dr. Lion's bungalow because "She allowed me access to her extensive library. I could read to my heart's contentment late at night, much of the time by flashlight....One day I selected Ina Seidel's *Das Wunschkind*, the story of a love-child born out of wedlock." Dr. Lion confiscated it. "I was surprised at her restriction, the first I had ever experienced in my life. It was years later when I was in graduate school, that the book fell into my hands and I became aware of the reason for her prohibition and of the suppression of sexuality in the school."[31] Wolf recalled, "By the time I reached the farm, at age fourteen, I'd picked up all sorts of sex information from raising rabbits, observing farm animals, and by learning from other boys. The Cockney Boy Scouts from the East End of London, with whom we camped, were a great source of information. In many ways they were our opposites: Heroes of the Blitz, but scared to death of spiders; ignorant in all that Stoatley Rough taught, but sophisticated in the ways of sex. Eventually someone on the farm acquired a Ministry of Information brochure on

---

[31] Renate Dorpalen [Dorpalen-Brocksieper] *Stoatley Rough Newsletter*, Issue 7, February. 1995, p. 15.

Sex Education. The Ministry did a good job. Anyway, we boys and girls knew about sex but stressful situations at the school were rare."

Scandal was partly avoided owing to the phenomenon that makes pals and buddies out of people who live closely together, for example co-ed college dorms. The student body at Stoatley Rough was family to each other, and it was only a newly arrived girl who most attracted attention. In his teens, Martin had one girlfriend after another, most of whom were recent arrivals. Goldy wrote, "Sex seemed to be totally ignored as well, at least for us boys. The girls and boys in the school were often more like brothers and sisters to each other, even though teenage romances blossomed here and there. For us boys it was sometimes difficult to ignore our sexual urges when the developing girls were wearing sweaters which they had long outgrown but could not replace because clothing was rationed….We often had crushes for the same girl, but that did not seem to matter because such things had to be kept very secret. The response to these awakening sexual feelings was to basically ignore them and to discourage situations where a boy and girl would be left alone too often and for too long. We did receive dance lessons by one enterprising teacher but the preferred dance was mostly the waltz because the centrifugal force of spinning a girl around almost eliminated body contact. Certainly the tango would have been frowned on."[32] Peter adds, "In a setting where boy-girl relationships were not encouraged nor special opportunities for such provided, the pool was one of the few places where the teenager could daydream." Wolf believed that "the sexual restraints which seem odd in retrospect were as much caused by inexperience, lack of information, the students' acute sense of insecurity as to their future and intuitive understanding that making commitments was too risky, as by School-imposed restrictions."

Night walks gave children freedom to explore relationships. Although Dr. Lion prohibited them, Nore, the enforcer, turned a blind eye. Many Roughians have written of delightful hours on the heath under the stars. Edith Hubacher [Cristoffel] recalled having to be awakened to go on the night walks because she was always falling asleep before the

---

[32] Hans [John Goldy] Goldmeier, *Memoirs* Part 1, p. 55.

appointed hour. She tied a string to her big toe and hung it out of her window. When her friends tugged on the string, she woke up and joined them. Barbara Gerstenburg [Prasse] wrote, "It is hard to describe our friendship given the ethos of to-day's teenagers. It was caring, loving, tender and very romantic. Surprisingly enough, we were so young that we never went beyond a chaste kiss or an embrace. ... We set an alarm and snuck out a kitchen window and then walked in the surrounding commons open fields and sat on a bench in the moonlight. When Ed and I went to Haslemere in 1972, I found the bench still there."[33] As noted earlier, at least two liaisons led to marriage: Herta Lewent and Hans Loeser, and Lilly Wohlgemuth and Peter Gluecksmann (both lifelong unions).

With no access to mass media (except the BBC radio) to enlighten youngsters about adult sexuality, childhood for these children was extended compared to that of children in today's world. Physical and emotional maturity occurred much later in the 1940s, compared to the cases where many (some blame it on the steroids in processed meats) reach pubescence at ages nine or ten. The authorities also shifted children around, policies that discouraged intimacy, even in same-gender friendships. Barbara Gerstenburg [Prasse] wrote, "I did not make any close girl friends at school, in fact, I believe we were not encouraged to do so. We were moved around, so that we always had different roommates and never became too close to any one."[34]

Teachers handled questions in class about sexual matters with more evasion, conflation and denial than wielded by the most skillful politician. Wolf was once sitting in class when the following dialogue took place. "Our teachers were not particularly informative about matters of sex. In English Literature one day, we were discussing Pope's "Rape of the Lock".

Girl Pupil: "What does <u>rape</u> mean?"

Teacher": "Rape is, you know, it's just one of those words that want to make you squirm!"

---

[33] Baerbel Gerstenberg [Prasse] 'Reminiscences, 1990" Boston, 1991.
[34] Ibid.

"On another occasion, the word <u>virgin</u> had come up:

Girl Pupil: "What's a virgin?"

Teacher: "A virgin is a young girl who hasn't, you know, who doesn't - well, you're a virgin and Elsie (not her real name) here, she is a virgin."

Elsie: (waking up from a daydream, emphatically): "I am <u>not</u>!"

And then there was the discussion during one of Dr. Lion's occasional classroom appearances, about the great German philosopher, Emmanuel Kant. Wolf recalls,"I don't mean to imply that the girls were more naïve than the boys. One of the more sophisticated girls broke into uncontrollable giggles in class when Dr. Lion told us about a man who had devoted his life to studying Kant. She was speaking English but pronounced the philosopher's name correctly, in the German manner."

The authorities were determined to keep the facts of life away from the younger students yet toward the end of the war, they allowed unsupervised teenagers of both sexes to live in the Farmhouse. Wolf reminds that "any reader who expects lurid confessions will be disappointed. The atmosphere of Stoatley Rough simply did not lend itself to improprieties. How, then, did we handle our growing sexual awareness? Simply getting information was a hit-or-miss affair. In a school run entirely by single women, we could sense stresses and strains among the staff. Sex was so delicate a topic that it was best avoided." At least once, Stoatley Rough offered a version of sex education that may have raised more questions than it answered, in Wolf's opinion. "Shortly after my arrival at age ten, the boys of my class were one day separated from the girls and confronted by a formidable German-speaking lady who announced that she would enlighten us *("aufklären"* was the word.) She solemnly produced a large German book with pictures of human fetuses in the womb, in various stages of development. How they got there, she did not say. She left us with the admonition not to play with ourselves (*"Also, hört zu! Vor Allem: Spielt nicht!"*) [So Listen up, all of you! No playing!]. A few years later, the girls were taken aside by the Haslemere District Nurse. Wolf reported, "I don't know what she told them, but for a couple of weeks the girls gave us boys a wide berth and strange looks."

To the boys, anything with the slightest connection to sex was infinitely fascinating. In the summer of 1944, Martin got a part-time gardening job at a place in Haslemere known euphemistically as a "home for wayward girls," where unmarried young woman stayed for the duration of their pregnancy. Every day he would return from work to his friends, who always asked the same question: what did you see? Every day came the same answer: nothing. It didn't matter. The subject was so full of potential that the boys speculated endlessly during the three months Martin's dull job lasted.

Wolf was once subjected to an agonizing experience that only a young man in the throes of adolescence could appreciate. Dr. Lion had made an arrangement with a private girls' school nearby that started having groups of girls walk over to swim at the pool once a week. A new boy had joined the Hut, Herbert Zwergfeld [Fielding] whom, having arrived with a mop of long hair, the boys instantly dubbed "Beethoven." Wolf moved to live on the Farm along with Beethoven early in 1943. "When Beethoven and I were on the Farm, we noticed that, on a certain afternoon of the week, our swimming pool would be visited by girls from Inval St. Hillary, a girl's school so strict that no contact with males was allowed. (My brother, Gerd, took his School Cert. exams there, in segregated conditions and under guard). Under those circumstances, there was no need for the girls to have bathing suits. And they didn't. Beethoven managed to borrow a pair of high-powered binoculars from Mr. Obee, issued to him by the ROC. [Royal Observer Corps]. Then he spent the afternoon by a window of the farmhouse, ogling the girls cavorting at the pool. BUT THE STINKER WOULD NOT SHARE THE BINOCULARS WITH ME! (He claimed that Mr. Obee had made him promise not to let them out of his hands!)"

There were the occasional accidents, when boys and girls were rewarded a brief glimpse of each other in the nude. Peter Gaupp remembered, "For some reason the boys and girls had to switch baths for a time, and the boys got to use the larger one. ... There was great excitement among the boys when they learned that out of habit, one of the younger boys had barged into the girls' bathroom. He was said to have seen a number of naked girls. The girls were reported to have been outraged that he just stood at the open door with his mouth open while they screamed for him to get out. The older boys declared the incident was "wasted on him." Once a girl barged in on Peter himself when he was sitting in the tub – fortunately with his back to her."[35] Another time Wolf burst into the Girls' bathroom (known as the white bathroom) expecting to see the barber. He was stunned to see a naked girl "facing me, standing up. I couldn't recall a thing. She later confessed to having blushed all over." The younger boys played a game with the girls called "ball-over-the-string." They were awed when the girls provocatively caught the ball against their chests. And then there was the time that Peter had to endure the same face off with the same tomboy who had wrestled Obo to the ground two years earlier. The girl picked on the newcomers it seems. Peter was standing near a group of thirteen-year-old girls on the terrace, waiting for dinner. The tomboy called him over. At eleven, Peter was shy and unsure of how to act, but dutiful and curious, he approached. The girl told him she was sure she could wrestle him to the ground. Peter prided himself on his wrestling skills, but this was an outrageous idea. He had been brought up with the idea that one did not ever touch girls. He tried to find excuses but they shamed him into accepting the challenge. So, he asked himself, how to wrestle a girl without touching her? Several children watched from the terrace as he and the girl squared off on the lawn. She had her arms about him and he flailed, trying not to put his hands on her. As he put it, "It was a terrible way to wrestle" and she had him down in no time. She even sat on him. Peter concludes, "No greater shame has a boy endured than that."

Sometimes someone fell in love. Love required an antidote. Wolf reports. "One of my classmates was smitten by a somewhat older girl [Ilse Kaiser] who kept her distance. He literally pined away in the classic

---

[35] Peter Gaupp, "Adolescent Awakening", *Stoatley Rough Newsletter*, Issue 17, June, 1998. p. 29.

manner, becoming pale, thin and distracted. This was serious because he was due to take the school-leaving exam, the School Certificate. It was a matter of great pride to Dr. Lion that no Roughian had ever failed the School Cert. The boy's love eventually literally rendered him 'pale and lifeless,' a true Byronic lover suffering from unrequited love. I worried that he'd become a ghost of his former self, and it got so bad that Dr. Lion gave me five shillings ($1.00) to take him to the movies in an effort to shake him out of his depression. The film version of "Pygmalion" was showing in Guildford, so we cycled there, saw a matinee and dined off fish and chips served in folded newspapers. My companion passed the School Cert and I returned about a pence in change to Dr. Lion."

The wartime environment did not favor innocuous pranks by randy teenagers. The military base of Canadian soldiers in the small town of Hindhead, a few miles from Haslemere, was a particular source of concern to mothers and of course, to Dr. Lion who warned her girls to avoid any contact with the soldiers. Wolf describes an innocent prank that backfired when carried out in the generalized atmosphere of fear that prevailed at the time.

"It was 1944. I was living on The Farm, where Fred Drechsler was supposed to be in charge. He was the last Farm Boy, about nineteen. The ambush was his idea. To house an overflow, the school had rented a house on Farnham Lane, "Rowallan," for some of the older girls (about my age, 14 – 16). Miss Barnes was in charge. She had been raised in Canada and knew how to handle Canadians and would regale wide-eyed girls with her adventures on dates with Canadian soldiers. I'm sure Dr. Lion never heard these stories. Also those Canadians must have been pretty desperate for female companionship – Miss Barnes was a large lady with a moustache. Anyway, the girls became apprehensive about their nightly trek to Rowallan in the blackout,

about a half mile or more. Fred D. rounded up
Beethoven and me (possibly someone else) to hide in the
bushes and waylay the girls. When a group approached,
he said, 'Hello, Sweetie,' in his best North American,
probably picked up in movies. The result was explosively
dramatic. The girls turned on their heels and ran back
to school, screaming at the top of their lungs. We ran
after them to shut them up. The girls never looked
back to see who was pursuing them, just ran faster and
screamed louder. By the time we caught up with them,
neighbors had called the police. Fred had made himself
scarce (we didn't squeal) leaving Beethoven and me
alone to face the music. We weren't punished but Dr.
L's wrath was unmistakable. One of the girls was Gerda
Stein [Mayer]; I don't remember the other victims."

Of such importance were girls to the boys (and vice versa) one day, the
Hut Boys decided to deal once and for all with the mysterious creatures
at their school. Peter recalled,

"One day five of the Hut Boys were lounging,
staring out of the hut window towards the front entry
of the school, when someone announced that they
had heard or read that we were of the age when one
is supposed to have a girlfriend. A novel idea which
had not crossed our minds before. There was some
disorganized ruminating as we tried to digest this. We
did not question it; rather, it was startling news. So what
do you do with this? It was actually a rather frightening
proposal. Girls were confusing. It was all right to share
classes, work, and even games with them, but nothing
too close. In retrospect, I have the feeling that none
of us were too enthusiastic about the business. (Note:
By the age of thirteen, quiet Martin, along with Tom
the Boldest, already had girlfriends, and were the envy

of the others.) Someone came up with a brilliant idea. Why not pick one girl, who could then be everyone's girlfriend? Sounded good and nominations were in order. Someone suggested Gina Schaefer. At first that had unanimous support. She was cute, our age, and friendly. But then a challenge came up. 'We can't do this because she is Felix's girlfriend.' No question about it. We knew he had expressed some interest in her and we had all witnessed him talking to her, in public, in the driveway by the front door. That clearly meant he had first claim and no gentleman interfered with that. As we pondered again, we looked across at Dr. Lion's bungalow. That was the answer! Mischi had recently been moved into the classroom which was at one end of the Bungalow 'because she was growing up.' We weren't quite clear about all of that but knew enough not to bother Mischi. In other words, her bedroom was directly in front of our window! She was nominated and, in a rush, approved as the group girlfriend. Next came the pledge to never tell her or anyone else. In a way this was a great relief. We had done our duty and as far as I can remember, the subject never came up again. If there were fantasies which followed this, they were personal and nobody's business. I don't remember if we ever told the other Hut Boys that they now had a girlfriend. They probably never knew that we had taken care of this for them."[36]

Felix and Obo were attracted to the same girl at the same time but the fact was scarcely a problem and in fact, it probably bonded the boys more closely together. Obo recalls, "We became aware of girls like Rosemary Ward, a very pretty English girl, whose reason for being at St.R. I never knew, and we would find excuses to follow her when she

---

[36] Ibid., p. 30.

went riding and discovered that she looked very sexy in her riding outfit. Then our interest of the opposite sex took a quantum leap to a very attractive young blonde English teacher named Miss Bailey (not Miss Bates). I don't know what she taught but she came to St.R. probably in late 1944 and had among other things, a great sense of humor and for some reason liked us. I remember that she must have been in the women's branch of the RAF because we thought she looked "smashing" in her uniform. Felix and I would frequently cross the Heath to the Corner Shop in Hindhead where we bought our cigarettes (where did we get the money?) and thought we were really going to score big points when we attempted to present Miss B with a 5-pack of smokes which of course she promptly refused to accept."

While the Hut Boys pondered the mysteries of adulthood, the war ground on. In January 1942, the first American forces arrived in Great Britain, bringing a whole new array of airplanes to be identified. Rommel began offensives and counter-offensives with a sequence of British generals in North Africa. In one of the countless shameful public acts of the Third Reich, SS Leader Heydrich held the Wannsee Conference, just miles from Wolf's former home, to coordinate "The Final Solution of the Jewish Question." Meanwhile the school carried on, continuing to cope with its high turnover of students. The boys in the Hut acquired a new supervisor, Miss Graetz (later Mrs. Herman). Wolf recalled, "She was in her early 20's; the Hut Boys were advancing through puberty and beginning to value privacy. Only her sense of humor saved her and us from embarrassments." The boys had begun to care about their personal appearance, and Goldy's hairnet became an object of particular interest, something he wore at night to tamp down his especially bushy mane. "We remember that Goldy wore a hair net to bed to keep his hair neat. Such garb was a novelty to the rest of us. As long as the girls did not see us wearing the hair net, some of us occasionally borrowed the net after washing our hair." [37]

---

[37] Wolf Edelstein [Elston], Martin Owens, Hans [John, Obo] Obermeyer, and Hans [John, Goldy] Obemeier, "Lifelong Friends," *Stoatley Rough Newsletter* Issue 19, August, 1999, p. 56.

The boys followed the field action on maps. German troops overran Odessa and reached Sevastopol in the Soviet Union in July 1942, while the Americans began to conduct sporadic air attacks on German-held cities in Europe in August.[38] The decisive months were October with Montgomery's victory over Rommel at El Alamein, and early November with Eisenhower's landing in then-French North Africa. By the end of the year, the Russians had surrounded the German 6th

---

[38] Wolf adds details of early American efforts in the war, hoping to counter one-sided perceptions borne in the movies. "The American raids of 1942 were feeble, ineffective, and costly, mainly for propaganda purposes. One exception: the disastrous raid on the Roumanian Ploesti oil fields, from North Africa. The US 8th Air Force didn't become effective until 1943. That's when we saw lots of B-17's.

In 1942 the RAF began major night raids (1000 scraped-together planes hit Cologne), with heavy losses. The RAF night raids didn't become effective until 1943 (air-to-ground radar, tin foil counter-measures); to this day there is controversy whether the enormous diversion of Britain's limited industrial resources harmed the Allies more than it hurt the Axis (Singapore lost in 1942 with 80,000 men for want of a few fighter squadrons while 1,000 bombers failed to cut Germany industrial production in Cologne). Beginning in 1943, the U.S. daylight offensive, like the British night offensive, was enormously costly. Churchill estimates both Allies between them lost 160,000 men (against fewer than 5,000 Germans in the Battle of Britain); about 600,000 German civilians were killed. The U.S. daylight raids became effective in 1944 after the Packard Motor Company in Detroit manufactured Rolls Royce Merlin engines under license. P-51's with Merlins and fiber-glass disposable extra gas tanks (build by British manufacturers of small boats, on the spot) were able to escort B-17's all the way to Berlin and back. At that point, Hermann Goering ...conceded that the war was lost but kept that piece of news to himself. In 1944-1945, American daylight raids finally picked a truly decisive target, the German synthetic oil plants. Eventually, the German military literally ran out of gas."

Wolf adds to make his point. "I saw the first few American planes – P-47 Thunderbolt fighters – on August 15, 1942, the day of the disastrous Dieppe raid – thousands of Canadians lost in their first European engagements. I mention these details to straighten out the current American impression of World War II: Things went badly until John Wayne and Steve Spielberg led the Greatest Generation to victory. The reality: along bitter and bloody struggle, with many blunders."

Army at Stalingrad. Goldy recalled, "We had maps with little flags where we followed the Russian, North-African and European theaters of operation as the front-line see-sawed back and forth. We learned the names of towns and cities where there was fighting, many that no one can recall any more. The big armies we followed were like the sports teams that we follow to-day."[39]

Every fourth Sunday was visiting day. Goldy's mother (who had found work as a day domestic servant nearby) would visit Goldy and notice Obo hanging around. In fact, she and Goldy might start to take a walk in the grounds, and there would be Obo, following them like a duckling follows its mother. The kindly woman began to include Obo in the little trips she made with Goldy outside the school. She knew that while letters kept arriving for Martin, Wolf, and the Gaupps, there were none for Obo. No one ever spoke to him about this worrisome fact. There was always hope. He knew his parents had by now joined his brother Arthur in Holland and presumably were safe. They just didn't have time to write. Obo continued to write letters to his parents and Arthur through the Red Cross.

In June of 1942, six months after Pearl Harbor, Herta received the news from Hans that he had enlisted in the United States Army, an act not only patriotic, but one that made him a citizen of the United States. In September, 1941, Herta had left the school and was living with her parents while doing secretarial work in London. Hans wrote about his new experience with the military, that he felt he was "an odd bird" with his German accent, but noting that the men seldom made fun of him. (He told her later that after basic training, he was assigned to the military police, and spent several months escorting ranking officers around town or riding shotgun on one of the trains that carried boisterous troops between southern training posts and New York.) It was wonderful to hear from Hans. Herta would never forget him, but now she had moved on and had begun to date young men she was meeting through friends in London. The pair had not pledged fidelity to each other when they had parted in late 1939, neither knowing if they

---

[39] Hans [Goldy John]] Goldmeier, *Memoirs*, Part 1.

would ever meet again. Herta wrote back to Hans about her job and of her life in the big city and about their mutual acquaintances. Neither dared to make long term plans. Their relationship remained suspended in the vacuum created by the intrusive, overshadowing, ever present war. All they could do was let their lives unfurl. And wait.

Big Jobs

n 1943 sixteen new students entered Stoatley Rough, and some of them were British. For the first time, children from the school's host country comprised a quarter of the total incoming group. The next year six, or about a third of the nineteen new students, were English. In 1945, of twenty-six newcomers, nine were English and by the end of the decade, England would be the predominant country of origin of the incoming pupils. Each year after 1943 the school's overall population declined, starting with the drop in 1944 from sixty-five to fifty-two pupils.

In 1943 the Hut Boys were fifteen, speaking with newly-deepened voices and thinking about their female classmates and teachers in ways other than brotherly. Permission to supplement their weekly chores brought new responsibilities and new privileges. Wolf said, they now "could walk to town by ourselves or ride our bikes. A group of Hut Boys would walk to the Hindhead Corner Shop on Sundays, to buy the *Sunday Express*. Goldy paid for it. I remember reading the exciting news of the victory of El Alamein and the Allied landings in North Africa. By 1943 I would regularly cycle to Haslemere at least once a week to run errands and replenish supplies for The Shop, run by Gina Schaefer [Mackenzie] and me."

The war was far from over. Early in 1943 U.S. and Commonwealth troops were heading for Sicily, still to fight many bloody battles. Wolf reminds us that "The U.S. Army under Patton and the Commonwealth 8th Army under his arch-rival, Montgomery raced to Palmero, with Patton winning by a couple of hours. In the meantime, the Germans escaped by sea in their version of Dunkirk. At this time came the news Wolf had been waiting for with a mixture of elation and dread. He would leave the school. With his parents safely in the U.S., they had been able to get visas for the whole family to join them although travel by sea was still prohibited as it was highly dangerous. Dr. Lion promoted Wolf to a higher Group level in order to help him get ready to take the school certificate examinations. "I was deemed to have outgrown the Hut and was transferred to the Farm. The Hut Boy gang broke up, as Squink (Peter Gaupp) left Stoatley Rough [for Shoreham] and Obo and Tom joined me on the farm." Long-haired Beethoven, after living on the Farm for two years, would leave within a few months. Wolf learned the pleasures of listening to the radio (for there was very little other entertainment for the children aside from the occasional excursion to the Rex Cinema). "The radio gave electric shocks to anyone trying to tune it, but it allowed us to keep up with the BBC news, listen to ITMA (It's That Man Again, the Tommy Handley Show), enjoy the latest hits played by Geraldo and his Band and the voice of Vera Lynn (The Forces' Sweetheart) and wait for Vic Oliver's inevitable father-in-law joke. Vic Oliver was the stage name of a fellow-refugee from Vienna who had done very well for himself. Everyone knew that his father-in-law was Winston Churchill. After the invasion of Normandy, we could listen to Captain Glenn Miller and his Band on the Allied Expeditionary Forces Program of the BBC until the sad day when Captain Miller was reported missing, presumed dead." The boys loved swing music. They were even motivated to consult the school's atlas to find out the exact location of Chattanooga, Acheson, Topeka and Santa Fe. Wolf continued, "Another favorite radio station was *Soldatensender* Calais, a BBC station masquerading as a German station for the *Wehrmacht*. Its barracks-room German made a nice contrast to genteel BBC English." [40] Martin said, "The program was broadcast widely on the Continent, intended to discourage German soldiers by giving real news about German defeats and Allied victories, all interspersed with skits, jokes and music."

---

[40] Wolf Edelstein [Elston] *Memories of Stoatley Rough*, 1990. p. 17.

Martin remained in the Hut with Felix, Goldy, and Francis Le Messurier, but older girls and other friends were also sent to live on the Farm, such as Ruth Lichtenstein (Ultman) and Ilse Meyer. Mr. Hughes, the sturdy Welshman, had left by then to further his farm training. That left eighteen-year-old Fritz (Fred) Drechsler [Fred Drexler] in charge, the last of the original "Farm Boys," who still ran what was left of the farm. With wonderful common sense logic, (after all, the kids had now been living years without parental supervision), the new "man" in charge made no attempt to enforce the rules that still reigned up at the main house. Wolf said, "Fred lived in a small room off the common room and had no objections to anything we did, as long as he was invited." Wolf also informs us that by then, "the Farmhouse also housed Benjy the Cat, and Fred's nervous dog, Betty, and her two pups, Winston and Franklin. I now had what I valued most: freedom from supervision." Such freedom once led to a mistake in judgment. Wolf and Beethoven decided they needed to do something about the cold. Beethoven went to the pump house to scrounge some diesel fuel. Mistakenly, he took fuel from the wrong barrel, bringing back petrol intended for the tractor. He "chucked it onto the wood stove and whoosh, the flames roared up to the ceiling." Some of the fuel spilled onto the floor and the wooden planks began to burn. The boys worked feverishly to extinguish the fire. Wolf grabbed a coat belonging to one of the Farm boys and began beating the flames. After a few minutes, they managed to put it out, burning their fingers in the process. They looked around at the damage, acutely aware that not only had they almost burned down the building, but that they had done so with rationed fuel, a serious matter. They set to work. First they scrubbed the floor clean of any charred remains and then checked the coat. Remarkably, it was not ruined. They managed to remove most of the gasoline smell from it with soap and water, and when the hapless owner came back, they concocted a story delivered so well that the boy believed them. They were able to extinguish the gasoline smell in the room by putting wet leaves on the fire, leaving the top off the stove and filling the room with smoke. Disaster had been averted, and no one in authority never knew of the incident. Wolf remarked with no facetiousness, "With Fred Drechsler in charge, nobody was in charge." The general lack of supervision of the Farmhouse children presaged an atmosphere of freedom that would characterize the whole school after the war.

The Hut boys took on new and larger responsibilities. Obo, in particular, was given more duties than seems reasonable. In one of Dr. Lion's intuitive (often mistaken) and irrevocable decisions about a child's future potential, she assigned Obo to be an apprentice to Mr. Phillips. Obo not only was destined to help with the gardening in the summer, but had to feed the coal furnaces in the winter. The "Ginger Nipper" so fondly named by the old man graduated, at fifteen, to a more dangerous responsibility – the operation and maintenance of the large and ancient kerosene-powered engine located just off the path to the Farm. This engine drove a deep-well water pump that served the main house. It had an enormous flywheel, a heavy wheel that spun and moved a belt that energized a pump that pumped water to the main building. "I don't know how I qualified for these pyrotechnic activities but I did learn something without ever becoming a fireman or arsonist." [41] This contraption was anything but safe.

> "At the bottom of the steep path just above the farm house was an old corrugated steel shed which housed a large horizontal single cylinder, kerosene fired engine with two six- or seven-foot in diameter flywheels ca.1895. In order to start this engine, a small chamber on the opposite end from the flywheels had to be preheated in order to compress the gasses derived from the kerosene. Once the kerosene was hot enough to give off the desired compressed gas mixture, Mr. Philips used a removable handle which he attached to the end

[41] Hans [Obo, John] Obermeyer, Stoatley Rough Newsletter, Issue 19, August, 1999. Wolf noted that the diesel engine was a true museum piece. "Unfortunately it was junked after the war. Its date, 1896, from memory, showed it was one of the first diesel engines made in Britain. Rudolf Diesel took out his original German patent in 1892." (note to the author)

of the fly wheel drive shaft and slowly started to turn it until the pressure of the compressed gas took over and the engine gained momentum, removing the handle as it came up to speed. He later showed me how to do this whole process and when the engine backfired, which it did quite frequently, it scared the hell out of the young Ginger Nipper and I ran for the door more than once. Talk about OSHA, I think they would have put a large padlock on the door. One of the flywheels drove a flat leather belt which in turn drove a pulley shaft, which in turn drove another shaft and pulley. That arrangement drove the water pump which supplied a good part of the water to the large tank on the top floor of the main building several times a week as well as a small tank located just outside the shed from which we got the farm house water supply. There were also the remains of a pedestal which at one time had a dynamo/electric generator mounted on it which presumably provided electricity to a large storage battery in the main house but this had not been there for many years....This pump, so necessary to the operational life of Stoatley Rough, was one of the things that I remember vividly and really got me interested in all things mechanical in later life."[42]

The Hut Boys had been Boy Scouts since later 1942 or early 1943, gaining merit badges. Martin recalls, "The Haslemere Fire Brigade trained us to fight fires. One Saturday we learned how to hook up a hose, jump from a tower into a round canvas held taut by waiting men below, and to carry each other up and down ladders." Martin was teased because during the instructions on handling the hoses, he called out, "Water on!" while pointing the nozzle straight at his face. "If they'd turned the water on at that moment, it would have knocked me clean

---

[42] Hans [Obo, John] Obermeyer, in an email to the author, June 8, 2006.

into next week." Scouting was not just a casual dalliance. The school must have recognized that scouting not only gave the boys male role models but also a way to earn recognition.

Martin, who after one summer at a Zionist camp had become fanatical about the Zionist movement, wrote, "During this time, I became a boy scout, patrol leader and then troop leader. My patrol was the Stork Patrol whose colors were blue and white, the colors of Israel." He thrived in scouts. "Our scoutmaster was a gem from Haslemere where he worked in a plumbing supply house. I remember he once took me for a ride in a truck and the gas tank was right under my seat. The gasoline leaked as I sat there, and my bottom was sore for days. We were an active troop, taking a lot of merit badges. We took the fireman's merit badge and also the handyman's badge. We learnt to tie knots behind our backs and we drilled, marching some intricate formations, which we exhibited, in town. I thoroughly enjoyed scouting and the drilling." Martin became a King's Scout, the equivalent of an Eagle Scout in America, an achievement of which he is still proud. Some time after Wolf had left the school in 1944, the Hut boys / boy scouts were granted permission to ride their bikes into London and back, a trip of forty miles one way. (Earlier attempts to get Dr. Lion's permission had been unsuccessful.) The merry pack set off with the promise to return in time for evening tea. They rode as far as Hyde Park in downtown London, and stopped en route to look at the King's Beasts at Hampton Court Palace. The trip was arduous, legs pumping sweating bodies up and down many hill along the way. On the return home, Tom Wongtschowski ran out of steam and fell behind. He dismounted, defeated, as the others circled around, egging him on. It was the good-hearted Goldy who chose to stay with Tom, coaxing him along, while the others heartlessly forged on toward home.

Martin and Goldy, at fifteen, became air raid messengers, a job that forced them to confront their fear. Air raids now occurred on an average of once every two weeks, (although from August, 1940 to May of 1941, there were hundreds). After the Battle of Britain the air raids became sporadic, they happened at night, and children only heard the airplane motors as search lights swept across the sky. The job of the air raid messenger was to show up at the closest neighboring house, a farmer's house just beyond the Farnham Lane estates, during each raid. Their job, in case of an attack on the school, was to get the message into Haslemere. The boys took turns getting out of bed and walking their bikes through the dark, blacked out landscape. The farmer's wife always gave them a cup of hot tea and cake before they returned home but neither enjoyed the trip, going or returning - after all, a German parachutist might lie in wait just beyond the next hedge.

Wolf described the experience of the war for the children as experienced in early 1944. "London had formidable defenses and the northern horizon (toward London from the school) would be red with flashes, probably from rocket and AA batteries (mostly in parks – all that hardware had to come down). There would also be flares, probably from German planes trying to locate landmarks. The morning after, we'd pick up strips of aluminum foil with paper backing (as in candy wrappers, but long and narrow) dropped by bombers to confuse radar. In 1943 while in bed on the Farm, I watched a German Dornier bomber (we learned its identity later) crash in flames. In 1944 we cycled to the Beacon Hill Golf Course, near Hindhead, to look at a crashed Heinkel 177, one of the few German four-engined heavy bombers. Dr. Lion heard about it and was not pleased."

Wolf began studying for his Matric, and Dr. Lion asked him and Gina Schaefer [Mackenzie] to co-manage the Shop. The Shop was an essential institution at the school, operational almost from its inception. Wolf recounts the details of his responsibilities:

> "My period on the farm was one of maturing in matters other than sex. Although my National Geographic card file showed little progress [Dr. Lion had asked Wolf to catalogue the contents of a huge pile of the old magazines], Dr. Lion promoted me to a position of real responsibility. Gina Schaefer (Mackenzie) and I were put in charge of the Shop, a weekly Wednesday evening

302

affair, where pupils and staff could buy necessities like pencils, toothbrushes, and the like. Most important of all, I was put in charge of the sweets (candy) ration of three ounces per person per week. One ounce was dished out free of charge for dessert, the other two were sold in the Shop. I was entrusted with the sweets-rations coupons for the entire school. The exercise of this new responsibility required much diplomacy. Gina and I operated under supervision of Miss Nacken, who believed in high thinking and plain living. Her idea of sweets was something nutritious, like plain dark chocolate. The kids much preferred something gooey, like Mars bars, even though they were said to cause pimples and rotten teeth. With Solomonic wisdom, I tried to get one-third of the ration in plain chocolate, to be handed out free of charge as dessert, and the rest as candy bars, which had to be bought with our meager pocket money, half-a-crown per month (fifty cents at the then prevailing rate of exchange). The soap ration was another point at issue. The plain soap that was issued free of charge was sufficient for us boys, but the girls had reached an age at which they demanded some choice. Miss Nacken approved, provided the alternative was a strong disinfectant soap. That was not what the girls had in mind. To please everybody, we carried two kinds of soap: a daintily perfumed variety, which sold briskly, and a smelly carbolic soap for Miss Nacken's eyes and nose. Nobody ever bought a piece, not even Miss Nacken."[43]

Wolf and Gina employed creative (but scrupulously honest) bookkeeping. "Miss Nacken taught Gina and me a simple kind of double-entry bookkeeping and inspected the books at the end of every month. Our

---

[43] Wolf Edelstein [Elston] *Reminiscences.*

total capitalization was exactly £11 1s 6d (about $45, pre-inflation) and on inspection day the value of our stock of merchandise plus cash in hand had to total that magic number. After much sweating, Gina and I always managed to balance the books, at which point I had a great urge to kiss Gina. I was much too shy and never did. Gina, what would you have done if I had? [Fifty years later, Gina met Wolf at a reunion and responded, 'I would have been honored.' Wolf's own response: 'Life's saddest words...Checkhov wrote plays about situations like this."]

"I will now reveal another secret for the first time: our books never balanced precisely; we were always a few pence over or under £11 1s 6d. Unknown to Miss Nacken, Gina and I had an old cigar box, into which we deposited the surplus of good months and from which we made up deficits. Fortunately, the box never ran out of change. It's too bad that the U.S. Treasury can't operate on the same principle. The shop gave me a great opportunity to get away from school and supervision. On Thursday afternoons, I regularly cycled down Farnham Lane to Haslemere, to replenish our inventory. Word soon got around and I was handed many other errands...shoes to be repaired, stamps to be bought, prescriptions from Boots the Chemist, groceries for the kitchen, etc. I got to know and respect many of the local tradesmen, like Boots' the chemist, which moved to the opposite side of High Street as of 204; Nobs the Stationers, still in business as of 2004; and Metcalf and Yates, the butchers (their former shop is now an expensive Italian restaurant). The carrier on the back of my bike was always loaded. Once, my cargo included a sick little girl to take to the doctor. She was obviously frightened to death but never let out a peep, even when the bike blew a tire. Another time, Miss Demuth asked me to pick up an order at the butcher's. It turned out to be about thirty pounds of bloody lengths [of oxtail] very difficult to balance on the back of a bike. They fell off a few times but made good soup anyway."

Sometimes the administrators asked the boys to pick up cigarettes for them. Obo recalled, "I think Dr. Lion smoked DuMaurier Ovals which came in a square box and the smaller quantities came in a cardboard box. I do remember going to the sweet shop next to the

Haslemere railway station to purchase smokes for her. I don't know why the man then already elderly, somehow didn't ask me how old I was. If I had discovered wine and beer I wonder what would have happened if I'd tried to buy some from him." Wolf remembered Dr. Lion making a little joke while buying candy in town. "Even before they were rationed, the limited supply was restricted to people with children. Not aware of the restriction, she tried to buy some and was asked, "How many children do you have, madam?" Her answer was, "Oh, about one hundred."

Wolf' reminds us that the children always walked or rode bikes; the single car at the school was the exclusive provenance of the adults. "The trip home was always the hardest since it was uphill all the way. Occasionally Dr. Leven would zoom by in the school car (gray Austin 8 convertible, license plate HPL 715–another piece of remembered trivia). She never stopped and never offered to carry my load, let alone the bike and me." In our era, where most parents have become obsessed with children's safety, it's hard to imagine the risks the staff allowed the children to take. Cycling into town with its numerous traffic junctions and roundabouts was potentially dangerous, yet according to Wolf it was not dangerous at all, just "little Haslemere with little civilian traffic." He was nevertheless not immune to the dangers of being hit by a vehicle. One day he was riding on what was called the High Pavement. "The narrow roadway was (and still is) flanked by a brick embankment more than 6 ft high. Unexpectedly encountering an outsize tank while riding a bike, a split-second choice had to be made: Get squashed or bail out and hit the bricks. I made the right choice but required stitches on my forehead. If you look carefully, you can still see a faint scar. The tank was unhurt." Wolf's comment about the incident: "I didn't feel that I almost got killed, just that I had made an obvious choice. In view of all the risks of the times – Nazis, bombs, etc., - the ordinary risks of daily lives seemed so trivial that we gave them little or no thought."

The Hut Boys recognized the historical significance of the war and the impact upon their lives. Wolf said, "In the midst of a pervasive war, we did not look on ourselves as sheltered. Planes, most of them friendly, were always within earshot as were training exercises of the Second

Canadian Armoured Brigade. One beautiful summer day, somebody remarked that 'if it weren't for the gunfire, you wouldn't know there's a war on.' No irony was intended. The Springs of 1943 and 1944 brought 'little *Blitzes*,' when the night sky was lit by flares and tracers and glowed red in the direction of London. One night, a flaming German bomber spiraled to earth. In excitement and immaturity, I cheered. The next day, one of the grownups sharply reminded me that men had died in that plane, men who might once have been neighbors. The incident brought home to me the dilemma of our times; our former neighbors served a cause dedicated to our extermination; the men who risked their lives to save ours might look on us as enemy aliens. We did not lead sheltered lives."[44]

Wolf began to think like an adult. "After our fifteenth birthdays, we became fire guards and stayed up all night once a month in an air raid; we were supposed to get on the roof of the main building and watch for incendiary bombs. Fortunately, there were no air raids when I was on duty, and I could use the long nights to satisfy my thirst for modern history in the school library....I tried, and am still trying, to discover the reasons behind the events that had placed us where we were. Nothing I read, then and since, has come close to conveying the feelings of what we saw and lived every day." Obo expressed similar thoughts. "I often think what did we really know and understand and relate to with regard to these horrific events during our stay at Stoatley Rough? For that matter what did the staff know and what should they have told us and if so, were we ready to understand and relate to it?"

In 1943, the Hut Boys were still speaking too much German with each other. Dr. Lion made them an offer. If they spoke only English for six weeks, she would reward them with cash. The boys decided to take up the challenge (in spite of the fact that Tom Wongtschowski would be a holdout. For those six weeks they had no trouble keeping their pledge during daylight hours, but at night with the lights out, Tom was always lapsing. By and large they managed to convert him and they were rewarded with a modest sum. They held a caucus to determine

---

[44] Wolf Edelstein [Elston] *On the Occasion of Eleonore Astfalck's 90ᵗʰ Birthday.*

what to do with their winnings. After much deliberation, they decided to become entrepreneurs. They would raise rabbits. They bought two females. Someone found a pamphlet on raising rabbits (probably a free pamphlet issued by the Ministry of Food) and the boys learned how to determine the gender of a rabbit through all that black and white fur. The boys built a hutch in front of the Hut and took turns rising at the crack of dawn to search for dandelion leaves or to beg vegetable scraps from the kitchen. When the does were old enough, they took them to a Shottermill school mate who owned a buck. "It was slam, bam, thank you ma'am, very educational." The stud fee was one of the litter. One day, Peter saw a young one fighting with one of the does. "We tried separating them but it did not work. And then, a few weeks later, one of them started getting fat – it was pregnant. It turned out to be female and the fighting wasn't fighting at all." One of the male offspring had impregnated one of the does, (one hopes not its own mother).

Over time, the boys grew tired of raising rabbits but for awhile, there was a time of real, if paltry, money-making. The first time they decided to sell a rabbit to the butcher in town, Wolf was chosen to take it in. He borrowed a bike, popped the rabbit in a burlap-covered box and cycled into Haslemere to the butcher shop. He carried in his bundle and handed it over, expecting to be paid and to get out the door. It was not to be. "The butcher dispatched it with a quick chop before my eyes, as soon as I handed it to him." Wolf was still in shock when the butcher handed over the money but quickly recovered at the thought of profit. "He paid us five shillings, equivalent to two months' pocket money." The rabbit family multiplied and Wolf got used to delivering the rabbits to town. One day he carried two rabbits in the burlap box. Riding down Farnham Lane, he met two strangers who stopped him for directions. He got off his bike and put the box on the ground. As he stood chatting, the box started jumping up and down "to the astonishment of the onlookers" until Wolf explained its contents. Even on their last journey, the doomed rabbits had found love.

The enterprise lasted through the next year, Obo and Wolf taking the rabbits with them to the Farm. When Wolf left the school in the

Fall of 1944, Obo became the sole proprietor of the remaining stock. It's not clear how many generations of rabbits the Hut Boys raised, or how successful an enterprise it was. We know that at least one time a rabbit ended up on the boys' dinner table.

Obo picks up the story. "The party was on the night of June 5-6, 1944, for my (June 2) and Martin's (June 16) birthdays. Afterwards, boys and girls went for a moonlight walk, interrupted by low-flying (under German radar) RAF heavy bombers, heading for Normandy. After awhile, we heard rumbles of distant explosions. As a joke, somebody said, 'it must be the Invasion." (We had waited for years and wondered if it would ever come.) The next day the sky was full of American and British planes, their wings painted overnight with black and white recognition stripes. The first news of the Invasion came from the German radio, but gave the wrong location, a successful Allied feint." Life was about to take a new turn for the denizens of Stoatley Rough.

But on the night before the invasion, the teen-agers had their party. One of the Farm boys butchered one of their rabbits for them while a few girls "liberated" some shortening and sugar from the kitchen. Still others stole apples for the feast they planned. The boys fried the pieces in stolen margarine. They all sat down at the table. Martin, unaware of the project, arrived from the Hut and sat down at the table, commenting on the delicious aroma of the "chicken". "When they told me what the main dish was, I was appalled. How could they have been so heartless? I jumped up and left the table, refusing to eat the vile thing, raising hoots and jeers from the others."

D-Day

Nineteen forty-four saw German losses (Italy had suffered in 1943 and was out of the fight. Wolf recalled that some Italian POWs worked on nearby farms), with Soviet troops advancing into Poland and Italy becoming the new major battleground. The British prepared to drop 3,000 tons of bombs on Hamburg as the Allies entered Rome. June 6, 1944 was momentous. It signaled the invasion of the Continent by way of Normandy - the push to Paris. [45] D-Day (not "debarkation day but merely a military shorthand to name events before an event such as D-3, D-2), was not only a thrilling turning point but also a time of reflection for the children at Stoatley Rough. It marked the beginning of the end of their life under the sheltering wing of their school and home. With the end of the war they would have to leave Stoatley Rough with its routines, familiar surroundings, friends and reliable and kindly adults. A reunion with family was for many a prospect loaded with uncertainty. Few wished to leave the security, the predictability and the familiar. Each child experienced this knowledge in his or her unique way.

The pupils knew for well over a year that the Allied attack was imminent. The buildup was all around them. For weeks the Allies had been steadily bombing the coastal areas of France, only seventy-five miles away from Stoatley Rough (thirty-five miles to Portsmouth,

---

[45] Hans Loeser points out that D-Day does not mean "Debarkation Day" but rather simply "day." It is merely the military's way of marking a planned event, to lock in a date without disclosing it, hence three days before the event is called D-3, then the next day is D-2, and so on.

forty miles across the channel). Goldy wrote, "We had been used to the constant sound of Allied planes which often had their rendezvous above us before they set out to bomb Germany as we guessed where they were going. Around D-day it was a little different, however. For one thing, the activity was so frequent that most of us had to sleep through it if we were to have any rest at all. It continued daily and by night for perhaps four weeks. Only on D-day was everyone up to watch a sky constantly full of planes, the DC-3's [C-47's] pulling gliders so low that the trees bent in their wake. The children saw massive ground mobilization as well. "D-day, and the days before and later were exciting ones for us. Tanks, trucks and masses of troops, mostly British, Canadians, and Americans, were noisily making their way down the crowded Portsmouth Road to the coast and this traffic went on forever."[46]

It was customary for students and teachers to listen to the radio every noon in the large Sitting Room of the main building. On June 5, 1944, pupils and adults grouped as usual around the large bay windows or by the fireplace; they stood or sat tucked in various places in the next room; some were on the terrace. Quotations were recited for the amusement and enlightenment of those who lived and worked on the Farm as well as the teachers and staff standing in attendance. Then Dr. Lion turned on the radio, the moment all had awaited. Would today be the day? The broadcast began with the usual anthems of the nations comprising the Allies. It was a game among the children to be the first to match the country to the anthem. Then came national and international events. (People living on the Farm were accustomed to listening to a second helping of news every night on the radio and, old enough to understand the larger dimensions of the war, they hung on every word, interjected their reactions, and held long discussions in the evenings when the news was over. They also greatly enjoyed the German propaganda broadcasts and scoffed loudly at their former countrymen.) But on that day, the news ended and everyone filed up the stairs to their designated tables. Dinner was served.

---

[46] Hans [John, Goldy] Goldmeier, *Memoirs* Part I p. 59.

Sometime around mid-morning the children learned the invasion had begun. The Supreme Commander of the Allied Forces, General Dwight D. Eisenhower, came on the radio to announce the fact, and when he finished talking, Beethoven's 5th Symphony flowed majestically through the airwaves.

On the night of D-Day some of the boys went to the Cooney's house on the edge of the Farm to listen to their radio. Once again Eisenhower's high pitched, constricted voice filled the room, and someone said, "He sounds just like Donald Duck," and someone else said, "Yeah, well he's American, isn't he?" [47] The comments about his voice intended no disrespect, although Wolf points out that the Cooneys weren't only making fun of Americans and their accents. King George VI had struggled all his life against stuttering and any public appearance must have been an agony for him. On the night of D-Day, he momentarily had to pause in the middle of his address. One of the Cooneys remarked, "Shouldn't we now be singing *God Save the King?*" Donald Duck, like Mickey Mouse and the rest of the Disney gang, were world-famous in the thirties, so famous that the youngest children recognized the voice of the frustrated duck. (On the same token, Laurel and Hardy were also loved, even by the Germans, whom they called *Dick und Doof* (Fat and Silly). But the voice of Donald Duck was the most imitated and many children tried to produce the sound. Before the war, the very young Peter Gaupp – he must have been six or seven - had gone to see a movie with his mother. The newsreel featured Joseph Goebbles, Hitler's powerful minister of Nazi propaganda, who also had a high voice. "I asked in apparently loud voice if that was Donald Duck. We left very quickly.")

Obo heard the aircraft that morning and had run outdoors to see the planes. "On the morning of June 6th, 1944, we saw thousands of

---

[47] Wolf makes it clear that there was no disrespect meant toward Eisenhower on D-Day. "People joked about speeches by big shots. That included King George VI, who manfully tried to control his stutter. When he momentarily had to pause, one of his loyal subject said: 'Shouldn't we be singing God Save the King?'" The point is that there was no universal reverence or unalloyed admiration for the Americans in the war.

Allied planes with black and white stripes painted on the underside of their wings, headed for the south coast of England. We knew then that D-Day had come and the Allies had landed on the coast of Normandy in France. Although the war was far from over, we could feel for the first time in five years that it was coming to an end." The planes carried tons of bombs intended for Normandy beaches, the largest of which could carry around eight tons. Painted stripes on the planes were intended to prevent them from being shot down by Allied guns. Martin, standing a little apart from the others, gazed up in wonder. His focus was on the hundreds of gliders being towed by the DC-3s that he knew transported men. There were thousands of missions flown on D-Day by U.S. and British planes, mostly fighters, with light and medium bombs and transports. The boys and girls saw it all.

D-Day brought private sorrow for more than a few. Fifteen-year-old Ruth Ultmann [Muessig] had lost her mother several years before she came to Stoatley Rough, but her father and young brother had made it to England. He planned to take the family to America where they would "have a future." She resisted the idea but he was adamant – he would go and she would have to decide whether to join him. She had no intention of going to America, a country she knew nothing about. All she wanted to do was to live at Stoatley Rough until she could find work in England. D-Day destroyed her security. "We were waiting for the news to begin and the usual voice came on: 'This is the BBC Home and Forces program. Here is the news and this is Robert Robinson reading it. Allied forces have landed on the beaches at Normandy and are making their way to the capital, etc. etc.' He spoke about soldiers being greeted by children strewing flowers on them and women throwing kisses as they marched towards Paris. There was a hush in the room and the next thing we heard was *The Marseillaise*. I for one silently burst into tears. I realized instantly it was the beginning of the end, and I was torn because I knew that also meant I would have to leave the family who had taken me in as one of their own, Stoatley Rough, my 'other home' and England which I loved so dearly. To this day I cannot hear the French National Anthem without thinking of that day. I know exactly where I was standing (in front of a bookcase next to the curtain that divided the Zoo from the Bower [girls' sleeping quarters in the manse] and I was not paying attention as usual, daydreaming, not even facing the way I was supposed to be until I heard those fateful first words. I remember later that day running out into the garden to be alone and going to the bench under the wall facing the Downs. I looked hard at them, because I wanted to remember them forever and I told myself that was what I was doing, memorizing that one peak on the right hand-side and the built-up part in the middle with the depression on the far left."[48] Stoatley Rough remained with Ruth long after she left the school. "One reason my little house here in Connecticut attracted me right away was that it faces a mountain, the Sleeping Giant, and it looks remarkably like the Surrey Downs. When my Public Radio station plays Beethoven's Fifth Symphony and I look out of the window, I am back in the Music Room at Stoatley Rough." (Ruth crossed the Atlantic on the Cunard liner, *Aquitania,* that had been converted into a troopship, in April, 1945. Later, Wolf, by then also in New York, occasionally ran into Ruth at Time Square subway station. "She'd be heading downtown to work and I'd head uptown to City College....I too was homesick for England in my first months in America...The smug attitudes of Americans toward the war – distant from the action, safe, well fed, obviously prosperous – came as a shock after the sacrifices and privations of shabby, rationed, black-out and bombed Britain." Wolf adds with uncharacteristic bitterness, "I was never homesick for Germany."

Wolf expressed his feelings about American attitudes toward the world wars. "The differences in experiences between Europe and America lie at the root of current attitudes and conflicts. Two World Wars, with millions of dead on both sides, have devastated and traumatized

---

48 Ruth Ultmann [Muessig] never fully accepted having to leave England in 1945. She reported from her home in Connecticut that after her husband had died, after her children had grown, and after she had become a grandmother, that she had never felt at home in America, that her heart remained in England and that leaving had been a lifelong regret. Ruth Ultmann [Muessig] letter to Martin Owens dated October 17, 2001.

Europe. On the plus side, the Europeans will not fight each other in a major war for the first time since the collapse of the Roman Empire.... By comparison, America got off lightly in two World Wars and mostly remembers the Greatest Generation, John Wayne and inevitable victory. For experiences comparable to the European, one has to go to the South after the Civil War. When I was in the Army, stationed in Virginia 1952-1955, the time of Brown v. Board of Education, we were treated as the Yankee Army of Occupation."

After the invasion started, life changed for Stoatley Rough, although the children would have plenty of time to adjust. The war still had to play out to its bloody (albeit inevitable) conclusion for almost another year, with squadrons of airplanes still blanketing the sky and convoys of war vehicles constantly moving through Haslemere. Goldy recalled, "I was at the Haslemere train station a few days after D-Day and saw long lines of ambulances, most of them American, waiting to pick up the wounded who were expected by train from Portsmouth."[49] Although it may have seemed that the end was in sight, there was much more blood to be shed, many more buildings to be destroyed. Wolf wrote, "For nearly two months, the German lines in Normandy held and the battle was in balance. Many more battles were to follow, e.g., the Battle of the Bulge. For American, especially, the climax came after D-Day. Until that time, British and Commonwealth troops had outnumbered Americans in North Africa and Europe. From the buildup after D-Day, Americans became dominant in numbers and in casualties." The war wasn't over and the children came to fear one last act of evil from the hands of Hitler via their new bomb, the V-1 rocket, or "doodlebug."

During the summer of 1944, the same summer the Nazis liquidated the town of Oradour-sur-Glane in France in retaliation for the murders of SS officers by guerilla resistance fighters, they also unleashed their first doodlebug on Britain, also called buzzbomb by American reporters. The bombs came flying toward London from various sites held by the Germans in Belgium and France in the form of small unmanned jet planes (the V-2 was a rocket), kept level by simple gyrocompasses.

---

[49] Hans [John Goldy] Goldmeier, Memoirs Part 1.

The bombs made an odd putt-putt sound before their motors stopped, ominous because one could hear it coming, then its motors conked out just before it hit, and one never knew exactly where it would explode.[50] The children of Stoatley Rough experienced sufficient near-misses to have good cause to be afraid. David King, who as a seven-year-old, was living in London at the time, was home alone when particular damage caved his house in around him. Instructed always to go under the big oak table if there wasn't enough time to get to a shelter, he dutifully had crawled under the oilcloth tablecloth taking with him his toy soldier, his little lead spitfire airplane, one blade of the propeller missing, and his "special torch which had a shaded light beam and a kind of brown paper over the glass." Ten hours later, he was rescued, unhurt, covered in plaster and dust, saved by the table that had withstood the blast that took down the rest of his house. He recalled the sound of the V-1 with clarity. "It starts to splutter when the propellant runs out. Then there is a terrifying silence; it lasts forever, or so it seems. This is followed by a screaming dive as the flying bomb heads for its target. If you hear the next thing then you live; it's a deafening explosion."[51] Obo remembered, "We could hear these pilotless bombs passing overhead and when their engines stopped we would hold our breath and hope they would glide far enough away so that when they hit the ground and exploded, we would have been able to take shelter." Martin happened to be standing in for an ailing teacher with a class of young children when the distinct sound of a doodlebug filled the school. At sixteen, Martin not only had the distinction of being head of student council,

---

[50] "The V-1 was an unmanned, un-guided, flying bomb. Although primitive by today's standards, it was the first of what we now call a "cruise missile." The Germans called it *Vergeltungswaffe* or "retaliation weapon," designated V-01 because it was the first of its kind. The V-1 was a liquid fuelled, pulse-jet drone aircraft that could carry a 2,000 lb warhead. There was no navigation system, so it was simply pointed in the direction of its target. " Simple gyrocompasses kept it level and range was controlled by the fuel supply. Its typical target was a city in southern England." http://www.aviation-central.com/space/usm10.htm Aviation-Central.com accessed May 27, 2005.

[51] David King, "Buried Alive for Ten Hours", *Stoatley Rough Newsletter*, Issue 18, September, 1998. p. 22.

but also he had earned the rank of Boy Scout Senior Patrol Leader, both achievements of which made him feel "very important". Things were well underway in the classroom when the buzzing started then stopped. All eyes looked toward the window. Martin yelled, "Dive!" Everyone disappeared under the table, waiting for the explosion. They waited and waited, and nothing happened. "Eventually I crept out from under my desk, the rest resumed their seats, and I finished the class. Afterwards I learnt to my embarrassment that it hadn't been a doodlebug at all, but rather a B-17 that had lost a propeller as it flew by." [52] At the same time, Wolff was in Dr. Wolff's French class, so absorbed in the literature that she failed to note at first that the students had all scuttled under the table. "When the noise stopped, we all dived for cover. Dr. Wolff, who was hard of hearing but refused to admit it, hadn't heard a thing. She got excited and angry. She thought we were playing a trick."

The summer months proved to be a time of contemplation and anxiety for those who knew they would leave. Wolf wrote, "What I had heard about American high schools was not reassuring and I was determined to finish my secondary schooling in Britain." My goal was to take the School Certificate Examination in June 1944, two months short of my sixteenth birthday. The School Certificate, I should explain, was then the standard school-leaving examination throughout the British Empire. It was set by the universities (Cambridge, in my case) and, if passed at a high standard, entitled one to matriculate at a university. In order to prepare, my period of contemplation came to an abrupt end in late 1943. For many months, I studied hard far into the night. The time of the exam coincided with the weeks immediately after D-Day and the beginning of the V-1 flying bomb ("doodlebug") bombardment. A V-1 exploded during one of the tests; it raised adrenalin levels and cleared the brain. I passed with flying colors."

In his over twelve months prior to the exam, Wolf spent his afternoons at the Farm purportedly to study. "The greatest contribution to my maturing was the isolation of life on the Farm. On most days I went there after lunch ostensibly for prep. Actually I did very little work.

---

[52] Martin Friedenfeld [Owens] Stoatley Rough Newsletter, Issue 10, February, 1996.

Sometimes I read a non-required book; I remember pondering *The Bridge of San Luis Rey*. More often, I just wandered off. By the stream that fed the swimming pool, I watched frogs mate, tadpoles hatch, and newts and salamanders crawl. Mostly, I just walked and thought about whatever was important to me at the time. The thoughts allowed me to come to grips with who I was and how to cope with cruel and unusual times. My schoolwork suffered. Today, I would probably be classified as a withdrawn underachiever and potential candidate for the teenage ward of a psychiatric clinic. At Stoatley Rough I enjoyed a rare opportunity to mature at my own pace."[53]

A few months before his exam, Wolf studied very hard. He passed the matric and realized he was ready to leave Stoatley Rough. He was no longer a student there, and although Dr. Lion offered to let him stay to attend Godalming High School to study while working part time on the Farm, he knew it was time to leave. "The expected journey to America did not materialize because wartime conditions prohibited civilian travel. After much soul searching, I decided to leave Stoatley Rough, accept an invitation from relatives to live in Surbiton (a suburb of London) and attend Kingston-upon-Thames Technical College to make up deficiencies in physics and chemistry." Wolf left the school October 8, 1944. The next Hut Boy to leave the security of Stoatley Rough would be Goldy. Meanwhile, Hans Loeser was on his way from the United States back to Germany seven years after he had left. He was now a member of the Allied army that was on its way to crush the army of his former countrymen.

---

[53] Wolf Elston, "Memories of Stoatley Rough School, Haslemere, Surrey, England, 1939 – 1945. Written in honor of Nore Astfalck's 90th birthday and dedicated to the entire staff of Stoatley Rough." Albuquerque, New Mexico, December, 1990.

A Roughian Returns as a Yank

O ne of the more dramatic moments in the history of Stoatley Rough was the day Hans Loeser returned to the school in the uniform of an American Army officer. Not only would he go on to take part in the Battle of the Bulge, but the former Roughian was on a personal mission. He was to meet Herta Lewent in London.

Three years earlier, on September 3, 1941, Herta had given her notice after four years of service to Dr. Lion. (Katya Schaefer took her place.) At twenty-one, Herta had been more than ready to move out into the world. She took a secretarial job in London but continued to maintain contact with her friends, who included Nore Astfalck and Hanna Nacken, and she often returned to the school to sleep on the floor of their small room in the manse on weekends. Herta also did "war work" in Dundee, Scotland, for a stint, living with Margaret Dove [Faulkner] and her husband.

There are boundless stories of quiet sacrifice in wartime, and in 1939, Hans' family had benefited from one unsung hero, a lowly waiter, who lived in Philadelphia. "My parents found a black sheep cousin in America, a banquet waiter in Philadelphia, who gave an affidavit of support for the entire family. It was a generous and unselfish act by a virtual stranger. Supplemented by money from Walter Curchard, a second cousin, it did the trick."[54] The parents, who had emigrated to Tel Aviv, Palestine while they awaited visas to America, sold the Biedermeier furniture they had managed to save from their home in Kassel, and booked passage on the Dutch liner Staatendam bound for New York for

---

[54] Hans History, 1993.

themselves and their two children, Hans and his sister Liesel who had been working in England while Hans finished his studies at Stoatley Rough. They all docked in New York in December, 1939, to start afresh in America.

As the first bombs of the Battle of Britain dropped into London and Stoatley Rough prepared its air raid shelter, the Loeser family were settling into an austere apartment in Long Island City, New York. Hans and his older sister, Elisabeth [Lisel Loeser [Fontana], who also had attended Stoatley Rough for a brief time, took low-paying jobs while their father became a door-to-door Fuller-Brush salesman, enduring a humiliating and exhausting role that slowly killed the soul of the former owner and manager of his important department store in Kassel. This educated, elegant man, fluent in French, barely spoke the language of his new country. He later upgraded to another sales job, but like many refugee parents of Stoatley Roughians, he never adjusted to his reduced circumstances. "Though my father was saved from extinction in a place such as Auschwitz, he was clearly a victim of the Nazis. His six weeks in Dachau did impair his health, robbed him of energy and resilience, and speeded up the loss of self-confidence and belief in the future which had begun with the sale of his business."[55]

In the Fall of 1940, Hans enrolled in the City College of New York night school and Lisel learned she had received a full scholarship to Smith College. It had been arranged for her through a friend of Hanna Nacken who happened to be the president of the college. It's noteworthy that Lisel's academic preparation at Stoatley Rough was so good that she entered college as a junior. Hans worked by day restocking wallets and key cases in the luggage department of Gimbels' Department Store on 34th Street, next to Macy's on Herald Square. He attended school at night. He learned a new skill: how to interact with Americans by

---

[55] Hans' mother was responsible for getting her husband out of concentration camp. She approached the official with documents giving permission to emigrate to Palestine. By merest coincidence, years earlier the Loesers had donated money to plant a grove of trees in Palestine. This act made them eligible as 'landowners' to enter Palestine." In New York, Hans' father suffered from depression. He died of a heart attack at 56, in 1943, never to know of the victory of the Allies over Hitler.

"kidding around." He saw in this "important facet of American life the necessity for surface friendliness with everybody."[56] The family moved to Jackson Heights, made friends and assimilated, shedding their German clothes which represented the formality of the life they had left behind. (We are reminded of Wolf's father's displeasure when Wolf started wearing polo shirts and khakis to college classes. The old gentleman had the impression that Wolf had lowered himself by dressing like a "member of the proletariat"). Hans was promoted to assistant buyer at Gimbel's. All the while, he and Herta maintained their correspondence.

Five years and over 400 letters later, Herta knew Hans was coming to England. She must have wondered about his fate as she watched the planes fly overhead on D-Day, (just a few weeks before Hans was to arrive). Hans was now a part of military intelligence. It had taken the army a few years to appreciate what they had in him: after basic training the army assigned him to the military police; then they sent him to language school to learn Moroccan Arabic to prepare for the North Africa invasion (which happened before he graduated, in November, 1942). At last they placed him where he should have been all along, in Camp Ritchie, the military intelligence training camp in the Blue Ridge Mountains near Washington, D. C., a unit unique for its high number of future academics who "attained fame in the 1950's and 1960s."[57] Camp Ritchie was filled with other immigrants from Europe, like Hans, who would be used in the interrogation of captured Germans. A movie was made about these refugees who returned to Germany as U.S. soldiers, called, appropriately, *The Ritchie Boys*.[58]

---

[56] Op. cit.

[57] Walter Laquer *Generation Exodus*, P. 83.

[58] This film by Christian Bauer is the "untold story of a group of young men who fled Nazi Germany and returned to Europe as soldiers in US-uniforms. They knew the psychology and the language of the enemy better than anybody else. In Camp Ritchie, Maryland, they were trained in intelligence and psychological warfare. Not always courageous, but determined, bright, and inventive they fought their own kind of war. They saved lives. They were victors, not victims." http://www.ritchieboys.com/index.html. accessed April 19, 2006.

Hans' orders were to report to a private house in the small town of Broadway in the Cotswolds. Once he unpacked, the next action of the new Second Lieutenant was to secure a jeep, drive to a nearby town to find a telephone, and arrange to meet with Herta in London. Uncertain at first, they soon discovered that five years of separation had not diminished their love. They knew that "their lives belonged together." Under military rules, they had to wait ninety days before they could marry. So Herta went back to work while Hans joined the 82nd Airborne Division of seasoned veterans who had spearheaded the Normandy landings the night before D-Day. Accompanying them on their push through the Netherlands, Hans would interrogate prisoners of war with regard to the positions of their units and other such details, reading and analyzing written material that had been seized by the advancing American armies. Hans spent time translating captured German documents, and practiced riding in gliders that carried a squad of twelve men plus a pilot and copilot. While the uninitiated might think of a glider ride as a quiet, meditative experience, Hans reports that the ride was anything but silent or gentle, with the prop wash of the tow plane making any loose canvas slap against the steel frame, whipping the gliders up and down and sideways with sickening consequences to the passengers.

On September 16, 1944, his Division joined the 101st Airborne's assault to retake Holland in what would be known as Operation Market-Garden, portrayed in the Cornelius Ryan book of 1977, and later film, *A Bridge Too Far.* [59] His glider unit joined hundreds of planes and gliders in an enormous formation, his plane arriving in the second wave, (which Herta and most residents of south England surely watched), a horde of planes with parachutists and planes towing gliders as far as the eye could see. Hans wrote, "As we headed towards the Continent hundreds of fighter planes came from all over England to fly cover above us and

---

[59] The 1977 film directed by Richard Attenborough. Its stellar cast, including Michael Caine, Sean Connery, James Caan, Dirk Bogarde, Anthony Hopkins, Liv Ullman and Gene Hackman, portrayed the failed attempt to capture several German bridges. IMDb http://us.imdb.com/title/tt0075784/ accessed January 10, 2007.

our fighter bombers paved the way below us. It was an unbelievably spectacular event. I know that many people in England who saw it from the ground will never forget the sight."[60] He described the flak around the plane once his glider plane passed the coast.

> "One didn't hear them and seldom saw the flash of the gun muzzles. What we did see was the puffs of smoke in the air where the shells exploded. Occasionally, we saw a plane or a glider get hit and go down, but mostly the formation held...Very shortly before we got to our drop zone, my tow plane's right wing was cut off by what looked like machine gun fire from the ground. There were certainly no German fighters in sight. We saw it happen and our pilot cut us loose, putting us in a steep dive down while the formation went on very briefly and then cut loose its gliders and dropped its paratroopers. We could see this in the distance as our glider lost altitude...A slow landing glider is a sitting target. Our pilot headed for what seemed like a lonely farmhouse, tried to land in its garden, but would have hit the house if, in the last minute, he hadn't been able to lift the plane just over the roof of the house with its last bit of lift and then plunked it down in front of the house....The farmer and his wife were flabbergasted to see us there but once they collected their wits were enormously helpful. ...We managed to tow the glider, the canvas of which was in shreds, into a barn tail first, with the wings sticking out. We packed down a lot of bushes and trees to cover the wings..so that they would not be easily discerned from the air."[61]

---

[60] Hans Loeser, *Hans History*, Cambridge, MA, p. 105.
[61] Hans Loeser *Hans History* p. 106 Cambridge, MA

Hans and his comrades soon caught up with his Division, then he settled in a Dutch house at Nijmegen for work as interrogator of German prisoners for the next two months. Later he relocated to Reims, France. "Life was easy, the champagne flowed freely. Officers were given a free ration of two bottles of liquor of their choice per month and could buy more at the PX or from the French people. The great champagne cellars of Reims had been raided by the first troops...You waded in champagne. The soldiers had often broken the necks off bottles, drunk a little and tossed it away. Much went on that, in retrospect, one couldn't be particularly proud of. French girls were hungry and lonely and Americans were big and well fed and had food and nylons to give away. The synergies were clear."[62]

In December 1944, the 90-month waiting period was up. The Chief of Staff of his Division summoned Hans to his office. "Lieutenant, do you still want to get married?" "Yes sir". "All right. There is a troop carrier command pilot who also wants to get married .... I will issue orders for both of you to proceed to England on temporary duty...Your duty will be to get married as promptly as possible, have a few days with your bride and then get your asses and the airplane back here to us. Take off!"

Hans could not return to England without paying a visit to Stoatley Rough. He drove up and we can only imagine the excitement in the school, the younger boys crowding around the grown man who had once been a Hut Boy like them, one of their own returning as an officer in the US army. Wolf recalled, "I remember his visit. I was greatly impressed by his reappearance in the glamorous uniform of an American officer, made familiar by Hollywood. I suspect we all were. Here's a fantasy I cherished every time I pumped up Farnham Lane on the heavily laden one-speed bike borrowed from Felix (a green Hercules), after my weekly quest to replenish The Shop: One day I'd return, rich and famous, in a plush car. I wonder if Hans felt a sense of fulfilled fantasy."[63]

After a civil wedding on December 11, 1944, and a brief honeymoon in Torquay on the south coast of England, "the warmest place we could

---

[62] Ibid. P. 108.

[63] Wolf Edelstein [Elston] email to the author, April 21, 2006.

think of in England in December," Hans and Herta finalized their vows in a Jewish ceremony in London performed on December 14 by a Catholic U.S. Army chaplain. Hans returned to take part in the Battle of the Bulge (Battle of Ardennes), in a region covering parts of northern France, Belgium and Luxembourg. Hans was based just behind the lines.

"There was deep snow on the ground and we had to sleep in foxholes in the snow and mud. It was cold and miserable...We were under almost constant artillery fire. Day in and day out and throughout the night shells landed haphazardly among us, causing serious casualties even at Regimental Headquarters level. The combination of being cold and wet and being shot at is not a good one. The nights in particular were miserable and scary... Yet once again I must emphasize that what I suffered was nothing compared to the front line troops who lived in equally miserable or worse foxholes but were, in addition to artillery fire, exposed to machine gun and small arms fire, had to go on nightly patrols to feel out where the enemy was, and were constantly subject to being attacked, overrun and killed by the still advancing Germans." ...One night we ran into and captured alive the German Adjutant of a regiment of the 2nd S.S. Panzer Division. He was riding in a motorcycle side car. He had on him ...detailed plans..their routes to Liege and on towards Antwerp. My men and I were the first to understand the significance of that capture. It proved of great help to our superiors. All our training and experience paid off generously that day. We were delighted and were commended, though the real commendation and medals went, as they should have, to the patrol that captured that officer and his driver alive.[64]

---

[64] Hans Loeser, unpublished memoir, Hans Story. Copyright 1993. The entire account of Hans' experience with the Battle of the Bulge is taken from his memoir.

A new kind of danger took center stage. Hans spoke English with a German accent. It was a chilling fact that Germans deployed men in American uniforms who spoke perfect English. Hans once ran into a group of such men with their throats cut, killed by U.S. paratroopers. (A similar murder of Germans masquerading as G.I.s is depicted in Episode Three of "Band of Brothers," the eleven-episode series produced by HBO in 2001). Richie Boys such as Hans were instructed never to stray from the base, nor to walk alone and he never had any problems. On New Year's Day, 1945, the Battle of the Bulge was over. There were 80,000 American casualties, of whom 16,000 had been killed.

For the victorious troops, life became easy (in stark contrast to the vanquished German citizenry). Hans had a treat when he was in Rheims. Ingrid Bergman staged a special performance for the troops. It gives you an idea of the confidence of this man when he relates that he asked her to dance at the party afterward, and she accepted. Later he was sent to Cologne where he learned FDR had died. By then, the war for him was "almost fun." There was little resistance as the Allies moved toward Berlin, and much of the German army consisted of "pitifully young and old men, the old ones looking to surrender, while the sixteen- and seventeen-year-olds were still fanatically loyal to the Reich."[65]

Hans, however, was not allowed to escape one horrifying reality of the war. On May 2, 1945, the U.S. 82nd Airborne Division liberated 3,500 survivors of the Wöbbelin concentration camp, a satellite of the Neuengamme extermination camp near Ludwigslust in western Germany near Hamburg. "The stench alone was so strong that the protestations of the Ludwigslust inhabitants that they knew nothing of what went on were laughable. There were hundreds of dead bodies in the striped concentration camp uniforms stacked up several meters high and deep. There were also hundreds of almost starved to death people within the camp. It cured our GIs at least for some time from having any relationship with the Germans. We brought out the entire population of the town at gunpoint, paraded them past the bodies, facilities and survivors, then had them dig graves in the most beautiful

---

[65] Hans Loeser, Hans Story, unpublished memoir,

place we could find, the estate of the Duke of Mecklenburg. Many threw up as they were forced to bury the bodies, at the butt of the rifle. Every last person of the town was forced to attend the funeral." Hans' Division was selected to guard the American sector of Berlin, an honor, and when Hans arrived, he found the city "one huge pile of rubble, nothing standing in the center of town."

Herta asked Hans to find Nore Astfalck's brother and his wife, and to deliver food packages to them. German civilians were starving. He did so, and he also located an old school friend of Herta's, Gabi Landsberg, in a miserable basement room. She was half Jewish but had survived. The Germans in Berlin were in rags, starving gaunt shadows of people, pushing carts of pitiful belongings. Russian soldiers were everywhere, and everybody dealt with the black market, trading watches, army issue underwear, and other scarce items. Hans found himself translating for Russians (those who knew German) as well as for Americans, but one incident soured him. An American soldier had complained that a Russian MP had forced him to hand over his watch at gunpoint. A Cossack Brigadier took the GI and Hans to find the man and there he was, still directing traffic where he had taken the watch. "The General got out of his Jeep, walked up to the MP and spoke to him in Russian. Then we saw him pull out his revolver and shoot the man dead at point blank range. Then he came back grinning and said, 'That's what we do with thieves in our army.' Undoubtedly, he wanted to impress us. We were shocked to the core but there was nothing we could do. All this for a lousy GI watch."[66]

The Wannsee Yacht Club, where the Wannsee Conference of January 20, 1942, settled on the logistics of carrying out the Final Solution (the various family men representing the railroads, post office and telephone communications, etc. referring to their victims as *Stuecke*, i.e. pieces), now became an officer's club for the Allied Forces. Formerly owned by a wealthy Jewish family, the mansion had been turned into an R and R resort for SS officers. It is now a museum that Wolf visited it in 2002 as a guest of the city of Berlin. Hans took out a sailboat many lazy

---

[66] Ibid. p. 118.

afternoons while posted there. He worked in prisoner interrogations and became disgusted with those who said they didn't know or hadn't wanted to know what had happened to the Jews. "It was obvious that thousands of people were involved in loading and driving and scheduling the trains that ran endlessly to the extermination camps, others were involved in the arrests and in providing guards and the meticulous planning that went into the construction and erection of the camps and ovens. These people knew; they were not just SS members. They were civil servants and employees of companies and government agencies who did the dirty work.[67] Hans also took time to revisit his old hometown of Kassel. In a tragic twist of fate (and not uncommon), he located an old friend and was able to rejoice with him for having survived Auschwitz. The tragedy was that the friend's son, who had escaped to the United States before the war, had joined the army and returned to fight in Holland, and died in battle. Thus it was that Hans, as authentic an American soldier as one could be, had a front-row seat in the liberating of Europe from Hitler.

In order to live with her new husband, Herta joined the US army in the fall of 1944 as a mail censor, went to Paris, and managed to get assigned to Munich. Hans had himself transferred out of the 82nd and moved to Munich as well ("only a little sorry that he had to leave the 82nd since it had been selected to lead the great VE victory parade planned for New York"). The couple worked side by side, she as a censor, he as a de-Nazification officer, and they "had a wonderful time." In 1945 they returned to Boston and Hans prepared to enter Harvard Law School, their first child on the way.

---

[67] Ibid. Hans' experience confirms the thesis of GoldXX in *Hitler's Willing Executioners*.

Leaving Stoatley Rough

I n December of 1944, as Hans left Herta from Boston to join the 82nd Airborne Division in the Battle of the Bulge, sixteen-year-old Goldy was ready for his Cambridge University Matriculation. "This exam included Math, (Arithmetic, Algebra, and Geometry;) English (writing, grammar and comprehension;) English literature including thorough knowledge of two plays by Shakespeare (Hamlet and Richard II, that year); British and European History from 1689 to 1914; and German as a foreign language." Goldy was also tested on his electives, French and Scripture. He had prepared himself during a winter of deepest deprivations at the school. Renate Dorpalen [Dorpalen-Brocksieper] wrote, "Christmas was very cold and the most miserable one of the war. Five years of marginal diet, bombing defeat, and humiliation made everyone feel that his strength was sapped. There was only one wish – for the war to be over."[68] After his exams, Goldy celebrated with his teachers at Stoatley Rough over tea and "biscuits" [cookies] in the school library. It was a bittersweet time for the boys because now Goldy was soon to leave. After him, only Obo and Martin would be left at the school; stragglers of their old gang.

U-boats menaced the Atlantic to a lesser degree than in 1944 and consequently, visas to the U.S. came through for Goldy's mother, Goldy and his brother Ralph. (In fact, however, commercial ships were not safe on the water. Wolf's ship - in April, 1945- the *Aquitania*, was chased by U-boats, only to be rescued by the arrival of ships of the Royal Canadian

---

[68] Renate Dorpalen [Dorpalen-Brocksieper],"Stoatley Rough Remembered," *Stoatley Rough Newsletter*, Issue 9, October, 1995, p. 35.

Navy from Halifax, Nova Scotia.) Travel was contingent upon the availability of berths on the liners that had begun to cross the Atlantic again. Britain meted out bookings for passage. People were not told ahead of time the name of their ship or the port of departure for security reasons. Although the war was winding down in the European theater, a certain number of German U-Boats still prowled the Atlantic, mostly seeking to avoid prosecution. Granting of visas was not a predictable or timely process and people had no choice as to the carrier they were assigned to. Instead of waiting at the school, like Wolf before him, Goldy felt it was time to leave Stoatley Rough, allowing himself a short period of respite between the rigor of his final studies and the voyage that would begin his new life in America. He made his farewells and boarded a series of trains toward Yorkshire. His former hosts met him at the station and kept him well-fed for a few months.

On February 2, 1945, Goldy, his mother, and Ralph reported to Paddington Station to learn the point of departure of the ship assigned them. Their ship was in Wales, a 12,000 ton Cunard merchant ship that once had carried bananas from Jamaica. It now carried coal. There was room for only 150 passengers. The little family made the trek to their port in Wales and watched, for seven days, as coal poured into the hold from freight cars making a "deafening noise." Goldy picks up the story. "We moved out into the Atlantic Ocean where we circled until we were about sixty ships, mostly going to the United States in convoy." The ship cruised by the Azores where they picked up air cover and then went to Bermuda for more air cover. En route, an enormous storm overtook the voyagers. "It tossed the ship like a cork, plates crashing, and waves so high that they reached above the bridge. A day or two later we were almost alone in the ocean. The convoy had dispersed to avoid collisions and every ship was on its own. We zigzagged north along the American coastline, and while aboard, I tasted Coke for the first time and ate a banana, something I hadn't had for six years. The captain piped music and news from local stations through our public address system." After twenty-five days at sea the ship docked in Halifax. The family still had to catch a train to Montreal, from which they went to enter the U.S.

through St. Albans, Vermont. It was decidedly unglamorous to arrive in the United States in the middle of the night, with no vision of the Statue of Liberty to cheer them on. But the unsentimental Goldy and his family pushed on. With little fanfare he wrote, "Finally, we were in America. We arrived about 8 a.m. at Pennsylvania Station in New York City and were met by Uncle Carl and his wife, Alma. So here we were."[69]

With victory in Europe a certainty, other residents of Stoatley Rough were also making plans to leave. Since the prior September, the blackout in Great Britain had been officially relaxed to dim-out, with some street lighting allowed. The English began to feel fairly sure that enemy planes would no longer approach their country.

The Board of Governors of the school took up an important topic at their spring meeting. Should the school continue or was its work done? When the war ended on the European front, the other large German-English school, Bunce Court, was quickly disbanded and its leader, Anna Essinger, was more than happy to retire and return to Germany. She had helped over 800 Jewish children who otherwise might have perished. Her work was done. But Dr. Lion was younger than Miss Essinger and was not ready to retire. She saw her work unfinished. The indefatigable Miss Bracey sided with her. "Did we wish to carry on with our experiment as it is now or should we wish to include it into a larger Scheme? The future need would be very great in the matter of the care of children from the Occupied Countries, International Centres of Education for Children and Adults and the vast problem of the Orphans in Europe."[70] The Board decided that the school would forge ahead, offering a new kind of refuge while at the same time, assuring Drs. Lion and Leven and others of continued employment.

The war continued to play itself out. In the first months of 1945, the Allies successfully drove back German forces. The Russians advanced from the east, and the British and U.S. closed in on Berlin from the south and west. This was good news. There was also bad news, as word began to trickle in about the death of parents of Roughian children. It

---

[69] Hans [John Goldy] Goldmeier, Memoirs, Part 1.
[70] Stoatley Rough Archives, File 8/2, London School of Economics.

was to be a terrible time at the school for many. It was a spring day that Renate Dorpalen had been dreading. "I remember the day I received the letters as vividly as few others. It was one of those sparkling spring days that only England can offer, with the warm air permeated by the scent of blossoming bushes. The meadows were covered with bluebells, cowslips and primroses and the greening trees were full of chirping birds. In this incredibly peaceful atmosphere, in a quiet corner of the garden, I read and reread the shattering news of my parents' death in a grim, hostile environment." What is particularly poignant is the fact that Renata's mother had been dead for almost two years.

Renate learned from friends of her parents who had survived Theresienstadt (her mother died a year and a half after her father). These pages only reached Renate on April 27, 1945. She wrote later that when the films came out about the German concentration camps, "the picture of what my parents' last months of life might have been like was to become my recurring nightmare for years. Often in my dreams I was with them in the camp."[71] On May 7, Germany surrendered unconditionally to the Allies, the same day Theresienstadt was liberated by the Soviet army, "where of more than 140,000 deportees to the model ghetto, 33,529 had died of overcrowding, disease and starvation and another 88,000 had been sent to the gas chambers in Poland."[72] Renate was able to share her grief with one of her brothers who had fought with Patton in the American army and by then was stationed in England. The Western world was celebrating what everyone called V-E Day (Victory in Europe). Three months later on August 6, the U.S. dropped the A-Bomb, "Little Boy," onto Hiroshima, killing 70,000 people, followed by "Fat Boy" on August 9, which devastated Nagasaki. Japan surrendered on August 15.

Stoatley Rough was not to be left out of the victory party. Renate recalled wild celebrating all over England on V-E Day. Stoatley Rough threw a festive picnic, "dipping deep into our food ration reserves."

---

[71] Renate Dorpalen [Dorpalen-Brocksieper], Stoatley Rough Remembered", *Stoatley Rough Newsletter*, Issue 9, p. 40.

[72] Ibid. p. 43.

Some of the younger boys were emboldened to scale the steep roof of the mansion to hoist the Union Jack and a Scout flag. Hanno explains their adventure. "We (Andreas [Hanno] Pilartz, Uli Hubacher and Eddie Behrendt) "climbed out of the "Lookout" window to hoist the only two flags we could get hold of (a Union Jack and a Scout flag) onto the pinnacle of the building. We floodlit the flags by converting a number of pineapple tins into spotlights, providing enough light to make the flags visible from downtown Haslemere. [73] When she learned of such foolishness, Dr. Lion gave them a dressing down about climbing on the roof. But she was pleased. The stunt "even received a favourable mention in the *Haslemere Herald* the following day." Eddie said, "The [flags] were put up, along with the lights, to celebrate the end of the war and the end to blackouts. I seem to remember the lights as more important then the flags. I am not sure, but I don't think that I was all that patriotic. It was a big and very exciting lark for me. To this day I remember being somewhat scared climbing along the roof. It was of course a very crazy thing to do, but I had done it a couple of times before successfully, so that I didn't have to think about it too long. This time though I seem to remember it was dusk whereas the other times it was on a weekend during daylight. One could only get on the roof through the "Lookout Window" which was rather small and I believe had a couple of bars across it which we had to wiggle through. It was a typical thing for me to do since I was considered more of a mischief maker than someone worthy of education at the time. I was nearly always in trouble."[74] The same troublemaker loved to tell people the last thing Dr. Lion said to him before he left the school: "Eddy, you will make a fine practical worker." Eddie went to America and received a master's degree in social work, Dr. Lion's own field. The "practical worker" went on to build a distinguished professional career and became the well-known

---

[73] Andreas Pilartz, email to author.

[74] Eddie Behrendt in an email to the author, May 13, 2005.

founder of the American Kindertransport Association, established in 1989.[75]

After war's end, Hanno and Uli were granted the privilege of living in an outbuilding of the farm called The Black Hut, a shed that held hay for the School's horse and cow. Part of the shed had been fixed up as a hideaway for [Nore] Astfalck and [Hanna] Nacken. "It was a sort of Paradise for us – we even installed a cooker." [76] One day a few months after the war had ended, the boys encountered a serious brushfire on the lower property. "Dr. Lion got more or less the whole school to the blaze and organized a chain of buckets to supply us with water from the swimming pool...All the main fuses for the farm including our Black Hut were destroyed and it took a few months for the current to be restored." Uli wrote, "We ...practically extinguished it before the fire brigade, with no proper access road in the farm valley, reached the site." Wolf, who by then had left the school, explains, "It would indeed have been a difficult place to reach by fire truck – up Bunch Lane and then muddy farm paths, through several gates."

With the war over and the oceans once again reasonably safe, the mass exodus began. Those who were too young to live on their own and whose parents had not survived stayed on at the school, and some children left to live with relatives who found their way to England or

---

[75] With help from the Simon Wiesenthal Center, Eddie set up the organization to search for Kindertransport children living in America. The mission was to provide a venue for reunions, to educate and inform the next generation about the Kindertransport and Holocaust, and to provide funds for needy children regardless of race, creed or country of national origin. After four years in the United States Army, he served as Director of Personnel for the American Home Products (Wyeth) Corporation in New York for many years, but it was his role as teacher of the truths about the Holocaust that led him to travel the country to speak to High School students for several years as part of a program he founded from Eugene, Oregon, known as "Reach and Teach." He died in November, 2006. "His fervor for the world to know and accept responsibility for the mass annihilation of a people was overwhelming." The Kindertransport Association website, http://www.kindertransport.org/eddy_behrendt.html accessed August 2, 2007.

[76] Uli Hubacher, email, May 12, 2005.

sent for them. For any student who had matriculated, there was no delaying. It was time for the Hut Boys and the Household Girls to leave. "We'll Meet Again" was played over and over on the radio (sung by Vera Lynn, the "Forces' Sweetheart") as if to chronicle the inevitable end of an era and the parting of fast friends.[77] It also spoke to those who had lost loved ones.

"We'll meet again / Don't know where / Don't know when.
But we know / We'll meet again / Some sunny day."

The young people at the school had a sense of foreboding about the future. Peter Gaupp recalled, "None of us had any idea of what was going to happen to us after we finished school. I had a very quiet terror about the uncertain future. Who would tell me where I should go, how I would earn a living, how I could survive without adults telling me what to do? I certainly had no idea of going on to higher education since I was very doubtful that I would pass the School Certificate Exam. Who would find me a job and a place to stay? After all, I had been a shy, retiring child and teenager and totally relied on adults for every decision up to now."

Nore Astfalck and Hanna Nacken prepared to return to Germany. They both had parents and brothers still in Germany and they were eager to help their former countrymen. Right after the war, expatriates were not allowed back into the country right away and the women had to wait for the bureaucracy to give permission. Under mysterious circumstances, they quietly left for London. There was no going away party for either woman. Nore spoke frankly of leaving the school without ceremony, without formal acknowledgement and gratitude, and without even sufficient time to pack. In fact, once they had made their intentions to return to Germany clear, she and Hanna were asked to leave before they were ready to do so. Dr. Lion failed, in the end, to acknowledge the invaluable contribution Nore had made to the school. (See "The Interloper.") She and Hanna left the premises quietly in the summer of 1945 and took lodgings in London. Quakers in London

---

[77] Written in 1939, the music was written by Ross Parker and words by Hughie Charles. A movie of the same name came out in 1942, starring Miss Lynn.

asked "whether we were willing to help them in training German people who wanted to go to do the most urgent things in the way of social work. We agreed, and we also found a very good opportunity to work as helpers in the wartime kindergarten of Anna Freud. Then we moved to rooms in a settlement in Hoxton, the working class district of London."[78] They had to wait for more than six months. With the help of Hans Loeser, who by then, as an officer of the occupation army in Bavaria, knew how to pull strings, they were finally given the go-ahead. "Miss Nacken and I and two other people were the very first permitted to go back to Germany to stay there." They left, as she quaintly phrased the date, "on Whitsuntide, in forty-six."[79]

Many children who had found sanctuary at Stoatley Rough were disturbed at having to leave. Baerbel Gerstenberg [Prasse] (who, like Hans and many others, left for America before the war began) wrote about the pain of leaving, of real trauma.

> "I did not want to leave Stoatley Rough. It was home! I had had to learn to live without my parents and was apprehensive about moving back into their lives. I did not want to go to America. It seemed so far from not only England, but from Europe. But, of course, I could not stay and so in August of '38, I had to say "good-bye. I have come to the conclusion that I have had too many good-byes in my life, too many times of putting down roots and having to tear them up again. It hurts to do that. Stoatley Rough had been home and I had to leave it…I do not recall that anyone at the school, i.e., any one of the adults helped me or others to understand or to deal with our feelings. It was not only the British "stiff

---

[78] Eleonore Astfalck, *Oral History.*

[79] Whitsunday is the seventh Sunday after Easter; "White Sunday" commemorates the emanation of the Holy Spirit to the apostles in the Christian doctrine. Whitsuntide would be the week in which this celebration takes place. Wolf adds, "Whitsunday (*Pfingsten* in German) was (and probably still is) a popular holiday in Germany. Easter often is too cold for outings that are traditional at *Pfingsten.*

upper lip," but in retrospect there must have been other reasons. Perhaps it would have been too overwhelming to take the cork out of the bottle of all those pent up feelings of displaced, confused and often, I am sure, homesick children. There were no support groups, no therapy sessions, no reflections on what was happening to all of us. We simply went on with our lives as best as we could and maybe that was the only way to cope. In any case, I could not really voice my conflicting feelings about leaving Stoatley Rough and I do remember crying into my pillow the last night there, trying not to wake Herta, who was my roommate. I have no recollection where I sailed from or how I got there. My memory stops with that last night at the place that had been my home for two years and starts again with the next chapter in my life, i.e., America."[80]

It was Obo's turn to leave. "Since any funds that were deposited for me for tuition and board at Stoatley Rough were gone, Dr. Lion said rightfully that it was high time for me to earn a living. So in April 1945 I was sent to a youth hostel where a counselor found an apprentice job for me at the British Small Arms (BSA) factory (a former bicycle factory) that made mechanical and hydraulic components for military equipment. I started out by sweeping the shop floor, grateful to have been given a chance to make a new life for myself. I knew that this was the first step to a profession. Pretty soon I graduated to operating some of the precision metalworking machinery and apparently I was pretty good at it so that they enrolled me in their apprentice program and sent me to night school, the British Central Technical College." Obo wrote to Dr. Lion at the time, complaining, sounding a bit snobbish, about the types of people he had to work with. "I do not like the people because they are honestly very uneducated, especially the girls. In other words a

---

[80] Baerbel Gerstenburg [Prasse] Reminiscences on the Occasion of the School's 1990 Reunion.

bit common I suppose. [They like] dancing, pictures, Jazz, etc. That's all for them."[81]

Three weeks after Obo left the school the International Red Cross confirmed that his parents and brother Arthur had died in a concentration camp. He was an orphan and most of his friends had already gone to America. Obo was invited to move to the United States.

> "Meanwhile my father's brother, who had escaped from Generalissimo Franco's Spain to New York, asked me whether I was interested in coming to the US. In December of 1946 I received my immigration documents and $10 'traveling money.' I boarded a US Liberty ship which was returning GIs home from W.W.II. The eight-day voyage was, for the most part, uneventful and not particularly luxurious. One of the things I was unable to understand was the segregation of the "colored" soldiers from the white, especially those "coloreds" who were returning home with their British and other European war brides.... I arrived in the early morning hours of January 29, 1947 and after the excitement of seeing the Statue of Liberty and the lower Manhattan skyline, had the feeling that I was going to like my new home in a new world full of excitement and opportunities....It was not easy to bridge the age gap between an eighteen-year-old boy whose hormones were racing and was eager to start a new chapter, and an old world seventy-year-old intellectual gentleman [and newly-discovered uncle] who was now deprived of all the comforts and culture to which he had been accustomed for much of his life in Europe. But we worked it out."[82]

---

[81] Hans [John, Obo] Obermeyer, letter to Dr. Lion, Stoatley Rough Archive 3/28, London School of Economics.

[82] Hans [John Obo] Oberrmeyer in an email to the author, April 21, 2006.

Wolf and Goldy (and later Martin) re-established contact with Obo in New York, and others came to frequent reunions: Susanne Horn [Schapiro], Ruth Lichtenstein [Ultmann], Evi and Putti Cassel [Wronker], Hanna Untermeier, and Hanna Katz. The boys' families treated Obo as one of their own. A photo dated just after Obo arrived in the U.S. shows a group of young people – the girls inordinately pretty, the boys smiling and handsome, as sleek, affluent and confident young people.

It is well-established that many displaced children of the Holocaust and their parents who reunited years later suffered a special kind of hell, arising from the inability on both sides to bridge over the estrangement that had occurred during their period of separation. Diane Samuels' play, *Kindertransport,* explores this theme. It depicts a grown survivor who, as a girl, had been sent out of Germany to live with an English family. Now a middle-aged matron, she has blocked out her entire German past until her daughter finds a box of letters that reveal the fact that her mother is not the person she believed, but a child of the Holocaust. Flashbacks in the play depict the naturalized English woman as a teen-ager whose biological mother has returned from concentration camp to claim her. The girl finds her birth mother a stranger and wishes only to continue in her English life. She even tells her birth mother that she already has a mother, her English mother. The pain experienced by both of the mothers and the refugee daughter is wrenching to witness.[83]

There was at least one such case at Stoatley Rough, documented in the archives, and probably dozens of others left unrecorded. In September, 1945, a certain young woman's mother wrote from Hamburg asking Dr. Lion to intercede for her: her daughter (whom we shall call

---

[83] The play, *Kindertransport,* deals with the theme of separation and reuniting of children and parents after the Holocaust; The author states: "What I wanted to make into a play was an exploration of the universal human experience of the separation of parent and child." One character, "whose menacing presence runs throughout the whole play," is a German fairy tale character, the "Ratcatcher"a man who steals children and whose role is based on the Pied Piper myth. Octagon Theatre (Bolton, England) review of the play, accessed May 29, 2005. http://www.madstheatre.org.uk/kindertransport.html

Lisel Goldschmidt) did not want to see her. The mother wrote to the child's sponsors who suggested that she reassure Lisel that there was no question of her returning to live in Germany. The mother wrote, "It is very hard to understand from a mother's point of view whose child is her own flesh and blood. ...I think I will find a way to approach Lisel and ...will come to England when traveling possibilities will be available again. ...It is not my intention to take the child back to Germany or to interrupt Lisel in her education...for which I have to be extremely grateful to you for ever." The mother then asks Lisel's sponsors to discuss the matter with distant relatives as intermediaries. The sponsor then became angry and wrote to Dr. Lion: "Lisel is not going to be tricked or exploited by anyone, myself included. LISEL WILL DO AS SHE WISHES WHEN THE TIME COMES. If Lisel of her own free will elects to keep in touch with her mother I have no objection but I do object to intimidation or any interference. Do you think you could write to her mother pointing out the legal position, and ask her to stop meddling!" The sponsor's wife adds her own hand-written thoughts, "After being with us for six years, as you can imagine, she has completely forgotten her mother, and shewed not the slightest interested when we told her that her mother was alive and well. Her only reaction was that she did not want to go back. Her father died in 1942." Dr. Lion wrote the sponsors that she understood "a mother's longing for her child after all these years," and that she also understood the sponsors' "being anxious not to let the child get back to Germany in the near future." She referred them to a woman of the Refugee Children's Movement, Bloomsbury, House "who will probably have a number of similar cases."[84]

Wolf was worried. "One cause for emotional turmoil was the realization that I would soon be reunited with my parents in America. How could I relate to them? Our experiences of the intervening years had been so different. Would they still look on me as the ten-year-old they had last seen in 1939? ...I had mixed feelings about emigrating to

---

[84] Letter in Dr. Lion's file, Stoatley Rough archives, File 3 / 4 (ii), London School of Economics.

America. How could I adjust to yet another country?" It turned out that Wolf's reunion was fine. "It went smoother than expected even though there were rough spots. I had adopted English (and later, American) ways of thinking and behaving. My parents were forty-six years old when they came to America and set in their German ways. (Even today, when I visit Europe, I feel at ease in England and like a foreigner in Germany, even though linguistically I could more easily pass there as a native. In England, my acquired American accent would give me away as a foreigner.) The actual meeting with our parents in Penn Station was easier than [expected]. ...We recognized them right away (they had sent us pictures from America). Mainly I remember strange sounds coming from my father – a mixture of laughing and sobbing. The taxi ride to our new home was terrifying, all that NYC traffic on the wrong side of the street. Mainly I remember being dirty and dead tired after three nearly sleepless nights. During our last night at sea, we had to sleep in our clothes with life preservers at hand. That was followed by two nights of sitting in a train [entering the U.S. from Montreal, by the back door, at St. Albans, Vermont], and there was no chance for shaving (by that time I needed to do that) or shower."

Dieter and Peter Gaupp would also go to America, but having left Stoatley Rough earlier, did not express anxiety or sorrow, but rather eagerness to see their parents again who had waited out the war in Switzerland. While working his day job at the optical company in Bristol, Dieter took correspondence courses and passed the Matric. Peter also passed the Matric and stayed on at Shoreham for one more semester. He floundered, unable to attend Cambridge or Oxford, the colleges for which he had qualified, because of the planned trip to America. "They did not know what to do with me. I waited to be told. I was called into Mr. Bruder's officer (Headmaster) who asked me what I wanted to do with my life. ... In desperation I said I wanted to be an engineer and build bridges. So they kept me on for that extra summer, the only student at an empty school, while Mr. Bruder gave me science tutorials in the laboratory. I walked his Corgi [and] helped him clean his fish tank...Eventually he told me he had enrolled me in the Joseph

Lucas Trade School in Birmingham (England) where I could learn to be a toolmaker [while I took] engineering courses at night…In some ways it was almost an Oliver Twist experience. Sometimes I would miss some meals to save enough money to go to a concert with Obo and Dieter. (Obo was working at the local BSA factory.)" Peter concludes this phase of his life with characteristic wit. "The J. Lucas administration was impressed with my I.Q testing and proposed to train me to become their director of research to help them move into the jet propulsion field. I was terrified.[85]

Since the elder Gaupps would leave for America before the boys' visas were available, the family arranged to meet first in Switzerland, the first time they would be reunited after six years of separation. The brothers took a train to Zurich and when they arrived they began searching for their parents in the crowded station. They were looking for the tall, robust people they had last seen so many years earlier. Their parents were looking for their two little boys. When they all finally found each other, Peter was shocked to discover "two people who looked not as I remembered them at all but two aged, small people." The senior Gaupps, in turn, said they were amazed to see nearly-grown men.

Visas arrived in September, 1947. Dieter and Peter set sail on a freighter headed for Georgetown, Texas, home to Southwestern University. Herr Doktor Gaupp was already there with his wife, ready to start his position to teach German (and Italian Renaissance history, if the college required it.) It was when Herr Gaupp had been incarcerated in Italy upon the occasion of Hitler's state visit that he befriended the people who arranged for his teaching post in America. Knowing little English, he tried to learn the new language en route on his ship to America using a child's U.S. history book. He quipped about the United States, "I did not know they *had* any history."

The Gaupp brothers were unfortunate to have been assigned to an empty freighter returning from Holland after having hauled carbon black (a fine partially-burned carbon used in the manufacture of rubber tires and other products) from the Gulf coast. Peter recalled, "The

---

[85] Peter Gaupp, email April 21, 2006.

crew kept busy trying to clean up the carbon and Dieter and I started looking like coal haulers. Everything one touched turned black. There were about eight of us living in the officers' quarters. After we passed the half way mark, things changed amazingly. The crew started playing children's games (dominos) and the Captain's Table served curried rice for breakfast EACH DAY. (I still shy away from curry.) Then we started to run away from a hurricane and headed towards Galveston. That poor old ship had been through rough wear and it shook noisily as it tried to get up speed. The vibration and noise were scary - I kept wondering if things were going to fall apart. It did not help that one of the sailors, who I had befriended because he said he was a Boy Scout Ranger, told me that things were not holding up too well in the engine room. There was a period when the waters got rough and we were told to keep in our bunks...hard on the stomach! Well, the ship did hold together and we eventually enjoyed watching the dolphins escorting us into the Gulf of Mexico. Seeing the lights of Galveston from the distance was emotional. We parked a long way away from the coast and next morning we were told to appear in the Captain's cabin to meet with American Officials. SCARY! I don't know about Dieter, but I saw visions of being turned away. They were public health officials who checked out if we had the uglies...and passed us! Eventually we got to a cargo dock and exited on wooden planks." Peter adds to the story that when their parents met the boys, they hardly recognized them for the black grease on their faces they had been unable to remove with soap and water. It took days to get the carbon black from their skin and hair.[86]

Martin's departure was without incident. His crossing, in fact, was a sublimely happy one for him. "I planned to take my matriculation for Cambridge University in June, 1945. In March of that year, however, I received notice that I would leave for the United States to join my family in April. It was a big adjustment for me to give up my Cambridge plans, on the one hand, while contemplating leaving England [along with] all my friends. Perhaps it was that conflict that gave me the chicken pox, causing me to miss the boat I'd been booked for (the *Aquitania*).

---

[86] Email January 18, 2007

I did, however, catch the next one in May, the month the war ended in Europe, and I left on a troop ship that carried happy members of the US Army Air Corps. They were forever arguing about the merits of the airplanes that they had flown, notably the B-17 and the B-24. They were a very funny bunch and I literally laughed my way across the Atlantic. They also taught me to love Peppermint Patties. We were in one of the last convoys because there were still U-boats out there and we were the slowest ship in the convoy. It took us eleven days to cross from Liverpool to Brooklyn where we landed at the Army Base. Also on the ship was Susi Horn from Stoatley Rough. She was older than I, and she fell in love with one of the airmen who promptly jilted her the moment the ship docked."[87] When Martin's ship landed in Brooklyn, he disembarked and stood amidst the swarming crowds on the pier with his luggage. There was no sign of his mother or sister or his mother's new husband, Henry Owens [ne Oppenheimer]. Most the crowd disappeared. Still no family. Then he heard a cry. It was his sister who had spotted him. "a budding twelve –year-old, wide-eyed and adoring. Apparently, they had almost given up finding me among the throngs." There was discomfort in the reunion. Like the character in *"Kindertransport,"* Martin felt estranged. "My mother seemed capable of picking up where we had left off seven years earlier when I was ten, and tried to baby me. To me, she was almost a stranger."

(Martin and his parents never discussed how they came to their decision to send him away. He does not know who in fact sponsored him, whether it was Dr. Eisenklamm or one of the relief agencies. The family never talked about their uprooting; Martin says he does not recall his mother ever asking him about his seven years in England, leaving him with a measure of disappointment and a sense of something left unfinished with her. Understanding that she herself faced tremendous hardship after losing her privileged status in Vienna, he says she acted as if the hiatus in their lives had not happened at all, tucked under the rug and forgotten. For the rest of her life, his mother tried to baby him

87 Marti Friedenfeld [Owens] Recollections July 3, 2004.

although to Martin, she was never again the beloved *Mutti* he had left behind in the *Bahnhof*.)

Wolf had left a month before Martin. He had left the school and enrolled at Kingston-upon-Thames Technical College. While he was living with his relatives, a doodlebug hit his home. "After much floundering," he moved to a boarding house in Guildford, near Haslemere, "for 30 shillings a week (meals included)" and he started taking classes at Guildford Tech. In late March, 1945, his visa cleared and he was assigned to his ship. He had to say good-bye to the boys and to the teachers, to Dr. Wolff and especially Dr. Lion, who had been so tolerant and indulgent of him as he grew into manhood. "I received word to report forthwith for travel to America. One last time I cycled twelve miles to Stoatley Rough to say goodbye to friends and teachers. The last one was Dr. Lion. She met me at the door of her Bungalow and, as always on emotional occasions, spoke in Hamburg German. *'Na, Junge, mm, mm, mach's gut, halt' die Ohren steif und nimm dich vor den Weibern in acht!'* (Difficult to translate; approximate meaning: 'Now, boy, good luck, don't let anyone get you down, and be on your guard when it comes to females!') With that advice, she sent me out to face the world."[88]

---

[88] Wolf Elston, *Memories of Stoatley Rough School*, etc. Nore Astfalck's 90th birthday, December, 1990.

EPILOGUE

Part I: The School

Three Phases

The end of the war marked the third phase in the life of Stoatley Rough School. Phase 1 had been a harmonious, utopian experiment for upper middle-class children that unfolded from 1934 to 1938. Phase 2 began when children were sent in waves from Nazi-threatened countries. The school's capacity stretched to bursting after the *Anschluss,* and *Kristallnact:* the tiny Camelot was replaced by a full-bodied, down-to-the bones institution, filling several houses chock full of children. The school's leaders gravitated to the expedient and practical, balancing child-centricity with funding and provisioning needs. Those who had been at the school in the early days had to realign their priorities. Children were taught to care and take responsibility for each other. Renate Dorpalen [Dorpalen-Brocksieper] arrived in 1939, on the cusp of the change. "I felt like an outsider and intruder...With wartime, there were no more festivals and summer holidays. The new order of business at the school was to make do, to scrimp, sacrifice, and to perform that wonderfully British activity of carrying on. ... After 1939, the school adapted to a very different mission...providing a safe haven for children who had often suffered severe emotional trauma."

Phase 3, post war, saw a virtually new school, with a slightly less homogenized cohort of pupils that spanned the years from 1945 to 1960. In 1945 Dr. Lion was fifty-one. She apparently never considered returning to Germany, although she was too young (and lacked the means) to retire. She faced substantial challenges in both staffing and recruiting for her school now that sanctuary was no longer the first goal of potential pupils. Through word of mouth, modest brochures and British relief agencies for displaced people, she kept the doors open by admitting significant numbers of day students. Annual enrollments between 1945 and 1960 averaged around seventy pupils, with a ratio of boarding-to-day pupils around 4:1.[1] When the school closed in 1960, there were only thirty-six boarders (one as young as five) and about the same number of day students. It was tough sledding. Dr. Lion wrote in 1952 she would take children "with nervous conditions" but not ones with serious mental illness. There is no evidence she brought in specially-trained staff to deal with a child's emotional problems.

The post-war population was a diverse group. At first comprised of foreign students, refugees, children of refugees and the deserving English poor, it evolved to encompass day pupils from nearby towns who either took cabs, carpooled, or walked up Farnham Lane from the bus stop each day.[2] Dr. Leven wrote that the post-war students "came from a lesser educated background than the refugee children, [which] made teaching, organizing, the relationships between pupils and grown ups often more difficult." The graduates of the post-war era have written that they felt they had "a certain inferior status" to those who had come before them, deferring in newsletters to war-time pupils whom they perceived to have suffered more. Some felt that their experiences were "trivial" in comparison to those of earlier pupils.

The post-war school's identity was no longer one formed through shared suffering and displacement. In fact, by the early nineteen fifties, the historic roots of the school seem to have been consciously or inadvertently suppressed. Surprisingly, some post-war pupils never knew why the school had been founded, and had no idea of its links to the Third Reich. Dr. Lion spoke accented English, wrote herself notes

---

[1] In 1949 there were seventy-three pupils (sixty-two boarders, eleven day). By 1954 the numbers dropped to sixty-five pupils (fifty boarders, fifteen day).

[2] In 1951, Dr. Lion wrote, with a touch of cynicism, that her pupils were "..partly those of refugee parents and partly those who are sent by Authorities in the new boarding out scheme – children deprived of home life who are supposed to be worthy of grammar school education."

in a mixture of German and English, and usually spoke German to German-speaking refugees and Dr. Leven. Yet the entire *raison d'etre* for the school and its tumultuous history were ignored, forgotten, or simply considered inconsequential. Richard Greenwell, who attended Stoatley Rough between 1954 and 1958, mused, "I don't recall hearing anything at all about the Holocaust while at Stoatley Rough, directly or indirectly. The Holocaust (actually this specific term wasn't yet being used at that time) was never discussed in any class that I had, and no teacher or fellow student ever mentioned it .... To me, Stoatley Rough was simply another (my third) boarding school that I had lived in since I was about six years old – although I was much happier there than at the others – and I had no knowledge ...that its creation had anything at all to do with Nazi Germany." He then explains that he "must have led a very sheltered life at Stoatley Rough. In fact, I sometimes wonder if, by the mid 1950's, that's what Dr. Lion may have wanted, in order to protect us a little from even the knowledge of such evil." This gentleman studied twentieth century German history to compensate for all that "youthful ignorance" and, as an amateur historian, he reported, "the World War II section of my personal library contains about seven hundred and fifty volumes (including on the war's causes and aftermath), about eighty volumes of which deal specifically with the Holocaust."[3] Although Stoatley Rough's direct association with the Holocaust seems to have become unlinked from its postwar pupils, the school never lost its association with the wider world. Brochures in the late forties and fifties claimed the school would "provide a sound education and training for children of both sexes and more especially ...for the children of parents who are or at any time were refugees in England....According

---

[3] Ignorance can never be overestimated. This Roughian had the good fortune to be seated next to Elie Weisel, Nobel Prize winner and professor of Humanities at Boston University, on an airplane. He mentioned to the flight attendants that there was a celebrity on board, but when he mentioned the name, one said, "Oh, is he a rock star?" He relayed this fact to Dr. Wiesel who commented, "I suppose I missed my calling." Mr. Greenwell would always grateful that he had had the opportunity to tell the story to the "distinguished humanist." [From Stoatley Rough Newsletter Issue 7, February, 1995. pp.10-11.]

to school historian Michael Johnson, by 1959 the school had become "an international school following a grammar school curriculum with special stress on languages and music."

The post-war school suffered from the absence of Nore Astfalck and the healing presence of the Household Girls. A social chasm grew between the boarding population and the day pupils. Michael Johnson wrote that it took courage for a day pupil to ask the residents for the location of the Day Boarders' loo. Along with the loss of the Farm program and morning run, perhaps most significant, the school lost its sense of community. Now boarders and day pupils formed their own groups. An older boy supposed to be Michael's big brother told him on his first day that children were locked into the Schoolroom as punishment – "'been there myself several days,' he said cheerfully," leaving Michael with a slight fear of incarceration throughout his years at the school. The ethic of looking out for the smaller, younger ones had vanished, at least in this one case.

Music appreciation remained important. Dr. Leven's influence spread wide and deep, perhaps the single most conspicuous characteristic of the school's lasting legacy. The custom of quotations also survived. Superficially, the school inched toward incorporating the character of traditional English boarding schools. It started a prefect system whereby older children performed administrative duties. But Dr. Lion was no longer as strong a presence in the day-to-day affairs of the school, and without Nore's omniscient presence, the train now headed down the tracks almost on its own momentum. No longer did the adrenalin born of survival and idealism fuel the decisions of the aging Headmistress - she seems to have delegated many of her responsibilities. An open, casual, almost unstructured atmosphere took shape with diminished supervision of the children, a situation that most children loved yet one that allowed the shadowy presence of corporal punishment to creep in. At least one time a sadistic teacher administered a brutal beating to a big boy who had thrown spitballs at a girl during church services as others, told to wait their turn just outside the closed door, bolted in fear upon hearing the dreadful cries of the victim. It is doubtful that Dr. Lion was aware of the incident. Academic standards slipped. In 1950 a letter to Dr. Lion from parents reported bullying at the school. Dr. Lion wrote at least one letter to a former student forbidding him from bringing his friend to the grounds again for some unnamed but serious prior misdemeanour.

That the school's academic and general environment had deteriorated from its pre-war standard is evident in the alumni evaluations of the school reported in the Newsletters. Yet there was something special about the school that transcended the usual features by which a school is judged. The pupils simply loved the school. Stefan Lacey recalled, "an indifferent education, awful living conditions, and an administration which almost fifty years later I still consider a disgrace.....I always had the idea that the school was way out of their control." Yet the same boy went on to say, "I feel honoured and lucky to have spent my youth there; without doubt, it was one of my father's best decisions to send me there. ..It taught us self-reliance, to deal with the knocks of life without fluster, to try, try and try again till we succeed – to view a task or problem in different lights and angles, to perceive a solution where few others could." In fact, the majority of post-war pupils fiercely defend their years in Haslemere as happy and worthwhile, as if original values of self-esteem and independence had seeped into the walls of the structure itself and went on to nourish its post-war children. David Kirby-Burt called Stoatley Rough "a shambolically happy place," and many others exulted in the open environment. Ruth Morgan [Roberts], a day student, wrote, "I actually loved the school so much I begged to board and came up voluntarily on Saturdays and stayed as late as possible after school."

Early in the spring of 1960, Dr. Lion, now sixty-seven years old (Dr. Leven was sixty-one) circulated a letter declaring her retirement and the closing of the school.[4] She asked that there be no special celebrations.

---

[4] A draft of Dr. Lion's announcement read, "Dear Parents and Friends, It is with great regret that we announce that Dr. L. Leven and I want to retire at the end of the summer 1960. The School will cease to exist. This decision has been taken after careful consideration with our Chairman and the other members of the Bd. of Governors..."We were glad, Dr. Wolff included who had to retire earlier – that

She helped pupils to find other placements, and the school closed for good that summer.

As a Headmistress, Dr. Lion was flawed - insecure in her personal relationships, capable of vengeance. She was judgmental and often wrong in her evaluation of a child's potential. She showed unhealthy favoritism toward some pupils and she may have pushed the law to the limit in her use of Household Girls. Yet she also did the best she could with a fate she had hardly imagined for herself, let alone had been prepared for when as a young intellectual, she first launched her career in welfare and women's issues in Germany. This shy, unimpressive woman was supposed to live out her days writing and managing teachers like herself, dedicating her life to women's welfare issues. Instead, she ended up in the midst of displaced children with needs that only her school could uniquely meet. At forty years old, she built a school from scratch in a new country. She kept her Board happy, acquired and monitored an ever-changing stream of dedicated and often, superb teaching staff, and showed a willingness to improvise to achieve her goals. No mere ideologue, she was also practical in her way, yielding to the forces of history that could have swamped the school at any point. She had to badger, bully, and scrounge but she kept her school running for twenty-six years and she did so with honor. She literally saved many lives, helped hundreds to find jobs, and loved her large brood even more after they had left her protection. Most who passed through her tutelage express undying appreciation for her efforts. She never lost her love of growing things and always appreciated the humorous, the ironic. She wrote a letter to Peter Strauss in 1948: "The garden has improved since last year, especially our vegetable garden now under the care of a former MP, who puts his potatoes in such order, just as if they had to go on parade with the parsnips and the radishes! At the moment we

we could help in a small way, children and this country. Difficulties for the working of an independent school are mounting and we are not as young as 25 years ago – May we thank our most helpful board, esp. Miss Fearon, for their continued assistance. Stoatley Rough has been our life, now we want to have an active retirement. Please, remain our friends!" Stoatley Rough Archives, London School of Economics.

are over-run with lettuces but luckily some raspberries picked from the garden break the monotony in the diet of spaghetti and tomato juice, and a rather dry second course."[5]

It is much to the credit of Dr. Hilde Lion that the pupils loved the school. Edith Hubacher [Cristoffel] constructed a new word, perfectly grammitcal in German, to express her feelings about Stoatley Rough School: *Zusammengehoerigkeitsgefuhl: Zussamen* – together, *Gehoerigkeit* – sense of belonging together and *Gefuehl* – feeling, emotion.[6]

Dr. Lion and Dr. Leven

Upon retirement in 1960, Drs. Lion and Leven became naturalized citizens of Great Britain, a decision that allowed them to travel to Italy in 1948, and later, to Switzerland, the United States (twice) and Canada. The couple also spent time each winter in Las Palmas (Gran Canaria) visiting Hilde Lion's half-brother. Dr. Lion had written about her brother's son in May, 1941, in one of her *Rundbriefs*, "My nephew came in full uniform to see us and to let us share a little in his military life."

One occasion reconnected Dr. Lion and Dr. Leven with their past. They returned to Krefeld, Germany, Dr. Leven's home town, in September, 1951, to celebrate the seventieth birthday of a close friend who had asked Dr. Leven, who was now fifty-two, to conduct a Women's Choir for an audience of over 400. She was to lead the singers in a composition she had conducted in that town in 1931. Dr. Lion, fifty-eight traveled with Dr. Leven for the performance and was profoundly moved by the experience. Unprepared for the flood of memories, she found forgiveness for her native country in the experience. One senses wistfulness in her report, words that shine a light on the emotional cost of her exile. "A thunderous, nearly tumultuous applause spontaneously broke loose...Tears came to my eyes...The hall was filled with an

---

5   Lion, Hilde, letter to Peter Strauss dated July 15, 1948. Stoatley Rough School Archives, LSE, Box 3/45 (iii).

6   "I just made up a word that expresses the way Roughians feel about each other:" Edith Hubacher-Christoffel quoted by Wolf Elston in *Reminiscences*, 1992.

atmosphere of veneration. The last remnants of suspicions, distrust, petty excuses were blown away, we were no longer accusers or accused by human beings before a new beginning. On this summer night one had the feeling of suddenly being young again as in the spring of one's life."[7]

In 1960, the women used their reparation monies and pensions ("shockingly small" according to Dr. Leven) to build a house with two self-contained apartments at a "beautiful and secluded" site in Hindhead. They received many former pupils (some of whom had financed one of their trips to the U.S.). Dr. Lion died at the age of seventy-six, on April 8, 1970. Dr. Leven wrote to Martin Owens explaining why she had been unable to visit with him when they were in Boston and enclosed a clipping from the local newspaper about Dr. Lion's death. True to form, she complained that the reportage had been inadequate . She concluded, "Life is hard for me now. We built a beautiful house in Hindhead in 1960 and enjoyed it and the garden for nine years. Now I am alone and must let the furnished top-flat which, fortunately, has its own kitchen and bathroom, before the winter."

Dr. Wolff

Emmy Wolff never took British citizenship. She clung, to the end, to her idealized vision of a Germany resplendent in literature and culture, willing the beauty of art to transcend the ugliness of history. She managed to bring her mother to England during the war and would never return to Germany. After serving for twenty-two years at the school, she retired in 1956 and continued to write poetry. She died on September 9, 1969 in Haslemere, leaving more than 400 poems, translations and articles. Dr. Lion wrote in a letter about her friend that Emmy was "a fire-brand, often torn to and fro between the loyalty to the country she had to leave, the land of German Humanism, and England, the land of tolerance and freedom...Several times a week Emmy visited her mother, usually on her own, without a hat in all weathers. On her

---

[7] Hilde Lion, from "Luise Leven's Story, op. cit.

way she recited poems from Goethe to Ricarda Huch and on to Rilke, poems of early French to Verlaine, from Shelley to Auden. She has been an excellent translator, and some of her translations have been published in England and German....The inner richness helped her to accept her gradually increasing deafness and loneliness. She never talked about it. She was [un]compromising – at times stubborn, she was fond of her friends and she loved her family, keeping in close touch through unusual vividly descriptive and deeply moving letters. She was a fearless woman who slept alone in her house with windows wide open throughout the night."[8]

Eleonore Astfalck and JoHanna Nacken

Nore and Hanna were among the first ex-patriots to re-enter Germany after the war, by-passing the red tape for most returnees with the help of First Lieutenant Hans Loeser. After they visited Hanna's parents in Wurtemburg and Nore's brother in Berlin, they set about helping where they could do the most good. The educator Minna Specht, having also returned to Germany from exile, asked the two women to help her reclaim the *Odenwald Schule* near Heidelberg, a facility that had become a Nazi boarding school and later, a hospital.[9] (While Nore does not specifically address her relationship to Minna Specht while in England, she implies in her oral history that there was communication among the various German refugee educators. Dr. Lion was a firm friend of Bunce Court's Anna Essinger and probably corresponded with Minna Specht as well.)

Nore wrote about the deprivations of post-war-ravaged Germany. "Everybody got one potato and some boiled turnips for lunch and we had to scavenge the nearby woods for fuel but it was stripped clean."[10] She recalled there were only enough boots or shoes for half the school, and so they made the children share, some going around unshod while

---

8 Hilde Lion, Stoatley Rough archives, op.cit.
9 Ibid.
10 Eleonore Astfalk, *Oral History*

the other half went on an excursion wearing the shoes. Even one of the male teachers couldn't go to a conference because, he said, "I have no shoes." She wrote of the importance of CARE packages from America that brought honey, corn flakes and dried milk.

In 1950, Nore was asked to direct the rebuilding of *Immenhof,* part of a larger worker's welfare organization, the *Arbeiterwohlfahrt,* a self-help organization something like the Red Cross. It offered Kindergarten, speech therapy, and even a walking school for people injured during the war. It also brought in troubled girls formerly living in foster homes with the goal of educating them without locked doors and windows. Later the *Immenhof* offered domestic science training and provided a home for poor mothers to have a holiday (*Muttergenesungswerk* [Mothers' Recuperation]), a brainchild of Nore's. Over the years, the indefatigable Nore instituted other programs: training for mothers of handicapped children; a recreation program for blind mothers, and experimental programs dedicated to giving very poor people a holiday.

Hanna Nacken died in April, 1963, in her sixty-seventh year. Dr. Lion and Dr. Wolff had known Hanna as a feminist activist in Berlin. The two collaborated on a tribute, harkening back to their own salad days. The following was translated by Martin [Friedenfeld] Owens. "We knew Hanna in the days of the youth movement when she was still wearing wooden beads in her hair. She had the simplicity and love of nature of a *Wanderfogel.* She associated with the social youth organizations...expressing a new generation. We worked then at practical tasks and also tried to solve philosophical issues...Hanna, the daughter of a pastor, ...was opposed to strict and narrow religious dogmas. Inner truthfulness ... was something she did not question." In their final lines of tribute, Dr. Lion and Dr. Wolf pay respect to Nore as well. "Hanna had no visible ambition. She was more capable than her modesty allowed, she was clever, musical, and had good taste. With her Rhenish humor and sharp wit she laughed difficulties away. For those she loved, her financial largess knew no bounds. She and Nore helped so many not just with advice but also with action."

Nore was now alone. She stayed on at *Immenhof* for seven more years. In 1970, at seventy, she planned to retire and join her brother and his wife in Berlin. But she had more to give. She took a job at a *Schule fur Frauenberufe* [School for Women's Professions] that provided training for social workers, household workers, and cooking and sewing lessons. She worked full time for another seven years. Still healthy, she started a children's club for Turkish and German children. She said what was most valuable about her work was reaching out to the parents. In her eighties, she met a convict (she was doing volunteer work at a prison) who needed someone to accompany him when he traveled under his parole rules. They became friends. She enjoyed traveling with him for several years. She often said there was no such thing as old age. When she mused about the role ordinary Germans played in the war and Holocaust she refused to heap blame on her countrymen. She said, "You can't pass on what really happened, because if you are honest with yourself, you have to say you cannot understand it. It's not possible to understand what human beings have done to other human beings even when they were not forced to do it."[11] Eleanore Astfalck, a most loving woman, died in her sleep at the age of ninety. Months before, she had been feted at a reunion of Stoatley Roughians in Guilford.

---

[11] Ibid.

Part II: The People

W hat follows is a detailed look at the lives of a few of the many who voluntarily shared their stories for this book, many of whom offer a final word about the impact of Stoatley Rough on their lives.

Renate Dorpalen-Brocksieper (1922-2017)

Renate returned to Germany as a civilian Civil Censor Division of the US Army and at her first opportunity, she traveled to Berlin to find her family's beloved Aryan nanny, Mŭrt. Renate met her friend at the site of her former home now a part of the rubble that was Berlin.)

> "I had returned after seven years that seemed an eternity. How often had I pictured in my mind this return, never with the reality that was to confront me. In my dreams time had stood still.. The bombed-out cities of England, the ruin of Munich, had not prepared me for the destruction of Berlin. The formerly vibrant city was barely surviving. Once-crowded streets were empty, filled with silence, the avenues, robbed of their majestic trees, were overgrown with weeds; the parks had turned into wasteland....The few passers-by hurried along with downcast looks as if they dreaded to leave the safety of their shelters. ...children were rummaging

for food everywhere, or begged for cigarettes, which had become legal tender on the black market....The silhouette of the mighty tower of the Kaiser Wilhelm Memorial Church stood ghostlike above the ruins of its sanctuary, looking down the *Kurfürstendam* that had also lost its soul. The jagged tower had become a memorial to the drama performed by fearless, unshaken ministers of the confessional church and other righteous Christians."

Renate struggled to articulate her feelings during long hours she stayed with Mürt. She recalled sitting outdoors on a curb with the aging housekeeper who had relayed messages to various parts of the dispersed family. She was the one who had notified the children of their parents' deaths in Theresienstadt. The old woman was dressed in proper black with a white lace collar, her cane and pocketbook beside her, while Renate, young and fresh in her American military uniform, sat by her side. Able at last to unburden her heart, Renate reminisced about the life she had left behind. "My dominant feeling on encountering German men and women was one of distrust, as I could not help but wonder what part they had played in the sadistic drama. What I felt most, however, was an immense sadness." She talked about "the wrecked members of the master race...I felt no pleasure in watching the misery of the masses, who had once shouted *'Sieg Heil, Jude Verrecke'* [Hail Victory, Jew die]. They were not reduced to suffering the fate of the haunted, the displaced, the homeless. Here were people who had willingly followed their Fuehrer to conquer the world; these people who years before treated me as an outcast, were now ingratiating themselves to me. It was such a strange situation that I could hardly interpret my own feelings. I was supposed to hate them with all my strength. But I could not hate, or was it in the face of such suffering hatred was silent? I would neither sit in judgment nor would it be in my power to forgive and forget."[12]

---

[12] Renate Dorpalen [Dorpalen-Brocksieper], "Stoatley Rough Remembered" *Stoatley Rough Newsletter* Issue 9, October, 1995, p. 15.

Renate emigrated to the United States in 1947 and settled in New York City. After a stint as governess, she worked in New York City's Settlement House by day (one of several centers established to help recent immigrants to acclimate) and attended Hunter College by night.[13] She graduated with a BA in Sociology and History in 1950 earned a Master's degree in Social Work at Western Reserve in Cleveland, Ohio. She moved on to postgraduate work at the University of Michigan where she met her husband who was completing his PhD. When he moved to Yale University, Renate accepted a position in New Haven, Connecticut as a social worker in the department of Psychiatry. The couple had one son, George. Despite many academic and professional achievements, her United States naturalization papers remained her most valued possession.

Renate served on one of the planning committees for the Special Olympics World Games in New Haven, Connecticut in July of 1995, and was a delegation host for the German team for that event. She recalled having witnessed the 1936 Olympic Games in Berlin as a child. "All signs of Jewish persecution disappeared temporarily. From the balcony of friends on the *Kaiserdamm* I saw the marathon runner carrying the torch to the stadium. ...Jesse Owens, a Negro on the United States team, won four gold medals, astounded the world and upset Hitler's Aryan theories of superiority. While practically living with the German team for ten days on the Yale University campus, I surprised myself once again with thoughts of wondering what part the grandparents, maybe great-grandparents of the athletes, their coaches and the German officials had played in the sadistic drama of Hitler's 'Thousand Year Reich.' Reconciliation with our past is an intellectual accommodation but will never let us forget the emotional experiences."[14] Throughout her career and through her volunteerism, Renate believed in the power of community and was a tireless advocate for children.

---

[13] Ibid.
[14] Ibid.

Hans Loeser (1920-2010)

Hans joined his family in New York and set about becoming a U.S. Citizen. His first job was to serve in the U.S. Army as a Richie Boy, an elite group of German-speaking soldiers whose job it was to interrogate captured Germans. He served in the 82nd Battalion and recalls the Battle of the Bulge. While in France, Hans and his fellow German speakers were cautioned to refrain from straying from the camp, aware of authenticated stories that U.S. soldiers would seize and kill men wearing the U.S. uniform who spoke English with a German accent.

Hans married Herta Lewent while still serving, and took up his civilian life upon returning to America. Hans graduated from Harvard Law School in 1948 with honors, having received the prestigious invitation to join the board of the Harvard Review. Although he was offered a position with a prominent firm in New York City, he chose to join Foley, Hoag and Eliot in Boston. He helped the firm grow into one of Boston's finest and became managing partner. He commented that in those days, many large firms in New York and Boston "wouldn't look at Jews," a recognition of the active anti-Semitism in America in the fifties. Along with his lawyerly duties, Hans presided over the Cambridge Civic Association and the Arts and Crafts Council of Boston, the latter position taken owing to Herta's active role in that organization.

While privately accepting many pro bono cases along the way, he worked actively to end the Viet Nam war, starting Lawyers Against the War in Vietnam. He later claimed he was proud to have managed to get himself onto Nixon's enemies list. Hans co-founded Lawyers Alliance for Nuclear Arms Control, was Special Assistant to the Dean of Harvard Law School for long range planning and was appointed honorary consul for the Republic of Senegal. One of his most gratifying moments came the day his client walked into the room where three SEC lawyers waited, prepared to do battle. His reputation for fairness was such that the lawyers clapped their hands in appreciation.

Hans took many trips to England and Europe, primarily to ski and to look in on old Roughian schoolmates. In 2007, at eighty-six, this robust gentleman finally gave up his yearly ski trips to Europe but continued to coach his younger colleagues.[15] Hans published his memoirs *Hans's Story*, iUniverse, 2007, which is filled with fascinating tales of his life in Germany before the war during the period of racial laws that led to the Holocaust, as well as his work in Boston as a young lawyer.

He and Herta delighted in their eight grandchildren and spent many summers with them at their house on Martha's Vineyard.

Herta Lewent [Loeser] (1921-2014)

Herta left Stoatley Rough before the war ended, taking secretarial positions in London but maintaining her close friendships with Nore Astfalck and Hanna Nacken. She stayed many weekends with them at the School back in Haslemere. She also kept up a running correspondence with her former boyfriend, Hans Loeser, but each had determined to lead independent lives upon separating. But when Hans returned to England in uniform, he lost no time in requisitioning a jeep from his base to reunite with her. They knew immediately that they were destined to be life-long mates. They received permission to marry, were given a long weekend for a honeymoon in Southern England before Hans returned to his duties. After the Germans surrendered and the war was over, Herta joined the post-war scene in Europe to become an official translator/censor of German mail in the Civilian Censorship Division of the U.S. army. She emigrated to the US on a war brides ship in 1944.

Profoundly affected by the Women's Liberation Movement in the late sixties, Herta came home one night and said to Hans, "there's a revolution going on." She became involved in helping women find meaningful work, echoing Hilde Lion's own activities during the Depression in Germany at the same age. Herta always felt grieved by

---

15 Hans Loeser. Privately published "Hans History;" also recorded interview taken March 2, 2001, "Legal Oral History Project, Pennsylvania Law School."

her fate not to have been afforded a university education, yet she took leadership in a variety of volunteer positions in Boston.

Herta was asked to co-chair Boston's Civic Center and Clearing House, an organization that placed volunteers into hundreds of charitable opportunities and she received the prestigious honor of admission to the Radcliffe Institute for a year during which time she wrote *Women Work and Volunteering* (1972). The book sold over 4,000 copies before going into paperback. She became the President and Director of the Society of Arts and Crafts, America's oldest non-profit crafts organization in Boston, and said she was "happy that [she] knew very little about running a craft gallery." She rescued the fine institution from going under by raising its standards and for over ten years she steered it back into the black

Herta spoke about the difficulties she faced. "Everything we did had to be fought for and it was never, as I said, credentialed; it was always, in my case at least, hit or miss and unconventional...." Again her words reflect her disappointment at being denied a fulfilling education by Dr. Lion, who needed her in the office. Profoundly affected by her experience of being wrenched away from home so early, she noted that traveling later in life was not easy. "Even now when we go off to Greece and everybody says how wonderful,...it's always difficult for me....I think that it had to do with having to go on a big trip and never being able to go back."[16]

Martin Friedenfeld [Owens] (1928 - 2018)

Upon arriving in the US, Martin re-united with his mother, his new stepfather, Henry [Oppenheimer] Owens, and his sister, Lisa, in the Jackson Heights section of Queens. He graduated from Queens College with degree in Psychology. As searcher at the New York Public Library, he served on a committee that persuaded Boris Karloff to attend a gala staff party, and he found Frankenstein's monster the kindest, most

---

[16] Herta Lewent Loeser, Oral History p. 8.14.

courtly of gentlemen. Martin spent summers working along with Obo and Wolf as a busboy at the Breezy Hill Resort in the Catskills, stating that it only slightly resembled the resort made famous in the movie, *Dirty Dancing*. Most of its guests were German-Jewish survivors.

After a one-year deferral to attend graduate school at Western Reserve University in Cleveland, Martin volunteered for the Air Force and trained as Electronics Countermeasures Officer, flying as a 1st Lieutenant out of Puerto Rico for two years on RB 36s. In 1956 he joined the System Development Division of the Rand Corp and would later spend the last twenty-seven years of his career with the MITRE Corp. in Bedford Massachusetts. He married and had five children with his wife, Jane Passant.

Martin headed "Adventures in Music," a volunteer group that organized symphony orchestra concerts for middle school children; and, upon discovering the joys of sailing, became an instructor and national officer in the United States Power Squadrons., A self-described "aging jock," Martin, also skied, and taught skiing at the Nashoba Ski Area in Westford, Massachusetts, into his eighties. Although his favorite musical is *Sound of Music*, he did return to Vienna, although he stated "The duplicity of the Austrians made a profound impression on me, and I never wanted to return to Vienna. It took me fifty years to muster the courage to return. I admire the buildings and historic palaces, and the coffee houses and the food, but I can't ever forgive the Viennese for giving up their country so easily."

More than many other Hut Boys, Martin chose to leave behind his past. With his anglicized name and lack of accent Martin was always taken as American-born. If you were to ask him for his primary identity – Austrian, British, American - he answered he was a Jew. A new friend once remarked that Martin had the exquisite manners of an Austrian and the formality of an Englishman. Martin recognized he was a private man. Having lost so much so early in life, he always said his greatest fear was of losing people dear to him.

Wolfgang Edelstein [Elston] (1928 - 2016)

Wolf graduated *cum laude* from City College with Honors in Geology in 1949, earning the Ward Medal. After summers as a busboy in the Catskills, he taught evenings at CCNY before pursuing graduate studies at Columbia. After earning his PhD, he was drafted into the US Army the day after commencement to become a "highly educated dishwasher, potato peeler and cleaner of grease traps in the mess hall of Camp Crowder, Missouri....I went in as a private, came out as a private two years later because I was classified SPP (Scientific and Professional Personnel), which kept me from getting a permanent assignment until two weeks before discharge. No assignment, no promotion. I was, however, eligible for a Low IQ Discharge because I hadn't made PFC in 18 months. (I was tempted to apply)." He married Lorraine Hind, a Columbia journalism student, and followed his "inglorious military career as a tester of nylon socks and petroleum products."

Wolf accepted a position at the University of New Mexico earning numerous academic honors in his career: Founder and Coordinator, University of New Mexico-Los Alamos National Laboratory Volcanology Program, 1990 – 1999; fellowships from the Geological Society of America, Society of Economic Geologists, American Association for the Advancement of Science, and the Meteoritical Society. The New Mexico Museum of Natural History dedicated a symposium to him in 2001. He devoted his later years on a project in the Bushveld in South Africa, thinly slicing rocks for scrutiny by electronic microscope for evidence of an asteroid that hit the earth two billions years ago. He said, "I'm one of the lucky people whose vocation is also their avocation."

Wolf spoke fluent German and said that "The five and a half formative years at Stoatley Rough have remained a powerful influence on my life. Without knowing it, we Hut Boys were a support group without equal; it's no wonder we have remained friends for life. The strong women who ran Stoatley Rough had their quirks, but where would we have been without them? They not only gave us a safe home, they put us on paths to productive lives. Concerns for others that was instilled by community life at Stoatley Rough, have prompted modest efforts in furthering minority students and in speaking to school children about a childhood in Nazi Germany.... My public presentations end with a troubling question: How would I have acted if fate had given me ancestors considered 'Aryan' by Hitler's perverse definition?"

I'm deeply grateful to the people of Britain, who accepted us 'enemy aliens' at a time when their own national survival was at risk. America has become my country; it has given me home, family, citizenship, social acceptance, and incredible educational and professional opportunities. As a child it was described to me as "*das Land der unbeschränkten Möglichkeiten* (the land of unlimited possibilities)," and so it has turned out to be.

Hans Obermeyer (1928 -)

Obo arrived in New York City in January, 1947, to live with his elderly uncle, his only living relative. He worked at various jobs while attending a vocational trade school taking machine shop and allied courses. In October 1950 Obo was drafted into the US Army and was sent to Germany for two years. He was awaiting citizenship. He wrote, "My feelings were of course very confused. On the one hand the nightmare of having had to leave my parents some eleven years earlier and having learned of the horrors of the Holocaust and the death of my family at the hands of the people to whose country I was about to be sent still plagued me. On the other, I had escaped ...and I was grateful for having been given a second chance at life in my newly adopted country."

His return to Germany was difficult. "Once I overheard the Germans on public transportation as we were passing through the still partly-destroyed neighborhoods, talking about how tough they had had it during the war and what the Allies and especially the Amies (GIs) had done to their beautiful cities and how stupid those soldiers were. I stared them in their faces and left no doubt that I understood what they were saying. I think one time I spoke up and said how unfortunate it was that the Russians didn't advance far enough to the west. More than once I was asked to accompany the Military Police when they were called out to defuse a fight between the GIs and the local police at pubs and elsewhere." Obo revisited Bad Salzuflen. "Note I am avoiding the word 'hometown.'.....Basically very little had changed except that my parent's nice stucco house was now a private hotel presumably still owned by the Nazi hotel family to which my father had to sell it in 1937... Everything looked gray and depressing and badly in need of a coat of paint. We drove to my father's former place of business, a hardware and housewares store which he was forced to sell at a ridiculous price. After wrestling with my thoughts I went inside and immediately recognized a number of former employees who, presumably because I was in GI uniform and all grown up, at first did not know who I was. When I identified myself they seemed genuinely happy to see me and were glad that I had survived the war. They then wanted to tell me about their experiences under the Nazis and who of the former staff was killed on the Russian front. By then I was more than ready to leave town... In 1977, I paid the town another visit with [my wife] Joan and I had matured and had a different slant on life."

Obo became a manager for the DoAll company, a distributor of machine tools. When he became a grandfather at seventy seven, Obo doted on his new little "Ginger Nipper" grandson. He remarks on his past life. "Through the 'miracle' of the computer I keep in touch with several of the Hut Boys who have remained my best and lifelong friends. I have attended some of the reunions and have told my story to various groups of school children and adults as part of the *Kindertransport* experience. ... Life has been good to me after an uncertain and perilous start both in England and the US. I am thankful to Great Britain for saving my life and the US for having given me the opportunity to build a career and the security everyone can achieve in this country if one is willing to work for it."

Dieter Gaupp (1925 -)

Dieter enrolled at Southwestern University, Georgetown, Texas, in 1947 and received his undergraduate and masters degrees in Social Work. He became a social worker in the Dallas area. One summer, three co-workers invited him to join them in a cross-country trip to California during which he fell in love with one of them, Fannie Belle Peak, a native of Texas, to whom he was married for over forty-six years. Dieter's career was launched firmly in the public service camp: he ran children's agencies, worked at a medical school in Dallas evaluating children, and became coordinator for clinics for the state. He never forgot his Stoatley Rough introduction to carpentry. He has enjoyed wood-making projects throughout his adult life, forever indebted to his earliest mentor, Hanna Nacken, for showing him that wood is beautiful.

Dieter had an opportunity to heal old wounds within the Gaupp family that had been inflicted over Nazi membership in Germany. While his mother had been born Jewish, his father's people were Aryan, and certain allegiances through the years remained unhealed when the war ended. Dieter had never gone back to Germany until an elderly aunt encouraged him to re-establish contact with an estranged cousin whose father had been a member of the SS. On their return Dieter and Fanny Belle stopped over in Berlin. "There we met my cousin, embraced and have been very close ever since...When he came to the States he asked if he could meet my mother. She welcomed him into her home, whereupon he burst into tears."

Dieter lives in the Dallas area, and visits their son, Bill, as often as possible. "While I was at STRS [for] less than three years, my experiences there have lasted me a lifetime.... Having come to the school some five years after leaving Germany, it took me some time to integrate back into a German culture and I did not embrace it readily. I also felt at times that the adults in charge did not really understand me as a teenager, so that the close bonds I formed with friends offered me the security I needed and a way to express myself... I know the staff did their best and meant well and cared about me; they just didn't quite know what to do with me. Thus, when I was ready to take the matric exam, they did appreciate that I could do so with success but instead, denied me the opportunity. Stoatley Rough was for me a very special place and a very special part of my life."

Peter Gaupp (1928 -)

Peter enjoyed a loving reunion with his parents in Texas where his father had accepted a teaching professor at one of the Universities. After working consecutive jobs as Boy Scout camp program director, liquor clerk, shoe salesman, and recreation therapist with emotionally disturbed adolescents, Peter enrolled in Southwestern University in Georgetown, Texas, and studied physics, mathematics and later sociology and psychology. "The Dean's secretary was a stunning red-head and a music education major and I married her." With his bride in tow, the former Jo-Lou Meitzen, Peter went to work as a recreation worker at a large children's institution. He later moved to Austin, Texas and the couple became a family with the birth of their son and daughter. He became a psychiatric social worker in a Federal research psychiatric prison hospital for narcotics addicts before earning a Ph.D. in community planning, research and public health at the University of Pittsburgh. He directed a psychiatric research foundation back in Texas and later worked as a community health planner, "developing innovative public services such as the first family court services in this region." He is most proud of his efforts to develop *avant guarde* public services such as the first regional mental health and mental retardation center system and a network of community health centers for the poor. He joined the faculty of the nearby State Graduate School of Social Work where he taught Master and Doctoral students, did research, and organized a state-wide planning and development agency within the University. He established services in public health, preschool education, housing for the poor, delinquency prevention, and banking for the poor. He received a commendation medal from the US Surgeon General and retired as a Professor Emeritus in December 1993.

"It's gratifying how several of my programs, so controversial when I first developed them, are now well-accepted mainstays of the community and are doing a great job...[including] bringing down the mortality rate."

Peter is an active member of a Christian Protestant church, and he never lacks the time to visit and support his three grandchildren.

Hans Goldmeier (1928 - 2001)

Goldy emigrated with his mother and brother to New York. Upon arrival, his family had expected to claim a cache of $200 his father had entrusted to the brother of a friend in England, now living in New York. When the man denied receiving the money, the Goldmeier family resorted to the ancient custom of Beth Hadin, a Jewish system of justice in which three rabbis decide disputes. "This system still existed in New York and had been a way Jews solved legal problems in Russia and other countries where they wanted to remain inconspicuous or thought they could not obtain justice from biased judges in the regular courts."[17] The Goldmeiers won.

The diligent Goldy embarked on a rich succession of part-time jobs, from apprentice diamond cutter to fur coat salesman. (In that capacity, he caught a glimpse from his showroom of Frank Sinatra being mobbed by screaming girls.) "It made me think that American girls had lost their sense..... For me, life had always been serious."[18]

Goldy attended evening classes at City College in New York City over the next several years all the time working a dizzying string of occupations: retail clothing clerk, door-to-door magazine salesman (he never sold even one subscription), pots and pans salesman, peep-hole salesman and waiter. "They offered too many pies that I did not know, like lemon, apple, cherry, lemon meringue and so on. When I could not recognize one, I just said we had run out, an evasion that worked until

---

[17] John [Hans Goldy] Goldmeier, Memoirs, p. 67.
[18] Ibid. p. 69.

a customer noticed his pie being delivered to another table. So this job ended." As process server (he once served a summons to the Broadway theater owner, Mr. Shubert), he was paid to shout "present" when the case was called, after which he called the lawyer on the pay phone to come to court. He worked summers in the Catskills with Martin and Obo at Breezy Hill Hotel, and with Wolf one summer at the Majestic Hotel. "We all had to speak German so that the guests could feel free to speak German;…they had definite habits, from the food they ate to what time they would get up in the morning [and ordered at will,] such as having wine at the table just like in the old country. ….As for our working conditions, we cheerfully lied to the Department of Labor inspectors that we had a day off when we never did, and that our accommodations were fine when we were really crammed like sardines into hot lofts."

After Goldy received a Masters of Social Work from Tulane in 1952, he entered military service as a heavy weapons infantryman. He qualified as an interpreter in French and German and was sent to Bremerhaven, Germany. He decided he was not willing to remain in Germany, so he got himself transferred to La Chapelle St. Mesmim, France. As a Second Lieutenant he was put to work in the neuropsychiatry department troubleshooting mental health problems. His one "MASH" incident came about the night a high-ranking General called to demand a veterinarian. The General's dog had swallowed a chicken bone. Goldy and his buddies searched all the bars in the area with no luck. "We all made a strategic decision to let the dog run around a bit longer, coughing away. The story ended happily; the dog got rid of the bone and the General went away pleased."[19] In 1961 Goldy he spent a year at Columbia University and married the daughter of a German Jew, Dorothy Fried. The couple had three children. Goldy earned a PhD from the University of Chicago, School of Social Work, in 1963. He took a position as Associate Professor in the School of Social Work at the University of Maryland and as full Professor, published many books and taught for thirty years. Goldy wrote was grateful for the ideas [of]

---

[19] Ibid.

Dr. Lion [such as] ..."open inquiry, respect for others, and seeing the dignity of people in a world where this was all but forgotten at the time. I am grateful for that."[20]

In 2001 Goldy died before he could pursue this final dream of wanting to "pay back" for the many opportunities that he was granted to advance himself in his life.

Margaret Dove Faulkner (First English teacher)

Margaret Dove was born in London to a physician and his wife. She took Honors English at Westfield College, London. She taught at Calder Girls' School in the north of England then at Stoatley Rough School, Haslemere. She married Ewan, a Cambridge maths graduate, and bore four children in Dundee, Scotland where she taught English at the College of Commerce. She was local secretary for 20 years for Amnesty International, and worked all her life for human rights.

Margaret wrote in 1990 about her impressions after the Stoatley Rough Reunion of 1990. "To me, who had been a very young English teacher from 1937 – 1939, the Reunion was partly the privilege, denied to most educationalists, of seeing how my pupils had "turned out'; but mainly a proof that people can overcome sorrows and difficulties that could have been insurmountable and overwhelming. These children who had been separated from their parents, some of them forever, who had left the school with little money and few friends, to face a world to some extent prejudiced against both Jews and Germans, had become useful citizens, some really outstanding ones. .... The childhood experiences of the Old Roughians had probably enhanced their sensitivity and their intuitive sympathies; they had certainly contributed a great deal to society. I am sure that those who came after them at Stoatley Rough caught something of the spirit of the school and were helped to overcome some of their own very different problems."

---

[20] Religion at Stoatley Rough, Stoatley Rough Newsletter Issue 18, September, 1998, p. 34

REFERENCES

Bielenberg, Christabel, *The Past is Myself,* Oxford Clio Press, 1970.

Fox, Ann L., *My Heart in a Suitcase,* Valentine Mitchell, London, 1996

Elston, Wolfgang E., "Goldschmidtschule, Berlin-Grunewald, 1938 – 39" Article in *Passages from Berlin*, by Steve J. Heims, Atlantic Printing, South Berwick, Maine, 1987.

Epstein, Helen, *Where She Came From: A Daughter's Search for Her Mother's History,"* A PLUME BOOK, Penguin Putnam, 1998.

Epstein, Helen, *Children of the Holocaust,* Penguin Putnam, 1979

Experience and Expression Women, the Nazis and the Holocaust, Ed. Baer, Elizabeth R., and Goldenberg, Myrna Wayne State University Press, Detroit, 2003

Feidel-Mertz, "Integration and formation of Identify: Exile Schools in Great Britain" from *SHOFAR:* Fall 2004, Vol. 23, No. 1.

Clare, George, *Last Waltz in Vienna,* Avon Books, New York, 1983. (originally published in Germany, *Das waren die Klaars*, 1980.)

Goldhagen, Daniel Johah, *Hitler's Willing Executioners: Ordinary Germans and the Holocaust* Vintage Books

Goldmeier, John, "Memoirs" Part I, Columbia Maryland, January, 2000

Gorell, The Rt. Hon. Lord, C.B.E.M.C. Chairman, A GREAT ADVENTURE The Story of the Refugee Children's Movement, Bloomsbury House, London (M3206, Box 6)

Holton, Gerald, and Sonnert, Gerhard, "What Happened to the Austrian Refugee Children in America? A Report from Research Project

'Second Wave'," (Preliminary Report) Department of Physics, Harvard University, Cambridge, MA 02138, June, 2003.

Jeffreys, D., "Some Earlier History of Stoatley Rough," June, 1965, Archives, LSE 11/12.

Kubicek, Peter, 1000: 1 Odds: *Memoir of a World War II Childhood* Information Economics Press, 2002.

Laqueur, Walter, *Generation Exodus* Tauber Institute for the Study of European Jewry Series, Brandeis University Press/University Press of New England, 2001.

Leverton, Bertha and Lowensohn, Shmuel, editors, *I Came Alone, The Stories of the Kindertransports* London, 1990

Loeser, Hans F., *Hans's Story,* iUniverse, Lincoln, NE, 2007.

Loeser, Hans F. and Loeser, Herta, editors, *Since Then..." Letters from Former Stoatley Roughians,* Copyright 1971 Boston, Mass, Autumn, 1971.

Loeser, Hans F., Legal Oral History Project," Interview with Hans Loeser March 2, 2001. The University of Pennsylvania Law School

Loeser, Herta and Tom, *Oral History Recorded During the Winter of 1988 between Herta and Tom Loeser* Cambridge, MA, 1988.

Loeser, Hans F., and Herta Loeser, and Astfalck, Eleanore, *Oral History of Eleanore Astfalck, 1900 – " Recorded July, 1985.* Cambridge, MA, 1990.

Megged, Aharon, *The Story of the Selvino Children* Vallentine Mitchell London2002, Trans. From Hebrew by Vivian Eden

Meyer, Gerda, *Prague Winter* Hearing Eye, London, 2005

Milton, Edith, *The Tiger in the Attic: Memories of the Kindertransport and Growing Up English.*

Samuels, Diane, *Kindertransport* Nick Helm Books, 1993

Siegel, Lore, Other People's Houses

Simmel-Joachim, Monika, "Background of the Five Principal Refugee Teachers of Stoatley Rough School from Nazi Germany" from an article that first appeared in *Ariadne* (no 23) 23 May, 1993, Almanac of the German Women's Movement in German, translation by Gerda Haas.

Shirer, William, L., The Rise and Fall of the Third Reich, Simon and Shuster, 1960

Speer, Albert, *Inside the Third Reich*, The Macmillan Company, 1970

Seligmann, Matthew, Davison, John, McDonald, John, Daily Life in Hitler's Germany, Thomas Dunne Books, St. Martin's Press, 175 Fifth Avenue, New York, NY 2003.

Whiteman, Dorit Bader, *The Uprooted: a Hitler Legacy* Insight Books, Plenum Press, 1993

Newsletters from Stoatley Rough School 1934 – 1960, Vols. 1 – 23, December, 1992 - September 2004

On Other Schools
Part 3, from The Essingers by Tamar Duk-Cohan, Boston, USA, accessed November, 2004
http://www.egu.schule.ulm.de/wsignals/wsignals9/aessi04.htm

Jüdische Privatschule von Dr. Leonore Goldschmid
© Edition Luisenstadt, 1998 - 2003 15 Mar 2004, www.berlin-geschichte.de
http://www.luise-berlin.de/Gedenktafeln/cha/j/juedische_privatschule_
von_dr.htm
accessed October 28, 2005

On the Battle of Britain
The Battle of Britain 1940 "http://www.battleofbritain.net/0020.html"
www.battleofbritain.net/0020.html Battle of Britain Historical Society,
Education and Research for Students

On the Quakers
Quaker Refugee Projects from We Bring History to Life, accessed
November, 2004, http://www.traces.org/quakerrefugeeprojects.html

On the Blitz
"The London Blitz, 1940" EyeWitness to History, 2001. Accessed
October, 2004. http://www.eyewitnesstohistory.com

The Institute of Contemporary History and Wiener Library, 4
Devonshire Street, London W1W 5BH
Tel: 020 7636 7247 Fax: 020 7436 6428 e-mail: info@wienerlibrary.
co.uk web: www.wienerlibrary.co.uk
How to cite articles found on web:

"The London Blitz, 194," EyeWitness to History, www.eyewitnessto
history.com (2001).

Other Books Consulted

Stilben, R. Gabriele S., Is the War Over? Postware Years of a Child Survivor of the Holocaust Fithian Press, McKinley, California 2004.

Nicholas, Lynn H., *Cruel World, The Children of Europe in the Nazi Web*, New York, 2006

Bikales, Gerda, *Through the Valley of the Shadow of Death*, !Universe, Inc., Lincoln, NE 2004

Winter, Miriam, *Trains*, Kelton Press, Jackson, MI, 1997

Tayar, Enzo, *Days of Rain*, Yad Vashem, New York and Jersualem, 2004

And Life is Changed Forever Holocaust Childhoods Remember, Edited by Martin Ira Glassner and Robert Krell, Wayne State University, 2006

APPENDIX

Introduction

S tudents who passed through Stoatley Rough dispersed widely. Many acquired new surnames and new identities. Some totally disassociated themselves from Stoatley Rough. Many have died including at least four who are known to have committed suicide. In 1980 a core group of Roughians in England formed a steering committee to preserve the legacy of the School and hosted several reunions, after which several more reunions took place in the US. The committee raised sufficient money from the alumni to fund a cataloguing of the large body of materials placed in the archives of the London School of Economics; today all but the personal files of individual students are open to researchers.

General statements can be made. Many former pupils expressed passion about their time at the school. They also were grateful to the people of Great Britain for taking them in. They retained a lifelong appreciation for classical music and art; they revered neatness and thrift. Many shared a philanthropic, politically liberal attitude toward the less fortunate. Many maintained their ability to speak and read German; many shared their histories as speakers to high school students. And many returned to inspect their former homes in Germany, each in his or her own way attempting to come to terms with what happened. Many went on to higher education to earn PhDs, MDs, law degrees, and worked in the healing arts. It is my perception that a high percentage of Roughians rose to prominence in their fields whether it be business, science, technology, banking, or teaching and other areas.

The views in the book are not the whole story. They reflect the thoughts of those who chose to write. Countless former students remain unrepresented, some of whom may disagree with my interpretation of the school. Lacking the existence of complete records, I cannot, nor do I claim to account for, all of the people who passed through the mansion's halls or for the forgotten value they were to the community. But what follows are names of some of the people who were present at one time or another at the School.

First Pupils

These are some of the children who arrived at the School between 1934 and 1936.

Feldman, Eva
Halls, Laurie
Lewent (Loeser), Herta
Horkheimer (Hawkes) Fred
Isler, Ellen
Padolinsky, Ayosdo
Padolinsky, Alika
Loeser, Hans
Looman, Roswilla
Saul, Lotte
Wilzak, Ernst
Zedner, Klaus

Pupils During the War

Names of some pupils may have changed since their time at Stoatley Rouch. Parentheses enclose women's married names.

Bayer (Tuchman), Ruth
Behrendt, Eddie
Chasanowich, Lillian

Deutsch, Ruth
Deutscher, Kurt
Feldstein, Ilse
Finkler, Arthur
Friedenfeld, Martin Owens
Galligan, Angela
Gaupp, Dieter
Gaupp, Peter
Gerstenberg (Prasse), Baerbel
Gluecksman, Marianne
Goldmeier, Hans
Gumpel, Rosemarie
Hamberger (Pavlowsky) Inge
Heinsheimer (Pring-Mill), Bridgette
Henschel, Lili
Herold, Renate (Richter)
Hershkowitz, Inge
Hubacher, (Christoffel) Edith
Hubacher, Uli
Kassel (Wronker), Lili "Putti"
Kauffman, Liselotte
Kaiser (Neivert), Ilse
Kogut, Margot
Kornberg, Hans
Landau (Kanes), Eveline
Lassow, Peter
LeMesurier, Francis
LeMesurier, Claire
Lichtenstein (Ultman) Ruth
Lesser, Kate
Mazur (Hubner), Rosa
Obermeier, Hans
Pachmayr, Hans
Packmayre, Heinrich

Pilartz, Andreas "Hanno"
Pniower, Blanca
Pniower, Renate
Rapkin (Amerikaner), Franceska
Rosenthal, Peter
Roussel, Edward
Schafer, (MacKenzie) Gina
Schafer, Katya
Selo, Ursula
Solmitz (Frankenstein), Renate
Schleimer, Inge
Stein (Meyer), Gerda
Ultmann (Muessig), Ruth
Weissrock, Susi
Wilcynski, Kaethe
Wolff, Gerhard
Wongtschowsky, Tom

Post War Pupils

Mentioned here are those pupils who provided valuable observations and served on the post-war steering committee.

Danziger, Marion
Fielker, David
Fieldker, (O'Brien) Marian
Hering, Anna
Kann, Karla
King, David
Meyer, (Whittaker), Katharine
Schneider, Jan
Szajnzicht, Cecia
Szajnzicht, Heniek
Szajnzicht, Moniek
Townson, Chris

Household Girls

This category includes girls who came to the School primarily to work as Household Girls, but also those who started as academic students and at age sixteen with no place to go, became Household Girls.

Bauer, Ilse
Bing, unknown
Dorpalen (Bocksieper), Renate
Gans, Gertrude
Gluecksman, Marianne
Kaiser (Neivert), Ilse
Klein (unknown)
Koehler (unknown)
Lilienthal (unknown)
Neufeld, Lisel
Neufeld, T, (Unknown)
Selo, Ursula
Steinberg, (Unknown)
Wohlgemuth (Gluecksman), Lilli

Farm Boys

Refugee boys who were accepted at the School specifically to work on the Farm (in exchange for room and board) were given classes in English and farming-related subjects. This list does not include the names of older boys and girls who were moved into the Farmhouse from the Mansion to make room for younger children at the height of the war period.

Finkler, Arthur
Packmayr, Heinz
Dreschler, Fred
Ernest, Franz Otto

Guggenheim, Heinz
Houser, Goetz
Heinz, Hans
Lewent, Helmut
Rosenfeld, Peter
Roussal, Ernst

Teachers and Staff

The people here were mentioned in various documents as having been at the School sometime during the span of the School's life. As in all of these lists, we lack a record of their full names, their dates of service, and their functions.

Bailey, Miss (unknown) (teacher)
Bates (Miss (unknown) (teacher)
Bibbe, Mr. (Maintenance)
Bluhm, Dr (Mathematics and Science)
Brewley, Miss (Quaker, pre-war)
Corfield, Mr. (Farm Instructor)
Debenham, Miss (unknown)
Demuth, Miss (unknown) (Cook)
Dove (Faulkner), Margaret (English)
Graetz, (Herman) Eva (unknown)
Grimshaw, Basil (Teacher)
Hetherington, Miss (Teacher)
Hugh, Mr. Edward (Farm Manager)
Humby, Miss (unknown)
Krohn, Miss (adult post-war refugee)
Leven, Dr. Luise (Music)
Lewent, Dr. Kurt (Goldschmidt School)
List, Miss (Teacher)
May, Mr. Victor (Teacher)
Miss Pelmar (possibly Miss Pelmore)

Phillips, Mr. (Gardner)
Railing, Mrs. A.H. (Farm Chair)
Sileezinski, Miss (Art)
Taylor, Mr. (unknown) (teacher)
Temple, Miss (unknown)
Van Hollick, Miss (unknown) (teacher)
Von Gierke, Therese (Unknown)
Weissrock, Charlotte (Unknown)
Wilcynski, Kaethe Miss (Art)
Wolff, Dr. Emmy (Literature, German Literature, French)
Woolgar, Miss (unknown) (Farm Horticulturalist and
Land Army Girl)

Benefactors

Early letters and committee reports reveal the following collection of the names of Quakers, the Jewish Refuge League, members of the British Peerage, School Council members and others who contributed their energy, wealth and time to create and ensure the existence and success of Stoatley Rough School.

Alexander, Miss B. (unknown)
Bracey, Mrs. Bertha
Catchpool, Corder
Catchpool, Mrs. Gwen
Day, Miss (unknown)
Deeds, Sir Wyndham
Fearon, Miss A.R.
Frey, Miss Isabel
Gilbert, Dr. Mary
Goldschmidt, Dr. Leonor
Gooch, Prof. G. P.
Hayward, Miss Mary
Leon, Arthur

Monfiore,Leonard
Nicholson, Sir Walter
Nonnemacher, Hermann
Omerod, Miss (unknown)
Parmoor, née Ellis, Baroness Marian Emilly Cripps
Pentland, (née Gordon), Baroness Marjorie Adeline Sinclair
Pnieower, Mr. (unknown)
Sileezinski, Miss (unknown)
Sprigge, Lady (unknown)
Sprigge, Lord (unknown)
Stein, Dr. (unknown) (Rabbi)
Vernon, Marjorie